Language and Sexuality

Language and Sexuality

Contesting Meaning in Theory and Practice

edited by
Kathryn Campbell-Kibler
Robert J. Podesva
Sarah J. Roberts
Andrew Wong

CSLI
PUBLICATIONS
Center for the Study of
Language and Information
Stanford, California

Copyright © 2002
CSLI Publications
Center for the Study of Language and Information
Leland Stanford Junior University
Printed in the United States
06 05 04 03 02   5 4 3 2 1

Library of Congress Cataloging-in-Publication Data

Language and sexuality : contesting meaning in theory and practice /
Kathryn Campbell-Kibler ... [et al].
p.   cm.
Includes bibliographical references and index.

ISBN 1-57586-319-7 (cloth : alk. paper)
ISBN 1-57586-320-0 (paper : alk. paper)

1. Language and languages–Sex differences. 2. Sociolinguistics.
3. Gays–Language. I. Campbell-Kibler, Kathryn, 1977–
P120.S48 L346 2001
306.44′086′64 — dc21   2001043827
CIP

∞ The acid-free paper used in this book meets the minimum requirements of the American
National Standard for Information Sciences—Permanence of Paper for Printed Library
Materials, ANSI Z39.48-1984.

CSLI was founded early in 1983 by researchers from Stanford University, SRI International, and Xerox
PARC to further the research and development of integrated theories of language, information, and
computation. CSLI headquarters and CSLI Publications are located on the campus of Stanford University.

CSLI Publications reports new developments in the study of language, information, and computation. In
addition to lecture notes, our publications include monographs, working papers, revised dissertations, and
conference proceedings. Our aim is to make new results, ideas, and approaches available as quickly as
possible. Please visit our web site at
http://cslipublications.stanford.edu/
for comments on this and other titles, as well as for changes and corrections by the author and
publisher.

Contents

v

Contributors

RUSTY BARRETT: Department of Linguistics, University of Michigan, Ann Arbor, MI 48109, USA, rustyb@umich.edu

KATHRYN CAMPBELL-KIBLER: Department of Linguistics, Stanford University, Stanford, CA 94305-2150, USA, kcat@stanford.edu

PENELOPE ECKERT: Department of Linguistics, Stanford University, Stanford, CA 94305-2150, USA, eckert@csli.stanford.edu

HEIDI FRANK: Department of Anthropology, Northwestern University, Evanston, IL 60208-1330, USA, h-frank2@northwestern.edu

YOONHEE KANG: Department of Anthropology, Yale University, New Haven, CT 06510, USA, yoonhee@pantheon.yale.edu

SCOTT F. KIESLING: Department of Linguistics, University of Pittsburgh, Pittsburgh, PA 15260, USA, kiesling@pitt.edu

DON KULICK: Department of Anthropology, New York University, New York, NY 10276, USA, kulickdon@hotmail.com

BILL LEAP: Department of Anthropology, American University, Washington, DC 20016, USA, wlm@american.edu

ANNA LIVIA: Department of French, University of California at Berkeley, Berkeley, CA 94720, alivia@uclink.berkeley.edu

SALLY MCCONELL-GINET: Department of Linguistics, Cornell University, Ithaca, NY 14853, USA, smg9@cornell.edu

BONNIE MCELHINNY: Department of Anthropology, University of Toronto, Toronto, Ontario, Canada, bonnie.mcelhinny@utoronto.ca

ROBERT J. PODESVA: Department of Linguistics, Stanford University, Stanford, CA 94305-2150, USA, podesva@stanford.edu

ROBIN QUEEN: Department of Linguistics, University of Michigan, Ann Arbor, MI 48109, USA, rqueen@umich.edu

SARAH J. ROBERTS: Department of Linguistics, Stanford University, Stanford, CA 94305-2150, USA, sarahjr@stanford.edu

HARRIS SOLOMON: Rollins School of Public Health, Emory University, Atlanta, GA 30322, USA, hssolom@emory.edu

ANDREW WONG: Department of Linguistics, Stanford University, Stanford, CA 94305-2150, USA, andrewdw@stanford.edu

Acknowledgments

The editors thank all of the contributors for their hard work and engaging research and especially Penny Eckert for pushing to make this volume a reality. We would also like to express our gratitude to CSLI Publications for casting their net broadly enough to include work in sociolinguistics and for recognizing the importance of this particular subject matter. Finally, we owe a special debt to all those who participated in the inaugural International Gender and Language Association (IGALA) conference, as most of the papers appearing herein developed from presentations at the conference.

Acknowledgement

1

Speaking of Sex*

ANDREW WONG, SARAH J. ROBERTS, AND KATHRYN
CAMPBELL-KIBLER

In academic discourse and in the real world, sexuality is the site of numerous meaning-making struggles. As researchers interested in studying the
interaction of sexuality with linguistic practice, we find ourselves engaged at
once on two levels. We seek to document and explain the ways in which
meanings are established and contested within communities under study. At
the same time, we are contesting how to study and discuss sexuality. In
negotiating the object and methods of study, we are contributing to the ongoing discourses surrounding sexuality.

The establishment of identities around particular sexual object choices
has been a central issue in the development of the field of language and
sexuality. Research on this has tended to focus on central examples or behaviors, asking questions about the construction of gay or lesbian identities,
or representation in media or the historical development of words or signs
referring to sexual minorities (see, e.g., Leap 1995, Leap 1996, and Livia
and Hall 1997).

Other areas of negotiation around a sexual domain of meanings have
been less fully explored. Nonetheless, questions of ethnicity, nationhood and
gender (among others) intersect crucially with notions of sexual object
choice, socio-sexual life choices, sexual performance, and sexual tastes.

* Our names appear in random order. Thanks to Kira Hall, Bill Leap, and especially Penny Eckert and Don Kulick for their comments on earlier drafts of this chapter. All errors are our own.

Language and Sexuality: Contesting Meaning in Theory and Practice.
Kathryn Campbell-Kibler, Robert J. Podesva, Sarah J. Roberts and Andrew Wong (eds.).
Copyright © 2001, CSLI Publications.

This volume combines analyses of the use and contestation of sexual meaning in practice with theoretical papers participating in an ongoing debate of the goals, methods and subject matter of the study of language and sexuality. In the following discussion we point to some areas of struggle or fluctuation in the field, and bring up issues that highlight the centrality of contestation and our role within it.

1   The Debate over 'Gay Speech'

What is sexuality? Since the publication of Kulick's (2000) review article on gay and lesbian language, this question has been more widely debated in sociolinguistics and linguistic anthropology than ever before. One approach to the question is to view sexuality as something that has to do with sex. For instance, Webster's College Dictionary defines 'sexuality' as 'the quality or state of being sexual' and 'sexual' as 'of, relating to, or associated with sex or the sexes' or 'having or involving sex.' Another approach is to regard sexuality as (non-normative) sexual identity, as in 'a person's sexuality is a private matter.' This is an implicit assumption underlying much research in the study of language and sexuality (see, e.g., various chapters in Livia and Hall 1997). Studies that adopt the latter approach, Kulick argues, are marred by a fatal flaw: the non-existence of the object of inquiry. In what he calls 'Darsey's theorem' he condemns the overly simplistic methodology of matching sexual orientation to linguistic practice and claiming success: 'The fact that gays do X does not make X gay' (p. 259). Instead, he insists that one must prove that X is used by all and only gay people to 'make claims about gay or lesbian language' (ibid.). Kulick makes an essential point that researchers cannot limit themselves to describing the speech of self-identified gay or lesbian people and naming all the features found there as gay. This confuses a symbolic resource (which, he points out, people of any sexual orientation may appropriate) with an empirical phenomenon: 'the actual language practices...of individual gays and lesbians' (p. 257). It is indeed important not to conflate the empirical with the symbolic (or the ideological), but it is equally important to see the ways in which the two influence each other in the production and interpretation of identity.

An aspect of linguistic practice may legitimately be considered gay if gay people use it and perceive it as a 'gay marker', even though it is used by others for the same or different purposes. One example is in-group assumptions of perpetual lateness. The phenomenon itself is overwhelmingly common, and group after group has coined joking terms to refer to it. There have been CPT (Colored People's Time), Academic Time, Jewish Time, and of course, Gay Time and more recently, QST (Queer Standard Time). This functions even at a very local level, as when members of particular social networks use specific variants for their social group or particular members ('Well, they're only thirty minutes late, and by Chris and Pat time, that's fifteen minutes early.') This phenomenon fails the 'all and only' test, since many people in different communities use it. And yet in all instances, it marks members as belonging to a particular group. Using Gay Time means gay, in some experiential way for the participants, as shown in one coming-out story where a young man tells of going to his first meeting of a campus gay group: 'I came late on purpose, and I didn't realize, you know, being late wasn't like being gay late, 'cause gay late's very late' (Liang 1997:297). In this case, this speaker is describing something that is not unique to gay men (being consistently later than a stated time). Nonetheless, he is using it to mark in-group knowledge that he lacked as an outsider but that he now possesses.

In a similar vein, certain linguistic features may become markers of different social groups, even if they are not used by all and only members of the groups which they symbolize. The use of *y'all* as the second-person plural pronoun in southern United States has been widely noted and is perceived as a feature of southern speech. Likewise, *hella* – an adverbial quantifier and intensifier that has been grammaticalized from *hell of* – is often recognized as a feature of Northern California youth speech (Bucholtz 2001). Neither one of these features is used by every member of the social group that it is tied to. Nevertheless, at least at the ideological level, it would be difficult to deny that *y'all* and *hella* are markers of the speech of U.S. southerners and Northern Californian teenagers respectively. Researchers need to explore the ideological processes through which certain linguistic features become markers of particular social groups. Irvine and Gal (2000), for example, identify three semiotic processes that forge the ideological links between linguistic forms and the social world: iconization, fractal recursivity, and erasure. Most relevant to the present discussion is the third process. Erasure occurs, 'when an ideology simplifies a sociolinguistic field, forcing attention on only one part or dimension of it, thereby rendering some linguistic forms or groups invisible or recasting the image of their presence and practices to better fit the ideology' (Gal 1998:328). Thus, in the two examples mentioned above, erasure makes invisible U.S. southerners and Northern Californian teenagers who do not use the stereotypical features in question, thereby emphasizing the ideological associations between *y'all* and southern speech, and between *hella* and Northern California youth speech.

The above discussion of ideology foreshadows our point with regard to the important distinction between ideology and practice in language use.

Perhaps this distinction can best be illustrated by the debate over 'Gay Speech.' In the last few years, scholars (see, e.g., Crist 1997; Gaudio 1994; Rogers, Smyth and Jacobs 2000) have focused on identifying the linguistic features that constitute a style of speaking often referred to as 'gay speech' or the 'gay accent.' They have argued that it differs from other speaking styles at the lexical, phonetic and discourse levels. However, as Podesva, Roberts and Campbell-Kibler (this volume) point out, the assumption that there is only one gay way of speaking erases the diversity within the 'gay community.' It amounts to the belief that there is only one way to be gay and that this gay identity is indexed through the use of 'gay speech.' Yet the gay community encompasses myriad social groups such as leather daddies, clones, circuit boys and gay activists. The distinctions among these social groups are constructed through dress, beliefs, values, linguistic styles and other social practices. In other words, gay styles are diverse and multifaceted.

It might be advantageous to bring 'imagined community' (Anderson 1983) and 'community of practice' (Eckert and McConnell-Ginet 1992) into the discussion. One might say that while 'gay speech' corresponds to the imagined 'gay community,' different gay ways of speaking (i.e., different gay styles) correspond to different communities of practice organized around same-sex desire (e.g., gay activist groups, gay men's choir). According to Anderson (1983), an imagined community exists in *the minds of its members*; it emerges when individuals experience a strong sense of commonality with others who presumably share the same background – whether it is race, gender, class, national origin or sexual orientation. Despite the absence of direct social intercourse with other members, individuals feel a strong emotional attachment to the imagined community due to their common (but often separate) participation in similar activities or their common use of cultural artifacts that have acquired symbolic value. The concept of 'imagined community' privileges putative shared beliefs and ideologies over shared practice. On the other hand, the concept of 'community of practice' is more concrete. A community of practice is '...an aggregate of people who come together around some enterprise. United by this common enterprise, people come to develop and share ways of doing things, ways of talking, beliefs, values – in short practices – as a function of their *joint engagement in activity*' (Eckert 2000:35; our emphasis). Thus, the difference between 'gay speech' and different gay ways of speaking is the difference between ideology and practice. The 'gay speech' that many have endeavored to identify is an ideological construct that symbolizes the imagined 'gay community,' and the linguistic features of this ideological construct in turn provide some of the resources that are used in the construction of different gay styles – either personal styles or group styles that symbolize various communities of practice within the 'gay community.'

We do not imply that the search for the linguistic features that constitute 'gay speech' is a fruitless endeavor. Our point is that it is important to distinguish between ideology and practice. Perhaps the debate over 'women's language' can shed light on this issue. About thirty years ago, Robin Lakoff (1972) identified various features of 'women's language' – for example, the frequent use of hedges, 'empty adjectives' (e.g., *nice*) and standard language. Since then, her findings have been criticized on all fronts. Most notably, scholars (e.g., Nichols 1983) have pointed out that Lakoff's 'women's language' is an idealized version of the way white middle-class women talk, and in fact, many women – especially women of color – do not use the linguistic features that Lakoff identified. As Cameron (1985) and Hall and Bucholtz (1997) rightly claim, the 'women's language' described by Lakoff is an ideological construct rather than a realistic reflection of the way women talk; it is an ideal that women often try to attain or avoid. Although it is not a fair representation of women's diverse speaking styles, it has a tremendous influence on the actual linguistic practices of women. 'Gay speech' is likewise an ideological construct associated with the imagined 'gay community,' in that it merely represents what many perceive as sounding gay. Many gay men may not adopt 'gay speech' as their speaking style, perhaps because they do not want to be identified as 'too gay.' For instance, the gay attorney in Podesva et al. (this volume) does not exploit pitch or the duration of /l/ to produce a gay style, even though these linguistic features have been linked to 'gay speech.' Thus, looking for the linguistic correlates of 'gay speech' is important, but it is not enough. To truly understand how language is used to construct different gay identities, it is important to examine the ways in which gay men belonging to different social groups draw on 'gay speech' as a linguistic resource to construct personal and group styles. Several questions that might lead to productive research have not been adequately explored. For instance, how and in what settings do gay men exploit 'gay speech'? Under what circumstances is the use of 'gay speech' underscored? While ideology is important, actual linguistic practices cannot be ignored.

2   What's in a Name?

Not only can the study of language and sexual identity contribute to our understanding of the relationship between ideology and practice in language use, but it also addresses other fundamental issues in linguistics as well. Studying the use of different sexual identity labels can shed light on questions regarding semantic variation and change – an area that has remained by and large unexplored in sociolinguistics. For instance, what conditions make possible the process through which different meanings are attributed to the same label? How does one meaning win acceptance, while alternative meanings are marginalized? To answer these questions, it is necessary to examine the polysemy of labels and the politics of signification – that is, the various ways in which the social practice of meaning-making is controlled and determined.

Although it has long been acknowledged that words may have multiple meanings, only recently has polysemy been given center stage (see, e.g., Cruse 2000). In fact, polysemy – or synchronic semantic variation – is considered a necessary condition for semantic change (McMahon 1994) and makes meaning contestation possible in social discourse. Contrary to the implicit assumption of many linguists, words are not given fixed meanings. As McConnell-Ginet (this volume) points out, words do not really have much meaning at all – they are assigned interpretations when used; and the interpretations given to a particular word can vary from one context to another. The case of social category labels (e.g., *gay, lesbian* and *queer*) is particularly telling. Labels draw on social stereotypes, moral attitudes, old connotations and future possibilities – in short, ideologies of various kinds. *Gay* and *lesbian* are not only labels for male and female homosexuals respectively, but they carry more complex meanings as well. *Gay* – a relatively non-judgmental term – can become a derogatory descriptor. For instance, when teenagers sneer 'That's so gay', 'gay' does not necessarily denote male homosexuality; rather, it can be glossed as 'uncool' or 'gross' (ibid.). This reflects negative attitudes toward gay men – for example, the belief that gay men are effeminate and flamboyant; and such qualities are deemed undesirable for men (see, e.g., Cameron 1997). Different social and moral ideologies are associated with the use of the label *lesbian*, as Livia (this volume) illustrates. In *Lesbia* (a popular lesbian magazine in France), many personal ad writers include 'butches,' 'truck drivers' and other 'masculine women' in their lists of exclusions, thereby erasing them from the imagined community created in *Lesbia* and stating implicitly which qualities are considered undesirable. This practice, which attempts to delimit who can be counted as a lesbian in *Lesbia*, is constantly challenged by the editors of the magazine. The personal ads in this magazine are disrupted by the presence of NDCs or *notes de la claviste* 'notes from the keyboarder' which are separated from the main text by parenthesis. In addition to making verbal jokes and pointing out good matches, NDCs offer supportive comments to writers who confess to negatively regarded qualities (e.g., being plump) and provide covert criticism of the list of exclusions (e.g., masculine women, butches, mannish women, boyish women, truck drivers and women wrestlers). In this way they serve the function of countering the attempt of many personal ad writers to exclude 'masculine women' from the imagined community in *Lesbia*. Frank (this volume) similarly discusses the meanings associated with lesbian identity in Japanese women's magazines. In this context, 'lesbian' means more than just sexual orientation; it implies modernity and Western orientation as well. In two magazines – namely, *Labrys Dash* and *TypeMx*, the use of *katakana* (i.e., the Japanese script used for loanwords) indexes a certain lesbian identity through modernity and Western orientation indirectly (see Ochs 1991). These magazines employ more *katakana* and do so more innovatively (e.g., using *katakana* in *kanji-katakana* compounds and for non-loanwords). These three examples show that *gay* and *lesbian* mean more than what they denote; the use of these labels often brings to mind a host of beliefs, attitudes and ideologies as well.

Perhaps the label *tongzhi* 'comrade' can further illustrate the fact that what underlies a social category label is less like a definition than ideologies associated with the social category. *Tongzhi* is arguably the most popular contemporary Chinese label for those with same-sex desire. The label itself has a long history. First adopted in Republican China as an address term for those involved in the Nationalist Revolution, it was taken up by Chinese Communists to refer to those fighting for Communist ideals. After 1949, *tongzhi* was used as an address term not only by Chinese revolutionaries, but also by the general public. Since the opening up of the market economy of China in 1978, it has become disfavored due to its original political connotations (Fang and Heng 1983). In the late 1980s, it was appropriated by the gay and lesbian communities in Taiwan and Hong Kong to refer to those with same-sex desire; and it has positive connotations of respect, equality and resistance (Wong and Zhang 2000). Chou (2000:2) claims that *tongzhi* – with its positive cultural references and gender neutrality – is preferred over *gay* and other labels imported from the West. In addition, the use of *tongzhi* highlights the differences between the home-grown *tongzhi* ideologies and the gay and lesbian ideologies imported from the West. The two differ most significantly in their orientation toward the relationship between kinship and sexual identity. While gay and lesbian ideologies underscore the importance of expressing sexual identity openly through coming out, those who embrace *tongzhi* ideologies claim that the Western notion of 'coming out' privileges sexual identity over family identity and therefore is not applicable in the Chinese context. Instead, they advocate the indigenous strategy of 'coming home' which can supposedly reclaim *tongzhi* not by denying family-cultural identity but by integrating *tongzhi* into the family and cultural context (ibid.:259). Thus, *tongzhi* emphasizes the cultural specificity of same-sex desire and provides an indigenous identity for integrating the sexual into the social. In recent years, mainstream print media in Hong Kong also started using *tongzhi* to refer to those with same-sex desire.

However, the label has gained negative connotations in this context – in particular, *tongzhi*s are those who refuse to acknowledge their 'original gender roles' and consistently look for easy victims to recruit into their community (Wong, this volume). Therefore, what underlies the label *tongzhi* is not just its definition (i.e., those who desire the same sex) but ideologies that the *tongzhi* community and mainstream print media have attached to the social category '*tongzhi*.'

One source of information about the ideologies associated with social category labels comes from what linguists may charmingly refer to as 'folk theories' of linguistic structure and use. These ideologies about language have been crucial in the debate over the expansion of the 'gay community' into the GLBT(QQF) (gay, lesbian, bisexual, transgendered, queer, questioning, and friends) community. This is an easily observed process by those working at universities, as campus groups post flyers and host debates with each name change. By giving informed and detailed accounts of the linguistic ideologies at work, activists have a good deal to offer to linguists (and vice versa):

> When the question of who got to define the word *lesbian* arose, one of the bi-phobic lesbians came up with this solution: 'The lesbians will define who is a lesbian.' Now, in a purely semantic sense, this is a meaningless statement, even an absurd one, the sort of thing you might see in a lesbian version of *Alice in Wonderland*. But the sense is not, in fact, meaningless. The implied meaning is crystal clear: 'Women who do not and will not ever have sex with men will decide whether women who do or might have sex with men may be defined as lesbian.' Or to put it another way, 'The people who fit the most narrow definition of the word will decide whether or not the definition is to be expanded.' (Christina 1997:33)

Examined and analyzed carefully, 'folk theories' can complement the data on the speakers' tacit and practical understanding of linguistic structure or use – that is, data collected by studying language use itself (e.g., how social category labels are *actually* used in conversation). There is also evidence that some lesbians, gay men and other queers have put into practice ideologies about social category labels developed in academia. Theorists have long discussed the radical potential of the word *queer* as 'a signifier without a signified.' Although many in the community use 'queer' in a more concrete sense (i.e. referring to specific marginalized sexualities), writer and activist Pat Califia (1998:231) brings the idealized 'queer' to life in a piece of erotic fiction where one of the characters addresses the issue of sex between lesbians and gay men simply: 'She's queer, like you boys. Queers have sex with other queers, right?' This political edgeplay turns on the historical context of the word *queer* and the community it represents to the reader, circumventing the definition squabbles of the 'Label Wars.' This expansion is a literal and sexual instantiation of the queer theorists' obsession with subversion, as some queers or sex radicals seek constantly to reinvent sex, using it each time to build structures of understanding that they will smash in the next iteration.

While the discussion above shows how the polysemy of labels arises, one central question regarding the contestation of meaning remains: How does one meaning win acceptance over the others? The answer to this question lies in the fact that the contestation of meaning is intimately linked to the contestation of ideologies. Those with meaning-making power (e.g., the media) attempt to naturalize their own ideologies about the social category that a given label denotes. Naturalization works by making ideologies appear to be natural and spontaneous representations of 'reality,' thus creating what Stuart Hall (1982) calls 'the reality effect.' Dominant ideologies that are naturalized become literal meanings of the label. Perhaps McConnell-Ginet (1989) offers the best account of how the naturalization of dominant meanings works in everyday interaction. Using the example of *hussy* (once merely a synonym for *housewife*), she shows how labels can acquire negative connotations as a result of the way they are used. According to McConnell-Ginet, it is plausible that a certain ideology of the speech community was that sexual wantonness was a characteristic of the housewife. Those who embraced this ideology would say *hussy* and rely on their addressees to invoke that characteristic when interpreting the utterance. Although the addressees might not accept this ideology, the insult would work as long as they were aware of it and as a result, understood it as an insult. When enough uses of *hussy* to insult succeeded, subsequent language users would be able to interpret the insult without relying on any extralinguistic attitudes. The stereotype might fade, but the meaning that *hussy* as an insult conveyed becomes part of the literal meaning of the word (ibid.: 44). Like *hussy*, other words such as *mistress* might have undergone a similar process and gained negative connotations (see also Schulz 1975).

Yet, due to the polysemous nature of words, alternative meanings can never be totally erased. As a result, the 'reality effect' is something that needs to be worked at constantly. As far as social category labels are concerned, meaning is often the result of social struggle and the politics of signification is always contested. The label *queer* is a prime example. Even though *queer* has recently been reappropriated by those with same-sex desire to counter homophobia and to subvert the heterosexist system, this re-signifying practice works only because of the history of the label. As McConnell-Ginet (this volume) rightly claims, the fact that 'We're here, we're queer, get used to it!' is more effective than 'We're here, we're gay, get used to it!' is due to previous (and present) uses of the label in gay-bashing; the power of the label for lesbian and gay men to affirm their same-sex desire rests on its power to insult. The ideologies associated with *queer* (e.g., *queer* as a label to describe those who should be despised for their same-sex desire, *queer* as a 'non-identity' for those who defy categorization and resist heteronormativity, and *queer* as an umbrella term for bisexuals, lesbians, gay men, transexuals and transgendered people) contribute to the semantic indeterminacy of the label. This semantic indeterminacy is vital to the political utility of the label. As Butler (1993:228) points out:

> If the term 'queer' is to be a site of collective contestation, the point of departure for a set of historical reflections and future imaginings, it will have to remain that which is, in the present, never fully owned, but always and only redeployed, twisted, queered from a prior usage and in the direction of urgent and expanding political purposes.

While the study of sexual identity as a conveniently pre-packaged social category is fraught with problems, the investigation of sexual identity as a social phenomenon and a site of contestation shows significant promise. If nothing else, sexual identities are bound to have interesting linguistic correlates as a result of their checkered history and conflict-filled present. In the most frequently quoted line of his seminal *History of Sexuality*, Foucault (1990[1978]:43) describes a particular historical point in European-American sexological understanding: 'The sodomite had been a temporary aberration; the homosexual was a species.' Since that time, the homosexual has evolved into an identity with a body of literature, music, fashion, consumer goods, and of course, linguistic practices.

3   Desire, Gender, and Other Things

Nevertheless, sexuality is not just about sex, nor is it only about sexual identity. As Weeks (1989) explains, sexuality refers to the cultural ways of expressing our bodily desires and pleasures. In a similar vein, Kulick (2001) argues that the study of language and sexuality should not be limited to the study of the language use of lesbians and gay men; rather, it should endeavor to examine how language is implicated in the construction of the myriad elements that make sexuality sexuality, i.e. fantasy, desire, pleasures and the unconscious. Kang (this volume) shows how language is used to invoke sexual desire. She focuses on a Petalangan (Sumatra) women's genre of 'obscene magic spells' called Monto Cabul to illustrate how sexual desire is represented and projected in linguistic practices. Petalangan women use these magic spells to invoke more the desire of their husbands than their own sexual desire; this shows how conventional notions of gender relations are deeply embedded in the magic spells. In Petalangan society, men are more mobile than women. While women cannot socialize freely, men can go anywhere they want and are more likely to meet other women outside the village. Magic spells are the only resources available to Petalangan women for dealing with the fear of being abandoned by their husbands. The importance of magic spells can be summed up in a Petalangan women's saying: 'City women put on make-up, while we wear magic spells.' Kang shows clearly the centrality of desire and more importantly desirability in the construction of a sexual self for Petalangan women.

While desire is an important facet of sexuality on both individual and cultural levels, there are important aspects to sexual domains of meaning which do not focus on either desire or the identity issues touched on above. Sexuality may be used in the service of non-sexual desires, or in the construction of other emotive stances or identities. Eckert (this volume) gives two examples where sexual meanings find a use in putatively non-sexual domains. She tells of one girl's use of sexual experience (and a performance of her 'loss of virginity' story) as a method of claiming a particular brand of 'tough girl' Chicana identity. In this discussion she highlights the fact that Angela's story minimizes sexual desire and the sexual experience itself, focusing instead on the social moves involved and their results, including the 'scariness' of the boys she became involved with, the concern of her friends and the envy of enemies. This is not to claim that Angela had no experience of or opinions regarding the physicality of sexual involvement. Rather, Eckert is making the point that 'sexuality is not just about sex.' Another example she gives is 'sexy voice' quality which, though iconically linked to sexual arousal, may be used for a range of performances from sexual harassment to expressing strong desire for a car, or chocolate.

Gender is another field of meaning which is intimately tied to sexuality. One of the central tenets of queer theory is the separation of gender and sexuality. As Livia and Hall (1997) point out, this is neatly summarized in Eve Kosofsky Sedgwick's Axiom Two:

> The study of sexuality is not co-extensive with the study of gender; correspondingly, antihomophobic inquiry is not coextensive with feminist inquiry. (1990:27)

Undoubtedly, sexuality is qualitatively different from gender, and collapsing sexuality with gender may lead to undesirable consequences. For instance, the fight for equal rights for lesbians and gay men is related to but different from the fight for gender equality. However, taking this too far and treating sexuality as a separate domain, we may run the risk of losing sight of the important connections of sexuality with kinship, religion, and most important of all, gender. In fact, sexuality often mirrors gender; it is associated with prevalent notions of masculinity and femininity. The popular conception is that while heterosexuality corresponds to hegemonic masculinity and femininity, homosexuality is linked to marginalized masculinity and femininity (Connell 1995). Kiesling (this volume) illustrates this point, examining the narratives told by a group of men belonging to the 'greek' letter society system. This system is arranged through an ideology of sexual difference, so that fraternities are all-male and sororities all-female. Kiesling argues that 'fuck stories', which are on the surface about sex and sexuality, serve the purposes of constructing hegemonic masculinity and maintaining one's power within the same-gender group. Fuck stories – often told at the end of Sunday meetings – are about the narrator's sexual exploits over the weekend; they are rather graphic and portray women as sexual objects. However, Kiesling points out that these stories are not as much about the actual relationships the narrator has with women as the relationships he is creating with other men. They are used to create status among peers and 'to display power over other men (and women) to other men.' The masculinity that the members construct through the telling of 'fuck stories' is not fundamentally sexual in nature, but sexuality is integral to the way in which this masculinity is presented.

Kiesling's chapter in this volume is also an important contribution to an area that has been little explored in the study of language and sexuality: heterosexuality. Unstudied and naturalized, heterosexuality is classed as a sexual identity or orientation more out of a concern for fairness than theoretical principle (though to whom the fairness is directed shifts):

> My friend Will Roscoe once told me his theory of homophobia: Straight people, he said, are jealous of us, because we have a sexual orientation and they don't. In our sexual otherness, we have to learn to talk about sex; it defines us in a way it doesn't define heterosexuals, and in the process of becoming a community, we learn comfort with the language. (Queen 1997:p.xiii)

We cannot close the book on sexual identity before we have determined (or at least sweated over) whether the vast majority of the population even possesses one. Many who are seen by (queer) others as heterosexual do not experience themselves as heterosexual, or do so without any internal connection with the concept (see Kitzinger and Wilkinson 1993 for a detailed discussion of this discomfort on the part of feminists). This work could be usefully informed by the discussions of Whiteness in the literature on linguistic productions of race. The 'not an identity' feeling has an analogue there: some researchers in education warn against providing an 'other' category in multiple-choice ethnicity questions, as the bulk of the respondents will be 'White with an attitude'.

As a 'non-identity,' heterosexuality (like hegemonic gender roles) is too easily assumed to be the same cross-culturally. Exploring sexual minority identities on a global scale has been acknowledged as a controversial endeavor. Particularly in terms of word choice, care has been exercised much more extensively on non-normative identities than normative ones. Weston (1998) comments 'when it comes to gender, many analysts continue to use 'man' and 'woman', like 'masculine' or 'feminine', as though the meanings of these categories were uncontested' (p.157). In addition to *heterosexual*, this warning applies to words like *sex* and *sexual*. Just as we cannot declare a given person gay or straight on the basis of 'what they do' without an in-depth understanding of the system of meanings they are operating with, we cannot assume that we know what it is they're doing, merely because it looks just like something we recognize.

One of the ways that heterosexuality has been addressed within the field of language and sexuality is through the queer theory concepts of parody and subversion, as developed most fully by Judith Butler (see, for example 1990, 1993). This focus on the potential for subversion turns our attention away from heterosexuals and heterosexual behavior, and seeks illumination in instances of parody within queer worlds. Butler mentions the potential for including in the term queer 'straights for whom the term expresses an af-filiation' (Butler 1993: 220, discussed extensively in Thomas 2000). Her point is a good one, that same-sex sexual practice or attraction is not a pre-requisite for engaging in parody, the central form of subversion she dis-cusses. But of course, as Butler acknowledges, there is more to parody than simply 'doing it wrong,' namely, a subversive effect. Conversely, there is more to being a good heterosexual member of society than not parodying it successfully. Instead of inquiring how heterosexuals for whom the term queer 'expresses an affiliation' may go about being good straight queers, at some point shouldn't we ask how heterosexuals for whom the term holds no appeal whatsoever go about being good straights? What does it take to suc-cessfully establish oneself as a heterosexual in various communities, and what does it mean to fail in that performance? And how does being a meaningfully sexual being differ from being a meaningfully gendered being (see Rubin 1984)?

An interesting consequence of the focus on identity within language and sexuality studies is the overwhelming construction of sexuality as an attrib-ute of individuals. This theoretical stance is odd, given that at least in the U.S., sexuality is commonly seen as the province of couples. Kulick sug-gests a focus on desire, which as a transitive relation would improve on this model somewhat. But desire too is a characteristic of an individual, though it has an object. In popular discourse, however, sexuality frequently inheres in the couple as a unit (as in the phrase 'our sex life'), and sociologist such as Laumann et al. (1994) point out that the sexual dyad as a social relation-ship is central to sexuality and sexual behaviors. The ramifications of these different understandings, and the forms of sexuality associated with each could represent a beginning step towards a more nuanced understanding of the largely implicit conceptual models that people use to reason about sex.

In the struggle to define what sexuality is, institutions – particularly nation-states – play a key role. Solomon (this volume) demonstrates that how institutions perceive AIDS (what is seemingly about sex and sexuality) involves how they perceive gender differences as well. Focusing on the language use of several AIDS educational pamphlets published by the Israel AIDS Task Force, he shows how the use of various discourse strategies in these pamphlets reflects the temperament of AIDS education in Israel. In particular, there are noticeable differences in the presentation of messages based on the gender of the intended audience. First of all, these pamphlets exploit the use of optional vowel diacritics to underscore the gender of the intended audience. While nonvocalic written Hebrew is used to reach an audience that includes both men and women, gender marking through the use of vowel diacritics becomes important when the educational messages are tailored for a single-sex audience. In addition, the texts of the pamphlets tailored for men and women differ in style and tone. Pamphlets targeted toward gay men encourage the reader to consider an HIV-antibody test, but they do not discuss the emotional factors involved in the process of acknowledging one's HIV-positive status. Moreover, they emphasize the physical nature of the HIV virus. On the other hand, pamphlets that address a female audience highlight the emotional aspects of AIDS – they are more affect-focused than those tailored for a male audience and they often discuss issues such as fear, loss of control and the emotional impact of AIDS on the everyday life of an HIV-positive woman. Thus, the accentuation of different AIDS educational messages seems to be influenced by predominant Israeli concepts of masculinity, femininity and homosexuality.

There has also been exciting work on the use of sexuality in the production of ethnic pride or nationalist discourses (Puri 1999, Boyarin 1997). Stoler (1995) provides a thorough discussion of the ways in which the Native other in the colonialist enterprise was central in the development of the bourgeois *scientia sexualis* described by Foucault. In addition to being an individual characteristic, sexuality is a force through which religious and political movements may build credibility and influence behavior. Rubin (1984) discusses at some length the phenomenon of recurring moral panics about sex, in which the fears of a nation take shape as the sexual deviant of the moment. In this way language and sexuality are curiously alike, since grammar is used similarly to embody fears about society, often by the same people (Cameron 1995).

4   Queer Linguistics

The study of language and sexuality is a young discipline and as the previous sections show, it is one still endeavoring to define its object of study and methodology. Much of the debate hinges on how crucial terms are defined and how they reflect our epistemological assumptions: What is meant by *sexuality*? Does it refer to a sexual practice, identity, or something else entirely? Should the term be scrapped in favor of *desire*? Is identity something one *has* or what one *does*? Do we accept *queer* as a useful analytic concept and in what sense? Such conflicting meanings arise from the use of these terms in different theoretical paradigms that already occupy the academic terrain: queer theory, linguistic anthropology, variationist sociolinguistics, language and gender studies, among others.

Interestingly, one of the central assumptions of queer theory is that meaning is unfixed and constantly subject to disruption, complication, and reformulation. Some of the papers in this volume observe the contestation of meaning in language use (see McConnell-Ginet and Wong, this volume), and this is indeed a fruitful area of research. As linguists, it is easy to forget that we are also engaged in this practice ourselves. The contributors to this volume, as well as other like-minded researchers, are all participating in a social project of carving out a space within linguistics for the study of language and sexuality. Many come to this task with very different theoretical perspectives and thus there is still no consensus on methods, approach, and terminology. This tension was brought into focus in the panel session at the first IGALA (International Gender and Language Association) conference, held in May 2000. The topic for the panel was 'The Future of Queer Linguistics' and the participants included Robin Queen, Don Kulick, Anna Livia, Rusty Barrett, and Bonnie McElhinny. Expanded versions of their papers appear in the first section of this volume, along with invited papers from Penelope Eckert and William Leap. Although these papers draw on different (and often conflicting) perspectives, they collectively contribute to the metadiscourse on disciplinary priorities and work towards bringing the study of language and sexuality into greater conceptual coherence.

As Robin Queen points out in her paper, the title of the session forced the participants to contemplate two things: the name of the academic enterprise and its future. These concerns are not independent since the name makes particular claims on what the enterprise is about, depending on how the words are interpreted. 'Queer linguistics' is certainly a controversial name, involving an expression recently reclaimed from derogation (yet still widely in use as an epithet), rejected by some self-identified gays and lesbians, and used in highly specific ways in activist and academic discourse. 'Queer linguistics' is therefore a rather ambiguous name for a subdiscipline and may mean different things to different people: It is the study of language as used by 'queers' (invoking 'queer' in the sense as an identity label), it the study of language and sexuality informed by certain insights from queer theory (invoking 'queer' as a shorthand for 'queer theory'), it is really just a covername for 'language and sexuality studies' but sounds cooler and more academic (hinting at 'queer theory' but not really incorporating any of its assumptions as basic principles), it is the sociolinguistic study of any language use without recourse to identity categories and following the basic paradigm of queer theory (invoking 'queer theory' to the fullest extent, as it has a lot to say about social processes apart from sexuality), it is an applied form of linguistics embedded within queer activism, and so on. On the basis of Livia and Hall (1997), 'queer linguistics' may be interpreted as an approach to language and sexuality which shares certain concerns with queer theory, but the agenda and methodology of 'queer linguistics' has not yet been clearly worked out.

Barrett (this volume) enthusiastically endorses the application of queer theory to sociolinguistics in general (in effect, 'queering' linguistics). He identifies several key weaknesses in traditional sociolinguistic theory which need to be corrected: reliance on 'unanalyzed' identity categories which obscure the role of ideology in structuring discourse and smuggle the researcher's own biases into the analysis, description of the meanings associated with variables without probing how the relationship between variables and social meaning is formed, and an unawareness of the sociolinguist's role in creating the social structures which get analyzed (i.e. the observer's paradox). Identity categories are still significant as semiotic constructs cited in linguistic practice, but the sociolinguist no longer must assume the independent existence of categories in order to proceed with a linguistic analysis. Queer theory also allows the researcher to discover the citation of identities marginalized, obscured, or ignored altogether in traditional correlational approaches, such as the existence of genders formerly sublimated into a binary model of sex-gender and sexual identities labeled in terms of Western white middle-class constructs of homosexuality. Barrett envisions queer linguistics as not a specific subdiscipline within linguistics but as a basic approach to language which recognizes categories as 'ideological constructs produced by social discourse,' an approach which can benefit linguistics in general.

Leap (this volume), on the other hand, cautions against replacing existing approaches in language and sexuality studies with queer theory. While the latter may highlight identities otherwise neglected in other approaches, it privileges the study of these transgressive, marginal, and unrealized identities at the expense of 'mainstream' gay/lesbian experience. Leap notes that queer theory is primarily concerned with broad social processes and has little to say about the individual subject. In Leap's reading of queer theory, this results in a disjuncture between individual lived experience and social practice, a disjuncture which places queer subjectivity beyond the reach of many gays and lesbians. Leap argues that as a theoretical focus, queerness is too inclusive to be of much help in addressing various questions relating to the lives of gays and lesbians.

Kulick (this volume) does not question the importance of queer theory to the study of language and sexuality (indeed, he regards indexical performativity as an obligatory starting point), but he asks how 'queer linguistics' as currently practiced can be queer at all if queer cannot be defined a priori. He points to the following paradox in linguistic methodology: If 'queer linguistics' putatively displaces research from identity categories, and since *queer* emphatically is not synonymous with *gay* or *lesbian*, then why do researchers still resort to these categories when choosing informants or situating speech in a model of 'queer' community? Kulick recommends that we think more carefully about what *queer* means before deciding to call our enterprise 'queer linguistics.'

Queen (this volume) discusses the profound indeterminacy of meaning in the term 'queer linguistics' and concludes that this term actually conflates two separate, but important, enterprises: a queering of linguistics in general (as recommended by Barrett and which is already in progress) and research into the linguistic construction of sexual identities (which often, though not necessarily, draws on queer theory). Queen's emphasis on sexuality as 'sexual identity' contrasts sharply with Kulick's focus on sexuality as 'desire.' Kulick (2000) suggests that the psychological underpinnings of desire might shed more light on language use than correlation with identity categories, but Queen argues that such an approach is unnecessary. Like Barrett, Queen argues that identity categories do impact language use and need not be reified for linguistic analysis. Queen regards research into the indexing of sexual identities by linguistic resources as a disciplinary priority. Another priority is the consolidation of language and sexuality studies ('queer linguistics' in the second sense) into a disciplinary home that secures a legitimate 'identity' to the enterprise.

Livia (this volume) recognizes queer linguistics as a sub-field of language and gender studies which imparts to the discipline an understanding of identity in terms of indexical performativity. However Livia asserts that queer linguistics must conceptually stray from classic 'lit crit' style queer theory if it is to account for speaker intentionality. Queer theorists place intentionality outside the scope of critical inquiry (as subjects are semiotically constituted and significant only as citers of pre-existing performative acts), but Livia contends that speaker intention is a chief concern of linguists working with actual informants because it helps explain the rationale behind a speaker's choice of performatives within a situational context. Livia believes that only intentionality can explain the difference between 'passing' and 'dragging' in different 'trans' identities, for instance. She therefore suggests that the theory is somewhat ahead of linguistic methodology, raising questions on how queer linguistics might best be conducted.

Eckert (this volume) comments on Kulick's attempt to shift the theoretical focus of language and sexuality studies to desire and warns that this move, if unchecked, can open the door to essentialist discourses on gender and sexuality. Such discourses mystify desire merely as individual physical experience, thereby circumventing the many social aspects of sexuality. She also argues for an increased focus on how identity categories are constituted and challenged through linguistic practice, as well as their function in social structures such as the heterosexual market. Understanding how linguistic and sexual practices lead to the formation of categories such as 'slut' and 'good girl' may shed light on how other sexual categories are constituted.

Finally, McElhinny (this volume) sees the value of queer linguistics as, among other things, recognizing identity as produced through social inequities and not attached to individuals. This broadens the horizon of queer linguistics to include the consideration of institutions and discourses that promote and sustain inequality. According to McElhinny, queer linguistics needs to examine how different inequalities stratify sexuality in different ways and employ methodologies that get at identities otherwise obscured by hegemonic discourses. The academic project is, therefore, a much richer one than merely correlating variables with hegemonic sexual categories.

5   What Lies Ahead

The object of inquiry in our own community of practice (whether we call it queer linguistics or otherwise) may thus be regarded as an ideological construct necessitated by the demands of our profession, as academic disciplines require definable, fixed foci for research and study. Like the imagined 'gay community' with regard to ideological constructs such as 'gay' identity and 'gay speech,' our discipline would remain undefined and, in a sense, unnamed, until we settle on a fixed object of study. Whether such an outcome is desirable, of course, depends on our stance towards disciplinary ideology. The lack of consensus on the meaning and desirability of the label 'Queer Linguistics' reveals clearly that our object of inquiry is currently undergoing contestation in our academic practice. The contestation of meaning, after all, is the contestation of ideology.

The academic debate over what constitutes the field's object of inquiry is not much different from other struggles to fix, unsettle, and reformulate meaning. Like word meanings, the abstract constructs we linguists employ in framing our analytic methodology are constantly being contested, rejected, and reworked. The papers in this volume all take sex or sexuality as their point of departure, but by framing sexuality differently from a variety of perspectives they shed light on far more aspects of sexuality than a single-focus approach would be able to do. The question of priorities, however, is a very important one for the field since our joint enterprise is situated within an academic social structure that demands a certain degree of coherence, fixity, and stability. Working out the tensions among our varying agendas, methodologies, and theoretical assumptions is a project that will no doubt continue in the future.

References

Anderson, Benedict. 1983. *Imagined Communities: Reflections on the Origin and Spread of Nationalism.* London: Verso.

Boyarin, Daniel. 1997. *Unheroic Conduct: The Rise of Heterosexuality and the Invention of the Jewish Man.* Berkeley: University of California Press.

Bucholtz, Mary. 2001. Word Up: Social Meanings of Slang in California Youth Culture. Language and Culture Symposium 8. http://www.language-culture.org

Butler, Judith. 1990. *Gender Trouble: Feminism and the Subversion of Identity.* New York: Routledge.

Butler, Judith 1993. *Bodies that Matter.* New York: Routledge.

Califia, Pat. 1988. *Macho Sluts.* Boston, MA: Alyson Publications.

Cameron, Deborah. 1985. *Feminism and Linguistic Theory.* London: Macmillian.

Cameron, Deborah. 1995. *Verbal Hygiene.* New York: Routledge.

Cameron, Deborah 1997. Performing Gender Identity: Young Men's Talk and the Construction of Heterosexual Masculinity. *Language and Masculinity*, ed. Sally Johnson and Ulrike Meinhof, 47-64. Oxford: Blackwell.

Chou, Wah-Shan. 2000. *Tongzhi: Politics of Same-sex Eroticism in Chinese Societies.* Binghamton, NY: Haworth Press.

Connell, Robert 1995. *Masculinities.* Berkeley, CA: University of California Press.

Crist, Sean 1997. Duration of Onset consonants in Gay Male Stereotyped Speech. *University of Pennsylvania Working Papers in Linguistics.* 4(3): 53-70.

Cruse, Alan. 1992. Monosemy vs. polysemy. *Linguistics* 30: 577-599.

Eckert, Penelope 2000. *Language Variation as Social Practice.* Oxford: Basil Blackwell.

Eckert, Penelope and Sally McConnell-Ginet 1992. Think Practically and Look Locally: Language and Gender as Community-based Practice. *Annual Review of Anthropology* 21:461-490.

Fang, H. and J. Heng 1983. Social Change and Changing Address Norms in China. *Language in Society* 12: 497-507.

Foucault, Michel. 1990 (1978). *The History of Sexuality: An Introduction.* Volume 1. Trans. Robert Hurley. New York: Vintage Books.

Gal, Susan. 1998. Multiplicity and Contestation among Language Ideologies: A Commentary. *Language Ideology,* ed. Bambi B. Schieffelin, Kathryn A. Wooolard, and Paul V. Kroskrity, 317-331. New York: Oxford University Press.

Gaudio, Rudolf 1994. Sounding Gay: Pitch Properties in the Speech of Gay and Straight Men. *American Speech* 69.1: 30-57.

Hall, Kira and Mary Bucholtz 1997. Introduction: Twenty Years after *Language and Woman's Place. Gender Articulated: Language and the Socially Constructed Self,* ed. Kira Hall and Mary Bucholtz, 1-22. New York: Routledge.

Hall, Stuart 1982. The Rediscovery of 'Ideology': Return of the Repressed in Media Studies. In M. Gurevitch et al., eds., *Culture, Society, and the Media.* New York: Methuen.

Harvey, Keith. 1997. 'Everyone loves a lover'. *Language and Desire: Encoding Sex, Romance and Intimacy,* ed. Keith Harvey and Celia Shalom, 60-82. New York: Routledge.

Heywood, John. 1997. The object of desire is the object of contempt: Representations of masculinity in *Straight to Hell* Magazine. *Language and Masculinity,* ed. Sally Johnson and Ulrike Meinhof, 88-207. Cambridge: Blackwell.

Irvine, Judith and Susan Gal 2000. Language Ideology and Linguistic Differentiation. *Regimes of Language: Ideology, Politics, and Identity,* ed. Paul Kroskrity, 35-84. Santa Fe, NM: School of American Research Press.

Kitzinger, Celia and Sue Wilkinson. 1993. Theorizing Heterosexuality. *Feminism and Psychology* 2.3:293-324.

Kulick, Don 2000. Gay and Lesbian Language. *Annual Review of Anthropology* 29:243-285.

Lakoff, Robin 1975. *Language and Woman's Place.* New York: Harper and Row.

Laumann, Edward, John Gagnon, Robert Michael and Stuart Michaels. 1994. *The Social Organization of Sexuality: Sexual Practices in the United States.* Chicago: University of Chicago Press.

Leap, William 1995. *Beyond the Lavender Lexicon: Authenticity, Imagination, and Appropriation in Lesbian and Gay Languages.* Amsterdam: Gordon and Breach.

Leap, William 1996. *Word's Out: Gay Men's English.* Minneapolis, MN: University of Minnesota Press.

Livia, Anna and Kira Hall 1997. It's a Girl!: Bringing Performativity back to Linguistics. *Queerly Phrased: Language, Gender and Sexuality,* ed. Anna Livia and Kira Hall, 3-18. New York: Oxford University Press.

McConnell-Ginet, Sally 1989. The Sexual (Re)production of Meaning: A Discourse-based Theory. *Language, Gender, and Professional Writing: Theoretical Approaches and Guidelines for Nonsexist Usage,* ed. Francine Wattman and Paula Treichle, 35-50. Commission on Status of Women in the Profession, Modern Language Association of America, New York.

McMahon, April 1994. *Understanding Language Change.* New York: Cambridge University Press.

Nichols, Patricia 1983. Linguistic Options and Choices for Black Women in the Rural South. *Language, Gender, and Society,* ed. Barrie Thorne, Cheris Kramarae and Nancy Henley, 54-68. Cambridge, MA: Newbury House.

Ochs, Elinor 1992. Indexing Gender. *Rethinking Context: Language as an Interactive Phenomenon,* ed. Alessandro Duranti and Charles Goodwin, 335-358. Cambridge: Cambridge University Press.

Pendleton, Eva. 1996. Domesticating Partnerships. *Policing Public Sex: Queer Politics, and the Future of AIDS Activism,* ed. Dangerous Bedfellows: Ephen Glenn Colter, Wayne Hoffman, Eva Pendleton, Alison Redick and David Serlin, 373-393. Boston: South End Press.

Puri, Jyoti. 1999. *Woman, Body, Desire in Post-colonial India: Narratives of Gender and Sexuality.* New York: Routledge.

Queen, Carol. 1997. *Real Live Nude Girl: Chronicles of Sex-positive Culture.* San Francisco: Cleis Press.

Rogers, Henk, Ron Smyth, and Greg Jacobs 1999. Sounding Gay, Sounding Straight: A Search for Phonetic Correlates. Paper presented at New Ways of Analyzing Variation in English 28, Toronto.

Rubin, Gayle. 1984. Thinking Sex: Notes for a Radical Theory of the Politics of Sexuality. *The Lesbian and Gay Studies Reader,* ed. Henry Abelove, Michele Barale and David Halperin, 3-44. New York: Routledge.

Schulz, Muriel 1975. The Semantic Derogation of Women. *Language and Sex: Difference and Dominance,* ed. Barrie Thorne and Nancy Henley, 64-75. Rowley, MA: Newbury House.

Stoler, Ann Laura. 1995. *Race and the Education of Desire: Foucault's History of Sexuality and the Colonial Order of Things.* Durham: Duke University Press.

Thomas, Calvin. 2000. Introduction. *Straight with a Twist: Queer Theory and the Subject of Heterosexuality,* 11-44. University of Illinois Press.

Weeks, Jeffrey 1989. *Sexuality.* London and New York: Routledge.

West, Candace and Don Zimmerman. 1987. Doing Gender. *Gender and Society* 1:125-151.

Weston, Kath. 1998. *Long Slow Burn: Sexuality and Social Science.* New York: Routledge.

Wong, Andrew and Qing Zhang 2000. The Linguistic Construction of the *Tongzhi* Community. *Journal of Linguistic Anthropology* 10.2:248-278.

Part One:

Contesting Meaning in Theory

2

Is Queer Theory Important for Sociolinguistic Theory?*

RUSTY BARRETT

> 'There is neither Jew nor Greek, neither slave nor free person, there is not
> male and female; for you are all one in Christ Jesus.'
>
> – Paul's letter to the Galatians 3:28

1   Introduction – Queering Linguistics

I begin this paper with an epigraph from the Bible to underscore two basic
points about identity categories. First, the desire to free ourselves from the
constraining and dominating nature of identity categories does not originate
in (and is not exclusive to) queer theory. Second, the queer theoretical
stance of deconstructing identity categories and pointing out their role in
dominant discourse has implications well beyond the realm of understanding
the behavior of individuals who might be thought of as somehow 'queer'.
This is a basic point within queer theory; the goal of such research is not
intended simply to increase understanding of 'queer' behavior, but to increase understanding of human behavior and to question exclusionary theoretical assumptions across academic disciplines. If one accepts the decon-

* Thanks to the participants at the first IGALA conference, especially the graduate students at
Stanford, for helpful discussions on these issues. I am also thankful to Robin Queen and Keith
Walters for their comments on drafts of this paper.

Language and Sexuality: Contesting Meaning in Theory and Practice.
Kathryn Campbell-Kibler, Robert J. Podesva, Sarah J. Roberts and Andrew Wong (eds.).
Copyright © 2001, CSLI Publications.

struction of identity labels so common in queer theory, one is left with two basic options in moving this acceptance into sociolinguistic research. One option would be to simply give up on identity altogether and attempt to focus on something else (such as the proposal of Kulick 2000). Another option would be to attempt to rework the traditional view of identity that has predominated in sociolinguistic research and attempt to find an understanding of the relationship between language and identity that does not reproduce exclusionary categories.

The stance of questioning the normativity (and normalness) of particular interpretations of behavior goes to the very root of social science disciplines. As Michael Warner writes, 'If queers, incessantly told to alter their 'behavior,' can be understood as protesting not just the normal behavior of the social but the idea of normal behavior, they will bring skepticism to the methodologies founded on that idea' (Warner 1993: xxvii). This is what is commonly referred to as *queering* a particular academic discipline or methodology. It would be possible to interpret what follows as a queering of sociolinguistics in that it uses a viewpoint drawn from queer theory to question the assumptions underlying sociolinguistics as a discipline. As such, it is not intended solely for the interpretation of language as it relates to sexuality, but rather to enhance our understanding of the role of language in society in general. Thus, the aim here is not so much to define queer linguistics (or the study of language and sexuality), but to propose a queer-based repositioning of the assumptions surrounding linguistics itself. As such, this paper is not intended to critique the work of any particular researcher or research paradigm, but rather to raise questions about the discipline itself. Indeed many of the questions raised here are beginning to surface in a variety of research within sociolinguistics and linguistic anthropology.

2   Queer Linguistics

A common misunderstanding is the idea that queer linguistics is somehow equatable with the study of language use by some externally definable group of 'queers,' such as the study of gay and lesbian language. Such an assumption is basically equivalent to saying that feminist linguistics is somehow the study of language use among feminists. Just as feminist linguistics suggests the study of language (where language is taken to mean *all* language) enhanced with understandings gained from feminist theory, queer linguistics is the study of language augmented with ideas from queer theory. As such, queer linguistics has the potential to contribute to our understanding of language use in general terms (the subject of linguistics itself) and cannot be limited by application to a particular identity category. In fact, such a move would be counter to many of the basic ideas within queer theory. One of the main points of queer theory is to demonstrate the ways in which (hetero-normative) assumptions concerning definable identity categories are part of a larger social discourse[1] of domination. For 'queer linguistics' to focus on such predefined categories would simply reinscribe that domination.

The use of the term 'queer' throughout queer theory can be seen as a linguistic experiment in which an attempt has been made to reclaim (and hence redefine) a pejorative term so that it has no referent, but is a purely indexical sign in both form and use. In other words, the signifier 'queer' is intended to have no corresponding real-world signified, but rather 'queer' is intended to index an imagined and undefined set of sexual practices (and individuals associated with those practices) that fall outside of the hetero-normative assumptions of dominant societal discourse. Through an ideology of domination, constructions of 'difference' are used to delimit norms of acceptability in which any identity category based on 'difference' will by its very nature exclude potential category members. The desire to associate a particular externally-defined social group as queer is the desire to 'fill in' the missing signified, but it is also a desire driven by a dominant ideology that demands that limitations be placed on acceptable practices and identities.

It is doubtful that this linguistic experiment could succeed (and many would argue that it has already failed), given the difficulties involved in sustaining a purely indexical sign in the minds of speakers, who typically demand direct connections between linguistic signifiers and a signified entity. Without a corresponding signified, 'queer' is destined to always be defined in terms of a realm of possibilities. As David Halperin argues, the term 'queer' 'does not designate a class of already objectified pathologies or perversions' instead it 'describes a horizon of possibility whose precise extent and heterogeneous scope cannot in principle be delimited in advance' (1995:62). The power of the term 'queer' derives directly from the absence of a signified. The defiance of 'queer' derives from its resistance to a dominant ideology of 'difference' that depends on the construction of definable identity categories which, once defined, place restrictions on social acceptability, excluding those who cannot (or refuse to) place themselves within any pre-defined category. As it is used in queer theory, the term 'queer' can only succeed as a purely indexical sign and its usefulness is destroyed when it becomes tied to an externally-definable signified. As Judith Butler argues:

---

[1] I use 'social discourse' to mean the broader, socially-oriented sense of 'discourse' as used in critical theory as opposed to 'discourse' as used in linguistics to describe the structure of particular texts or interactions.

> If the term 'queer' is to be a site of collective contestation, the point of departure for a set of historical reflections and futural imaginings, it will have to remain that which is, in the present, never fully owned, but always and only redeployed, twisted, queered from a prior usage and in the direction of urgent and expanding political purposes. This also means that it will doubtless have to be yielded in favor of terms that do political work more effectively. (1993: 228)

The goal, then, of queer linguistics cannot be the study of the language of a pre-defined set of 'queers' (since such a set cannot be defined), but rather a linguistics in which identity categories are not accepted as a priori entities, but are recognized as ideological constructs produced by social discourse. The distinction here is between a traditional approach which assumes identity as an inherent (albeit constructed) characteristic of an individual to an approach in which we acknowledge that identity is usually assigned by researchers to a given individual in order to place individuals into definable categories. If we acknowledge that identity categories serve to simultaneously construct and constrain acceptable behaviors for particular individuals, we must also acknowledge that these categories will always be exclusionary both in terms of their assignment to individuals and in terms of any linguistic data 'explained' by attributing behavior to category membership. Any explanation based on an assumption of category membership will not only exclude those who do not 'fit' the normative assumptions of what constitutes membership in an identity category, but will also serve to perpetuate predominant ideologies of normativity and acceptability by simultaneously reiterating and delimiting the norms of behavior associated with the (inherently exclusionary) categories themselves. By shifting our focus from how language *reflects* a priori identity categories to how language *constructs* identity categories we might be able to develop a more nuanced understanding of the relationship between language and identity that is not based on biased and exclusionary assumptions concerning identity itself. Here, sociolinguistics has a rare opportunity to enhance social theory, particularly theories that are built upon the idea that identities and behaviors are controlled through the performative role of language.

3   Identity, Performativity, and Indexicality

Within queer theory, Austin's (1975) concept of performativity is applied to the concept of identity (cf. Butler 1990, 1993, 1997). In addition to performatives such as 'I now pronounce you domestic partners' or 'I bet you five dollars,' there is a set of performatives related to identity categories. Statements such as 'It's a girl!' or 'I am a lesbian' have an illocutionary performative effect in that they immediately cause a change by placing an individual within a given identity category. Other uses of identity labels ('Ice skat-

ers are all gay,' 'Asians are nice people,' 'Women can't work in construction' etc.) are often interpreted as performative as well in that they also work
to construct an imagined referent for a given identity label. This second type
of performatives may be seen as perlocutionary speech acts in that the
change they effect may not be immediate, but may initiate a particular set of
consequences (by associating stereotypes to particular identity categories).[2]
Just as with other performative statements, all performatives using identity
labels operate through citation. Through the iterativity of such statements a
referent for particular identity categories is constructed both in the minds of
speakers and in a larger social discourse. In other words, identity categories
are created through repetitions of the assignment of individuals to particular
categories and repetitions of statements attributing particular social attributes or practices to a particular category.

In addition to the linguistic performatives of identity categories, queer
theory views other aspects of social practice as performative as well, in that
they create similar associations through citation. Butler (1990) argues that
gender is a performance without an original. The meaning of gender (or any
other social category) only exists through the citational character of its performativity. This process of citations not only constitutes the identity categories themselves, but it also sets limits on acceptability, constraining an
individual by placing boundaries around possible identity categories and the
practices associated with those categories. As Butler writes:

> Performativity cannot be understood outside of a process of iterability, a
> regularized and constrained repetition of norms. And this repetition is not
> performed by a subject; this repetition is what enables a subject and con-
> stitutes the temporal condition for the subject. This iterability implies that
> 'performance' is not a singular 'act' or event, but a ritualized production, a
> ritual reiterated under and through constraint, under and through the force
> of prohibition and taboo, with the threat of ostracism and even death con-
> trolling and compelling the shape of the production, but not, I will insist,
> determining it fully in advance (1993: 95).

Thus, the citational nature of performatives constructs the concepts of
'difference' that are associated with particular identity categories. These
notions of difference simultaneously constitute and constrain identity. This
is the reason 'queer' was taken as a purely indexical sign. The dream of
queer was to demonstrate that all identity category labels are signifiers without a signified. They operate as indexical signs which point to particular
performative practices and performative statements which, through repeated
citation, have come to be associated with a particular category. The choice

---

[2] There is debate as to the potential felicity conditions for performatives of this type, particularly when they might be seen as 'hate speech.' Butler (1997) discusses this debate, particularly
the distinction between Derrida's (1978) focus on the role of iterability of the citation versus
Bourdieu's (1991) focus on whether or not a speaker has the authority to make such citations.

to place one's self in the category *queer* or *lesbian*, *Mexican American* or *Chicano, white* or *European American* is the choice between signs that index distinct sets of associatiòns constructed through citation and the historicity of the sign. These choices may display markedness (Myers-Scotton 1993, Barrett 1998) with regard to when and where particular identity categories are used for self-reference, as particular citations may seem more suited for particular social contexts.

Uses of identity categories in social science research can thus be seen as a class of performatives that also serve to constitute and constrain their subjects. In the majority of sociolinguistic research, the range of possible identities considered has been quite limited. This is particularly true of quantitative research, where the use of statistical analysis forces the creation of category distinctions (cf. Eckert 1989). Typically, sociolinguistic studies examine a single identity category based on a single point of difference along lines of class, gender, or ethnicity. Studies focusing on a single point of difference are by their very nature exclusionary, as a study of 'women's conversation' allows the women in the data (usually white and middle-class) to stand in for the entire possible range of (potential) women. This is how the field of language and gender (like most other areas of social science) fell into heteronormativity where the idea of cross-gender communication could become a focal point for reconstructing heterosexuality as the center of a research paradigm. While such research might provide insight into how gender is imagined (both by speakers and by researchers) it remains exclusionary. Sociolinguistic studies with a focus on two points of difference tend to arise only when the subjects of a study are neither male nor European American, (such as studies of 'Mexican American women's speech'). Thus, in determining a research focus, particular identities are typically left unmentioned unless they index some opposition to an unspoken norm. The number of points of difference found in the title of a sociolinguistic study typically corresponds to the degrees of difference from a white heterosexual male norm. Thus, we rarely see studies claiming to look at European American straight men's speech (since this is covered by 'English syntax')[3], studies of European American straight women's speech are labeled as 'women's speech,' studies of African American straight women's speech are labeled as 'African American women's speech', and studies of Mexican American lesbians' speech would be labeled as such. This correspondence between points of difference noted in describing a research focus and distance from a white heterosexual male norm serves to reinforce the role of identity catego-

---

[3] The emergence of sociolinguistic studies of men's speech are typically, like the entire field of 'men's studies' a response to feminist research and tend to reproduce the ethnocentricism and heteronormativity found in early studies of women's speech.

ries in constructing representations of whiteness and heterosexuality and further restricts identity categories that are already marginalized. Recently, sociolinguists have begun to recognize the ways in which their research serves to construct and constrain conceptions of identity categories. Consider, for example, Morgan's (1999) discussion of how research on African American Vernacular English (AAVE) is constructed in a way that excludes women, Mufwene's (1992) discussion of the role of ideology in studying the history of AAVE, and Walters' (1995) discussion of how linguistic discussions of AAVE serve to construct representations of whiteness and exclusionary categorizations of African Americans. Another positive move in this direction can be seen in the work of researchers who consider the place of the individual (e.g., Johnstone 1996) and researchers who have focused on emic identity categories that emerge through local practice as opposed to relying on traditional externally-defined identity labels (e.g., Eckert and McConnell-Ginet 1995, Eckert 2000, Bucholtz 1999). The move from etic to emic categories opens the door to a realm in which identities are not restricted by the assumptions of the researchers and the focus is placed on the local construction of particular identities. One must be cautious, however, of the possible ways in which the use of emic categories operates in the construction of the Other ('we don't have a word for them, but they call themselves X'). As Kath Weston points out, this is especially true of 'indigenous categories' (such as *hijra* or *travesti*) where 'the use of "foreign" names constructs the subject of inquiry as always and already Other' and serves to 'reify differences and buttress ethnographic authority' (1993:348).

Despite the move toward emic categories, the majority of researchers in sociolinguistics have done little to question the ways in which the discipline itself serves to construct and place boundaries around identity categories. As Eckert (1989:247) has noted, researchers tend to fall back on 'unanalyzed notions' of basic categories such as sex (which are felt to be externally definable) and fail to consider aspects of identity that do not have direct correlations with the data in question. In Tannen's (1999) recent work on gender in the workplace, for example, she uses Goffman's notion of analyzing data in terms of 'sex-class-linked' features, recognizing that the 'class' of men and the 'class' of women are socially constructed. Tannen (1999:223) also recognizes the exclusionary nature of such classes, arguing that this approach 'does not mean that every individual in the class will exhibit those behaviors' associated with the class. Yet, having gone this far, Tannen adds a note of caution, that we should not overlook the importance of biology, arguing that the distinction between sex and gender 'serves to reinforce a false ideology that biological and cultural factors can be distinguished' (1999:223). While I would agree that biological and cultural factors cannot be fully distinguished, I would argue that the relationship between the two is not that socially-constructed categories are based on natural measurable biological differences (i.e., the biological influences the cultural), but that our understanding of biological differences is based on socially-constructed concepts of sex itself (i.e., the cultural influences the biological). Reducing a biological continuum to a binary opposition of two extremes excludes everyone who doesn't fall at one of the two end-points.

The distinction between sex and gender, in which sex is natural and biological and gender is socially constructed allows researchers to 'fall back' on 'unanalyzed notions about gender' (Eckert 1989:247) precisely because we have seen gender as intrinsically tied to sex and have not questioned the category of sex itself. When it comes to other biological-cultural oppositions, such as race/ethnicity, such oppositions have fallen into disfavor long ago. I would hope that all sociolinguists would be horrified by a researcher reminding us that in analyzing the relationship between ethnicity and language use we must not forget the biological correlates of race. It is important to recognize that, like race, the concept of biological sex is itself largely socially constructed. If we learn anything from the transgender movement, we should learn that the social construction of biological sex is itself clearly exclusionary. This is surely the case both for transgendered individuals (those with gender identity in conflict with the sex they were assigned at birth) and intersex individuals (those born with some combination of male and female genitalia), as well as those who are both transgendered and intersex.

Devor (1989) discusses the limitations of examining sex (and gender) as a dualistic binary opposition. She demonstrates these limitations by pointing out the error in assuming that the difference between the sexes lies in a difference between XY versus XX chromosomes. The numerous children born with sets of XXX or XXY chromosomes are (like all children in American society) assigned a sex based on the physical appearance of their genitalia. Those with XXX chromosomes are typically assigned to the male sex and often display hypermasculine gender including violent behavior (making it clear that possession of a Y chromosome is not the basis for maleness). Similarly, in Western societies, children born with 'ambiguous' genitalia (intersexed individuals) are typically put through sex-assignment surgery to make them unambiguously male or female. Thus, where biological fact does not mesh with cultural ideology, the biological is changed (through surgery) to meet cultural expectations. As Geertz (1983) has noted, this attitude toward hermaphrodite children is a cultural trait of Western societies (and hence is driven by ideology of gender rather than a natural biological opposition). The mere existence of 'third gender' categories in other cultures, such as the hijra (Hall 1998) and the 'yan daudu (Gaudio

1998) should tell us that our Western opposition of male and female is a culturally-based binarism. In other words, the 'biological' concept of sex is the culturally-based opposition between male and female imposed onto bodies that exist in a physical range that is much broader than a basic binary opposition between male and female. Thus, the concept of sex itself is a category developed through cultural expectations of gender. To quote Butler yet again:

> It would make no sense, then, to define gender as the cultural interpretation of sex, if sex itself is a gendered category. Gender ought not to be conceived merely as the cultural inscription of meaning on a pregiven sex (a juridical conception); gender must also designate the very apparatus of production whereby the sexes themselves are established. (Butler 1990:7)

Thus, even the most basic forms of difference (male versus female) are formed through cultural and ideological impositions of identity onto the bodies of individual subjects. If we continue sociolinguistic research based on the assumption that such points of difference are natural (rather than constructed through ideology), our work is destined to only reproduce our own cultural ideology, not to fully understand that ideology itself. In the following section, I will outline some implications of a view of language and identity based within an understanding of the performative nature of language. This view is not intended to solve the problems created by studying language through a fixed view of identity, but to provide a starting point for producing a more nuanced view of the language/identity relationship.

4   Sociolinguistic Variables and 'Performative Indexicality'

Linguistic variables and stylistic choices operate as a system of indexical signs. It is traditionally held that these signs index a particular identity category, typically one referring to broad groups defined around gender, ethnicity, or class. In the type of sociolinguistics proposed here, there is a conscious recognition that this set of indexical signs operates as performative language, the very means of constructing and constraining the categories themselves. Such an interpretation would turn focus away from the behavior of the category members as a class and instead examine how such categories are actually created through language, especially through the variation inherent in language.

The nature of sociolinguistic variables could thus be interpreted in terms of *performative indexicality*. As noted before, a statement like 'I am a lesbian' is a performative speech act in that it effects a change by placing an individual into an imagined social category and (through citation) reestablishes the imagined category itself. Sociolinguistic variables have the same performative effect in that they convey social information that aligns speakers with particular identities. As with other performatives, they operate through citationality and in contrast to citations tied to other imagined categories (producing a complex system of oppositions constructed through multiple citations). The variable must have been used previously and carry the 'authority' necessary to actually effect change through conveying identity. Unlike identity labels, however, linguistic variables do not directly serve to construct identity categories; they are indirect indexical signs (Ochs 1990). As the relationship between a variable and an identity category is itself indexical, the variable constructs associations with the individual and her or his desire to convey a particular social attribute (which may in turn be associated with an imagined social category). Thus, linguistic variables are performative indexicals because they 'point to' a change in the making rather than directly cause the change itself. They do not directly construct identity categories, but as with other forms of social practice they (through citation) serve as the building blocks with which those categories develop over time.

A speaker may use the performative indexicality of linguistic variation to convey her or his desire to be seen as a particular type of person in a particular situation. It is only by associations made by the listener (or researcher) that this type of person is tied to a particular social category. In order to make the association between the linguistic variable and a particular identity, the listener must first recognize the variable itself (and notice it in speech) and then recognize and be aware of the citational nature of the variable, what associations it indexes, and determine whether or not the speaker has the authority to make such citations. Thus, the relationship between a linguistic variable and a social category is not direct. As the citational nature of the variable must be recognized (and its authority accepted), the use of sociolinguistic variation (like other performatives) may be felicitous or infelicitous. Thus, if the listener does not recognize the variable or lacks knowledge of its previous citations, the performative will be infelicitous.

One might expect infelicitous performative indexicals to be quite common in cases of exploratory style-switching (Myers-Scotton 1993), such as 'covert communication' among lesbians and gay men (Painter 1981, Leap 1996). In such cases, a lesbian (for example) may use language in a particular way to index her identity as a lesbian. The language chosen in such cases usually has a fairly narrow range of citation so that it is recognized as having performative indexicality primarily by other lesbians and tends not to be recognized by heterosexuals. This reduces the threat of violence associated with direct questions, such as 'Are you a lesbian?' and saves face for both speaker and listener. Because many listener's would not recognize the variable in question, such cases might produce numerous infelicitous performatives.[4] Other cases of infelicitous performative indexicals might arise in cases where the listener recognizes the citation involved but does not accept the speaker's authority to make such a citation. These would be cases in which, for example, the listener does not feel that the speaker has the 'right' to index associations with a particular identity. One instance of such cases would be failed strategies of condescension (Bourdieu 1991), such as cases in which an Anglo American attempts to speak poor Spanish to a Mexican American and receives a reply in English (cf. Peñalosa 1980, Pratt 1987), basically conveying the listener's opinion that the speaker does not have the citational authority to index those properties associated with Spanish.

I noted earlier that the relationship between a sociolinguistic variable and social identity is not direct, because the citational nature of the performative must be recognized by the listener. Similarly, the relationship between the social identity and an identity category may not be direct either. The association reconstructed by the listener may not directly index an identity category, but perhaps some other social attribute. Thus, a particular variable may index attributes such as educated, street-smart, strong, hip, friendly, powerful, etc. Consider if you will, Sapir's (1949 [1915]) description of 'abnormal' speech in Nootka. In his examination of person-implication in Nootka, Sapir notes that linguistic forms distinguishing social groups typically involve either sex-discrimination or rank-discrimination. In other words, variable forms of language typically index gender or status. The 'abnormal types of speech' found in Nootka are abnormal because they index a variety of social types that are atypical (i.e., not related to gender or status). In Nootka, suffixation and consonant mutation are used to convey the fact that the addressee or referent belongs to a social group distinguished by some feature other than status or gender. The categories indexed include 'fat people or people of unusual size' (181), 'people who are abnormally small' (182), 'people suffering from some defect of the eye' (but not the blind) (182), 'hunchbacks' and 'lame people' (183), 'left-handed people' (183), 'circumcised males' (184), 'greedy people' (184), and 'cowards' (184). Sapir's description of Nootka suggests that the possible range of social attributes that may be indexed through language is, at the very least, much broader than sociolinguists have traditionally acknowledged. This is not to suggest that we begin to look for linguistic correlates of handedness or circumcision in the study of American English, but to convey the breadth of indexical power that a language may contain. Limiting our research to specific predetermined identity categories forces this range of indexical

---

[4] This, of course, complicates the notion of felicity conditions as part of the goal is to keep 'outsiders' from recognizing the citational nature of the performative (which is achieved in cases where the performative is infelicitous).

power into tight categories in which anything not fitting our prejudices about what constitutes an acceptable identity is either ignored or labeled as 'abnormal.' Thus, we should be open to the possibility that language may be used to index social attributes that are new even to researchers. These forms in Nootka also suggest that language may index particular social attributes rather than full-blown identity categories (assuming that 'greediness' is a personality trait rather than a social identity in Nootka culture). If the speaker associates a variable with such a social attribute (rather than with a full-blown category), it is only when this attribute is also tied to a particular identity category that an actual association with an identity category will result. The possibility of indexing social attributes (rather than identity categories) has not been widely considered in sociolinguistic research, outside of matched-guise tests, which have typically been applied to entire languages rather than to single linguistic variables.[5]

Speakers may also use very specific forms of language to index the social attributes typically associated with a particular category without claiming membership in the category itself. For example, Sunaoshi (1995) found that female managers in a Japanese camera shop used some (but not all) features of Motherese when giving directives in the workplace. Sunaoshi notes that giving the full range of Motherese would sound condescending, but that a specific subset of Motherese forms was able to convey the authority associated with motherhood without fully indexing the asymmetrical status relationship between mother and child. Similarly, in my own work (1998, 1999), African American drag queens use some forms of language stereotypically associated with European American heterosexual women to index particular class and ethnic conceptions of femininity. By using a subset of the forms associated with the category of 'white women', the drag queens were able to draw associations of femininity from a social category without actually placing themselves in that category. Similar relationships have been discussed in the use of gendered language in Lakhota (Trechter 1999) and in the use of African American Vernacular English by European American teenagers (Bucholtz 1997). This is also true of Jane Hill's work on Mock Spanish (1993, 1995, 1998) which demonstrates that the use of Spanish by Anglo Americans can be used to indirectly index negative stereotypes of social attributes that Anglos associate with Latinos. Thus, we must bear in mind that although a particular linguistic variable is associated with an identity category it may also index social attributes (or personality traits) associated with prototypical members of the category and need not

---

[5] This distinction between identities and attributes could, for example, be examined through matched-guised tests of computer-altered samples which differed only in terms of a single linguistic variable. Such studies might show exactly what attributes speakers associate with a given variable (such as t/d-deletion for example).

always index the category itself. Some directions for future study might be to determine when and how language indexes these social attributes, how and when it directly indexes a particular identity, how the relationship between the two develops historically (i.e., how attributes become dissociated from identity), and what role language socialization plays in acquiring the associations themselves.

Another distinction between the forms of speech in Nootka and the traditional Labovian linguistic variable is that the Nootka forms index addressee or referent, rather than speaker. In other words, the citational power of a performative indexical need not be self-referential. In this sense they are similar to forms found in honorific languages (such as Japanese and Javanese), which classify addressee or referent with regard to their solidarity and status relationships with the speaker. Yet it would be possible for even highly self-referential forms of language to be used in the construction of referent identity. Trechter (1999) has shown, for example, that the supposedly 'gender-exclusive' (i.e. non-variable) forms in Native American languages operate as performatives that are citational in nature and may be used to appropriate social attributes associated with a particular gender (without placing one's self in the other category). The 'gender-exclusive' forms in Lakhota are used when quoting another speaker, thus they may serve to construct referent identity as well as speaker identity. Trecther's analysis demonstrates that a form typically described as being non-variable and exclusively tied to a particular sex actually operates as a performative indexical which, in part, constructs gender categories through citation.

Despite the importance given to addressee in Western sociolinguistic research (cf. Bell 1984), the traditional focus has been the construction of identity for speaker, with little attention paid to how language constructs identity for addressees or referents. In language variation as audience design, a speaker is choosing performative indexicals in a particular way so as to construct an identity that will be acceptable for a particular listener. In addition to constructing one's own identity, the speaker's self-censorship (Bourdieu 1991) chooses citation from a particular set of performative indexicals in order to construct the listener as a person with a given set of expectations. The speaker's choice reflects a reaction to the assumed identity of the listener that may consist of meeting the listener's expectations or attempting to undermine them. Thus, linguistic forms are based not only on speaker identity, but on the speaker's assumptions concerning the identity of the listener and the listener's position in the history of discourse (with it's myriad citational possibilities). Many of the problems associated with the genre of the research interview (cf. Briggs 1986, Paredes 1993 [1977], Walters 1999) derive from the lack of attention researchers have given to the construction of listener identity, which in the case of the sociolinguistic interview amounts to the subject's construction of the researcher's identity. Consideration of the ways in which language constructs listener identity would produce an entirely different set of assumptions on which one could interpret particular data. Labovian hypercorrection (1972), for example, could not be simply attributed to the 'insecurity' of the middle class. We would also need to question the degree to which such 'insecurity' is the result of the linguistic construction of the listener/researcher (as a person with a given set of expectations for the production of minimal pairs). The point here is not that our approach to the study of language variation is wrongheaded, but that we have failed to fully consider our own role in the production of conclusions that have implications beyond the research itself. We must confront a fuller understanding of the observer's paradox. It is not just that our presence as researchers influences language use in the collection of data, but that our presence as individuals with a particular set of assumptions regarding the possible citational range of indexical language influences the interpretation of data, including the choice of research paradigm, the choice of the data, the way in which data are presented, and the conclusions drawn from the data themselves.

The regulation and control of performative indexicality in language variation forces us not only to question our own position within a complex system of citations, but also to use our research to produce a better understanding of the performative nature of indexical signs. Such research could examine the ways in which citation of linguistic variables may vary in their indexical power. When does performative indexicality construct/constrain self-reference? When does it construct/constrain an addressee? When does it serve to construct/constrain a third party not present in an interaction, as is the case with the indirect indexicality of Mock Spanish (Hill 1995, 1998)? Other important issues (which have already begun to be addressed) include how citational authority is regulated by means of language ideology (cf. Woolard and Schieffelin 1994) and appropriation, how is the range of possible citations circumscribed by social discourse that enforces discrimination (Lippi-Green 1997, Zentella 1995), and how is citational power constructed across time (Silverstein and Urban 1996).

5 Conclusion

In his letter to the Galatians, Paul notes that 'neither circumcision nor uncircumcision counts for anything' (Galatians 5:6), but that righteousness can only be obtained through inner faith. He argues that the decision to become circumcised will not bring one closer to God without a corresponding spiritual change. Paul's message to the Galatians stresses that external physical distinctions and the social categories built upon them are unimportant when compared to the inner spiritual life of an individual. Yet Paul's message and that of countless others who have stressed the risks involved with judging people on the external basis of identity, is rarely taken to heart.

It is clear that individuals rely on externally-defined identity categories in their use of language and their attitudes about language varieties. This is why the issue of identity is central to so much work in linguistic anthropology and sociolinguistics. This should not mean, however, that we as researchers should simply follow 'common sense' thinking and make similar judgements based on the same social categorizations. As social scientists our goal should be to understand the ideology behind the workings of society, not to simply reproduce that ideology in our research.

Numerous academic debates about the construction and propagation of discrimination center around issues of language. This is true of debates ranging from issues of 'political correctness' to issues of sexual and racial harassment and hate crimes. As linguists, we should contribute to (if not control) discussions regarding language. Yet for the most part (and there are numerous exceptions), sociolinguists and linguistic anthropologists have had relatively little to contribute to the debates that center around issues of 'difference.' If we wish to have something meaningful to contribute to such debates, then we should take the message of queer theory seriously and critically examine the ways in which language serves to construct social difference and enable discrimination based on that difference.

To return to the question posed in the title of this paper, 'Is queer theory important for sociolinguistic theory?', the answer to such a question must, of course, be subjective and depends on the degree to which the other questions raised here have importance for sociolinguists themselves. I would hope, however, to have demonstrated that queer theory *is* important, if not for sociolinguistic theory, at least for understanding sociolinguistic practice. If we, as sociolinguists are content with a research paradigm that places individuals in exclusionary categories that simply reinscribe prejudiced cultural assumptions about appropriate and 'normal' behavior, then queer theory is not important at all. If, on the other hand, our desire is to truly understand the role of language in society without simply reproducing cultural ideology (and the prejudice, exclusionary practices, and methods of social domination inherent in that ideology) then queer theory might indeed prove to be very important. A growing number of researchers have begun to approach many of the issues I have raised, suggesting that whatever one's attitude towards queer theory might be, it has already had an impact on the theoretical make-up of sociolinguistics and linguistic anthropology. As was the case with queer theory's predecessor feminist theory, it is likely that the influence of queer theory will eventually come to be more and more accepted and its contribution to theories of language will be recognized. Once researchers have begun to take questions drawn from queer theory seriously, it is unlikely that these issues can be openly ignored. Thus, as the cheer of early queer politics pronounced – it's here, so get used to it.

References

Austin, John L. 1975. *How to Do Things with Words.* Cambridge, MA: Harvard University Press.

Barrett, Rusty. 1998. Markedness and Styleswitching in Performances by African American Drag Queens. *Codes and Consequences: Choosing Linguistic Varieties,* ed. Carol Myers-Scotton, 139-61. New York: Oxford University Press.

Barrett, Rusty. 1999. Indexing Polyphonous Identity in the Speech of African American Drag Queens. *Reinventing Identities: The Gendered Self in Discourse,* ed. Mary Bucholtz, A.C. Liang, and Laurel Sutton, 313-31. New York: Oxford University Press.

Bell, Alan. 1984. Language Style as Audience Design. *Language in Society* 13:145-204.

Bourdieu, Pierre. 1991. *Language and Symbolic Power.* ed. John B. Thompson, trans. Gino Raymond and Matthew Adamson. Cambridge, MA: Harvard University Press.

Briggs, Charles. 1986. *Learning How to Ask: A Sociolinguistic Appraisal of the Role of the Interview in Social Science Research.* Cambridge: Cambridge University Press.

Bucholtz, Mary. 1997. Borrowed Blackness: African-American Vernacular English and European-American Youth Identities. Ph.D. Thesis, Department of Linguistics, University of California at Berkeley.

Bucholtz, Mary. 1999. 'Why Be Normal?': Language and Identity Practices in a Community of Nerd Girls. *Language and Society* 28.2:203-23.

Butler, Judith. 1990. *Gender Trouble: Feminism and the Subversion of Identity.* New York: Routledge.

Butler, Judith. 1993. *Bodies that Matter: On the Discursive Limits of 'Sex.'* New York: Routledge.

Butler, Judith. 1997. *Excitable Speech: A Politics of the Performative.* New York: Routledge.

Derrida, Jacques. 1978. Structure, Sign and Play in the Discourse of the Human Sciences. *Writing and Difference,* by Jacques Derrida, trans. Alan Bass, 278-94. Chicago: University of Chicago Press.

Devor, Holly. 1989. *Gender Blending: Confronting the Limits of Duality.* Bloomington, IN: Indiana University Press.

Eckert, Penelope. 1989. The Whole Woman: Sex and Gender Differences in Variation. *Language Variation and Change* 3:245-269.

Eckert, Penelope. 2000. *Linguistic Variation as Social Practice: The Linguistic Construction of Identity in Belten High.* Malden, MA: Blackwell Publishers.

Eckert,, Penelope and Sally McConnell-Ginet. 1995. Constructing Meaning, Constructing Selves: Snapshots of Language, Gender and Class from Belten High. *Gender Articulated: Language and the Socially Constructed Self,* ed. Kira Hall and Mary Bucholtz., 469-508. New York: Routledge.

Gaudio, Rudolf P. 1998. Not Talking Straight in Hausa. *Queerly Phrased: Language, Gender and Sexuality,* ed. Anna Livia and Kira Hall, 416-29. New York: Oxford University Press.

Geertz, Clifford. 1983. *Local Knowledge: Further Essays in Interpretive Anthropology.* New York: Basic Books.

Halperin, David. 1995. *Saint Foucault: Towards a Gay Hagiography.* New York: Oxford University Press.

Hall, Kira. 1998. 'Go Suck your Husband's Sugarcane!': Hijras and the Use of Sexual Insult. *Queerly Phrased: Language, Gender and Sexuality,* ed. Anna Livia and Kira Hall, 430-60. New York: Oxford University Press.

Hill, Jane H. 1993. Is it Really 'No Problemo'?: Junk Spanish and Anglo Racism. In *SALSA I: Proceedings of the First Annual Symposium about Language and Society, Austin,* ed Robin Queen and Rusty Barrett, 1-12. Austin, TX: University of Texas Department of Linguistics (*Texas Linguistic Forum* 33).

Hill, Jane H. 1995. Mock Spanish: A Site for the Indexical Reproduction of Racism in American English. Electronic Document: http://www.cs.uchicago.edu/ discussion/l-c.

Hill, Jane H. 1998. Language, Race, and White Public Space. *American Anthropologist.* 100.3:125-34.

Johnstone, Barbara. 1996. *The Linguistic Individual: Self-Expression in Language and Linguistics.* New York: Oxford University Press.

Kulick, Don. 2000. Gay and Lesbian Language. *Annual Review of Anthropology* 29:243-85.

Labov, William. 1972. *Sociolinguistic Patterns.* Philadelphia, PA: University of Pennsylvania Press.

Leap, William. 1996. *Word's Out: Gay English in America.* Minneapolis: University of Minnesota Press.

Lippi-Green, Rosina. 1997. *English with an Accent: Language, Ideology and Discrimination in the United States.* New York: Routledge.

Mufwene, Salikoko S. 1992. Ideology and Facts on African American English. *Pragmatics* 2.2:141-66.

Morgan, Marcylena. 1999. No Woman, No Cry: Claiming African American Women's Place. *Reinventing Identities: The Gendered Self in Discourse,* ed.

Mary Bucholtz, A.C. Liang, and Laurel Sutton, 27-46. New York: Oxford University Press.

Myers-Scotton, Carol. 1993. *Social Motivations for Codeswitching: Evidence from Africa.* New York: Oxford University Press.

Ochs, Elinor. 1990. Indexicality and Socialization. *Culutral Psychology,* ed. James Stigler, Richard A. Shweder, and Gilbert Herdt, 287-308. Cambridge: Cambridge University Press.

Paredes, Américo. 1993 [1977]. On Ethnographic Work among Minority Groups: A Folklorist's Perspective. *Folklore and Culture on the Texas-Mexican Border,* by Américo Paredes, ed. Richard Bauman. Austin, TX: Center for Mexican American Studies, University of Texas at Austin.

Painter, Dorothy S. 1981. Recognition among Lesbians in Straight Settings. *Gayspeak: Gay Male and Lesbian Communication,* ed. James W. Chesebro, 68-79. New York: The Pilgrim Press.

Peñalosa, Fernando. 1980. *Chicano Sociolinguistics: A Brief Introduction.* Rowley, MA: Newbury House Publishers.

Pratt, Mary Louise. 1987. Linguistic Utopias. *The Linguistics of Writing: Arguments between Writing and Literature,* ed. Nigel Fabb, Derek Attridge, Alan Durant, and Coin MacCabe, 48-66. Manchester: Manchester University Press.

Sapir, Edward. 1949 [1915]. Abnormal Types of Speech in Nootka. *Selected Writings in Language, Culture, and Personality,* by Edward Sapir, 179-96. Berkeley and Los Angeles, CA: University of California Press.

Silverstein, Michael and Greg Urban. 1996. *Natural Histories of Discourse.* Chicago: University of Chicago Press.

Sunaoshi, Yukako. 1995. Your Boss is Your 'Mother': Japanese Women's Construction of an Authoritative Position in the Workplace. In *SALSA II: Proceedings of the Second Annual Symposium about Language and Society, Austin (Texas Linguistic Forum 34),* ed. Pamela Silberman and Jonathan Loftin, 175-88. Austin: University of Texas Department of Linguistics.

Tannen, Deborah. 1999. The Display of (Gendered) Identities in Talk at Work. *Reinventing Identities: The Gendered Self in Discourse,* ed. Mary Bucholtz, A.C. Liang, and Laurel Sutton. New York: Oxford University Press. 221-40.

Trechter, Sara. 1999. Contextualizing the Exotic Few: Gender Dichotomies in Lakhota. *Reinventing Identities: The Gendered Self in Discourse,* ed. Mary Bucholtz, A.C. Liang, and Laurel Sutton, 101-22. New York: Oxford University Press.

Walters, Keith. 1995. Contesting Representations of African American Language. *SALSA III: Proceedings of the Third Annual Symposium about Language and Society, Austin. (Texas Linguistic Forum 36),* ed. Risako Ide, Rebecca Parker and Yukako Sunaoshi, 137-51. Austin: University of Texas Department of Linguistics.

Walters, Keith. 1999. 'Opening the Door of Paradise a Cubit': Educated Tunisian Women, Embodied Linguistic Practice, and Theories of Language. *Reinventing*

Identities: The Gendered Self in Discourse, ed. Mary Bucholtz, A.C. Liang, and Laurel Sutton, 200-20. New York: Oxford University Press.

Warner, Michael. 1993. Introduction. *Fear of a Queer Planet: Queer Politics and Social Theory*, ed. Michael Warner. Minneapolis: University of Minnesota Press.

Weston, Kath. 1993. Lesbian/Gay Studies in the House of Anthropology. *Annual Review of Anthropology*. 22:339-67.

Woolard, Kathryn A. and Bambi Schieffelin. 1994. Language Ideology. *Annual Review of Anthropology*. 23:55-82.

Zentella, Ana Celia. 1995. The 'Chiquitafication' of U.S. Latinos and their Languages, OR Why We Need an Anthropolitical Linguistics. *SALSA III: Proceedings of the Third Annual Symposium about Language and Society, Austin. (Texas Linguistic Forum 36)*, ed. Risako Ide, Rebecca Parker and Yukako Sunaoshi, 1-18. Austin: University of Texas Department of Linguistics.

3

Not Entirely in Support of a Queer Linguistics

BILL LEAP

Queer linguistics is an academic project about which I have profoundly mixed feelings. The domain in question is not unfamiliar. I have explored intersections of queer theory and language research in several publications, e.g. Leap (1996, 1997, 1999, in press). And I agree that the transgressive stances of queerness provide helpful alternatives to the essentialized treatments of sexuality and gender which still dominate conversations in linguistics, anthropology, and women's/gender studies. But it is one thing to bring the destabilizing presence of queer theory into discussions of language, sexuality and gender. Treating queerness as an obligatory starting point for those discussions, or as the cornerstone for the intellectual enterprise of which the discussions are a part, is an entirely different matter. In fact, as I want to suggest here, foregrounding queerness in such fashion is likely to obscure critical social realities which progressive discussions of sexuality-gender need to expose.

1   Queer Theory – 'A Standpoint From Which to Analyze Social Dynamics'

It is fashionable in some circles to talk about queer theory as if it were a unified intellectual project, defined by an agreed-upon selection of primary sources. Examined closely, many of those studies present diverse and at

Language and Sexuality: Contesting Meaning in Theory and Practice.
Kathryn Campbell-Kibler, Robert J. Podesva, Sarah J. Roberts and Andrew Wong (eds.).
Copyright © 2001, CSLI Publications.

times conflicting points of view about sexuality and gender. Common ground is not always easy to locate under such circumstances, but certain issues can be identified to that end.

For one thing, most discussions of queer theory argue against reifying particular expressions of sexual/gendered identity and propose instead to study lesbian, gay, bisexual and transgendered experiences in relation to broader understandings and practices. Accordingly, while discussions of same-sex desire occupy prominent places in most forms of queer theory, so do discussions of the heterosexuality and the heteronormative. As Seidman (1996:13) argues,

> the study of homosexuality should not be a study of a minority – the making of the lesbian/gay/bisexual subject – but a study of those knowledges and social practices that organize society as a whole by sexualizing – heterosexualizing or homosexualizing – bodies, desires, acts, identities, social relations, knowledge, culture, and social institutions. Queer theory aspires to transform homosexual theory into a general social theory or one standpoint from which to analyze social dynamics.

But a general social theory cannot merely incorporate heterosexual and homosexual perspectives into the same analytical paradigm. To do so unavoidably subordinates understandings of same-sex experience beneath the authority of the heterosexual norm. As Eve Sedgwick (1990:41) observes,

> there currently exists no framework in which to ask about the origins or development of individual gay identity that is not already structured by an implicit, trans-individual Western project or fantasy of eradicating that identity.[1]

To avoid such outcomes, queer theory proposes to shift the focus of analysis away from prediscursive assumptions about sexuality and gender, and argues instead that sexuality and gender do not exist outside of the forms of social action through which they are created. As Butler explains (1990:25):

> there is no gender identity behind the expressions of gender; that identity is performatively constituted by the very 'expressions' that are said to be its results.

Hence, she considers (1990:33) gender as best understood as:

> a set of repeated acts within a highly regulatory frame that congeal over time to produce the appearance of substance. . . . A political genealogy of gender ontologies, if it is successful, will deconstruct the substantive appearance of gender into its constitutive acts and locate and account for those acts within the compulsory frames set by the various forces that police the social appearance of gender.

---

[1] This arrangement does not just pose problems for Seidman's 'general social theory.' As I have discussed elsewhere (Leap, 1996:125-139, 2000), it also frustrates attempts by social subjects to make sense out of unacknowledged, unnamed dimensions of personal sexuality during the 'coming-out' experience and during other transitional stages within their gender careers.

One of the first studies to discuss gender in performative terms was *Mother Camp*, Esther Newton's (1972) now-classic discussion of how the logic of 'drag' and 'camp' inform public performance of female impersonators in the US Midwest. Judith Halberstam's *Female Masculinity* (1998) and Jennifer Robertson's *Takarazuma* (1998) offer more recent discussions of similarly performative, transgressive sexuality/gender-themes.

By shifting focus away from context-free assumptions about sexuality and gender, and drawing attention to sexuality and gender as forms of social action, performativity studies have also underscored the mechanisms of normativity and the workings of inequality *as they are viewed from the vantage point of the quotidian, the subaltern, and the margin.* In queer-oriented literary and media studies, such analysis ponders how familiar narratives might read if the storylines were presented from the perspective of one of the minor characters. Brought into social analysis, this perspective encourages researchers to subvert the expected order of things by using silenced voices rather than mainstream discourse as the starting point for description and theory-building.

Phillip Brian Harper (1993) uses this perspective when he shows how tensions between masculinity and blackness, embodied in ideologies about valued speech and silence, 'produce a discursive matrix that governs the significance of AIDS' (1993:241) in African American speech communities. Martin Manalansan (1998) uses a similar perspective to explore the intersections of displacement, sexual desires, and national belonging which underlie claims to *bakla* subjectivity within the Filipino diaspora. And a similar perspective guides my insistence (Leap 1995, in press) that the lesbian and gay linguistic practices are best described as *language*, and not as 'dialect', argot, or some other subset of a more inclusive, normatively sexualized code.

Discussions of *mainstream* and *margin* are, of course, discussions of location, and recent work in queer theory has begun to show how normative understandings of sexuality and gender help to define features of place and space which conventional conversations about geography ordinarily takes for granted.

For example, Elizabeth Grosz (1995) argues convincingly that shelter, protection, and other foundation concepts in architecture do not have neutral meanings, but invoke connections between idealized understandings of constructed space and idealized descriptions of womanhood. By ignoring the feminine presence within the built environment, she continues, architecture affirms a disembodied femininity, and supports in other ways 'the cultural refusal of women's specificity or corporeal and conceptual autonomy and social value' (1995:47) which is already pandemic in contemporary society.

And in an ethnographically rich refutation of the 'lesbian invisibility' widely reported in urban studies literature, Tamar Rothenberg (1995) shows how women-identified women use communication networks (e.g. 'and she told two friends') to establish claims to place within the city – a different strategy from the foregrounding of landmarks and boundaries, which is commonly associated with the formation of male-dominated gay ghettoes.

Importantly, in this area of queer inquiry sexuality and gender have ceased to be the primary concerns of theory-building. The disembodiment and erasure which Grosz and Rothenberg describe are issues affecting a broad range of struggles over place and space in urban and other domains, and any number of individuals are regularly forced to claim residence within the social margins and shadows. Rather than limiting marginal geographies with forms of sexual perversion, *queerness* provides a space for anyone placed 'at distance' from the mainstream to begin to respond to, to critique, and to attack conditions of oppression. Returning now to Seidman's argument (1996:13) cited above, queer theory responds to this inclusion by broadening its commitment to general social theory and social dynamics, rather than focusing exclusively on particular claims to sexual/gendered identity, practice or desire. Or, as Michael Warner (1993:xiii) has explained:

> Being queer means . . . being able, more or less articulately, to challenge the common understanding of what gender difference means, or what the state is for, or what 'health' entails, or what would define fairness, or what a good relation to the planet's environment would be. Queers do a kind of practical social reflection just in finding ways of being queer.

2 But Who *Are* the Queers? Contesting Queer Homo-geneity

But who are the social actors who are mounting these 'challenge[s] [to] the common understanding of gender difference' and who become engaged in this 'practical social reflection' simply by 'findings ways of being queer?' Most work in queer theory gives leaves these questions unaddressed, primarily because queer theory's rejection of the gendered prediscursive leads to a refusal to anchor *any* form of experience in the particulars of social identity (Seidman, 1993:133). As a result, even though recent work in queer theory has produced a large number of 'essays, presentations and books on the subject of drag, gender, performance and transsexuality,' Ki Namaste (1996:183) reminds us that:

> these works have shown very little concern for those who identify and live as drag queens, transsexuals and/or transgenders. The violation of compulsory sex/gender relations is one of the topics most frequently addressed by critics in queer theory. Those discussions, however, rarely consider the implications of an enforced sex/gender system for people who live outside of it.

This omission of 'those who live outside' becomes all the more serious since, as David Eng and Alice Y. Hom have observed:

> Queerness materializes within a concretized space, and it asserts itself in the material realm only through its intersections with a wide range of social differences, frameworks and locations. (1998:10)

Yet as long as queer theory downplays attention to that 'range of social differences' and continues to privilege sexual/gendered transgression as the cornerstone of queer experience, 'the white, European, middle class gay man [remains] the unacknowledged universal subject of lesbian/gay *and queer* studies' (Eng and Hom, 1998:12, emphasis mine), and queer theory itself will 'continue to be, at best, "thin" on gender and race' and to present 'a false front of unity when diversity is the dominant flavor' (Ingram, Bouthillette and Retter, 1997:7).

3 Decentering the White Gay Subject and (His) White Gay Space: Studying 'Gay Space' in Washington DC

One of the most insidious expressions of this 'false front of unity' stems from the widespread use of 'ghetto' and 'community' as frames of reference when describing lesbian, gay and other queer geography. The terms draw attention to a singular location in physical and/or social terrain, which is occupied by a homogeneous constituency and maintained through shared forms of spatial practice. To be sure, the image which emerges here–a localized, unified sexual subject laying claim to a homogeneous sexual geography–is politically desirable. But the image is not consistent with details of queer-related, quotidian experiences attested in real-life settings of queerspace, nor are they confirmed within the language(s) through which queer individuals explore, engage and contest quotidian experiences within those domains.

Consider, for example, the diagrams presented in Figures 1-4, a selection of maps of Washington DC as a gay city which I have collected from gay-identified DC residents over the past five years.[2] Each of these diagrams displays important features of the city's gay geography as each respondent has come to understand them through their everyday activities and interactions within this terrain.[3] In other words, besides representing the city's gay

---

[2] These maps are drawn from a larger corpus of sixty maps, collected during interviews with DC-area, gay-identified White, African American and Hispanic men. Contrasts in map designs and differences in map-related narratives are even more noticeable when the corpus as a while is explored. See discussion in Leap (to appear).

[3] Commonly identified features include gay and gay-friendly bars and clubs, gay-oriented social centers and other meeting places, cruising areas and locations for public sex, sites of activism and protest, places where respondents fell in and out of love, met significant others, and the like.

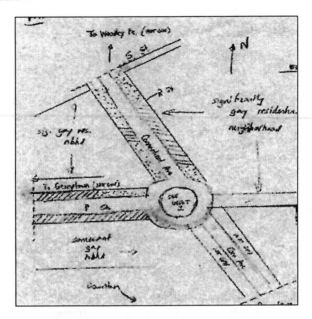

Figure 1. Harold's view of Washington DC.

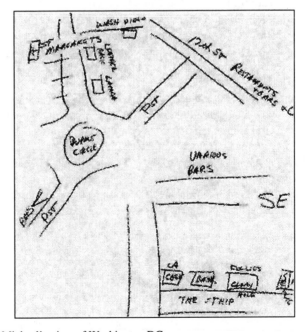

Figure 2. Michael's view of Washington DC.

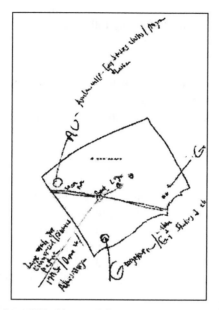

Figure 3. Turner's view of Washington DC.

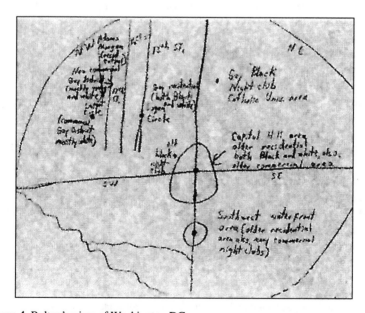

Figure 4. Bolton's view of Washington DC.

terrain, these maps visualize key moments in the respondents' autobiography, and (as is always the case in my follow-up discussions with each mapmaker), the maps provide incentives for story-telling through which respondents reveal much about their urban gender career.

3.1 Multiple mappings of queerness

Certainly, we can read these displays as statements of queerness in the sense outlined in the preceding section of this paper. That is, the maps are performative. That is, even though familiarity with local gay landscape influence how the maps are drawn and how they are read, understandings of gay landscape are themselves constructed through the process of map-making and map reading.[4] Further, the maps reflect a sense of the urban landscape not ordinarily included in conventional descriptions (e.g. roadmaps, tourist brochures, gay guidebooks) of the urban terrain. The authority of these maps, like the subject matter on which they are based, lies outside of the mainstream. And finally, the maps describe sites of experience which cut across connections between sexuality, gender, place and space in predictable and at times unpredictable ways. They are not, in that sense, restricted by familiar heterosexual/homosexual binaries.

But even if these maps present a recognizably queer perspective on urban gay geography, or could be considered 'statements of queerness' on other grounds, the details of that perspective are not expressed in terms of similar references and images. Instead, queerness is claimed *individually* and in some ways contrastively in these displays.

For example, Harold's map (Figure 1) concentrates tightly around the several residential and commercial areas adjacent to Dupont Circle.[5] This is the area of the city which many DC residents consider the local 'gay ghetto,' and the prominence which Harold gives to Dupont Circle gives support to this claim. At the same time, Harold's map also shows how Dupont Circle's gay-centered areas align with adjacent neighborhoods (e.g. Woodley Park, Georgetown, downtown DC), suggesting that gay presence may not be as tightly contained as 'ghetto'-like imagery implies.

Michael's map (Figure 2) identifies some sites in the Dupont Circle and adjacent areas, but also identifies sites adjacent to the Washington Navy Yard in close-in southeast DC. The map does not locate either area within

---

[4] Paralleling Butler's claims about gender, discussed above, these understandings are 'constituted by the very 'expressions' that are said to be its results' (Butler, 1990: 25).

[5] Brief remarks regarding respondent backgrounds will be helpful to this part of the discussion. Harold is white, in his mid-forties, blue-collar worker, and a DC resident since 1980. Michael is white, in his mid-forties, white collar employed, and a DC resident since 1985. Turner is African American, in his early thirties, blue collar private sector worker, and a DC resident since 1992. Bolton is African American, in his early thirties, white collar employed, and a lifelong DC resident. All four self-identify as gay men during the interview and in everyday conversation.

the larger urban terrain, or show how the areas are connected with other DC neighborhoods. Later in the interview, Michael explained that he included them in his map because these are the two gay neighborhoods which he frequents. Dupont Circle is 'where I go to relax', and Navy Yard is 'where I go to play.'

Turner's map (Figure 3) does not focus tightly on any single gay area, nor is it constructed primarily as a reflection of personal gay experiences. The map uses the District's boundaries to establish a sense of the city-whole. But the map also combines streets and merges familiar landmarks to produce a non-literal description of the District's gay geography. Dupont Circle is identified here, but so are locations which are not so closely associated with urban gay experience, e.g. American and Georgetown Universities, Adams-Morgan neighborhood. Overall, while this is a map of gay DC, the understanding of urban gay space which guides the display is not immediately clear (I return to this point below).

Bolton's map (Figure 4), in contrast to the others reviewed here, offers a much more literal reading of city geography. His display does not foreground any single 'gay area,' but locates gay-related sites throughout the city terrain. He also identifies the racial composition of the clientele frequenting these sites, allowing a sense of people as well as of place to emerge from this display, another feature not directly attested in the other maps examined here.

3.2 Conflicting descriptions of queerness

So while it is possible to refer to the maps in figure 1 as *queer* displays and as based on queer understandings of local geography, doing so anticipates that the maps will display much more similarity in their detail than actually proves to be the case. More seriously, perhaps, assertions of shared queerness do not prepare the analysis for the contrasts in understandings of place and space which emerge when respondents talk about these maps, describe particular locations, and explain why certain sites have been included or omitted from their displays.

Excerpts 1-4 present their comments on Dupont Circle, the area of northwest DC with a large number of gay- and gay-friendly commercial sites, and very visible gay component within the residential population. All of the respondents identified Dupont Circle on their maps, but each one did so with a particular understanding of that location in mind.

01 ... So the gay area of Dupont Circle is primarily the center part of it,
02 the fountain and the inner ring of benches. But if you move away from

03 Dupont Circle there are two [p]^6 primary [p] arteries where gay
04 businesses and activities are concentrated. To the east, P Street
05 heading toward Rock Creek Park and Georgetown, and to the north-
06 west, Connecticut Avenue. . .
07 [And he describes the various gay–oriented businesses along the P
08 Street corridor]
09 ... The northern boundary of what I call the gay area, commercially
10 anyway, is what I perceive to be S Street. There's a heavy concentra-
11 tion of gay activity on the east side of Connecticut Avenue. Lambda
12 Rising is there, the Circle Bar, the Leather Rack. I am trying to remem-
13 ber is there's just that one the Outlook store on the other side. And then
14 as you go southeast of the Circle on Connecticut Avenue, you go into
15 that transition area between Dupont Circle and the downtown area, and
16 gay activity drops off precipitously as you get down there, with the
17 exception of one one place which is on 18th Street, which is that Ozone.
18 And as you head east on P Street, the other significant corridor of gay
19 activity is 17th Street. Especially on the east side, there are many res-
20 taurants, bars, businesses that openly cater to gay people. And that is
21 where the majority of gay pedestrian traffic is. ...17th Street being a gay
22 street, you'll see lots of gays, but the activity specifically geared toward
23 restaurants, bars, strolling, cruising, whatever, is on the east side
24 of 17th.

Excerpt 1. Harold ('If you move away from Dupont Circle there are two primary
    arteries').

01 ... There's St Margaret's where um I go to Dignity. There's the Leather
02 Rack where I pick up toys. There's Lambda where I go to find uh read-
03 ing material, just hang out. There's Washington Video where I go get
04 videos. Uh 17th Street and P Street – I'm not much of a bar person, so
05 they're there. I put 'cruise street' on 17th Street because that is what 06
  happens, but I don't really frequent those places.
06 Q: ... how do you characterize this area – [pointing to Dupont Cir-
   cle/17th St]. If [Southeast DC] is where you go to play, this is –
07 A: Where I go to relax, if that makes any sense.

Excerpt 2. Michael ('[This is] where I go to relax').

01 I'll start with Dupont, Logan Circle, Adams Morgan area. What did I
02 write? [Reads from captions on his map] 'Large, openly gay, commer-
03 cial/residential presence. The gay pride flag is prominent in that. those
04 areas. A lots of stores have them coming out of their fronts or their win-

---

^{6} The [p] notation indicates a pause in the speech flow lasting longer than 3 seconds.

05   dows. Um, you see people walking, same-sex couples that is, walking
06   hand-in-hand, um, with relative ease and with relatively few people –
07   I've never seen anyone harassed. There may be second glances, but
08   it's pretty much the norm there, as opposed to people turning their
09   heads and saying, 'Oh my God, there's two people holding hands.'
Excerpt 3. Turner ('The gay pride flag is prominent in those areas').

01   ... because in my mind the largest aspect of commercial and residential
02   life in gay city focuses very close to Dupont Circle. So I identified Du-
03   pont Circle there and I put 'it's the commercial gay district.' It also hap-
04   pens to be very residential, as far as a lot of gay people live there. And
05   I said it's mostly white in commercial patronage and as far as residen-
06   tial living, too.
07   I identified Seventeenth Street primarily the strip between P Street
08   and Q, R, S Street which is in my opinion the new commercial gay dis-
09   trict, which has thriving new restaurants, new clubs, caters primarily to
10   a [swallows] younger crowd and primarily mostly a white young crowd
11   at that. I call it a *guppie* crowd.
Excerpt 4. Bolton ('The largest aspect of commercial and residential life in gay
        city').

Harold's remarks (Excerpt 1) address 'gay ghetto' themes, but he does
so by focusing his remarks on the area's streets, gay sites, and other prominent locations. While his map identifies areas adjacent to Dupont Circle as
'specifically gay residential neighborhood[s],' he says nothing more about
these neighborhoods or about the gay (and other – see below) people who
live there. In addition, his own location within this display is not specified in
these remarks. So we cannot tell whether the map is product of his own on-
site experiences or based on information from others.

Michael's comments about Dupont Circle (Excerpt 2) make clear that he
is using his own knowledge and experience as the cornerstone for his
Dupont Circle description. His remarks are filled with references to 'where I
go...', 'where I do...', and other first person imagery. Consistent with those
references, Michael says little about other gay men who may also be making
use of Dupont Circle's gay resources. In effect, while Dupont Circle may be
public space, Michael describes it here as if its terrain was intended for his
personal appropriation.

Turner (Excerpt 3) also bases his remarks about Dupont Circle on his
own familiarity with the area. This is not the detached, objective statement
as in Excerpt 1, but it is not an extended claim to personal appropriation as
in Excerpt 2, either. Turner uses direct references (lines 5-8), indirect quota-

tion (line 9), and other techniques of narrative description to acknowledge that others are also 'on the streets', making use of the local geography. According to these remarks, gay sites are an important part of what makes Dupont Circle attractive, but the presence of gay and gay-friendly people is equally important in that regard.

Bolton (Excerpt 4) begins by positioning Dupont Circle within the broader domain of gay city; he is one of very few respondents in this project who did this, and I suspect that doing so is a reflection of his life-long residence in the city. Even so, and similar to the wording in Excerpt 1, Bolton does not specify his own location within the Dupont Circle setting; like Harold, he remains the detached observer. Yet unlike Harold (and also unlike Michael), Bolton acknowledges the presence of others, and presents a degree of familiarity with the area derived through his own on-site experience. And unlike the case in Turner's remarks, Bolton acknowledges Dupont Circle's gay residential presence, and does not focus solely on its gay commercial venues and gay street-presence.

3.3 Example: Queering dissemblance

But even with that broader focus, Bolton's description of Dupont Circle is still selective. He suggests (lines 5-6) that Dupont Circle is 'mostly white in commercial patronage and as far as residential living, too' and then adds (lines 9-11) that the concentration of gay-oriented businesses along Seventeenth Street:

> cater [. . .] primarily to a . . . younger crowd, and primarily mostly a white young crowd . . . a guppie crowd.

Measured against demographics of the Dupont Circle area, Bolton's remarks are problematic in at least two ways. First, by focusing his remarks on *white* gay presence, Bolton ignores the number of African American and Hispanic gay/same-sex identified men who regularly make use of Dupont Circle's gay resources.[7] Second, by focusing is remarks on gay/same-sex male presence, Bolton ignores the sizeable number of heterosexual women and men who live in the Dupont Circle area, many of whom are also African American.[8]

But even though these allusions to white presence and gay dominance are at variance with racial and sexualized realities of the Dupont Circle area,

---

[7] For example, gay bars and clubs along P Street have been popular meeting places for African American gay men since the mid 1970s, and the weekly Latino night (hosted by one of the gay clubs on 17th Street and featuring salsa music, Latin dancing, and drag performances filled with Hispanic entertainers) attracts gay/same-sex identified Hispanic men from the city and the distant suburbs.

[8] Limitations of space led me to concentrate on the erasure of African American presence. I shall defer a discussion of Hispanic erasure until a later time.

focusing attention on whiteness and gayness are consistent with a text-making strategy widely attested in African American public discourse, especially when the discourse is addressing highly personal, highly sensitive themes.

Darlene Clark Hine identifies this strategy as one of *dissemblance*, that is, a belief that some issues are better left 'unknown, unwritten and unspoken except in whispered tones' and an agreement that 'those who broke the silence provided grist for detractors' mills and, even more seriously, tore the protective cloaks from their inner selves' (1997:436). Hine suggests that *dissemblance* is widely attested in the life story narratives told by African American women. Constructing texts in this form, Hine explains, allows these women to 'create the appearance of disclosure or openness about themselves and their feelings' (1997:436), while downplaying direct references to the physical, sexual and domestic violence which has shaped their lives. And by doing so, African American women were able to by protect from outside scrutiny and critique the 'sanctity of inner aspects of their lives' (1997:436).

Phillip Brian Harper suggests that dissemblance has a broader occurrence in African American linguistic experience, in that:

> black people's successful participation in modes of discourse validated in mainstream culture – their facility in Received Standard English, for example – actually implicates them in a profound *silence* regarding their African American identity. (1993:243, his emphasis)

That *profound silence/dissemblance* is especially noticeable, Harper explains, in instances where homosexuality is a prominent theme in African American identity. As Bolton himself observed, during a later segment of his interview:

01 …there are pockets in the city – primarily around Dupont Circle – where
02 where there is such a concentration, centralization of the gay commu-
03 nity – you don't see it with the black gay community. It tends to be a lot
04 more fragmented. There tends to be pieces of it scattered about in
05 different areas. … (W)ith a lot of Black gay residents, they tend to be
06 just kind of mixed in with other working class families in uh row houses
07 in certain parts of the city. Their identities are kept kind of concealed.
08 There's, they seem to get along quite well, but as far as their openness
09 and their outness, not really. And people tend to respect them for not
10 revealing, quote, unquote, 'their business.'
11 … Black people don't tend to politicize being gay as much as white
12 people do. I think that for the longest time, and even today, that um
13 black communities have always seen being gay as a white thing.
14 They've always seen it as, they can't associate it with the black ex-

15 perience. Black people just did it; you don't talk about it, you just did it.
16 Um, you didn't try to identify it or to put a label on it, politicize it; it was
17 just done.
Example 5. Bolton.

At this point in the discussion, I asked Bolton whether this reluctance to 'put a label on it' (another form of dissemblance) might explain why rainbow flags and other gay symbols are so rarely displayed on houses and cars in African American neighborhoods. He agreed that such items were unlikely to appear there. 'So,' I continued, 'if you saw a rainbow flag in that area, what would you assume?' And he replied:

20   – [you'd] assume that this was a white,
21 because you have a lot of gay white individuals and couples who do
22 live in Black areas of the city. Yeah, I would definitely assume it was a
23 white resident
Example 6. Bolton (continued).

Bolton's references to Dupont Circle as *primarily white space* as well as his deletion of direct references to African Americans in that setting, are consistent with Hine's and Harper's remarks about dissemblance, and with his own incorporation of this text-making strategy at other points in the interview. That is, foregrounding Dupont Circle's gay whiteness in this fashion distracts attention from the Black gay presence in the area of Washington DC and maintains without disruption the agreed-upon silence surrounding African American homosexuality (see again Harper's remarks, above).

Like Bolton, Turner did not make any explicit references to an African American (or Hispanic) presence in the Dupont Circle area. Initially, given the absence of explicit Black (or Hispanic) reference, I read Turner's statements as a foregrounding of gay whiteness, and as a disguising of gay Blackness by means of dissemblance.

At a later point in the interview, I pointed out to Turner that he had not said anything about Dupont Circle's African American population. Turner replied to my remark with surprise, 'I haven't?,' and then assured me that he intended statements like 'same-sex couples walking hand-in-hand' (Excerpt 3, lines 5-6) to be comments about African American gay men. In fact, he continued, everything he had said about Dupont Circle was African American oriented, even if he had not marked the particulars of racial identity as such within the text.

Leaving race unmarked in such references is an effective way of achieving the 'secrecy' and 'self-imposed invisibility' (Hine 1997:436) which are prominent features of textual dissemblance. But if Turner was using textual dissemblance to structure his remarks about African American homosexuality in Dupont Circle, his use of silence and secrecy are very different from that attested in Bolton's text.

Generally in mainstream American English text-making, race is obligatorily marked in references to peoples of color and whiteness enjoys the status of unmarked referencing and, thereby, the default category (Wander, Martin and Nakayama 1999:15). In Turner's usage, African American gay presence preempts white gay presence as the unmarked, default category. As in Bolton's remarks, the 'unspoken' reference is still African American in focus, but under this arrangement, unmarked Dupont Circle is now a gay African American terrain, and the presence of whiteness in that terrain is now pushed into the sidelines of the textual reference.

Importantly, there are no structural clues in Turner's description of Dupont Circle which show that his use of dissemblance differs from Bolton's. It was my follow-up question brought the particular meaning underlying this usage into focus. Such similarities in textual form are consistent with the concealment of personal messages which is at stake in such text-making. The fact that I could gain access to the concealed message only by breaking the textual silence about African American gay presence is consistent with Hine's and Harper's claims that African American commitments to dissemblance have been successful in keeping dissemblance itself concealed from the prying eyes of (white) outsiders.

Harold and Michael also said nothing about the African American presence—gay as well as straight—in the Dupont Circle area. The absence of racial specifics in these remarks implies a focus on whiteness, and white gay experience, which is consistent with remarks elsewhere in their interviews. In theory, the absence of racial specifics within their remarks could also be read as moments of dissemblance. But such a claim would conflict with the point of view about same-sex desires proclaimed throughout these texts. There is nothing in the interviews to indicate that Harold and Michael are trying to maintain a *profound silence* (in Harper's wording, 1993:243) about African American homosexuality. But there is much in the interviews which locates homosexual experience within domains of white privilege.[9]

So here is another instance in respondent commentary where texts share an appearance of textual similarity—in this case, the absence of explicit references to African American gay presence in respondent descriptions of

---

[9] These markers of white privilege include: the close association of urban gay space and commercial location, the frequent references to economic consumption, the references to urban gay spaces as sites for 'playing' and 'relaxing', as well as the foregrounding of the narrator and his experiences as the focal point guiding spatial descriptions.

Dupont Circle; but where similarities in textual appearance actually disguise different understandings of sexuality, race and place. It is worth remembering that this domain of whiteness is also the area of the city which DC area residents generally refer to as DC's gay ghetto. To the extent that Dupont Circle-as-ghetto coincides with Dupont Circle-as-whiteness (and the overlap is strongly evidenced throughout the project's larger corpus), these differences in place-description speak even more powerfully to different formations of same-sex desire which are performatively constructed within this urban setting.

4 Diverse Voices vs. Queer Inclusion

There were moments in the map-drawing and the text-making (for example, Turner's inversion of the meaning of dissemblance) where presentations of specific features departed from or otherwise 'queered' the expected reference or conventional representation. And it is important to analyze those moments (as verbal or visual enactments of queer perspective and, thereby, as situated claims to queer subjectivity. But I see great danger in assuming, categorically, that all four maps, and/or all of the respondents' remarks about them, are in some entire sense best considered as statements of queerness. Yes, these texts enable performative claims to sexuality and gender, advance subaltern, quotidian perspectives on mainstream experience, validate transgressive claims to place, and/or otherwise incorporates issues and themes closely associated with queer experience in the theoretical literature. But even with those shared characteristics, and the shared foundation of queerness which they jointly imply, the maps and texts considered here conveyed rather diverse messages about sexualized geographies embedded within Washington DC's urban landscape.

In part, the diversity reflects differences in respondent backgrounds, the particulars of each respondent's sex/gendered experiences within the DC context, or is autobiographic in other ways. But linking differences in visual and verbal text-making to other components of respondent subjectivity simply underscores the points I want to make here: Queer references are not always totalizing, they do not automatically pre-empt other points of view – especially so, other points of view on queer-related themes.

Gordon Brett Ingram, Anne-Marie Bouthillette, and Yolanda Retter (1997), writing about struggles to claim spaces of queerness in urban settings, Alexander Doty (1993) writing about gender-bending messages in American television programs, Judith Halberstam (1998) writing about female masculinity, Rosalind Morris (1997) describing the transgressive significance of Thai *kathoey* for Thai people and gender theorist alike all insist that effective work in queer theory needs to be oriented in ways which show

how conditions of queerness to emerge from the text, rather than assume that textual queerness is always, already a part of the textual prediscursive and provide documentation accordingly.[10] I believe that the same argument should guide language-oriented studies of queerness. To assume otherwise is to impose equality onto textual expressions and attendant voices when real-life conditions of text and voice suggest otherwise.

5 Coda: If Not *Queer*, Then Why *Gay*?

One could argue that the fictional, erasive properties I associate with queer(ness) are attested just as strongly in discussions of sexual/gendered experiences framed in terms of *gay(ness)* and to *gay men*. These references also cut across divisions of race and class, lumping together experiences and understandings of desire and identity which are quite distinctive. But there is sense in which, these distortions notwithstanding, reference to *gayness* and to *gay men* are defensible actions in linguistic inquiry—at least, in the domains in Washington DC where my linguistic research unfolds. *Gay* is a form of vernacular self-description which extends widely across boundaries of race, class, and erotic orientation in DC settings, *Queer*, on the other hand, is a term of self-description confined largely to those in academic circles, some mainstream activist domains, and other privileged locations. Describing speakers in their terms of reference choice is a long-standing linguistic practice; imposing identities and labels onto respondents struggling to express subjectivities in their own terms has also been ethically unacceptable, up quite recently. I see no reason why those practices and ethical stances should be changed.

Understanding why speakers favor certain forms of self-reference and why they devalue other references are an equally important linguistic practice. But to address this task we need theory which resonates effectively with real-life conditions of desire, subjectivity and sexual practice. I do not see how the fictional inclusiveness of queer theory will help us unpack the workings of discrimination, homophobia, racism, sexism, class privilege, and other themes which structure conditions and languages of everyday experiences for so many women and men (same-sex oriented and otherwise) in late modern society.

---

[10] I made the same point in an earlier (Leap, 1997) discussion of the *performative effect* of gay English usage in otherwise not-gay or anti-gay settings.

References

Butler, Judith. 1990. *Gender Trouble.* New York City: Routledge.

Doty, Alexander. 1993. The gay straight man: Jack Benny and the Jack Benny Program. *Making Things Perfectly Queer: Interpreting Mass Culture,* 63–80. Minneapolis: University of Minnesota Press.

Eng, David L. and Alice Y. Hom. 1998. Q&A: Notes on a queer Asian America. *Q&A Queer in Asian America,* ed. David L. Eng and Alice Y. Hom, 1-23. Philadelphia: Temple University Press.

Grosz, Elizabeth. 1995. Women, *chora,* dwelling. *Postmodern Cities and Spaces,* ed. Katherine Gibson and Sophie Watson, 47-58. London: Blackwell's.

Halberstam, Judith. 1998. *Female Masculinity.* Durham: Duke University Press.

Harper, Phillip Brian. 1993. Eloquence and epitaph: Black nationalism and the homophobic impulse in responses to the death of Max Robinson. *Fear of a Queer Planet,* ed. Michael Warner, 239-263. Minneapolis: University of Minnesota Press.

Hine, Darlene Clark. 1997. Rape and the inner lives of Black women in the Middle West: Preliminary thoughts on the culture of dissemblance. *The Gender/Sexuality Reader,* ed. Roger N. Lancaster and Micaela di Leonardo, 434-439. New York City: Routledge.

Ingram, Gordon Brett, Anne-Marie Bouthillette, and Yolanda Retter. 1997. Lost in space: Queer theory and community activism at the fin-de-millenaire. *Queers in Space,* ed. Gordon Brett Ingram, Anne-Marie Bouthillette, and Yolanda Retter, 3-15. Seattle, WA: Seattle Bay Press.

Leap, William. 1995. Introduction. *Beyond the Lavender Lexicon,* ed. William Leap, vii-xx. Newark: Gordon and Breach Publishers.

Leap, William. 1996. *Word's Out: Gay Men's English.* Minneapolis: University of Minnesota Press.

Leap, William. 1997. Performative effect in three gay English texts. *Queerly Phrased,* ed. Anna Livia and Kira Hall, 310-325. New York City: Oxford University Press.

Leap, William. 1999. The queerness of queer space: Review of: *Queers in Space,* ed. Gordon Brett Ingram, Anne-Marie Bouthillette, and Yolanda Retter. *Sexual Geographies,* 37: 133-136.

Leap, William. In press. Studying lesbian/gay languages: Vocabulary, text-making and beyond. *Out in Theory,* ed. Ellen Lewin and William Leap. Urbana: University of Illinois Press.

Leap, William. To appear. *Gay City: Sexuality, Space, and the Language of Sites in Washington DC.* Minneapolis: University of Minnesota Press.

Manalansan, Martin. 1998. *Remapping Frontiers: The Lives of Filipino Gay Men in New York.* Unpublished doctoral dissertation, Department of Anthropology, University of Rochester.

Morris, Rosalind. 1997. Educating desire: Thailand, transnationalism, and transgression. *Queer Transexions of Race, Nation and Gender*, ed. Phillip Brian Harper, Anne McClintock, Jose Esteban Munoz, and Trish Rosen. *Social Text*, 52-53: 53-79.

Namaste, Ki. 1996. 'Tragic misreadings': Queer theory's erasure of transgender subjectivity. *Queer Studies*, ed. Brett Beemyn and Mickey Eliason, 183-203. New York City: New York University Press.

Newton, Esther. 1972. *Mother Camp: Female Impersonators in America*. Chicago: University of Chicago Press.

Robinson, Jennifer. 1998. *Takarazuka: Sexual Politics and Popular Culture in Modern Japan*. Berkeley: University of California Press.

Rothenberg, Tamar. 1995. 'And she told two friends': Lesbians creating urban social space. *Mapping Desire*, ed. David Bell and Gill Valentine, 165-181. London: Routledge.

Sedgwick, Eve Kosofsky. 1990. *Epistemology of the Closet*. Berkeley: University of California Press.

Seidman, Steven. 1993. Identity and politics in a 'postmodern' gay culture. *Fear of a Queer Planet*, ed. Michael Warner, 178-192. Minneapolis: University of Minnesota Press.

Seidman, Steven. 1996. Introduction. *Queer Theory/Sociology*, ed. Steven Seidman, 1-29. London: Blackwells.

Wander, Phillip C., Judith N. Martin, and Thomas K. Nakayama. 1999. Whiteness and beyond: Sociohistorical foundations of whiteness and contemporary challenges. *Whiteness: The Communication of Social Identity,* ed. Thomas K. Nakayama and Judith N. Martin, 13-26. Thousand Oaks: Sage Publications.

Warner, Michael. 1994. Introduction. *Fear of a Queer Planet,* ed. Michael Warner, i-xxxi. Minneapolis: University of Minnesota Press.

4

Queer Linguistics?*

DON KULICK

In another publication (Kulick 2000), I have already presented work on the history of research on gay and lesbian language, pontificating about the past, and offering suggestions about the future. For that reason, I am going to be very brief here and focus only on one specific issue. I am going to play the role of a devil's advocate, while making it clear that I do so as someone who is enormously sympathetic to queer theory, and who has been teaching it and using it since about 1993.

What, I wonder, *is* queer linguistics? How does it differ from 'gay and lesbian' linguistics? Now one immediate answer to that question that I'm sure leaps to many minds is that whereas anything we would want the label 'gay and lesbian' linguistics attached to (or mired in, depending on your perspective), identity categories, queer linguistics will transcend those and attend not to how identity is *expressed* linguistically, but, instead, how identity is constructed or materialized performatively.

Yeah, sure, sure, I would respond. My question is what exactly is it that is *queer* about that? Because once we accept as axiomatic the observation that identities are discursively/performatively constructed (and I take it for granted that we all accept this), what, then, is the queer part? What does 'queer' mean? What is special or unique about queer? And most impor-

---

* Editors' Note: This paper is the text of Don Kulick's commentary given during the panel discussion on 'The Future of Queer Linguistics' at the first IGALA conference in April 2000.

Language and Sexuality: Contesting Meaning in Theory and Practice.
Kathryn Campbell-Kibler, Robert J. Podesva, Sarah J. Roberts and Andrew Wong (eds.).

tantly: if queer is *not* the same as lesbian, gay, bisexual or transgender – as all queer theorists insist that it is not – why, then, is the only language ever investigated to say anything about queer language the language of people who self-identify, or who researchers believe to be, lesbian, gay, bisexual or transgendered?

I have yet to encounter an adequate definition of queer in any of the literature on the topic. As those who are familiar with queer theory know, the way in which scholars love to answer the wide-eyed question: 'But what is queer?' is by shaking their heavy heads and responding, with the same kind of weary, indulgent smile that met the bald boy-David Carradine whenever he asked his Master a question on that old television program *Kung-Fu*: 'Ah, that, young grasshopper', the queer oracles intone, 'is not for anyone to say.' Queer, we are forever informed, is always that which exceeds definition, that which is undefinable. 'There is nothing in particular to which it necessarily refers' explains David Halperin (1995:62). 'It marks a flexible space for the expression of all aspects of non- (anti-, contra-) straight cultural production and reception,' Alexander Doty informs us (1993:3). It is both 'anti-assimilationist and anti-separatist,' says Rosemary Hennessy (1994:86-7). And in what gets my nomination as the single most annoying definition of queer that has ever been authored by anybody, Lauren Berlant and Michael Warner (in an otherwise quite interesting article, I should add, 1998:558) draw back the curtain to reveal unto us that 'The queer world is a space of entrances, exits, unsystematized lines of acquaintance, projected horizons, typifying examples, alternative routes, blockages, incommensurate geographies'.

Now all this sounds fabulous. But let's face it, it isn't particularly helpful and it doesn't always make a great deal of sense ('typifying examples'?). My concern is that this kind of obfuscation and breezy equivocality about 'queer' can easily lead us to avoid defining 'queer', even as we continue to use it in undertheorized, ad hoc, and ultimately extremely problematic ways. I do agree with those scholars who argue that one analytic advantage of 'queer' is precisely its semiotic slipperiness (Halperin's 'There is nothing in particular to which it necessarily refers' argument). But granting that, we need to remind ourselves that the key terms used in past studies of gay and lesbian language – terms like 'gay', 'lesbian', 'language', and 'sexuality' – are also slippery. And we ought to remember how those terms have been employed in past work: not as critical tools, but, rather, as largely unproblematized labels used on the assumption everybody simply shared an understanding of what they signified (Kulick 2000:273). I worry that the same problem may arise if we don't think very hard about what we mean when we say 'queer'.

Let me offer a quick example of what I am talking about, taken from a recent article by Robin Queen. I chose this example because I think that Robin Queen's writings (together with those by Rusty Barrett [1995, 1997], with whom Robin shares a theoretical project) are some of the most important now being published (see especially Queen 1997). Indeed, to the extent that we can speak of a 'queer linguistics' at all, I think Robin and Rusty's research constitutes part of the core of that emerging canon. I am, however, puzzled about one thing. Even though both Robin and Rusty both the word 'queer' liberally, I think it is not easy to see exactly how their use of that concept differs from 'gay and lesbian.' A main reason for this is because both Robin's and Rusty's research focuses exclusively on speakers who self-identify as gay or lesbian; something which, I think, is a real theoretical disadvantage, especially if we really are interested in developing a 'queer linguistics' that differs in any substantial was from a 'gay and lesbian linguistics.'

The problem becomes especially highlighted in Robin's recent definition of what she means by 'queer community.' She defines this by first explaining that she uses 'the term queer...to refer to lesbians and gay men.' But then she adds that she understands the term 'to refer potentially to any gay, lesbian, bisexual or transgendered people who see themselves as having their sexual orientation in common and who see that commonality as influential for their sense of culture and identity' (1998:203).

Now read that definition closely. What it means is that even though Robin, like Rusty Barrett, elegantly argues that the focus of research on queer language should be displaced from identity categories to signifying practices, her understanding of 'queer' rests precisely on identity categories ('gay, lesbian, bisexual or transgendered people'), and it definitionally excludes anyone who identifies as straight; including, apparently, straight-identified men and women who have same-sex experiences or relationships, and straight-identified transexuals and transvestites. So the important implication of Robin's (and Rusty's) arguments that the position 'queer' might be filled by a subject who is not gay, lesbian, bisexual or transgendered, remains not only unpursued, but even, it seems to me, given this kind of language, actually blocked.

I conclude by repeating that I am doubtful that something we can call queer linguistics even exists, and I am wary of proclaiming a future for it, especially if we are not able to come up with better definitions and understandings of 'queer' than what we have been working with so far. To the extent that we want to argue that 'queer' is a kind of 'exposure within language – an exposure that disrupts the repressive surface of language' (Butler 1993:176), and that a 'queer linguistics' would seek to identify those ruptures, account for silences that make them possible and give them meaning, and explore how they in important ways structure and are structured through (all kinds of) sexuality, then we are, I think, on firmer ground. We can then use 'queer' as a means of dramatically expanding the scope of our concerns, and of moving 'queer linguistics' beyond the study of the linguistic behavior people we know to be, or suspect might be, gay, lesbian, bisexual or transgendered. However, to the extent that we allow ourselves to invoke 'queer' just as a blithe new synonym for gay and lesbian, we risk recapitulating all of the problems that have plagued research we are trying to supercede. So if there is a future of queer linguistics, maybe it lies in first of all deciding what we might mean when we use that term. Even if we ultimately reject it, the debate will undoubtedly prove bracing.

References

Barrett, Rusty. 1997. The 'Homo-genius' Speech Community. *Queerly Phrased: Language, Gender and Sexuality*, ed. Anna Livia and Kira Hall, 181-201. Oxford: Oxford University Press.

Barrett, Rusty. 1995. Supermodels of the World Unite! Political Economy and the Language of Performance among African-American Drag Queens. *Beyond the Lavender Lexicon: Authenticity, Imagination and Appropriation in Lesbian and Gay Languages*, ed. William L. Leap, 207-26. Buffalo, New York: Gordon and Breach.

Berlant, Lauren and Michael Warner. 1998. Sex in Public. *Critical Inquiry* 24.2: 547-66.

Butler, Judith. 1993. *Bodies that Matter: On the Discursive Limits of 'Sex'*. New York and London: Routledge.

Doty, Alexander. 1993. *Making Things Perfectly Queer: Interpreting Mass Culture*. Minneapolis: University of Minnesota Press.

Halperin, David. 1995. *Saint Foucault: Towards a Gay Hagiography*. New York and Oxford: Oxford University Press.

Hennessy, Rosemary. 1994. Queer Theory, Left Politics. *Rethinking Marxism* 7.3: 85-111.

Kulick, Don. 2000. Gay and Lesbian Language. *Annual Review of Anthropology* 29:243-285.

Queen, Robin. 1998. 'Stay Queer!' 'Never Fear!': Building Queer Social Networks. *World Englishes* 17:203-224.

Queen, Robin. 1997. 'I Don't Speak Spritch': Locating Lesbian Language. *Queerly Phrased: Language, Gender and Sexuality*, ed. Anna Livia and Kira Hall, 233-56. Oxford: Oxford University Press.

5

A Matter of Interpretation: The 'Future' of 'Queer Linguistics'*

ROBIN QUEEN

1   A Matter of Meaning

When asked to participate in a panel at the first meeting of the International Gender and Language Association on the future of queer linguistics, I found myself rather perplexed by the title of the panel. My confusion centered on the two propositions contained in the title, namely that of 'future' and that of 'queer linguistics.' As is typical in calls for discussions of futures, there is an inherent instability embedded in the call, namely an uncertainty about whether there will be a future and if so, what its nature can or should be. The panel title also contained the presumption of a very particular kind of present, one that was knowable and that pointed to multiple possible trajectories, including the move to disband 'queer linguistics'. This is not to claim that I read this title as necessarily part of a disciplinary crisis since many discussions of futures offer visions of hope and new direction. The problem for this particular call and the source of my puzzlement were not in what

* I would like to thank the IGALA organizers for organizing the panel out of which this paper grew and the panel participants for an invigorating discussion. I would also like to thank Susan Garrett, Judith Irvine, Deborah Keller-Cohen, Alaina Lemon, Lesley Milroy and especially Rusty Barrett for helpful and enlightening comments on various drafts of this paper. Special thanks to Joy Rowe for invaluable research assistance. All errors in fact and interpretation remain, of course, entirely my own.

Language and Sexuality: Contesting Meaning in Theory and Practice.
Kathryn Campbell-Kibler, Robert J. Podesva, Sarah J. Roberts and Andrew Wong (eds.).
Copyright © 2001, CSLI Publications.

would come of talking about the future of a particular area of inquiry, but rather what I see as the area of inquiry's thorough uncertainty with respect to its present. This is a point to which I plan to return throughout the essay because there are existential questions at stake, questions that are fundamental to any discussion of a future. One of those existential questions in fact involves the second source of my puzzlement, the naming of the area of inquiry under discussion.

Although the term 'queer linguistics' has been floating around for some time, it has never been entirely clear what the term actually means, especially in that particular collocation. One certain resonance is a claim of alliance or affiliation with queer theory, which has been among the recent dominant theoretical paradigms in cultural studies and related fields. The alliance, however, has been a rather strange one because queer theorists and researchers in 'queer linguistics' have not been particularly successful at engaging in dialogue with one another. This situation arises not necessarily out of ill will but rather out of the fact that the two groups of scholars have relatively little professional contact (e.g., they attend different professional meetings, publish in different professional venues and are housed in different disciplinary homes). Additionally, the tenets of queer theory require a very different intervention into linguistics than the one that is reflected in the work typically considered under that label. In one way or another, most of the work that gets placed under the label 'queer linguistics' is not specifically queer theoretical but rather based on data from queer subjects. Although it is rarely specifically defined as such, the 'queer' of 'queer linguistics' has been fashioned so that an undergraduate of mine could reasonably claim that the article 'Performing gender identity: Young men's talk and the construction of heterosexual masculinity' (Cameron 1997) was not relevant to his interests in 'queer linguistics' because it concerned heterosexual men. The validity of this claim arises not out of some natural or actual delineation, but rather out of the social practice that uses the label 'queer linguistics' for work that queries language use as it is entangled with categories of social identity that revolve around non-heterosexual sexualities.[1]

In thinking about the present state of this area of inquiry, it is in fact critical to distinguish these two senses of 'queer linguistics.' As queer theory has importantly pointed out, all categories of identity are inherently regulating and exclusionary. Further, categorization based in identity tends to reproduce hegemonic discourses that rank and order particular types of desires and behaviors, rendering some modes of being exemplary and others deviant (e.g. Rubin 1984). A queer intervention occurs not only when these

---

[1] This labeling does not entail the exclusion of heterosexual identities by researchers themselves.

processes are interrogated, but also when the normalizing tendencies that typically result from these processes are deconstructed. As Barrett (1997 and this volume) points out, an actual queering of linguistics would entail a fundamental re-working of the underlying assumptions through which sociolinguistics and linguistic anthropology have typically operated, particularly with respect to the assignment of speakers to particular kinds of social categories. This represents an important theoretical move and one in which many sociolinguists and linguistic anthropologists have begun to engage. However, it orients around a fundamentally different project than work that seeks to examine the relationships between the symbolic resources available through language and the social identities available through socializing rubrics of sexuality. While it is most certainly the case that much work on language and sexual identity draws heavily from the tenets of queer theory, the two are not isomorphic.

A 'queer linguistics', then, would necessarily be quite different from the study of the ways in which language becomes a part of claiming a sexual identity as part of the sense of self. Any discussion of a future for this area requires first a clear demarcation of which future is in question. Blessed with the hindsight of the panel, it seems to me that the future in question is not the queering of linguistics, something which is well underway, particularly in sociolinguistics and linguistic anthropology, but the future (and the possibility) of investigating language and sexual identity. This is an unusually pressing future to discuss, as sexual identities have remained a focal point in the overall theoretical crisis over identity, particularly in cultural studies. For instance, in Don Kulick's recent review and critique of the study of language and sexual identity, he concludes the following (2000: 272):

> ... phrasing the enquiry in terms of language and sexuality might be counterproductive, especially because sexuality can easily segue into 'sexual categories,' which can lead us right back to 'sexual identity.' To forestall and avoid that slippage, it might be helpful to declare a moratorium on 'sexuality'...

While I do not agree that a moratorium on such studies provides the most fruitful path for continuing the exploration of the symbolic power of language, I would like to go into Kulick's argument in some depth because it well represents the sorts of issues with which any study of the symbolic resources associated with a social identity must contend.

2   A Matter of Naming

Kulick notes that despite a mini-explosion in this area of inquiry, research on language and sexual identity has had virtually no impact on sociolinguistics or linguistic anthropology. He goes on to suggest multiple possible reasons for this state of affairs, including discrimination about this work and its authors, the appearance of much of the work in obscure publications, the lack of an obvious disciplinary home, the vocabulary list nature of much early work and finally the conceptual difficulties that have 'plagued' the area (Kulick 2000: 246). Kulick focuses the bulk of his review/argument on the final possible reason for the lack of impact of studies of language and sexual identity. Without discussing why he sees this difficulty as paramount to the others, Kulick goes on to present his understanding of the problem and to propose ways of addressing it. He argues from the position that much of the work that has dealt with language and sexual identities has not taken seriously an exploration of what makes sexuality sexuality, namely, 'fantasy, desire, repression, pleasure, fear and the unconscious' (270). In his formulation, the social aspects of sexual identities have become divorced from the sexual. Rather than argue for a more thorough exploration of why this has happened, what it might mean, and whether it is useful to maintain such a distinction, he calls instead for a shift in focus away from sexual identities and heralds the emergence of a 'linguistics of desire.'

Kulick bases his position on two interrelated points. First, previous research has not identified any particular set of linguistic features (with the possible exception of lexicons) that is unique to gay men or lesbians and second, using data from those who self-identify as gay or lesbian tells us very little about queer sexualities (as sexual desire). While I generally agree with his first point, it is unclear to me how or why this should be a fundamental basis for calling for a moratorium on studies that look at sexual identity (unless of course one is interested in looking at something else). As much recent research in both sociolinguistics and linguistic anthropology has been at pains to show, few if any linguistic resources are uniquely tied to specific groups of speakers (e.g. Tannen 1993, Bucholtz 1999; Johnstone 1996; Barrett 1995, 1997, 1999, papers in Schieffelin, Woolard & Kroskrity 1998, Campbell-Kibler, Podesva & Roberts 1999, Eckert 2000 etc.). This theoretical point has not resulted in a call for a moratorium on studies of the language use of socially salient groupings, such as Wolof griots (Irvine 1989, 1998), jocks and burnouts (Eckert 1989, 2000), speakers of AAE (papers in Mufwene et. al. 1999) or Brasilian Travesti (Kulick 1998b). To the contrary, such work has been critical to showing how important an understanding of emic social categorizations is when exploring language use. In fact, it is these very studies that have demonstrated the fluidity with which people use and respond to symbolic resources when constituting and indexing social identities. Such work has also helped move scholarship away from the rather undertheorized ideas of the social typical in much work on language, culture and society and to a more sophisticated understanding of language variation itself as a social practice rather than simply a reflection of other social practices.

With respect to his second point, while it would certainly be enlightening to know how linguistic resources stereotypically associated with certain identities get used by those who do not claim the identity and what those usages might mean semiotically, it is rather odd to claim that the area is weakened specifically by its focus on those for whom a particular social category of identity has salience. For instance, it has been one of the guiding principles of recent work on African-American English that one need not reference other varieties of English in order to say something interesting about African-American English, a position which understands critiques to the contrary as evidence of an imposed normativity (e.g. Laboratory of Comparative Human Cognition 1997). Requiring reference to the language use of those who do not identify with the social discourses under discussion seriously reconfigures sociolinguistic and linguistic anthropological inquiry. For instance, without such reference it becomes quite difficult to develop an understanding of the processes through which features come to be used as symbolic resources in the first place or how various sets of symbolic resources might be related to one another. While it is obvious that neither individuals nor groups can be reduced to compartments of identities, recognizing that fact does not make the social salience of categories of identity disappear. Kulick's vision of the future not only removes the social from the psychological but also leaves little room for pursuing an understanding of sexuality as a social phenomenon.

Focusing on desire rather than sexual identity will not fundamentally attend to the dilemma of categorization because the mere act of focusing on desire necessarily begins a new process of categorization. The problem is not so much in categorization per se but rather in the normalizing and naturalizing effects of categorization, something that Whorf reminded us of long ago (Whorf 1956) and which many scholars have begun pursuing with renewed vigor (Lucy 1992, Silverstein 1979, 1993). Categorization of any sort inevitably leads to grappling with the tug-of-war between essentialism and constructionism, a battle that has been raging for some time within social theories that juxtapose the problem of difference and the problem of sameness. As Epstein (1987: 150) notes, however, neither essentialism nor strict constructionism can capture the ways in which people who question them conceive of categories like sexuality. He calls instead for a focus on the continuum of relative 'sameness-in-difference' and 'difference-in-sameness.' In other words, because the relational nature of categories of identity typically make the resources used for creating and reflecting those categories unique in degree rather than in kind, the particulars of such relationships typically emerge through the processes of selection and combination from among a variety of resources (e.g. Jakobson 1960, Queen 1997, Irvine, in press). Such a relational approach helps make sense of the rather peculiar fact that critiques of an identity label typically succeed by rallying around the label in question (Epstein 1987). Thus it would seem that one critical theoretical move with respect to language and sexual identity must be to understand the process of semiosis through which sexuality becomes a category of identity around which people orient rather than to decenter that sense of sexuality. This is not a new point and many researchers have begun to move in this direction with respect to identity more generally, particularly in work that explores language ideologies and indexicality (Silverstein 1979, 1993, Schieffelin, Woolard & Kroskrity 1998, Kulick 1998a, Gal & Irvine 2000, Irvine in press). It is within many of these theoretical approaches that I would look for resolution to the conflict over identity and its relationships to language use.

Within these models, the focus is not primarily on tying the psychological states of given individuals to language but rather on exploring how individuals and groups of individuals come to recognize language as a part of what it means to claim oneself as a particular kind of person (or not, as the case may be). As Povinelli (1999), writes:

> Sexual identities, the formalisms of love and desire, emotion talk, intimacy; all are instances of socially-mediated, institutionally regimented and regimenting, metapragmatic discourses. They evaluate and frame desires and attachments as more or less valuable and they are articulated in other discourses of costs, scales, benefits and risks. Whether implicitly or explicitly these discursive frames indicate how persons should calculate and calibrate the stakes, pleasures and risks of being a certain type of sexual form in a certain type of formed space.

Sexual desire does not represent a somehow more accurate rubric than sexual identity for understanding the symbolic resources of language as they relate to social life, but a different analytic focus. To focus on sexual desire is to 'allow analysis expanded scope to explore the role that fantasy, repression, and unconscious motivation play in linguistic interactions' (Kulick 2000: 274). However, the paths through which desires become social practice are not embedded in desires themselves but rather in the semiotics that categorize desires in some fashion, for instance as a concept of social identity. To focus on sexual identity as a part of a socialized sense of self, then, is to explore the multiple layering of indexical relations that hold not only between the linguistic and the non-linguistic but also between different parts of the linguistic and the non-linguistic. Ultimately, however, these theoretical matters will be worked out to the degree that this area, and scholars working in it, are nurtured and allowed to mature. Thus, the primary concerns for a future of the study of language and sexual identity lie not solely in the theoretical and methodological development of the area, but equally in the 'meta-narrative' of the inquiry. This meta-narrative includes the question of the inquiry's disciplinary home, the publication record for research in this area and the evaluation of the area and its authors.

In terms of disciplinary homes, the study of language and sexual identity presents a fairly complicated area of inquiry because, like queer theory and cultural studies more generally, it issues a strong challenge to the idea of obvious disciplinary boundaries. Problematically, however, it is precisely the obviousness of disciplinary boundaries that tends to award legitimacy within academia. For instance, within cultural studies, the critique of boundaries has itself become a disciplinary boundary and hence a naturalizing rubric. While cultural studies has played an important role in the re-alignment of academic disciplines, helping to blur the perceptions of what counts as history, political science, literary analysis, or art history, it has not typically included linguistics as a discipline with which it saw itself aligned.[2] Although there are obvious historical and epistemological reasons for this state of affairs, the point is that even as research has become increasingly interdisciplinary, the idea of disciplinarity of some sort has not disappeared.

In order for an area of inquiry to have an impact, it requires a home base from which to operate. The study of language and sexual identity, however, does not yet have an obvious home base, which contributes to my characterization of it as having an uncertain present. Although I find it crucial for language and sexual identity studies to maintain their interdisciplinary ties, for any meaningful discussion of the future of such studies to occur, one of the first steps must be to situate them disciplinarily, which means imbuing them with legitimacy. This position is not intended as a call for enhanced disciplinary policing or as a suggestion that the study of language and sexual identity is part of a winner-take-all system in which it 'belongs' to one discipline and one discipline alone. Rather it is to say that without the academic legitimacy that goes along with a disciplinary home, the future for the study of language and sexual identity is bleak indeed.

In part the problem for language and sexual identity reflects a more general problem concerning the home for the study of the intersections between language and social life. Although formal linguistics has not been particularly amenable to the exploration of these intersections, most sociolinguists nonetheless claim their legitimacy within linguistics, and the fact that many linguistics departments hire and tenure sociolinguists underscores this claim. While scholars in many disciplines lay valid claim to language, few non-

---

[2] As evidence of this boundary, I offer the comments of a colleague, who recently said to me: 'We've decided to include linguistics as part of cultural studies in our department. Although it is seriously unconventional, it seems to make sense in our case.'

linguists do so from a specifically linguistic perspective, by which I mean a perspective that focuses at least in part on questions related to linguistic form (e.g. phonetic, phonological, morphological, syntactic, discursive or narrative form).[3] Hence, sociolinguists typically claim their legitimacy within linguistics because their interests include a specific interest in linguistic form and/or function, their training is often in linguistics, their theories and methods relate (perhaps oppositionally) to those of linguistics and they see themselves as linguists. Similarly, linguistic anthropologists claim their legitimacy within anthropology because of the nature of their training, objects of inquiry, theories and methods and because they see themselves as anthropologists. Thus, while sociolinguists and linguistic anthropologists locate themselves in different disciplines and may orient around radically different theoretical concerns, they may nonetheless align themselves with one another when they have overlapping intellectual interests because their academic legitimacy is pre-established.

Returning to the question of a disciplinary home for the study of language and sexual identity, I would argue that as a starting point, this area of inquiry would be best served if it were to be accepted as an aspect of sociolinguistic/linguistic anthropological inquiry and hence situated within linguistics and anthropology. Such a positioning would be similar to that for the study of the relationships between language and social identities related to gender. The exploration of language and gender is perhaps an apt point of comparison because of the ways in which it has only relatively recently achieved an accepted legitimacy. In fact, its legitimacy is so well established that many researchers in linguistics now see the possibility of moving language and gender research from underneath the umbrella of sociolinguistics to a position as itself one of the sub-fields of linguistics.[4] This trajectory was neither obvious nor natural, and language and gender research had its own uncertain present that included struggles over legitimacy. The important issue for the analogy to language and sexual identity is that inquiry into the relationships between language and gender has had the time to mature within those disciplines that reflect the training, theoretical and methodological interests of the scholars engaged in them, even as those scholars reached beyond disciplinary boundaries for new insights. For language and sexual identity to have a discussible future, it too must mature from within a disciplinary home.

---

[3] Including linguistic form as a focus is not intended as a justification for autonomous linguistics or autonomous sub-fields of linguistics.

[4] Given somewhat different alignments within linguistic anthropology, it does not appear to me relevant to try and position language and gender research as independent of linguistic anthropology, though such a move makes sense within linguistics.

3 A Matter of Space: Publications

Related to the question of a disciplinary home for language and sexual identity is the distribution of publications in this area. Like disciplinary legitimacy, publications are an important gauge of the vitality of any area of inquiry. Publications in peer-reviewed journals and books published by a select set of academic presses represent the pinnacle of professional recognition, as evidenced for instance by standards for granting tenure and promotion at research institutions. While it may not be the case that publications in these venues actually represent the highest professional achievements or intellectual merit, it most certainly is the case that these venues offer the greatest academic currency. Further, publication in these venues typically engages a wide professional audience with specific inquiry, even when the area is new or controversial, and professional debates occur in part through such venues. There is a paradoxical understanding of the state of publication in the area of language and sexual identity as seen in the almost obligatory statement early in any discussion of language and sexual identity that notes both the relative paucity of information about sexual identities and language use and the relative 'explosion' of such materials in the last few years (Jacobs 1996, Livia & Hall 1997, Frenck 1998, Kulick 2000). The publication record for research on language and sexual identity is in fact complicated; however, in general, the bulk of the publications in this area have appeared in obscure or otherwise difficult to obtain publications and in conference proceedings. Such a record accentuates my characterization of this area of inquiry's uncertain present because it suggests that scholars have been presenting research at professional conferences, but that the work itself is not (yet) being published in high impact venues. In what follows, I will show in more detail how publications in this area distribute across the relatively high impact venues noted above.

I begin with a very brief overview of the type of work that has been published in this area. Although much early research and much of the research conducted by those who do not claim affiliation with linguistics has focused on lexical items, the range of linguistic work on language and sexual identity has been fairly broad, including phonetic studies, phonological studies, pragmatics, conversational analysis, narrative analysis and discourse analysis. This range of approach roughly mirrors the types of studies typically found in sociolinguistics more generally. Most, though by no means all, of the research has been based on data from white North Americans whose class positions are unspecified, a trend that is evident in much of queer theory as well. Research on data from gay males and lesbians predominates, with research focused on gay males comprising roughly half of all research in this area.[5] It is perhaps unsurprising that gay males represent the focus for much of this work given the relative salience of stereotypes about American gay males and their language use as well as the social positions within American society of gay males as males. However, I would also point out that the trend to focus on one particular social identity mirrors that of early work on language and gender that tended to focus on white, middle-class, North American women.[6] Just as language and gender research has moved beyond this narrow focus, the research record for language and sexual identity is not pre-determined and there is good evidence that research in language and sexual identity has moved to broaden its scope fairly quickly.

For instance, one of the few books that focuses specifically on language and sexual identities, *Queerly Phrased*, published in 1997 by Oxford University Press (Livia & Hall 1997), includes a broad range of foci, both in terms of analytic foci and in terms of the social groups represented, and its editors took great care in representing the continua of 'sameness-in-difference' and 'difference-in-sameness' suggested above. At the same time, the book itself was clearly located disciplinarily within sociolinguistics and linguistic anthropology. Of the 28 authors included in the book, 21 (75%) claimed training or affiliation in linguistics and/or anthropology.

Of additional interest for the purposes of this essay is the relative rank of the authors in that book. Among the 28 authors, only four of them were tenured professors or the non-US rough equivalent and one of those was an emeritus professor. Of the remaining 24, there were nine who were unaffiliated with academic departments, four graduate students and eleven assistant professors or the non-US rough equivalent. In other words, the academic positions of 86% of the authors in one of the most widely-cited books on language and sexual identity were at the time of publication institutionally insecure, a state of affairs that again underscores the relative 'youth' of this area of inquiry and hence the relative uncertainty of its present. Comparing the academic affiliations of the authors in *Queerly Phrased* to those of the authors in another collection, *Reinventing Identities*, recently published by Oxford University Press (Bucholtz, Liang & Sutton 1999) but framed in terms of language and gender, further underscores the relative 'youth' of studies of language and sexual identity. In *Reinventing Identities*, there are 20 authors listed (85% of whom have training or affiliation with linguistics

---

5 This assessment comes from an informal analysis of the Gay and Lesbian Language Bibliography (web site) as well as keyword searches on several index databases.

6 In fact, it mirrors virtually all new areas of inquiry within sociolinguistics and linguistic anthropology and is a problem that is typically responded to as the areas of inquiry achieve a certain legitimacy within their disciplines.

and/or anthropology). 40% were tenured professors or the rough non-US equivalent at the time of publication as compared to the 15% in *Queerly Phrased*, and all the authors had some sort of academic affiliation as compared to only 68% of the authors in *Queerly Phrased*. Like the state of publications more generally, the relative security of those who work on these issues is critical to any discussion of the future of the field. I will turn to some of the consequences of these positions later in the essay and return now to a discussion of the distribution of publications.

In addition to the book noted above, there have been three other books published since 1990 that focus on language and sexual identity. Of those, only one, *Word's Out* (Leap 1996) presents a single-author, book-length treatment of the issue while the other two, *Language and Desire* (Harvey & Shalom 1997) and *Beyond the Lavender Lexicon* (Leap 1995), comprise edited collections. Only one of these three books, *Language and Desire,* was published by a press, Routledge, that counts itself among the more highly ranked, international presses; however, it is not generally understood as rivaling academic presses such as Oxford and Cambridge. Interestingly, *Language and Desire* is also the collection that is the least focused on aspects of language and sexual identity that include specific linguistic forms, focusing more on semiotic treatments of language and textual analysis. While there is certainly no a priori critique to such an approach, it nonetheless differs in fairly significant ways from the fare presented in *Queerly Phrased*. As this discussion shows, there have been publications focused on language and sexual identity published by high impact presses. Overall, however, the book-length publication record is relatively sparse, a situation that is similar to that for peer-reviewed journal publications.

In order to assess the distribution of publications on issues related to language and sexual identity in peer-reviewed journals, a keyword search was conducted on the Linguistics and Language Behavior Abstracts database. The search was done on September 3, 2000 and included the following keywords: *lesbian, gay, homosexuality, sexuality, heterosexuality, transgender, transsexuality* and *bisexuality*. Neither this list nor the chosen database were intended to represent an exhaustive search, rather they were chosen as a likely set of keywords and a likely database that someone who was interested in language and sexual identity might consult. The combined searches resulted in 390 hits, with a 51% (197) overlap between different terms (e.g., the same article might come up under several of the keywords). Counting each article only once resulted in a total of 193 hits. An examination of the title and the short abstracts of each entry narrowed that number to 123, which represents only those articles that were actually relevant to one of the keywords (e.g., although someone whose last name is *Gay* hit during a keyword search of the word *gay*, that person does not write on issues of language and sexual identity). Table 1 below shows the distribution of these 123 entries.

Publication type	Percentage (raw numbers appear in parenthesis)
Peer-reviewed journals in linguistics, sociolinguistics or linguistic anthropology (e.g. Journal of Sociolinguistics)[7]	32% (38)
Peer-reviewed journals in non-linguistic disciplines (e.g. Journal of Homosexuality)	36% (43)
Book chapters [8]	13% (15)
Book reviews	13% (15)
Dissertations	10% (12)

Table 1. Results of a keyword search in the Linguistics and Language Behavior Abstracts database

From the subset of articles that have appeared in peer-reviewed journals of linguistics, sociolinguistics or linguistic anthropology, the data were further analyzed for articles that have been published since 1990 (which somewhat arbitrarily marks the establishment of queer theory with the publication of Judith Butler's *Gender Trouble* and Eve Kosofsky Sedgwick's *The Epistemology of the Closet*) in one of the following journals:

American Speech
Annual Review of Anthropology
International Journal of the Sociology of Language
Journal of Linguistic Anthropology
Journal of Linguistics
Journal of Pragmatics
Journal of Sociolinguistics
Language
Language in Society
Language Variation and Change
Linguistics
World Englishes

---

[7] The LLBA database does not include many non-peer-reviewed venues and those that it does were not among the hits received by the keyword search.
[8] Oddly, neither *Queerly Phrased* nor *Beyond the Lavender Lexicon* appears in the LLBA database.

Although by no means exhaustive (for instance it excludes journals such as *Discourse and Society* and the *TESOL Quarterly*, where scholars in this area might well publish), this list represents the high impact journals for sociolinguistics and linguistic anthropology. As of September 3, 2000, 15 articles had been published in one of these journals since 1990. Of those 15 articles, two were review articles and seven were part of a special edited edition of *World Englishes* that underwent a slightly different process of selection and review than is typical for single articles. This set of seven included an additional review article. The remaining articles are as follows:[9]

From *American-Speech* (3)

Long, Daniel. 1996. Formation processes of some Japanese gay argot terms. *American Speech* 71:2: 215-224.

Gaudio, Rudolf. 1994. Sounding gay: Pitch properties in the speech of gay and straight men. *American Speech* 69: 1: 30-57.

Shapiro, Michael. 1990. Gays and lesbians. *American Speech* 65:2:191-192.

From the *Journal-of-Sociolinguistics* (2)

Thorne, Adrian and Justine Coupland. 1998. Articulations of same-sex desire: Lesbian and gay male dating advertisements. *Journal of Sociolinguistics* 2:2: 233-257.

Jones, Rodney H. 1997. Marketing the damaged self: The construction of identity in advertisements directed towards people with HIV/AIDS. *Journal of Sociolinguistics* 1:3: 393-418.

From *Anthropological Linguistics* (1)

Mixco, Mauricio. 1992. The role of metaphor in Kiliwa kinship and religion. *Anthropological Linguistics* 34:138-158.

While these 15 articles and four books on language and sexual identity are certainly progress, they are far from representing an 'explosion' of research, particularly if one compares this record to the record for publication in queer theory during a similar timeframe. Similarly, comparing the record for optimality theory, an important formal linguistic paradigm that emerged in roughly the same timeframe as language and sexual identity, provides a striking contrast. A keyword search using 'optimality theory' performed on September 10, 2000 resulted in 465 hits. While it is no doubt the case that not all of those hits represent publication in high impact journals for formal

---

[9] Since the initial database search, an additional article has appeared in the *Journal of Sociolinguistics* (Moonwomon-Baird 2000) and an additional review has appeared in the *Annual Review of Anthropology* (Kulick 2000). I have also been told that several articles are currently in press.

linguistics, it is unlikely that the corpus of such articles is as small as that for language and sexual identity. Further, it is unlikely that 20% of those articles comprise review articles, as is the case for language and sexual identity.

The prevalence of review articles relative to non-review articles only serves to highlight the somewhat ambiguous nature of this area of inquiry's present more than to define possible trajectories for the future, as there is at this point relatively little to actually review.[10] Further, the prevalence of review articles suggests a rocky path for developments in this area because of the ways in which this prevalence implies a particular kind of knowable present, one that in my opinion has been falsely constructed to give the appearance of acceptance and stability for this work when the facts suggest otherwise. It may in fact be beneficial to call for a brief respite from reviews so that the area of inquiry can have time to mature in terms of the questions posed to it, the theoretical premises utilized by it, and the methods of investigation developed for it. Further, such a respite might allow for a more serious exploration of whether the current lack of impact for such work suggests a similar future lack of impact.

Without knowing how many articles are currently somewhere in the publication pipeline, my sense is that the concern over a future impact is manifold and includes skepticism about the validity of the object of study, uneasiness with the strong interdisciplinary nature of the work, particularly its use of social and critical theory, and concern of negative impact from those who consider writing on these issues. While it is typically the case that new areas of inquiry are received with a skeptical eye and their disciplinary appropriacy questioned, this area is somewhat unique because of the ways in which it confronts significant societal prejudice, including from within academia, concerning the very people who serve as the source of data. The fact that many of the scholars who write on these issues also themselves identify as belonging to the categories of identity under discussion further provokes the potential for prejudicial treatment. As Toni McNaron, the author of *Poisoned Ivy*, a study of gay and lesbian faculty writes (1997: 101), 'Thirty years of pioneering and substantial publication in the field of lesbian and gay history and culture has not eradicated the deeply held prejudices against such scholarship and its authors.'

4   A Matter of Space: Confronting Homophobia

As discussed above with respect to the authors whose work appears in *Queerly Phrased*, there are very few researchers of language and sexual identity in tenured or even tenure-track positions. In the past five years, only

---

[10] Naturally, this is a matter of opinion rather than empirically established fact.

one job advertisement for sociolinguistics or linguistic anthropology (for a temporary position in linguistics at Stanford University) has specifically mentioned sexuality as an area of interest for the hiring department. If my own experience of working on these issues while also developing an academic career is an accurate gauge of how this work is evaluated, then the marginalization of this area of inquiry presents one of the most formidable obstacles to the future of the inquiry itself. While it is certainly the case that my work in this area has been recognized and has brought me a great deal of intellectual satisfaction and growth, it is also clear that my path would have been a significantly different one had I not engaged in additional areas of inquiry as part of my research agenda.

Despite having been advised not to do so, I have included my work on language use among lesbians in all of my dossiers as I applied to academic jobs. Of the interviews that I have had (both on-campus and off), that work has never once been addressed or discussed in any of the official meetings with search committees or other faculty members. The two times it has arisen as a point of discussion were both in private conversations outside the boundaries of the 'official' interview. Further, although my work in this area has never been actively discouraged, I have been regularly counseled (beginning in graduate school, at each of my jobs and from colleagues at various institutions) to make sure that I had an additional body of work that was more 'mainstream.' I have regularly had the distinctly unpleasant task of asking colleagues (again at various institutions) if my work with lesbians was professional suicide. Thankfully, none has ever said yes; however, all have stressed the need for a 'mainstream body of work as well.' Anecdotal evidence from other colleagues who work or consider working in this area suggests that my experience is far from isolated and may sadly be the norm.

I assume that such advice comes out of a very real concern about the acceptability of this work to a broader audience and I have had no sense of malice behind the advice I have received. My senior colleagues appear to reflect the sentiments of Toni McNaron (1997:8), who writes

> Just the other day I had the unhappy job of advising a new Ph. D. in drama to wait until she had a job offer in hand before declaring her lesbian research and pedagogical interests .... A state university eager to bring her to campus is located in the rural Midwest, where her truest intellectual concerns are likely to be highly suspect because of their lesbian/gay cast. It would have been irresponsible for me to assure this woman that things are categorically better today than they were when I was being interviewed in 1963. I certainly do not wish to dampen individual or collective celebrations of gains on some campuses and within many professional associations. But the stories offered here are a reminder of the reality of homophobia, which still demands serious attention.

Like McNaron and my own mentors, I, too, have begun to advise students to be aware of the potential problems associated with working on language and sexual identity, particularly if they are interested in competing on the academic job market in linguistics.[11] While I find this position to compromise strongly my own ethics with respect to academic freedom and while I continue to encourage students to pursue questions related to sexuality and sexual identity, I find that I cannot in good conscience fail to remind them to consider seriously that their work in this area may be read with a less than favorable eye.

I have little doubt that, given time, many of the issues that I have discussed as critical to a sustainable future for the exploration of language and sexual identity will work themselves out, particularly as researchers continue to bring increased sophistication to the theoretical and methodological framing of those explorations. Without specific and concerted intervention into the problem of homophobia, both overt and covert, I have serious doubt about the ability of this area of inquiry to actually move toward that sustainable future. The time is now critical for those of us who are, or who become, institutionally secure to agitate forcefully against the pressures of homophobia. For the study of language and sexual identity has great potential to dramatically enrich the more general study of language, culture and society and at this point, realizing that potential remains within grasp.

References

Barrett, Rusty. 1995. Supermodels of the World, Unite!: Political Economy and the Language of Performance among African American Drag Queens, in Leap, 207-226.

Barrett, Rusty. 1997. The 'Homo-genius' Speech Community, in Livia and Hall, 181-201.

Barrett, Rusty. 1999. Indexing Polyphonous Identity in the Speech of African American Drag Queens, in Bucholtz, Liang, and Sutton, 313-331.

Bucholtz, Mary. 1999. 'Why Be Normal?': Language and Identity Practices in a Community of Nerd Girls. *Language in Society* 28:2. 203-224.

Bucholtz, Mary, A.C. Liang and Laurel Sutton. 1999. *Reinventing Identities: The Gendered Self in Discourse*. Oxford, Oxford University Press.

Butler, Judith. 1990. *Gender Trouble*. New York: Routledge.

---

[11] This advice appears to me to be somewhat less urgent for students in linguistic anthropology because of anthropology's generally wider acceptance of queer theory and other cultural theories typically included in work on language and sexual identity. This is not to suggest, however, that homophobia is not also present in anthropology, as the recent report by Commission on Lesbian, Gay, Bisexual and Transgendered Issues in Anthropology shows (URL: http://www.aaanet.org/aaareports/index.html).

Campbell-Kibler, Kathryn, Robert Podesva and Sarah Roberts. 1999. Beyond Lisping: A Preliminary Look at the Linguistic Correlates of Gay Styles. Paper presented at NWAV 28, Toronto.

Cameron, Deborah. 1997. Performing Gender Identity: Young Men's Talk and the Construction of Heterosexual Masculinity. *Language and Masculinity*, ed. S. Johnson and U. H. Meinhof, 47-64. Oxford, UK: Blackwell.

Eckert, Penelope. 1989. *Jocks and Burnouts: Social Categories and Identity in the High School*. New York: Teacher's College Press.

Eckert, Penelope. 2000. *Linguistic Variation as Social Practice*. Malden, MA: Blackwell.

Epstein, Steven. 1987. Gay Politics, Ethnic Identity: The Limits of Social Constructionism. *Socialist Review* 93/94: 9-54.

Frenck, Susan. 1998. Symposium on Linguistic Creativity in LGBT Discourse: Introduction. *World Englishes* 17:2: 187-191.

Gal, Susan and Judith Irvine. 2000. Language Ideology and Linguistic differentiation. *Regimes of language*, ed. P. Kroskrity, 35-84. Santa Fe, NM: School of American Research Press.

Harvey, Keith and Celia Shalom. 1997. *Language and Desire: Encoding Sex, Romance and Intimacy*. London: Routledge.

Irvine, Judith. 1989. When Talk isn't Cheap: Language and Political Economy. *American Ethnologist* 16: 248-267.

Irvine, Judith. 1998. Ideologies of Honorific Language Use, in Schieffelin, Woolard and Kroskrity, 51-67.

Irvine, Judith. In press. Style as Distinctiveness: the Culture and Ideology of Linguistic Differentiation. *Stylistic Variation*, ed. John Rickford and Penelope Eckert. Cambridge: Cambridge University Press.

Jacobs, Greg. 1996. Lesbian and Gay Male Language Use: A Critical Review of the Literature. *American Speech* 71.1. 49-71.

Jakobson, Roman 1960. Closing Statement: Linguistics and Poetics. *Style and Language*, ed. T. Seboek, 350-377. Cambridge, MA: MIT Press.

Johnstone, Barbara. 1996. *The Linguistic Individual: Self-Expression in Language and Linguistics*. Oxford: Oxford University Press.

Kulick, Don. 1998a. Anger, Gender, Language Shift and the Politics of Revelation in a Papua New Guinean Village, in Schieffelin, Woolard and Kroskrity, 87-103.

Kulick, Don. 1998b. *Travesti: Sex, Gender and Culture among Brazilian transgender prostitutes*. Chicago: University of Chicago Press.

Kulick, Don. 2000. Gay and Lesbian Language. *Annual Review of Anthropology* 29: 243-85.

Laboratory of Comparative Human Cognition. 1997. Paradigms and Prejudice. *Mind, Culture and Activity: Seminal Papers from the Laboratory of Comparative Human Cognition*, ed. by M. Cole, Y. Engström and O. Vasquez, 100-116. Cambridge: Cambridge University Press.

Leap, William (ed.). 1995. *Beyond the Lavender Lexicon*. New York: Gordon and Breach Publishers.

Leap, William. 1996. *Word's Out: Gay Men's English*. Minneapolis: University of Minnesota Press.

Livia, Anna and Kira Hall (eds.). 1997. *Queerly Phrased*. New York: Oxford University Press.

Livia, Anna and Kira Hall. 1997. 'It's a Girl': Bringing Performativity back to Linguistics, in Livia and Hall, 3-18.

Lucy, John. 1992. *Language Diversity and Thought: A Reformulation of the Linguistic Relativity Hypothesis*. Cambridge: Cambridge University Press.

McNaron, Toni A.H. 1997. *Poisoned Ivy: Lesbian and Gay Academics Confronting Homophobia*. Philadelphia, PA: Temple University Press

Moonwomon-Baird, Birch. 2000. What do Lesbians Do in the Daytime? Recover. *Journal of Sociolinguistics* 4:3:348-378.

Mufwene, Salikoko, John Rickford, Guy Bailey, and John Baugh. 1998. *African-American English*. London: Routledge.

Povinelli, Elizabeth. 1999. Review of Language and Culture Symposium #6. http://www.language-culture.org/archives/mailing-lists/lc/199911/msg00005.html.

Queen, Robin. 1997. 'I don't Speak Spritch': Locating Lesbian Language, in Livia and Hall, 233-256.

Rubin, Gayle. 1993. Thinking Sex: Notes for a Radical Theory of the Politics of Sexuality. *The Lesbian and Gay Studies Reader*, ed. H. Abelove, M. Borale and D. Halperin, 3-44. New York: Routledge.

Schieffelin, Bambi, Kathryn Woolard, and Paul Kroskrity. 1998. *Language Ideologies: Practice and Theory*. Oxford: Oxford University Press.

Sedgwick, Eve K. 1990. *The Epistemology of the Closet: English Literature and Male Homosocial Desire*. New York: Columbia University Press.

Silverstein, Michael. 1979. Language Structure and Linguistic Ideology. *The Elements: A Parasession on Linguistic Units and Levels*, ed. P. Clyne, W. Hanks, and C. Hofbauer, 193-247. Chicago: Chicago Linguistic Society

Silverstein, Michael. 1993. Metapragmatic Discourse and Metapragmatic Function. *Reflexive Language*, ed. by J. Lucy, 33-58.

Silverstein, Michael. 1998. The Uses and Utility of ideology: A Commentary, in Schieffelin, Woolard and Kroskrity, 123-149.

Tannen, Deborah. 1993. The Relativity of Linguistic Strategies: Rethinking Power and Solidarity in Gender and Dominance. *Gender and Conversational Interaction*, ed. D.Tannen, 165-188. Oxford: Oxford University Press.

Whorf, Benjamin. 1956. *Language, Thought and Reality*, ed. by John Carroll. Cambridge, MA: MIT Press.

6

The Future of Queer Linguistics

ANNA LIVIA

1 Gender and/or Sexuality

At the first International Gender and Language Conference (IGALA) held at Stanford University in the year 2000, a round table discussion was held to answer the question: What is the future of queer linguistics? The question presupposes that there already exists a field of enquiry recognisable as 'queer linguistics' and asks in what new directions it is headed. This turned out to be a highly controversial idea. Objections to the very notion of 'queer linguistics' took two main forms. The first revolved around the meaning of the term *queer* which, it was argued, was far too vague and all-encompassing, relating in some equally vague way to queer theory, itself an uneasy amalgam of theoretical positions rather than a cohesive discipline. The second objection concerned the communities who are generally lumped together under the umbrella term *queer*: transsexuals, sex workers, gay men, lesbians, and the sense that there are few, if any, shared values or attributes among them. Does queer linguistics study the language patterns of queer communities or does it refer rather to the research concerns of gay and lesbian linguists? Does the gender neutral term *queer* obfuscate power differences between men and women? Is it simply a useful shorthand for people who are not straight? Does a speech community need to recognise itself as queer for the term to be appropriate?

Language and Sexuality: Contesting Meaning in Theory and Practice.
Kathryn Campbell-Kibler, Robert J. Podesva, Sarah J. Roberts and Andrew Wong (eds.).
Copyright © 2001, CSLI Publications.

To answer some of these questions and pinpoint how queer linguistics might be useful and what it might be useful for, I believe it may help to consider for a moment the history of the concerns it seeks to address. Contemporary sociolinguistics has benefited from thirty years of research into language and gender, research which investigated many aspects of discourse from hesitations and interruptions, to pronunciation differences, to verbosity and turn taking. The data collected from attested utterances were analysed in terms of gender. Do men interrupt women more often than women interrupt men or each other? Are all interruptions equal, or do they perform different functions and achieve different ends (what Robin Lakoff and Deborah Tannen (1993) have termed *pragmatic homonymy* or the use of the same discourse device to widely different effect)?. The field of language and gender has been carefully assessed and reassessed to achieve finer and finer analyses. However, throughout most of its history, the terms *men* and *women* were assumed to be relatively unproblematic. If gay men and lesbians participated in the research, this fact was either not known or not seen as relevant. That the genders might 'cross-express,' or use the speech characteristics of the opposite sex, as is frequently the case among gay male drag queens, for example, was not considered an appropriate area of language and gender research.

Addressing the question of communities of speakers who do not fit easily into the existing gender categories, in 1997 Kira Hall and I published *Queerly Phrased*, an anthology of articles about lesbian, gay, bisexual and transsexual speech in different part of the world. Like most pioneering books, it was at first received with great applause and affection by other gay and lesbian linguists and scholars of queer discourse, broadly defined. Soon, however, as its position as the principal reference work for queer linguistics became established, and it came to be required reading on every course in this new sub-sub field, it found itself under attack as somehow unworthy of the attention it was getting. 'Undeserved popularity' is one of those interesting tautologies like 'unexpected windfall' that remain in currency because they express an emotional truism. Be that as it may, it was in the late nineties that the term *queer* as in 'queer theory' and 'queerly phrased' came under interrogation.

Recently, the sociolinguistic sub-field known as language and gender has added the concept 'sexuality' or 'sexual orientation' to its axes of inquiry, as may be seen from the call for abstracts of the first IGALA conference: 'we seek 20 minute papers that deal with language in relation to gender and/or sexuality.' What the sub-sub field we are now calling queer linguistics has contributed to the study of language and gender is a theoretical insistence on the performativity of gender, understood as the notion that cultural gender (as opposed to sex) cannot be indexed directly and unproblematically to a speaker's anatomical configuration. Thus, instead of being both cultural and linguistic anomalies, communities which do not fit easily into the usual dualistic vision of gender as composed of two terms: men and women, communities like the hijras (castrated males) of India or the cross-expressing 'yan daudu of Nigeria, are easily accommodated under an umbrella notion of gender as performed–or actualized–by the speaker who participates in a culturally intelligible semiotic system (see Livia and Hall 1997). Instead of creating refugee camps outside the gender paradigm in which to (temporarily and inadequately) house these differently gendered communities, we can analyze their speech using similar terms as those used to study that of heterosexually positioned fraternity brothers or, indeed, kindergartners.

2   Sex is Public

Instead of being an extreme case, transsexuals thus become part of the mainstream, a mainstream which has redefined its borders to include them. However, the term added was *sexuality* not anatomical configuration. It is easy to see that either special accommodation (the refugee camp approach) or redefinition is necessary if we want to include transsexual communities in the study of language and gender. It is less evident how gay men, lesbians and bisexuals — the differently oriented rather than the differently configured — fail to fit the old paradigm. This is because trans-ness is pretty directly about gender, whereas sexuality tends to get subsumed, and made invisible, under gender as though the relationship between the two were too hard to articulate. The Harvey Milk Institute in San Francisco, which offers courses to the gay, lesbian, bisexual and transsexual communities, asks its students to tick the box representing their gender. The options are F (female), M (male), FTM (female-to-male) and MTF (male-to-female). The possibility that someone has changed, or is in process of changing gender is recognized. Students are not asked to define themselves in terms of their sexuality, however, so, once again, this information is not collected. What sex you are, is, it seems, a public fact, like where you live and how old you are, whereas who you desire is private.

In her now famous axiom two, the prominent queer theorist, Eve Sedgwick, warns powerfully against equating sexuality with gender:

> Axiom Two: The study of sexuality is not coextensive with the study of gender; correspondingly, antihomophobic inquiry is not coextensive with feminist inquiry. But we can't know in advance how they will be different. (1990: 27)

Although this warning was written more than ten years ago, and is hardly unique in its decoupling of gender and sexuality, its ideological import and ramifications are so complex that they are still being worked out.

3   Fieldwork and the Question of Desire

In a textbook on methodology, *Introduction to Linguistic Field Methods* written by Bert Vaux and Justin Cooper at Harvard (1999), the following advice is given on deciding which native speakers to work with:

> First of all, it is generally a good idea to select an informant who is of the same gender as the field worker. Of course, in a society where more than two gender types are recognized, this maxim should be adjusted accordingly: the basic point here is that field workers should avoid selecting informants who might become sexually interested in them. (7)

Clearly Vaux and Cooper have heard of communities such as the hijras who are 'differently gendered,' but they still assume a baseline heterosexuality: informants who are of the same gender as the investigator will, a priori, not be sexually interested in him or her. There is no recognition of the fact that informants themselves may speak differently depending not only on their gender, but also on their sexual orientation, for the linguistic system used may be an important part of their representation of themselves as heterosexual or gay. As I argue in *Pronoun Envy* (2001a), the linguistic gender system in both English and French provides resources which are utilized by transsexuals, gay men, lesbians and many others who want to project an image of themselves which is at odds with the heteronorm. Methodology such as that taught by Vaux and Cooper provides no tools to collect data on this, let alone analyze it. Sexual desire is defined, a priori, as a problem to be avoided rather than data to be probed. Nor is there any sense that gender presentation may be part of a speaker's arsenal of stylistic effects.

4   The 'Sorta,' 'Kinda,' 'Y'know' Guy

Robin Lakoff, a pioneer in so many fields, has written of the transformation George Bush was compelled to undergo as part of his passage from Governor to President (Lakoff, 1990). Calling him a 'modern Tiresias,' she describes how stereotypically feminine his speech was during his election campaign. Dotting his utterances with lexical and discursive hedges, he was the 'sorta,' 'kinda,' 'y'know' guy who would ask for a 'splash more coffee' and talk to his running mate, Dan Quayle, 'about this vice-presidential thing' (273-4). This style, perceived by the electorate as feminine, uses features of upper-class speech, a code which was insufficiently familiar to most Americans and was therefore not comprehended as such. Bush's aides gave him a linguistic makeover, blunting his gestures and replacing his vagueness with authoritative facts and figures. Research like Lakoff's demonstrates that the performative function of gender is not only important to minority groups, but may be an important consideration in any discussion of language and gender. The fact that Bush Senior was able to respond to his gender lessons suggests that even deeply ingrained social codes and behaviors may be changed voluntarily.

5 Swarthy Legs are Masculine

This is, I believe, the current state of play in queer linguistics, and these are the current issues: creating, refining and revising concepts like gender and sexuality; finding ways to analyze and interpret the data so as to get at contradictions and show how different demographic axes, like race and class, intersect, overlap or collocate. For a long time it was assumed that members of oppressed groups had a similar relationship to the oppressor: that women, Black people and the working class were similarly disadvantaged and thus used similar discourse features. Yet sociolinguistic research has demonstrated that women tend to use more prestige features than men, that in many contexts, women's speech might in fact be defined as the prestige variant. If we add to this the fact that men who use upper class features are often perceived as effeminate, we see that upper class, female and male homosexual tend to collocate, while working class, heterosexual male and lesbian tend to collocate. How does the axis of race intersect with the others? Research like that of Rusty Barrett (1997) on the use made by African American drag queens of stereotypical 'white women's speech' suggests even more complex imbrications.

As I have argued elsewhere (Livia 2001b), femininity and whiteness collocate to a very high degree, while masculinity collocates with blackness. This means that when men cross-express as women, for example, they often combine stereotypical traits of femininity with Caucasian physical features. The feminist linguist Deborah Cameron quotes data collected by her students who were investigating the speech of male college students. In a conversation which Cameron has entitled 'The antithesis of man,' a group of young men, presumed heterosexual, discuss a 'really gay guy' in their class (1997: 53-54). The guy in question has skinny legs, no leg hair and wears women's shorts made of 'French cut spandex.' Bryan, Ed, Carl and Al work together to produce a collective portrait of their classmate. This culminates in the line 'his legs/very long very white and very skinny.' Although Cameron does not explicitly comment on this remark about light skin color, it clearly shows that the gay guy's effeminacy is increased by his white appearance. Swarthy legs are masculine; white legs are feminine.

6   What Do You Mean by That?

This emerging field is still very much under fire from linguists in related areas and even from language and gender theorists, who either disagree with its main tenets, or would prefer to see them included under a broader umbrella of sociolinguistic inquiry. What I have outlined is the position and some of the questions with which Kira Hall and I started when we edited *Queerly Phrased*. Some linguists have questioned the central place we give to intentionality, arguing that this concept, which explains the speaker's intention in making a particular utterance, is of little value since the utterance itself gains its meaning with relation to a complex, pre-existing semiotic network which cannot be controlled by the speaker. I disagree with this analysis. The concept of speaker intention is valuable precisely because it gets at distinctions in gender performance. If gender is seen as indexically derived from the anatomical configuration of the body, then intention is not so important, because the gender performance is not problematic. But, if we see gender as performative, actualized by the speaker, then we need to know which cultural codes they are citing.

Intentionality is, I believe, the key to distinguishing between complex phenomena like passing and dragging, sincerity and irony. A drag queen might use exactly the same traits of stereotypical femininity as a male-to-female transsexual. Either might exclaim over a friend's attire: 'What a lovely dress, that's organdy, isn't it?' (attested example, Marlene's drag bar in San Francisco, June 1994). But while the male-to-female transsexual, who is intent on passing as a woman, wants her comment to index her as female, the drag queen wants her comment to be understood as using femininity to index her as non-masculine, i.e., as disloyal to heterosexual masculinity. There is a necessary double-take to the drag performance: the speech is feminine but the speaker is masculine. This type of polyphony achieves its effect when the addressee recognizes the speaker's intention. Arguably, the distinction between irony and sincerity can only be made by addressing intentionality.

7   Authors and Schizophrenics

The question has been raised as to how intentionality is to be reconciled with performativity (specifically by the editors regarding an earlier version of this paper). I believe there is only a dichotomy between the two if we base our understanding of performativity on the way it is used in a cultural studies context which, due to Jacques Derrida's pronouncements on the irrelevance of author intention, banishes all consideration of intention in interpreting a text (1998). However, as linguists we do not interpret texts but human utterances in their social context. A literary critic and noted exponent of psychoanalytic readings of literature like Leo Bersani can quite reasonably assert that the incongruity and swift topic shifts in Lautreamont's *Chants de Maldoror* are not evidence of incoherence or lack of cohesion but a masterly command of language. The same flights of imagination, about turns and irrelevant responses when found in the speech of a schizophrenic patient are symptoms of mental illness. It would be acting irresponsibly to analyze them as literature. The difference is in the intention: Lautreamont intended to produce a work of art; the schizophrenic is doing his or her best to respond to the psychiatrist's questions.

The concept of linguistic performativity began life in the philosophy of language, in J. L. Austin's little book, *How to Do Things With Words* (1955, first published 1962), Austin is careful to distinguish between the locutionary (the simple uttering of a sentence), the perlocutionary (what is ultimately brought about by the words), and the illocutionary (the conventional act performed by the words). Austin points out that while the perlocutionary sense 'must be ruled out as irrelevant' (110) (for anything at all may ultimately be achieved), we must pay attention to the illocutionary force of our words. As he observes, 'unless a certain effect is achieved, the illocutionary act will not have been happily, successfully performed' (116). In a paper on meaning written two years after Austin had first presented his ideas on performativity at Harvard, Paul Grice (1957) points out that 'A must intend to induce by X a belief in an audience, and he must also intend his utterance to be recognized as so intended' (75). For Grice and Austin, and for the kind of queer linguistics that seems to me the most useful, meaning and intention are intricately related.

Linguistics and other social sciences like sociology and psychology are not the only disciplines to pay increasing attention to the intentions of their subjects. In law too gender is becoming a more and more problematic category with the increasing numbers of transgendered and cross-gendered citizens, and with children produced not only by the physical coupling of a man and a woman but by a range of medical interventions. In *In re Marriage of Buzzanca* (Doskow 1999), the 4th District of California was presented with the problem of deciding the paternity of a baby girl. Mr. and Mrs. Buzzanca, both being infertile, agreed to hire a sperm donor to fertilize the egg of one woman to be implanted in the uterus of a second woman. By the time the child was born, Mr. Buzzanca had left his wife and claimed that since he had no biological tie to the baby, he would not pay child support. There was now a collection of five possible parents in place of the usual two: Mr. and Mrs. Buzzanca who had both planned the procedure and intended to produce a child in this fashion but who had no genetic tie; the sperm donor; the egg donor; and the bearer of the egg. Although the latter three all had a biological link to the baby, the court found the two people who had intended to produce her were the legal parents. My aim in recounting this legal precedent is not merely to show that the California Supreme Court has itself been involved in issues of gender, but also that the law is increasingly recognizing intention as a more important principle than biology. In disciplines concerned with human subjects rather than with their cultural expressions, intentions cannot be set aside.

8   Between the Theory and the Method Falls the Shadow

On the level of theory, then, queer linguistics started off with a pretty hefty armory, borrowed in the main from literary theorists like Judith Butler and Eve Sedgwick. We are now reassessing how far theory which comes out of an engagement with literature can be of use to a social science-oriented discipline like linguistics. The dismissal of concepts like intentionality comes very much from a model of language as a set of signs which relate more significantly to other signs than to referents, i.e., a discipline in which the relationship between words takes precedence over their real-world consequences. Unlike our colleagues in lit crit, our research is data-driven, requiring field research with native speakers who talk in order to effect change. It is in the area of methodology that, I would argue, queer linguistics is falling short. Because our theory has mainly been developed from disciplines without complex field methods, this is the part of our research which has benefited the least from careful scrutiny. While our systems of interpretation have become increasingly sophisticated, our methodology has remained unchanged. We identify a linguistic community, we tape its conversations, we analyze the transcripts.

The further we move from a theory of gender as indexed by sex to one of gender as performative, the more care we need to take in our own relationships with our subjects because there is much greater leeway for getting things wrong, for misunderstanding an interaction or for misleading our subjects as to what we are doing. If gender is merely a formal device to index sex, then you do not need to ask what a person means by it. Conversely, the more gender is seen as part of a personal stylistic arsenal, the more possible meanings there are. Sexuality, often treated as so *personal* it should not be mentioned, defaults to heterosexuality with no other choices on the menu.

9 Different Time Zones

A few years ago I conducted some research on computer-mediated communication in the French gay community. I never met my subjects face-to-face but interpreted our interactions entirely according to their online personas, or projections of gender and sexuality. Ethical questions such as informed consent became more complex since it was not apparent to participants in an online forum how far their experience of our interactions differed from my own. My French subjects did not know, for example, that in my time zone it was early afternoon, that I was wide awake, that my university had prepaid all my interactions with them. For them it was late at night, computer interactions were expensive (in France you pay per minute of connection time—there are no free local calls) and they were sleepy. I would hypothesize that my very invisibility made them trust me more than they would in real life. They assumed I was like them because they could not see how different I was.

It may seem as though the question of computer-mediated communication is an extreme case in terms of sociolinguistic methodology. But research on the Indian hijras, or Bay Area transsexuals appears exotic too, until someone thinks of using the same types of analysis on mainstream figures like George Bush, and finds similar patterns of interaction. The problem of creating and deserving participant trust, of covert recording, which is so evident in computer-mediated communication, is just as pressing in face-to-face encounters. We need to take as much care of the way we set up our research projects as we do in interpreting them. How does this community define itself in distinction to others which seem to us contiguous? How is it defined by the wider society in which it operates? What do its members think of our own gender performance and construction of sexuality? What image do they have of our research project? If we are working within heavily marginalized communities: how does our research potentially endanger them, simply by calling attention to their existence?

10 Saving Face

In some field research I conducted in Paris and Lille in May 2000, I asked French lesbians how they interpreted descriptions of masculine women included among personal ads in *Lesbia*, a monthly cultural magazine (see Livia, this volume). The ad writers typically wished to exclude women of 'masculine' appearance from responding, using a series of highly pejorative terms like *diesel dykes*, *women wrestlers* and *kitchen dressers*. I asked my informants what picture they had of, for example, a *camionneuse* (diesel dyke). Some of my informants were adamantly opposed to using oppressive gender descriptions and said so most articulately. Yet the task I set them required that they enter into the spirit of the ad and explain what the writer meant by these terms. For me the point was to investigate the 'mythologies' of gender (in Barthesian terms) using the highly value-laden descriptions in the personal ads. A *camionneuse* is, for example, aggressive, masculine, over-muscled, beer swilling and loutish. For some of my informants, however, my question was a catch 22: if they were able to elaborate the cultural connotations of the term *camionneuse* then they reinforced irksome gender stereotypes. Yet if they failed at the task, they appeared to be cultural illiterates. We need to create a methodology that saves our subjects' face, and quote them as experts on their own language use, not as our dupes.

My friend Leigh Star, working on the methodology of infrastructure, laughingly refers to herself as a member of the interdisciplinary group for the study of boring things. Methodology is not nearly as sexy as the interpretation of sexuality, but the future of queer linguistics depends on our turning our attention to how we get our data as much as to what we do with it once collected.

References

Austin, John L 1962. *How to Do Things With Words*. Cambridge, MA: Harvard.

Barrett, Rusty. 1997. The 'Homo-Genius' Speech Community. *Queerly Phrased: Language, Gender and Sexuality*, ed. Anna Livia and Kira Hall, 181-201. New York: Oxford University Press.

Cameron, Deborah. 1997. 'Performing Gender Identity: Young Men's Talk and the Construction of Heterosexual Masculinity. *Language and Masculinity,* ed. Sally Johnson and Ulrike Meinhof, 47-64. Oxford: Blackwell.

Derrida, Jacques. 1988. *Limited Inc*. Evanston, IL: Northwestern University Press.

Doskow, Emily. 1999. 'The Evolution of the 'Second' Parent.' *San Francisco Attorney*. October-November. 26-29.

Gaudio, Rudi. 1997. Not Talking Straight in Hausa.. *Queerly Phrased: Language, Gender and Sexuality*, ed. Anna Livia and Kira Hall, 416-29. New York: Oxford University Press.

Grice, Paul. 1957. Meaning. *Philosophical Review* 66:377-88.

Hall, Kira. 1997."Go Suck your Husband's Sugarcane!': Hijras and the Use of Sexual Insult. *Queerly Phrased: Language, Gender and Sexuality*, ed. Anna Livia and Kira Hall, 430-60. New York: Oxford University Press.

Lakoff, Robin Tolmach. 1990. *Talking Power: The Politics of Language*. Basic Books: New York.

Lakoff, Robin and Deborah Tannen. 1998. *Gender and Discourse*. New York: Routledge.

Livia, Anna. 2001a. *Pronoun Envy: Literary Uses of Linguistic Gender.* New York: Oxford University Press.

Livia, Anna. 2001b. Camionneuses et dandies: la sexualite et la classe. *Desireuses: lesbiennes fems et lesbiennes butchs*, ed. Christine Lemoine and Ingrid Renard. Paris: Editions gaies et lesbiennes.

Livia, Anna and Kira Hall. 1997. 'It's a girl.' *Queerly Phrased: Language, Gender and Sexuality*, ed. Anna Livia and Kira Hall, 3-18. New York: Oxford University Press.

Sedgwick, Eve Kosofsky. 1990. *Epistemology of the Closet.* Berkeley: California University Press.

Vaux, Bert and Justin Cooper. 1999. *Introduction to Linguistic Field Methods.* Muenchen: Lincom Europa.

7

Demystifying Sexuality and Desire

PENELOPE ECKERT

1 Introduction

Don Kulick (2000) has proposed recasting the study of language and sexuality as the study of language and desire. This shift, he says, would move us away from a focus on identity categories (such as *gay* and *lesbian*), and from the enterprise of describing how people talk *as* members of these identity categories. In other words, he is calling for an avoidance of the category-bound pitfalls that haunt sociolinguistics, particularly the reduction of the social meaning of linguistic practice to an expression of membership in, or affiliation with, predetermined and fixed identity categories. He argues that by extending our interest to desire more generally, we will move away from a focus on the groups of people who engage in particular kinds of desire, to a focus on 'culturally grounded semiotic practices.' I certainly agree that a focus on the language use of identity categories in the study of sexuality (and indeed in the sociolinguistic study of everything) can be problematic. And I believe that viewing the study of language and sexuality as part of a wider study of language and desire is an interesting idea. What I wish to outline in the following pages is a set of pitfalls that await this change in focus – pitfalls that are not inherent in Kulick's proposal, but that surely await its implementation. We are all painfully aware of the problem of essentialization in the study of language and gender – the assignment of essential qualities to the two standard sex/gender categories, and

Language and Sexuality: Contesting Meaning in Theory and Practice.
Kathryn Campbell-Kibler, Robert J. Podesva, Sarah J. Roberts and Andrew Wong (eds.).
Copyright © 2001, CSLI Publications.

even the attribution of these qualities to our biological nature. The mystified status of sexuality in our culture renders the study of sexuality even more subject to this kind of treatment, and I will argue that if we turn our focus to desire, we need to be particularly vigilant of an increased danger of naturalization.

As Kulick argues (2000:271), the focus on identity categories distracts the analysis of language and sexuality from sexuality itself. But I doubt he is suggesting that we dispense with such categories altogether. If discarding an interest in identity categories presents the risk of discarding the social from the analysis of sexuality, moving to the study of desire intensifies this risk. As linguists, our interest in sexuality is in its social life – in how we use language to accomplish sexual ends, how we talk about sexuality, how we index sexuality when we talk about other things, how we use language in and around sexual activity, how we use language to organize ourselves socially around sexuality, and how we use language to organize ourselves sexually around sociability. Most readers will have no difficulty with this statement of the endeavor, and I believe that the statement demystifies the subject to some extent. But it is a little more difficult to recast this statement substituting *desire* for *sexuality*, because we can bring ourselves to conceptualize sexuality, but not desire, purely in terms of activity. And it is the activity that makes it easy for us to think of sexuality as social. We tend to view desire, on the other hand, as an individual, private, thing. It is desire, in other words, that brings the mystification into the study of sexuality, and it is in contemplating desire that we are inclined to fall into an asocial and naturalized view of sexuality. The challenge, then, is to adopt an approach that focuses on the social mediation of desire: to construct a view of desire that is simultaneously internal and individual, and external and shared. In the interests of such an approach, I wish here to explore the social nature of desire, and to expose the potential for the kind of mystification and naturalization that can stand in the way of this exploration.

2 Personae and Identity Categories

While Kulick does not intend it, his paper is apt to be interpreted as a denial that the study of identity categories and the study of culturally grounded semiotic practices can be compatible. I will begin by trying to rescue identity categories from the analytical trash basket, for while an exclusive focus on such categories is problematic, we cannot do sociolinguistics without them. The problem of working with identity categories in sociolinguistics in general lies not in attention to the categories, but in the way in which the categories are selected and the manner in which they are invoked. Problems arise when one limits attention to categories, takes them as given rather than as products of social practice, and focuses on boundaries rather than on what people do with boundaries.

The study of language and sexuality has to a great extent been dominated by a focus on the identity categories *straight, gay* and *lesbian*. Putting the sex/gender of people's sex partners at the center of the endeavor in this way folds sexuality into gender, and elevates a cultural preoccupation with choice of partner to a primary analytic scheme. The fact that these categories are actually lying on the ground – that this preoccupation exists – certainly makes them important analytic constructs. But their importance does not lie simply in their potential to yield ready-made categorizations of speakers. When categories are put at the center of analysis, they take on a significance that masks much of their functioning in practice. While indeed highlighted gay speech styles are prominent and interesting, their existence and their interest do not lie in category membership, but in the *idea* of category membership. The life of 'gay language' is in the complexity of the social landscape that ties people to each other and to the rest of the world as 'gay', 'not gay', 'maybe gay', 'aligned with gay', and as educated, artistic, political, biker, shopper, and any number of activities and characteristics that come somehow to be tied in some circumstances to gayness. People have quite different orientations to their own sexuality and that of others, and to the relation between that sexuality and the other things and people in their lives. There may be linguistic effects that one finds only within communities of practice that are defined by sexuality. And these linguistic effects may spread beyond these communities of practice to the extent that people wish to project affiliation with the practice of these communities, whether they are actually participants in them or not. And the practices that they affiliate with may not be the sexual ones, but something else altogether, as the categories defined by choice of sexual partner simply provide the background against which all kinds of meaning can be made.

In this volume, Robert Podesva, Sarah Roberts, and Kathryn Campbell-Kibler approach the study of 'gay' speech in terms of the use of a range of linguistic resources to position oneself in a variety of ways in a broader social landscape – a landscape that is peopled not by gays and straights, but by gays, straights, lawyers, liberals, conservatives, serious people, flamboyant people, etc. As they say, the idea of a 'singular gay way of speaking homogenizes the diversity within the gay community' and 'reifies as gay certain linguistic practices that are shared throughout society.' Examining the release of word-final stops in the speech style of a gay activist lawyer, they emphasize that while this feature has been frequently associated with gay speech, this lawyer's status as gay in this situation is inseparable from his status as an activist, a lawyer, a serious and articulate person. And his linguistic style conveys the entire package. But the fact that this feature has been found in the speech of gay people does not make it gay. That is, it does not mean that this feature means 'gay'. It is far more interesting than that. Sarah Benor (in press) has noted that the release of final stops is characteristic of 'Jewish speech' and Mary Bucholtz (1996) has shown its use by teenage girls in constructing a 'nerd' style. To say that stop release is 'gay' is both incorrect and uninteresting. It is the very fact that this linguistic resource is available to everyone, and used by a variety of people in constructing styles that makes it interesting. And the wide range of its use is what makes it useful for the construction of particular kinds of styles that include 'gay' as part of them. The question is, then, is the release of final stops associated with something like articulateness? And if so, what is the role of this meaning in the construction of different gay styles?

Note that as we talk about variation at this level, we move away from categories to something more like personae. The lawyer is presenting himself not as a gay man, or as a lawyer, or as an activist, but as a particular intersection of these – and no doubt other things. But the success of his presentation of a persona depends on his ability to call on categories to make that persona meaningful and recognizable. Personae are built against the background of a social landscape – a landscape that is rendered meaningful by categories in varying stages of reification. One might say that an identity category is a reified locus of iterability. *Gay*, *straight*, and *Jew* are what one might call major identity categories. *Nerd* is an identity category when people – including the nerds – make it one. What about compulsive shoppers? Shoe fetishists? To the extent that people identify themselves as aligned in some way by their habits of accumulation – with, for example, the help of the institutionalizing effect of such things as self-help books and support groups – they come to constitute identity categories. And as they constitute identity categories, they are no doubt more likely to develop common ways of speaking.

3   Naturalizing Sexuality, Desire and Emotion

As we move into the use of variables across the social landscape, we move the variationist enterprise closer to the semiotic practices that Kulick argues should be at the center of the study of language and desire or sexuality. But things such as stop release are still related to what one might call recognized properties of people, available for study divorced from the interactions they facilitate. But Kulick raises the interest of precisely the kinds of linguistic practices that resist association with categories of people:

...the sexual desire of a man for a woman is conveyed through a range of semiotic codes that may or may not be conscious, but that are recognizable as conveying desire because they are iterable signs that continually get re-circulated in social life. The iterability of codes is what allows us to recognize desire as desire. This means that all the codes are resources available for anyone—whether straight, gay, bisexual, shoe fetishists, or anything else—to use. (Kulick 2000: 273).

A focus on how people talk to their lovers, how they talk about sex, or what kinds of vocalizations they make when they're engaged in sexual acts is sociolinguistically interesting to the extent that it links these in a meaningful way to wider conventions of social and linguistic practice. What are the limits of these conventions? Just as variationists suffer from the tendency to think of identity categories in terms of those that appear in sociology textbooks, we also don't tend to pay attention to variables like voice quality or intonation – most of us are terminally stuck on apparent vowel changes in progress. It may well be that the linguistic units we are quantifying are not the ones that are actually doing social work. For example, the choice of phonological variables is often led by an interest in certain parts of the phonology – as in the case of the Northern Cities Vowel Shift in my own work (Eckert 2000) – rather than by virtue of their possible social meaning. The study of desire presents a particularly interesting challenge, not just because we begin with the social meaning to seek our variables, but because some of the variables that potentially signal affect may originate outside the linguistic system as currently defined. I would argue that when we move into the realm of sexuality and desire, we move into a new set of semiotic practices that will stretch the tolerance of sociolinguistics, particularly of variationist sociolinguistics. And I want to go there.

It is important to recognize the great potential for naturalization in the study of sexuality in its relation to language. And I would argue that this potential increases as our focus shifts to desire and to emotion more generally. The shift is likely to awaken the belief that there is something more 'real' or basic – something more sexy – about desire than about, for instance, identity categories. The naturalizing force of discourses of sexuality lies in the location of desire in the body. The focus on where our libido leads us – whether into identity categories or into expressions of desire – allows us to ignore that the centerpiece of sexual ideology is that sexual desire is *natural,* unfolding unmediated from a physiological and individual need. Cementing this centerpiece into place is the concern with the social allocation of libido: One must not have too much or too little libido for the social location of one's body. Women should have less than men, European Americans fear that African Americans have more than they do, and a classmate in college once told me that Jewish men had too much. In order to get on with it, we need to recognize that sexuality is eminently social, and that our desires and emotions do not form our social lives, but are formed by our social lives as well. But sexuality is not just about desire; it is also about undesire. For many, perhaps particularly victims of assault, abuse, and unwanted attention, sexuality can be as much about revulsion, fear, or lack of desire as it is about desire. It is all framed by desire, of course – and by what one might call the desire imperative – but we cannot study desire and be done with sexuality. So perhaps the study of sexuality is not located within a study of desire, but overlaps with it. Perhaps the study of desire is located within a more general study of affect.

So the study of sexuality will involve the social mediation of the 'natural'. Of particular interest in this regard is the potential for 'natural' sounds to be used as conventionalized expressions of inner states – for example, as what Erving Goffman (1981) refers to as *response cries*. Goffman argues that 'eruptions' such as *ouch!, oops!, shit!, brrr!, eek!* make a momentary and limited claim on the attention of others in the situation, displaying the utterer's alignment to immediate events (such as tripping on the sidewalk or walking out into a snowstorm). The response cry thus draws the attention of others to the utterer's inner state (or what the utter would claim to be his or her inner state).

> Just as most public arrangements oblige and induce us to be silent, and many other arrangements to talk, so a third set allows and obliges us momentarily to open up our thoughts and feelings and ourselves through sound to whosoever is present. Response cries, then, do not mark a flooding of emotion outward, but a flooding of relevance in. (Goffman 1981: 121)

In other words, response cries are not just socially mediated inner eruptions. Rather, the inventory of such cries constitutes a culturally sanctioned set of inner feelings – the broader set of 'unconscious foreclosures' (Kulick 2000: 274-5).

These sounds also can be exploited for more general variables. A moan can occur as a response cry marking sexual pleasure. It can also be built into voice quality, producing a variety of voice qualities that I will loosely refer to as 'sexy voice', and that many people adopt to 'do' sexually aroused. Producing sexy voice can be auto-erotic, it can arouse others, and it can signal arousal. People can use sexy voice independently of actual arousal to engage others in sexual activity, to harass others sexually, to present themselves as sexually aroused, or to mock someone who does not arouse them, to present themselves as a sexy person. Sexy voice can be used to express cathexis of all sorts – for things that feel good like food, perfumes, soft fabrics; and for more distantly desirable things such as articles of clothing, works of art, pieces of furniture, flowers, cars, buildings, jobs. And the repeated expression of cathexis for particular classes of objects can contribute to the construction of a persona – perhaps as a compulsive shopper, an artistic person, a sensual person. But that persona is derived from a quality shared with others, and that sense of sharing is the beginning of an identity category.

Semiotic practices are available – among other things – for the production and reproduction of identity categories. Sexy voice can be combined with other linguistic resources to construct a variety of styles, and it is a voice quality that one might adopt in making sexiness – or by extension promiscuity – central to one's persona. In this way, what is a strategic resource may become common enough in some people's speech that it can be said to be part of their style, and it may signal to others that they belong to a category of sexy or promiscuous people – whether or not, in practice, they are sexy or promiscuous.

We can identify semiotic resources, but trying to separate them from the people that use them is assuming a homogeneous speech community. Semiotic resources are laden with their social histories, relating what an individual does to things that categories of people do. Those categories may be the classical ones, they may be related to the classical ones, or they may lie somewhere else altogether. Right down to silence, sighs or grunts, we have some idea of how our vocalizations (or lack thereof) fit into common and uncommon practice. But the popular identity categories have a kind of public and ideological status that makes them a particular kind of social, hence linguistic, resource, both because they mirror the current focus of sexual ideology, and because the negotiation of membership and identity has far-reaching effects on language. But we're talking degree, not difference here. Moving from identity category as given to the use of semiotic resources in stylistic production focuses on the use of language to produce the fluid connection between personae and identity categories.

The very mention of the word *desire* invokes the specter of the natural. Society mystifies and romanticizes desire, and in the study of desire, we have to problematize not only its objects but its source. The expansion of focus from language and sexuality to language and desire should not extend naturalistic arguments into the study of desire but should, on the contrary, draw the study of language and sexuality away from such arguments. Perhaps, in fact, the analytic endeavor should be a study of naturalizable linguistic resources. The identity categories that dominate sociolinguistic work have varying potential for naturalization – gender has greater potential than age or race, which in turn have greater potential than class. The conventionalization of overall voice pitch builds on a statistical difference in post-pubertal fundamental frequency. But the availability of 'natural' sounds for conventionalization places sexuality in a privileged position – along with fear, sadness and anger. Indeed, it places sexuality in the complex of emotions, another area in which we have erased history. Emotions, like sexual desire, are commonly treated as unmediated natural responses. We read that as part of their socialization, boys learn not to cry when they're overcome with sadness. But we don't read that equally, girls learn *to* cry when they're not so overcome, and as they learn to cry they may eventually learn to be overcome. The management of emotion is not simply a matter of suppressing the 'natural' – but of constructing it. In fact, much of the study of development could well focus on the appropriation and construction of the natural. It is particularly important in this regard to recognize the extent to which the sexual order serves not only the gender order but the social order more generally.

4   Sex, Desire, Emotion and the Heterosexual Market

At the 1999 Linguistic Institute at the University of Illinois, I asked the students in my class on the ethnographic study of variation to think of an age-related social construct that could be important for the study of variation. One group suggested the loss of virginity. It was not the sexual initiation itself that they were viewing as related to language, but the social salience of sexual activity at a certain life stage. Indeed, during the life stage when people are expected to be moving into sexual activity with others, orientation to this activity becomes an important focus in the structuring of identities and alliances. And as time goes by, the female categories of *slut* and *nice girl* become major sexually defined categories, which in fact correlate locally with sociolinguistic variables.

My own recent work, in which I've followed an age cohort from late childhood (fifth grade) into adolescence,[1] tells me that heterosexual practice structures the emergence of the peer-dominated social order that separates adolescence from childhood. And its beginnings – and its middle – are anything but sexual. Rather, the adolescent social order emerges in such a way as to provide a structure in advance for organizing sexual desire.

During childhood, children's social lives in school are to a great extent circumscribed by the classroom unit, and dominated by the classroom teacher. In the transition from childhood to adolescence, the student cohort organizes itself into a peer-based social order through a process in which they jointly transcend the classroom, and appropriate power and authority from school adults. Fundamental to organizing a social order is the need to establish a locus for the negotiation of knowledge and value. This locus emerges in the elementary school in the establishment of a heterosexual

---

[1] This research has been supported by the Spencer Foundation.

market. It is well known that in late elementary school, a subset of kids begin a frantic and highly visible activity around forming boy-girl couples.[2] These couples form and break up at a dizzying rate – most last a few days, maybe a couple of weeks. But an alliance that begins in morning recess can easily be over by lunch.

Most of the alliances are achieved through one or more intermediaries, and have more to do with relations among intermediaries than with relations between the two people who are being paired up. The relationships themselves are almost entirely instrumental, and most of the activity is about getting together or breaking up rather than actually being together. In fact, the activity is engaged in, not by the members of the couples, but as a collaborative endeavor that defines a newly-formed heterosocial community of practice – an emerging popular crowd. As the first major girl-boy joint endeavor, this crowd represents to all the new social order, and the co-construction of social status and heterosexual practice. Adults view this frantic activity as evidence that kids don't know what heterosexuality is about. But in fact, it is very much about heterosexuality, for heterosexuality and the institutions that support it in adult society are also more about alliances and non-sexual matters than they are about sex.

The rapid activity of the early days lays down the foundations of a market, as a system of social value is created. People are elevated to status on the basis of their tradeability (whom they get paired up with) and of their role in effecting trades (their role as brokers). And in spite of all the breaking up, few people's feelings are hurt in the process, for this is a collaborative process for all involved, and the activity is not about relations between individual girls and boys, but about relations and alliances within the cohort more generally. The emotions that come into play in this market are not related to the relationship within the couple, but to the relationships of the people who are engaging in social engineering. Friendships and alliances can be volatile, they can break up with great passion, and friends can spend hours intervening for split-up friendship couples. But when a heterosexual couple breaks up, it is done in a matter of minutes – engineered by go-betweens – and with few regrets. At this early stage, the important social issue is both the creation of the market and the individual's relation to it. Whether a kid chooses to move ahead of the cohort or decides to lag behind, whether one becomes an *innocent,* a *slut* or a *stud,* is more important during this passage than most other aspects of social practice. But what is at stake is not sexual desire so much as social desire as it plays out in the sexual arena.

---

[2] This is discussed in some detail in Thorne (1993) and Eckert (1996).

It is significant that heterosexuality should be the underlying metaphor of the social order well before many of the participants become interested in their own sexual activity. In this way, the co-construction of status and heterosexuality, the sexualization of peer society, and the socialization of sexuality are well in place in time to organize kids' development of sexual desire for each other.

Angela had a long-standing struggle to get recognition from some of her gang-oriented Latina peers, who considered her uncool and white. One Saturday night she lost her virginity, and the following week she told me the long story, beginning with a flirtation with a boy, and the jealousy that his attention evoked from these tough Latina girls. The story moved on to another day and another week, through space as she walked the neighborhoods with a succession of cuter and scarier boys, under the eyes of more jealous enemies and worried friends, and ended up in an empty lot behind the hall where a party was taking place. The actual loss of her virginity was encapsulated in the final event of the narrative: 'and then we did it'. No carnal pleasure, only some disappointment that it hadn't amounted to much. This story was not about sexual desire or sensation. And it wasn't really about boys. It was about outdoing those girls who called her white. And indeed, as she told me this story, I heard a remarkable transformation of her speech, as she constructed her stance through the authoritative use of Chicano English in a startlingly contrast to the way she'd sounded in our conversations in the previous weeks and years. (I hasten to add that sexual engagement and Chicana identity do not necessarily go together – this is one particular tough brand of Chicana identity that Angela is after, and this is a strategy that Angela came up with to claim it.). Angela really had no particular desire to stay with this boy – beyond her desire to make the point that she could have him. And she had no particular desire to have sex again, beyond her sense that it accomplished social work for her.

This is not a story about a girl having sex to gain social status. It is about the fact that sexuality is not just about sex. And this leads me to my point – that if we focus on sexual desire, we're likely to make the same mistakes in the study of language and sexuality that have all too often been made in the study of language and gender. In this case, every act that indexes masculinity or femininity isn't necessarily about being male or female. And Angela's sexual activity is not about sex. It is about being Chicana, and about being tough. And if sexuality is about desire, the object of Angela's desire is not so much the boy or physical pleasure, but the girls' recognition and legitimization in the Chicano community.

5   Conclusion

In the study of desire, we need to recognize that the object of desire is not obvious. We do not engage in sexual activity only out of the desire for a particular physiological object, but for a social object. The notion of a "purely physical attraction" is a mystification – a dehistoricized version of what is in fact an eminently social course of learning. The general attraction of men to shorter women and women to taller men is one of the more overwhelming pieces of evidence that society structures sexual desire. While there is no biological reason for women to be shorter than their male mates, an enormous majority of heterosexual couples exhibit this height relation – far more than would occur through a process of selection in which height was random. Everywhere we look, we see images of the perfect couple. They are heterosexual. He is taller, bigger, darker than her. Standing or sitting, she is lower than him, maybe leaning on him, maybe tucked under his arm, maybe looking up to him (see Goffman 1976). And from the time we are very young, we have learned to desire that perfectly matched partner. Girls develop a desire to look up at a boyfriend. They see themselves leaning against his shoulder, him having to lean down to kiss her, or to whisper in her ear. They learn to be scared so they can have him protect them; they learn to cry so he can dry their tears. This concentration of desire is perhaps the most powerful force in the maintenance of the gender order.

Just as we insist that gender is not just about male and female, and that sexuality is not just about the choice of same-sex or other-sex partners, sexuality is also not just about sex. Sexuality bleeds into the rest of the world and the rest of the world bleeds into it. The study of language and desire opens up an area of linguistic investigation that is likely to uncover fascinating data, and raise new issues. But in this endeavor, we have to be even more vigilant than ever not to engage in, or be misled by, mystification.

References

Benor, Sarah Bunin. In press. Sounding Learned: The Gendered Use of /t/ in Orthodox Jewish English. *University of Pennsylvania Working Papers in Linguistics* 7.

Bucholtz, Mary. 1996. Geek the girl: Language, femininity and female nerds. *Gender and belief systems*, ed. N. Warner, J. Ahlers, L. Bilmes, M. Oliver, S. Wertheim, & M. Chen, 119-131. Berkeley: Berkeley Women and Language Group.

Eckert, Penelope. 1996. Vowels and nailpolish: The emergence of linguistic style in the preadolescent heterosexual marketplace. *Gender and belief systems*, ed. J. Ahlers, L. Bilmes, M. Chen, M. Oliver, N. Warner, & S. Werhteim. Berkeley: Berkeley women and language group.

Eckert, Penelope. 2000. *Linguistic Variation as Social Practice.* Oxford: Blackwell.

Goffman, Erving. 1976. Gender Advertisements. *Studies in the Anthropology of Visual Commmunication*, 3: 69-154.

Goffman, Erving. 1981. Response cries. *Forms of Talk*, ed. E. Goffman, 78-122. Philadelphia: University of Pennsylvania Press.

Kulick, Don. 2000. Gay and lesbian language. *Annual Review of Anthropology*, 29: 243-85.

Thorne, Barrie. 1993. *Gender Play.* New Brunswick NJ: Rutgers University Press.

8

Language, Sexuality and Political Economy*

BONNIE MCELHINNY

1 Introduction

Early sociolinguistic studies of gender were often built around a theoretical and methodological recommendation that was most clearly articulated by Brown and Levinson in 1983 when they said that gender was best studied 'in cross-sex interaction between potentially sexually accessible interlocutors, or same-sex interaction in gender-specific tasks' (Brown and Levinson 1983:53). Some queer theorists seem to have accepted this methodological recommendation and theoretical assumption as the principle necessarily underlying studies of gender, and thus have argued that although many gender-based analyses involve accounts of intragender relations, their definitional appeal 'must necessarily be to the diacritical frontier between different genders' (Sedgwick 1990:31) and thus they are not useful for explicating same-

---

* An earlier version of this paper was presented at a panel on "The Future of Queer Linguistics" at IGALA-1, May 1999, Stanford University. My thanks to the organizers of that conference for inviting me to participate in that panel. My thoughts on the issues this paper addresses have been developed over the years in conversations with Rudi Gaudio and Miyako Inoue. My thanks to them for their intellectual companionship. In 1997 Kira Hall invited me to co-teach a course on Language and Gender with her at the Linguistic Institute at Cornell. Some of the nuances in the argument here are due to what I learned from her as we prepared, taught and hashed over the course.

Language and Sexuality: Contesting Meaning in Theory and Practice.
Kathryn Campbell-Kibler, Robert J. Podesva, Sarah J. Roberts and Andrew Wong (eds.).
Copyright © 2001, CSLI Publications.

sex relations. Increasingly, however, feminist scholars in linguistics and other disciplines have questioned whether a focus on cross-sex interaction is the necessary centerpiece of studies of language and gender. Some of the critiques thus elaborated may also raise questions about whether the study of same sex relations should be at the center of queer linguistics.

There are at least four significant, and increasingly controversial, theoretical assumptions about sexuality and gender embedded in the methodological focus on cross-sex interactions:

FIRST: gender is closely wedded to sex, and the study of gender is closely wedded to the study of heterosexuality;

SECOND: gender and sexuality are attributes (rather than, say, activities or performances);

THIRD: the study of gender and sexuality is the study of individuals;

FOURTH: sexuality and gender are best studied where most salient.

I will have little more to say in this chapter about the fourth assumption (though see McElhinny n.d. for further exploration of it, and each of these other assumptions). I will, however, explore the implications of the first three assumptions for studies of language and sexuality.

Queer studies, like postmodern feminism, can be said to have been founded upon questions about the first theoretical assumption. The distinction between sex and gender is a long-standing distinction in Western feminist practice, which attempts to counter views which attribute all or many differences and inequalities between women and men to sex or biology. A typical definition of the terms is the following:

[Sex and gender] serve a useful analytic purpose in contrasting a set of biological facts with a set of cultural facts. Were I to be scrupulous in my use of terms, I would use the term 'sex' only when I was speaking of biological differences between males and females and use 'gender' whenever I was referring to the social, cultural, psychological constructs that are imposed upon these biological differences .... [G]ender designates a set of categories to which we can give the same label crosslinguistically or crossculturally because they have some connection to sex differences. These categories are however conventional or arbitrary insofar as they are not reducible to or directly derivative of natural, biological facts; they vary from one language to another, one culture to another, in the way in which they order experience and action (Shapiro, cited in Yanagisako and Collier 1990:139).

An increasing number of scholars argue that sex/gender models like Shapiro's are problematic, both in their conception of gender and in their assumptions about sex. To say that 'gender' refers 'to the social, cultural, psychological constructs that are imposed upon these biological differences' implies that there are TWO genders, based upon two sexes. Linda Nicholson (1994) calls this the 'coat-rack' model of sex and gender. This model suggests sex is a base upon which the superstructure of gender is built, with the result that 'assumptions about biological differences between males and females pervade the analytic concepts we use to study the cultural construction of gender relations' (Yanagisako and Collier 1990:140). This dichotomous picture of gender is problematic because it overstates similarity within each of the categories so designated, and understates similarities across these categories. Further, underlying the assumption that the sex-gender distinction is dualistic is an assumption that these differences are necessary for procreative sexuality, which is understood as heterosexuality.[1] The methodological recommendation to study gender 'in cross-sex interaction between potentially sexually accessible interlocutors' illustrates how the idea of just two genders can be conflated with a presumption of heterosexuality. Historically and crossculturally sexual attachment has not always been ideologically organized in terms of a dichotomy, but in Western capitalist countries at present 'objects of desire are generally defined by the dichotomy and opposition of feminine and masculine; and sexual practice is mainly organized in couple relationships' (Connell 1987:113).

Although several strategies are commonly used to address this problem, the one most commonly used in recent work in sociolinguistics in effect subsumes what was traditionally placed under the domain of sex into the domain of gender. Scholars with this view look at the social construction of 'sex.'

> [I]t is not enough to claim that the body always comes to us through social interpretation, that is, that sex is subsumable under gender. We must also come to explicitly accept one of the implications of this idea, that we cannot look to the body to ground cross-cultural claims about the male/female distinction. The human population differs within itself not only in social expectations regarding how we think, feel, and act, but also in the ways in which the body is viewed .... We need to understand social variations in the male/female distinction as related to differences that go 'all the way down', that is, as tied not just to the limited phenomena many of us associate with gender (i.e. to cultural stereotypes of personality and behavior) but also to culturally various understandings of the body and to what it means to be a woman or a man (Nicholson 1994:81-83).

---

[1] An example of the collapsing of sex, gender and heterosexuality is in Kapchan's 1996 study of changing gender ideologies for women in Morocco. She claims that 'It is appropriate to speak of two genders in the Middle Eastern context—the heterosexual dyad of male and female. For despite the largely homosocial context created by sex segregation, open homosexuality is taboo and considered deviant' (19, note 12). Kapchan here collapses sex, gender and heterosexuality into one. Sex (alluded to with 'male and 'female') becomes gender. Gender is tightly connected to heterosexuality, suggesting that one can only have more than one gender if one also has homosexuality (even though her book describes a wide variety of gender norms for different women: maids, educated working women, mothers-in-law, performers, women working in the market). Finally, her formulation accepts a hegemonic sexual ideology, and seemingly conflates it with actual practices and behaviors. Leap's (1996) study of 'gay men's English' also uses gender and sexuality interchangeably. Though Leap is clearly intent upon highlighting and at some points celebrating the practices of a sexual minority, this terminological decision seems to narrow the possibilities for understanding the relationship between gender and sexuality.

In addition to recognizing cultural differences in understanding the body, proponents of this view may argue that we need to look at how certain definitions of sex/gender become hegemonic and are contested within a given society.

Instead of asking what gender differences are, this approach (an approach which has been called post-structuralist or deconstructive feminist) leads one to ask 'what difference does gender make' and how it came to make a difference. To argue that differences found in people's behavior, including their speech behavior, can simply be explained by invoking gender is to fail to question how gender is constructed. Instead, one needs to ask how and why gender differences are being constructed in that way, or what notion of gender is being normalized in such behavior. This approach, then, proposes to investigate how categories like 'woman' are created and which political interests the creation and perpetuation of certain identities and distinctions serve. Within this approach, dualistic distinctions (including male/female, black/white, emotional/rational, objective/ subjective) are seen as evidence for attempts within a given culture to regulate and naturalize certain social identities in ways that make some identities and behaviors unimaginable (these are called *excluded identities*) and in ways that make it unimaginable that members of certain groups would manifest behaviors normatively associated with another group (these are called *repressed identities*—see Butler 1992:7). Where people's behavior does not conform to dominant norms of masculinity or femininity, it is rendered unintelligible or incoherent: such people are not recognized as legitimately human. Because they deviate from normative conceptions of how sex, gender and sexuality should be aligned they are subject to repercussions and sanctions which vary according to local context. Some are economic, with people being confined to certain kinds of work and expelled from others. In the U.S. women working as police officers often find themselves addressed as 'sir' and occasionally find that others assume they are lesbians, regardless of any other information about sexual identity, simply because of the work that they do. Others are physical interventions, in the form of violence or medical procedures: 'gay-bashing' is a form of physical violence directed against those seen as lying outside North American gender and sexual norms, while in North America intersexed infants are operated on in order to be easily categorizable as male or female. Yet others are emotional: witness the expulsion from biological families of many Indian hijras, Nigerian 'yan daudu and American gays and lesbians. That the boundaries of what is seen as appropriate gendered behavior are policed and sanctioned is seen as evidence that certain definitions of gender are used to maintain a certain social order. Nonetheless, the notion of social order often remains ill-defined, vague or abstract in many studies. As I'll suggest below, coupling the study of language and sexuality with the study of political economy may help to place contestations over sexuality and gender within more specific institutional, national, global and historical contexts.

Work critical of the second theoretical assumption is closely linked to work critical of the first. To challenge the idea that sex, gender and sexuality are things that one has is to suggest instead that they are activities one does. The extent to which these activities, or performances, or practices are shaped by individuals has been a question of active debate within feminist and queer theory.[2] In the nascent field of queer linguistics, it is therefore this theoretical assumption, that gender and sexuality are attributes, that has perhaps received the most elaborated critical attention. Some of the most careful work on the uses and limits of the notion of performativity and citation can be found in the work of key scholars working in queer linguistics (see e.g. Gaudio 1996, Kulick 1998, 1999, Livia and Hall 1997). In linguistics and elsewhere, this approach has led to a recent series of studies which focus on various kinds of sex/gender 'transgression', in part for what they help reveal about dominant norms of sex/gender/sexual identity. For instance, Hall's work with Indian hijras (ritual specialists, mostly men, who describe themselves as hermaphrodites but have often undergone a castration operation) highlights the process of socialization into gender: femaleness and femininity must be learned by hijras, much like others acquire a second language. Hall's work also interrogates the assumption that highly visible and culturally central gender ambiguity suggests higher cultural tolerance for gender variation, pointing out the range of exclusion and abuse experienced by hijras in India (Hall 1997, Hall and O'Donovan 1996). By looking at the ways that 'yan daudu (Nigerian men who talk like women, and often have men as sexual partners) transgress norms of gender and sexuality, Gaudio (1996, 1997) suggests how, even in a patriarchal society that in principle accords all men potential access to masculine power, this access is not equally distributed, nor unconditional. Cameron's (1997) study of college men watching a basketball game and gossiping about other men whom they label 'gay' shows how some men continually construct themselves as heterosexual and possessors of a hegemonic masculinity by denigrating other men. The men whom they gossip about are often labeled 'gay' in the absence of any information or even any indicators about their sexuality, but because their clothes or behavior or speech are perceived as 'insufficiently

---

[2] Though the concepts of activity, performance and practice are related, they are not identical, and placing any one at the center of one's analysis leads one in certain directions. McElhinny (1998b) represents one attempt to begin to sort out some of these differences, though much work remains to be done on this topic.

masculine.' Labeling others as 'gay' is here used to avoid being so labeled themselves. Kulick's work on Brazilian travestis addresses the question of what it is about the understanding, representations and definitions of sexuality and gender in Brazil that make it logical and meaningful for males who desire other males to radically modify their bodies (1998).

A critical interrogation of the first two theoretical assumptions does not, however, necessarily challenge the assumption that sexuality is primarily linked with individuals. Indeed, a focus on such issues leaves queer linguistics prone to precisely the same critique that Susan Gal offered of studies of language and gender about a decade ago, a critique which remains pertinent to feminist linguistics as well as relevant for queer linguistics. Gal pointed out that studies of language and gender encoded a preference for studying gender in 'informal conversations, often in one-to-one or small-group relationships in the family or neighborhood' (Gal 1991:185). This analytic preference then created the illusion that 'gendered talk is mainly a personal characteristic or limited to the institution of the family' (Gal 1991:185). As we shall see in the next section, this is a fairly precise description of the analytic focus of studies in queer linguistics at the moment. What such a focus forecloses is the possibility of studying language, sexuality and political economy, where political economy is defined as the economic processes governing the production, distribution and consumption of goods, including 'non-material' ones, and the patterns and culture of power that control or influence these processes (Friedrich 1989). It forecloses considering the ways that sexuality is a structural principle which organizes other social institutions and processes and serves as a way of allocating access to resources (see also Eckert this volume, Barrett 1995, Kendall and Magenau 1998, Morrish 1997). Eckert's (this volume) commentary on Kulick 1999 further underlines the need for such work. She argues that Kulick's proposal to organize queer linguistics around the study of desire rather than sexuality may not allow analysts of queer identities to go beyond the individual to look at heterosexuality and the institutions that support it in adult society.

2   Queer Peers: Studies of Same-Sex Interaction in Queer Linguistics

Before I consider what it might mean to study language and sexuality in political and economic contexts, let's briefly consider the advantages and disadvantages of an approach that places same-sex, peer interactions at the center of queer linguistics. Though queer linguistics is a very new field, there are a large number of studies which do precisely this (see e.g. Coates and Jordan 1997, Graf and Lippa 1995, Joans 1995, Leap 1996, Liang

1997, Miller 1995, Moonwomon 1995, Moonwomon-Baird 1996, Morgan and Wood 1995, Queen 1998). Though this is no doubt partly the result of methodological convenience (it has been easier for researchers to study their own peer networks than to gain access to institutions, for instance), these studies also seem to reflect an implicit theoretical and methodological recommendation which parallels Brown and Levinson's. If methodological convenience were the only explanation, one might also expect numerous studies on same-sex couples, in parallel with the large number of studies of heterosexual couples found in studies of language and gender. This, however, is not the case. The focus on queer peers occasionally includes couples (Cummings 1994), but much more often it includes groups of peers which have been called 'families we choose', i.e. families which include friends, lovers, ex-lovers and the children of all or any of these.[3] The reasons for making this decision are rarely made explicit in the sociolinguistic studies, but anthropologist Kath Weston (1998) has argued that amongst many of the queer San Franciscans she studied friendship was particularly important because it was seen to outlast many romantic relationships, and to be more reliable than the love of biological family, who may reject sons and daughters when they come out. These questions of how kinship is assessed have more than academic import since '[d]eterminations of who shall count as kin have material as well as social and ideological consequences.... For the person seeking access to a partner's health insurance plan or input into the treatment of a friend who lies in a coma, how family ties will be determined and what specific reconstructions of kinship will gain legitimacy remain compelling questions' (Weston 1998:80). This focus on 'families we choose' arises, therefore, at a particular historical moment, one when what it means to be gay or lesbian is much more intimately linked with being out, and being out to family, than in the past, and so at a moment in which many more people contemplate and risk alienation from biological families than before.

Studies which focus on queer peers do provide an important corrective to work that focuses largely on gender in heterosexual couples, but this challenge has remained implicit in the existing work on peer interactions in queer linguistics. Studies of peers do not, in their present state, challenge the idea that sexuality and gender is linked to individuals (though for an example of a study that does see Dunk's (1991) analysis of the ways that elaborate heterosexual displays in peer interactions by working-class men in northern

---

[3] Sometimes the community of peers includes 'all those who are out', a particular view of community that adopts a dominant/subordinate dichotomy which oversimplifies as it romanticizes social realities and practices.

Ontario are linked to their class, gender and ethnicity). Furthermore, a focus on peer interaction still aligns itself with long-standing sociolinguistic traditions (in variationist sociolinguistics and in conversational analysis) of treating interactions amongst peers as the 'most natural' form of talk (Labov 1972, Drew and Heritage 1992). The focus on peers thus fits neatly with prevailing cultural ideologies that distinguish between private and public spheres, where peer interaction is mapped onto the personal and the individual (McElhinny 1997). Such a distinction has, of course, been widely critiqued by feminist scholars (e.g., Cancian 1989, Dahlerup 1987, Hurtado 1989, Jaggar 1983, Pateman 1989, Rosaldo 1980, Strathern 1988, Yanagisako and Collier 1987). It remains a fraught distinction for queers too, since they've been subjected to enforced privatization and denied the legal rights of privacy accorded heterosexuals. 'Criminal prosecution, deportations, and less formal (but no less effective) methods of policing have subjected queers to the double move of enforced privatization and a withholding of the most protections of the privacy doctrine' (Weston 1998:90). Associating the most pure forms of social identity with private spheres can only ever be a fraught political strategy.

To assume that sexuality (or gender) is attached only to individuals, and to adopt the public/private split, is to adopt uncritically the hegemonic ideology of sexuality and gender in the U.S. One elegant exposition of this is in Ortner (1991). She argues that because hegemonic American culture takes both the ideology of mobility and the ideology of individualism seriously, explanations for nonmobility not only focus on the failure of individuals (because they are said to be inherently lazy or stupid or whatever), but shift the domain of discourse to arenas that are taken to be 'locked into' individuals—gender, race, ethnic origin, and so forth (171). Although sexuality is much less widely understood as firmly attached to individuals (one form homophobia takes is understanding sexuality as a lifestyle that people have 'mistakenly' chosen), sexuality is still rarely understood as embedded in institutions and relations of inequality.[4] We must be wary, I think, of accounts of social processes that uncritically adopt hegemonic American notions of social identity as attached to individuals in ways that fail to allow the theorizing of social identity as a structural principle or the interaction of social identity with systems of inequity. Our vision of queer linguistics should be sufficiently broad to consider what it would mean to study language and sexuality in and across all domains: labor, medicine, migration,

---

[4] Queer scholarship has for this reason found more comfort in a possible biological basis for queerness than, say, feminist, or anti-racist, or Marxist scholars have in a biological basis for gender, race or class, on a reading of biological that sees it as fixed and unchanging. The unit of analysis here remains linked to the individual.

colonialism, as well as theory and method.[5] In the remainder of this chapter I will offer a few examples of what such an analysis might look like in four of these domains in North America.

I hope it will be clear from this discussion that I believe that queer identities and queer scholars are at the center of queer linguistics, as women and female scholars are at the center of feminist linguistics, or Black women at the center of Black feminist thought (Collins 1990), or African-American scholars are at the center of the study of African-American English (Labov 1972). But this doesn't assume queers, or women, or Black women share an identity or an agenda, nor does it assume that a queer linguistics is only about queers, anymore than a feminist linguistics is only about women. *Heteronormativity* is one concept which has surfaced to describe the study of heterosexual norms and their effect on gays, lesbians and others, but it shares with the notion of patriarchy a simplistic dichotomous approach to the study of inequality. Heteronormativity assumes that the crucial axis is heterosexual and non-heterosexual, and associates all the privilege with the first term. I prefer instead *stratified sexualities*, which I define as the way that sexuality is understood or accomplished differently according to inequalities that are based on hierarchies of class, race, ethnicity, gender, place in a global economy, migration status and object of desire. Stratified sexualities are thus structured by multiple and perhaps conflicting social, economic and political forces.[6] This concept has the advantage of allowing one to investigate, rather than assume, the possible relationship between certain stigmatized forms of heterosexuality as well as homosexuality, and of considering possible hierarchies within heterosexuality and homosexuality.

3   Homo Economicus: Language, Sexuality and Work

A number of recent scholars have pointed out that when queer identities and economics are talked about together, they are usually talked about in terms of consumption (Badgett 1997, Gluckman and Reed 1997). Corporations, prompted by some gay and lesbian marketing groups, have decided that 'the profits to be reaped from treating gay men and lesbians as trendsetting consumer groups finally outweigh the financial risks of inflaming right-wing hate' (Gluckman and Reed 1997:519). This linkage between gays and consumption is problematic for a number of reasons, not least because the image

---

[5] My argument at this point is deeply indebted to Kath Weston's (1998) lucid introduction to *Sexuality and Social Science*. An important part of her argument in that chapter is that, counter to many recent claims in queer studies, including queer linguistics, the study of sexuality is not a recent arrival on the social science scene, but instead that the study of sexuality has deeply shaped modern social science from the beginning.

[6] This notion is modelled on Colen's (1995) definition of stratified reproduction.

of gay consumption has been quickly appropriated by groups intent on showing that gays and lesbians and other queers are far from disadvantaged or oppressed, because its homogeneous portrayals of gays and lesbians as well-educated, high income conspicuous consumers leaves out the many gays and lesbians and others who don't have disposable income pouring out of their pockets, and because it often relies on stereotypes of gays and lesbians as non-parents. The ways that such images get constructed, in a variety of different media texts, is a task that critical discourse analysis can help address (though the prevailing focus of critical discourse analysis on issues of class and ethnicity would need to be transformed in the process). But an even more important intervention may be to focus on language and production, for it is difficult to dismiss the effects of discrimination and occupational segregation on sexual minorities. See, for instance, the eruption of protests and demonstrations in 1991 when California Governor Pete Wilson vetoed a measure that would have banned antigay employment discrimination, a series of protests dubbed Stonewall II by some activists (Gallagher 1999b).

Though the study of work is a well-developed subfield in sociolinguistics, it has yet to be carefully linked to the study of sexuality. The exceptions are a small number of studies of sex workers (Kulick 1998, Hall 1995, Miller 1995). Indeed, the study of sexuality and work, and more broadly sexuality and political economy, remains an understudied area in social science in general, and not only in sociolinguistics (though see Barrett 1995, Woods 1997, Weston and Rofel 1998). The studies that exist tend to focus on lesbian and gay professionals (e.g., Woods 1993, Woods with Lucas 1997), and in this they compound the myopic focus of many sociolinguistic studies of work which also focus only on professional workplaces (see McElhinny n.d. for more on this theme). In the U.S. professional jobs account for only 15% of the jobs done by Black American women, only 10% of the jobs done by Black American men and only 25% of the jobs done by White men and women (Reskin and Roos 1990:5).

One rather lonely example of a study of sexuality and nonprofessionals is Kath Weston and Lisa Rofel's (1998) study of class and conflict in an auto repair shop owned by two lesbians, and employing lesbian mechanics and workers. They point out that the very categories of lesbian and work mirror the private and public dichotomy, since lesbian identity has historically been defined in terms of the sexual and personal while wage work is defined as public. Linking the two requires renegotiating the constructed boundary between the two. They argue this happened in this workplace by undermining the compartmentalization of lives and self that characterizes most workplaces. What exactly this means in interactional terms is a ques-

tion for further investigation—one of particular interest when so many studies of work define institutional talk over and against peer interaction or interaction in families (cf. Drew and Heritage 1992).

The integration of personal and work relationships had mixed effects in
this auto repair shop. On the one hand, it was experienced as affirming,
positive, and fulfilling, less alienating than other workplaces. On the other
hand, when conflicts began to develop between the two lesbian owners and
the lesbian mechanics, there was no compartmentalization of work and self
to protect the workers against the effects of power inequities. Indeed, 'the
personalization of work relations obscure[d] power differentials structured
through property relations and the division of labor' (Weston and Rofel
1998:123). A conflict over workplace policy developed as the company
grew that pitted owners/managers against workers. Ultimately it led to a
strike and the departure of many of the workers, with effects far more dev-
astating even than job loss usually is because of the expectations the job had
raised about what work could be like. Explanations that owners and workers
offered for the conflict drew upon different ideologies of communication,
and of the role of individuals in communication. For example, the workers
tended to explain the conflict in terms of miscommunication (Weston and
Rofel 1998:125). This allowed them to understand all the parties as rational
and equal and independent individuals, in ways that actively obscured class
relations, in part by ignoring the ways the owners got to set the terms for
communication. Indeed, class became understood according to individualized criteria (occupation, education, values, income) rather than within the
context of a division of labor and capitalist property relations. This miscommunication view did, however, recognize two parties to the disagreement: workers and management. Owners refused to recognize the solidarity
of workers by preferring a personality or provocateur theory of conflict, one
which suggested either that only the lazy, irresponsible and resentful workers were dissatisfied, or that some outside agent was bent upon destroying a
lesbian business. This interpretation, too, refused to attend to their role in
the conflict, as well as workers' solidarity in their demands. The ways that
such conflicts are resolved in radical institutions, like lesbian workplaces,
embedded in capitalist social relations remains a rich arena for sociolinguistic research, especially given the extent to which studies of institutional talk
have focussed almost entirely on mainstream institutions (McElhinny 1998a).

Most gays and lesbians do not, however, work in a self-consciously
queer workplace. Certain notions about heterosexuality and gender organize
a traditionally masculine workplace like the police department, a workplace
I've studied in some detail (1993, 1994, 1995, in press). The dominant
model of policing in Pittsburgh in the 1990s was a crime control, or milita-

rized model, which construes the typical police officer as a crime fighter extraordinaire, a seasoned, well-armed, professional soldier in an unending and savage war on crime. The ideal police officer was aggressive and tough, authoritative and male, all notions with clear interactional correlates (McElhinny, in press). Being a police officer and gay were seen as so incompatible in Pittsburgh that police officers contorted themselves to ignore stark evidence to the contrary. I asked one female officer if there were any gay men on the job. She said no. She said she'd once spotted one of her fellow officers in an area of town with some gay bars. Another man had his arm around him, and she thought, 'Ohmygod he's gay!' But then, she said, she decided that he was probably just drunk, and being helped home by a friend. And, in fact, he came up to her a few days later, and said, 'Hey I spotted you the other day when I was on X street, god I was so drunk, a friend had to help me home.' She seemed to accept his explanation without question. In traditionally masculine workplaces such as this where to be gay and a worker are seen as incompatible, received notions of both what it means to be gay and what it means to be a cop remain unquestioned.

Women working in traditionally masculine workplaces are often presumed to be lesbian, whatever their sexuality, in a view of sexuality that links homosexuality with gender inversion (see Sedgwick 1990 and Weston 1998:97 for discussion). Since for many people, the very term *lesbian* still works as an epithet (Pharr 1988), the risk of being so labeled and stigmatized is one way that all women are barred from lucrative skilled blue collar jobs.[7] This gender inversion model of sexuality works to bar women who are not seen as 'masculine' from certain forms of work, as it ignores all the lesbians working in traditionally feminine jobs. Sexuality, then, 'permeates conjecture about what people go best with what jobs, which qualities [including linguistic ones] come with which girls, and which girls are girls' (Weston 1998:98).

4 Stratified Sexualities: Language, Sexuality and Medicine

So far the studies of queer linguistics linked to medicine have focused on AIDS-related issues and thus largely on gay men (see e.g. Bolton 1995, Ibanez 1995, Leap 1996). However, there are a variety of ways in which issues of sexuality are linked to medicine. Presumptions of heterosexuality

---

[7] I didn't meet any women who were out during my year in Pittsburgh, and male and female officers alike laughed at the idea that all female cops were lesbian, but *lesbian* still operated as a signifier of masculinity.

can be life-threatening for lesbians (Gallagher 1999a:391-5). For many heterosexual women, access to the medical system is through birth control or child health care. Lesbians do not get screened for breast cancer as often as heterosexual women because of the presumptions of heterosexuality built into the structure of visits, but also into the case history questions doctors regularly run through: Are you married? Are you sexually active and on birth control? Some lesbians simply postpone their visits, given the choice of coming out to a provider, or educating them, or challenging them. Support groups with a heterosexual focus may not provide the kind of emotional support that lesbians diagnosed with breast cancer need, so that some lesbians have started up their own support groups, on-line and face-to-face. All of these interactions, with experts and peers alike, lend themselves to sociolinguistic scrutiny. Drawing medical practitioners' attentions to these interactions could be an important instance of applied linguistic inquiry.

Breastfeeding norms, though they may seem initially to be largely related to child nurturance, are part of the political and symbolic systems organizing gender relations and sexuality. Headlines that trumpet 'Good news for fathers—breastfeeding women are more sexually active than at any other time' (cited in Blum 1999:40) seem to suggest that the act of breastfeeding is the epitome of compulsory heterosexuality, but only detailed ethnographic investigation can highlight the actual meaning of breast-feeding for the women who do it. Many breastfeeding handbooks suggest that breastfeeding challenges certain forms of compulsory heterosexuality, if only because it challenges the normative notion that women's breasts are available largely for the heterosexual male gaze (Blum 1999:16-7). Breastfeeding handbooks provide ample advice on how to deal with the 'understandable' jealousy of the husband faced with the breastfeeding wife, advice which assumes in some ways husbands' ownership of their wives' breasts as it underlines the challenge nursing raises to that very idea (Blum 1999:39-40). Women whom I have talked to in the Metro Mother's Network, and in Toronto's public health postnatal groups, talk about the transformed attitudes they hold towards their breasts after prolonged breastfeeding: they now see them as entirely utilitarian, asexual body parts, desensitized to most touch sensation. Whatever initial reservations they had about public breast-feeding have been overcome: they now say they have no hesitation about whipping it out, any time, anywhere. Philosopher Iris Young sees the pleasurably nursing lesbian mother as doubly displacing her erotic relations from men, and thus as the ultimate affront to compulsory heterosexuality.[8]

---

[8] Despite the increased importance placed on breastfeeding in medical discourse, the practices of wet-nursing or shared nursing which were once commonplace in the West have not resurfaced. Blum points out that 'deeper anxieties about violations of compulsory heterosexuality

The case of Denise Perigo suggests the ways that supports or sanctions for breastfeeding are linked to stratified versions of heterosexuality in the U.S (see Blum 1999:96-97 for a fuller account). Denise Perigo, a single mother who was alarmed when she experienced sexual arousal while nursing her two and a half year old daughter, called a community volunteer center and asked to be put in contact with La Leche League (a breast-feeding support organization). La Leche League supports extended nursing in members (up to four or more years), and La Leche materials regularly reassure members that feelings of sexual arousal are normal and natural. Perigo, however, was put through to the local rape crisis center, where counselors interpreted her story as one of sexual abuse. Local police were dispatched to her home, she was arrested and her child placed in foster care. Criminal charges referred to inappropriate 'mouth to breast' contact. Though these charges were dropped, social services filed charges of sexual abuse and neglect and Perigo was only allowed to see her daughter in biweekly supervised visits. The family court focused on Perigo's suspect sexuality, specifically her 'failure' to wean, the fact that she was a single mother and that she was supposedly involved with a married man. Some La Leche League members are careful to distinguish 'sensual' and 'sexual' precisely because of the possibility of such sanctions.

The renewed popularity of breastfeeding is correlated with the rise of a cohort of certified professional experts (lactation consultants and midwives) and peer cohorts (like La Leche League), not to mention breast pump purveyors, obstetricians and self-help book authors, who offer advice on how best to do it. It also is linked to a rise of press coverage of cases like Denise Perigo's. All of this discourse, written and spoken, lends itself to linguistic analysis. Such professional advice establishes certain norms for how best (or 'most naturally') to be a mother (or a wife) which are often most easily and pleasurably fulfilled by white heterosexual middle-class married mothers. The promotion of what is most 'natural' (and thus presumably most healthy) for mothers and children suggests breastfeeding is outside the public realm, but also ends up suggesting that motherhood requires no significant resources and can be accomplished privately under any circumstances (Blum 1999:13). Most handbooks on breastfeeding (and pregnancy) assume women have a house and husband. The advice given ends up judging and marking as deviant those white working-class mothers who don't have the

---

encourage strict mother-baby fidelity as a parallel or mirror reinforcing the mother-father monogamous sexual tie–and this parallel importantly suppresses any suggestion of shared nursing' (1999:40). Breastfeeding also raises the charged issue of crossgenerational sensual ties (Blum 1999:17). Penelope Leach writes: 'your body is ready and waiting for him. Your skin thrills to his.' She is describing a woman about to breastfeed her newborn baby boy.

material conditions which afford them the time and leisure to breast-feed and breast-pump and who have good reason to be wary of the motives of the state and professional experts who long have intruded into their lives. Workers promoting breastfeeding may often treat African-American working-class mothers who reject breast-feeding as uneducated about its benefits rather than resisting the practice. Such mothers often reject outright the notions of 'natural' with which breast-feeding is promoted, quickly spotting links to notions of primitivism, animalistic and sexual which have long been problematic for them. They also often live in circumstances where breast-feeding is overwhelmingly burdensome or exhausting. Detailed analysis of the language and gender and sexual ideologies promoted in breastfeeding discourse will allow us to see how hierarchies of motherhoods are constructed, and how these are linked to forms of sexuality sanctioned or supported by medicine, the state, and other powerful societal institutions.

5 Sexuality on the Move: Language, Sexuality and Migration

Another topic which lends itself to sociolinguistic analysis is the effects of migration on speech. In one of the pioneering attempts to link political economic analysis with queer studies, John D'Emilio (1983) pointed out the ways that the general migration from rural to urban areas in the U.S. made possible the rise of modern gay and lesbian identities. Queer scholars have pointed to the dynamics of migration from rural to urban settings in North America since Stonewall, a phenomenon which has been called the great gay migration of the 1970s and 1980s.[9] Weston's 1998 analysis of coming out stories finds an urban/rural dichotomy as one of the crucial semiotic axes around which such stories are built. People begin their stories by talking about how they originally believed themselves to be 'the only one in the world.' They then undertake a quest for community, which ultimately takes many, at least for a while, to the city. The result 'is a sexual geography in which the city represents a beacon of tolerance and gay community, the country a locus of persecution and gay absence' (1998:40). This semiotics inverts a symbolic contrast that has developed around the city/country since the Industrial Revolution. Instead of condemning the city for its artificiality, anonymity and sexual license, and celebrating the country for its tradition, nature, and face-to-face interactions, the precise opposite occurs. The power

---

[9] Although migration to cities like New York and San Francisco has received the most scholarly attention, more regional movements (from, say, northern Pennsylvania to Pittsburgh) are also relevant.

of this semiotic contrast, and its manifestation in the discourse of coming out stories, suggests that this would be a particularly promising locus for investigation of how phonological variables might be used in the construction of queer identities. Since actual migrants may not find the utopia they anticipated upon arriving in the city, they might be expected to position themselves in relation to urban/suburban/rural values in a variety of different ways, in a variety of different situations. Penny Eckert's work (2000) on the ways that suburban teenagers construct group and gender identities by using phonological variables identified with an urban-suburban axis provides one rich model for such a study, as does Bortoni-Ricardo's (1985) study of the urbanization of rural dialect speakers, and the work of a new generation of scholars who are interested in how people use phonological variables to build personal styles of speech (Bucholtz 1996, Mendoza-Denton 1997, Podesva, Roberts, and Campbell-Kibler, this volume).

6 Carnal Power: Language, Sexuality and Colonialism

Studies linking migration and labor to sexuality remain, on the whole, rare. One of the best developed arenas for the study of sexuality may, however, be in studies of colonialism and post-colonialism (see McClintock 1995, Stoler 1991, 1995 for useful overviews). Foucault's work has been particularly influential here, as scholars have investigated how the nineteenth century penetration of social and self-disciplinary regimes into sexuality, as well as other forms of discipline for bodies, was linked to nation- and empire-building. This work has a two-pronged approach, one which considers how the discursive management of sexual practices of colonizer and colonized took place in colonies, but also the ways in which management of sexualities and bodies in the metropole was itself linked to the formation of subjects who would engage in, or support, empire-building. This work may also constitute one of the richest explorations of the interactions of race and sexuality, exploring as it does the linkages between the emergence of a highly biological notion of race in the 19th century alongside the emergence of the notion of sexuality as identity rather than practice.

As Stoler points out, colonial politics was not just about sex, and sex did not reduce to colonial politics. Nonetheless, 'sex in the colonies was about sexual access and reproduction, class distinctions and racial demarcations, nationalism and European identity' (1991:87). In the early days of colonialism, when European supremacy and control were not seen as in question, concubinage was promoted amongst colonial administrators. It was seen as cheaper than importing European women, as a way of promoting permanent settlement, as more stable and less health-threatening than prostitution, and as a strategy for preventing men from 'unnatural' liaisons with one another (a circumstance which men of different classes and nationalities were seen as differently prone to). Indeed, bachelors were actively recruited for colonial positions, and marriage was sometimes prohibited.

As, however, challenges to European control became more visible, concubinage, like adaptation to local food, customs and languages, was seen as a source of contagion, as loss of the white self. European women were recruited, and their presence was linked to increasing concerns about boundaries between colonizer and colonized. Relations with servants were codified, miscegenation was frowned upon, spaces designated as European and non-European were more carefully specified, and new social services were required. Charges of rape were often linked to perceived transgressions of social space by the colonized, and followed upon tensions in European community and their attempts to resolve them. In short, the presence of European women meant embourgeoisement of colonial communities and the sharpening of racial categories. The study of sexuality in colonial settings thus reveals 'how deeply the conduct of private life and the sexual proclivities individuals expressed were tied to corporate profits and the security of the colonial state' (Stoler 1991:62). What is unusual about sexuality in colonial settings is not, however, that it was imbricated with state and capitalist politics and with race and nationality, but rather that the relations between these are so clearly visible there. The study of sexuality in colonial settings thus provides a model for returning to metropole settings and beginning to unpack the relationship between these same institutions and sexuality in those settings. It only remains to consider what distinctive role sociolinguistics and linguistic anthropology can offer to these analyses.

Sexual control has been said to figure in the substance, as well as the iconography, of imperial rule. Edward Said has famously argued that the sexual submission and possession of Oriental women by European men stands for the relative strength of East and West. However, feminist critics, like Ann Stoler and Anne McClintock have argued that to treat sexuality only as a trope is to dismiss the significance of gender and sexuality, to subordinate them to racial, cultural and national relations, rather than considering their imbrication. Stoler (1991:52) argues that we need to treat the sexual and conjugal tensions of colonial life as more than a political trope for the tensions of empire; instead she investigates how gender-specific sexual sanctions and prohibitions not only demarcated positions of power but prescribed the personal and public boundaries of race. Nonetheless, as she points out, one of the key issues in the study of sexuality and colonialism is the question of where and when sexuality is used as a metaphor, and where discussed in its own right. This question is by no means straightforward to answer: 'Was the medium the message, or did sexual relations always 'mean' something else, stand in for other relations, evoke the sense of *other* (pecuniary, political, or some possibly more subliminal) desires? This analytic slippage between the sexual symbols of power and the politics of sex runs throughout the colonial record ....' (Stoler 1991:54). Repeatedly the task for colonial historians becomes unpacking what is metaphor and what is not. Since the pursuit of these questions means investigating records taken in a rather literal sense, as written accounts, these questions are eminently textual, and amenable to the kind of historical analysis of documents and ideologies of language and interaction that is being pioneered by such linguistic anthropologists as William Hanks (1986, 1987), Miyako Inoue (2000) and Joel Kuipers (1998).

7 Conclusion

This is a necessarily brief, and certainly far from comprehensive, tour of the issues that a queer linguistics attentive to political economy might attend to. I do not mean to suggest that such work is the only future for queer linguistics, but that a queer linguistics without it will be incomplete, and will risk uncritically adopting, disseminating and perpetuating hegemonic individualistic ideologies of personhood, which are necessarily and always linked to normative ideas about sexuality and gender, age and ethnicity, class and social relations. Rather than assuming the ideological segregation of sexuality from the rest of social life, the study of language, sexuality and political economy works to ask how and why sexuality is often so segregated, and to challenge this segregation.

References

Badgett, M. V. Lee. 1997. Thinking Homo/economically. *A Queer World: The Center for Lesbian and Gay Studies Reader*, ed. Martin Duberman, 467-76. New York: New York University Press.

Barrett, Rusty. 1995. Supermodels of the World, Unite! Political Economy and the Language of Performance among African-American Drag Queens. *Beyond the Lavender Lexicon: Authenticity, Imagination, and Appropriation in Lesbian and Gay Languages*, ed. William Leap, 207-26. OPA: Gordan and Breach.

Blum, Linda. 1999. *At the Breast: Ideologies of Breastfeeding and Motherhood in the Contemporary United States*. Boston: Beacon Press.

Bolton, Ralph. 1995. Sex Talk: Bodies and Behaviors in Gay Erotica. *Beyond the Lavender Lexicon: Authenticity, Imagination, and Appropriation in Lesbian and Gay Languages*, ed. William Leap, 173-206. OPA: Gordan and Breach.

Bortoni-Ricardo, Stella. 1995. *The Urbanization of Rural Dialect Speakers*. Cambridge: Cambridge University Press.

Brown, Penelope and Stephen Levinson. 1983. *Politeness*. Cambridge, MA: Cambridge University Press.

Bucholtz, Mary. 1996. Geek the Girl: Language, Femininity and Female Nerds. *Gender and Belief Systems: Proceedings of the Fourth Berkeley Conference on Women and Language*, ed. Natasha Warner, Jocelyn Ahlers, Leela Bilmes, Monica Oliver, Suzanne Wertheim and Melinda Chen, 119-32. Berkeley: Berkeley Women and Language Group, University of California Berkeley.

Butler, Judith. 1992. Contingent Foundations: Feminism and the Question of 'Postmodernism.' *Feminists Theorize the Political*, ed. J. Butler and J. Scott, 3-21. New York: Routledge.

Cameron, Deborah. 1997. Performing Gender Identity: Young Men's Talk and the Construction of Heterosexual Masculinity. *Language and Masculinity*, ed. Sally Johnson and Ulrike Meinhof, 47-64. Cambridge: Basil Blackwell.

Cancian, F. 1989. Love and the Rise of Capitalism. *Gender and Intimate Relationships*, ed. B. Risman and P. Schwartz, 12-23. Belmont CA: Wadsworth.

Coates, Jennifer and Mary Ellen Jordan. 1997. Que(e)rying Friendship: Discourses of Resistance and the Construction of Gendered Subjectivity. *Queerly Phrased: Language, Gender, and Sexuality*, ed. Anna Livia and Kira Hall, 214-32. New York: Oxford University Press.

Colen, Shellee. 1995. 'Like a Mother to Them': Stratified Reproduction and West Indian Childcare Workers and Employers in New York. *Conceiving the New World Order: The Global Politics of Reproduction*, ed. Faye Finsburg and Rayna Rapp, 78-102. Berkeley: University of California Press.

Collins, Patricia Hill. 1990. *Black Feminist Thought: Knowledge, Consciousness and the Politics of Empowerment*. NY: Routledge.

Connell, R. W. 1987. *Gender and Power: Society, the Person and Sexual Politics*. Stanford: Stanford University Press.

Cornwall, Andrea and Nancy Lindisfarne. 1994. Dislocating Masculinity: Gender, Power and Anthropology. *Dislocating Masculinity: Comparative Ethnographies*, ed. A. Cornwall and N. Lindisfarne, 11-47. London: Routledge.

Cummings, Martha Clark. 1994. Lesbian Identity and Negotiation in Discourse. *Cultural Performances: Proceedings of the Third Berkeley Women and Language Conference*, ed. Mary Bucholtz, A. C. Liang, Laurel Sutton and Caitlin Hines, 144-58. Berkeley: Berkeley Women and Language Group, University of California Berkeley.

Dahlerup, D. 1987. Confusing Concepts–Confusing Reality: A Theoretical Discussion of the Patriarchal State. *Women and the State*, ed. A. Sassoon, 93-127. London: Routledge.

D'Emilio, John. 1983. Capitalism and Gay Identity. *Powers of Desire: The Politics of Sexuality*, ed. Ann Snitow, Christine Stanesell and Sharon Thompson, 100-13. New York: Monthly Review Press.

Drew, P. and Heritage, J. 1992. Analyzing Talk at Work: An Introduction. *Talk at Work: Interaction in Institutional Settings*, ed. P. Drew and J. Heritage, 3-65. Cambridge: Cambridge University Press.

Dunk, Thomas. 1991. *It's a Working Man's Town: Male Working-Class Culture.* Montreal: McGill-Queen's University Press.

Eckert, Penelope. 2000. *Linguistic Variation as Social Practice.* Oxford: Basil Blackwell.

Friedrich, Paul. 1989. Language, Ideology and Political Economy. *American Anthropologist* 91.2:295-312.

Gal, Susan. 1991. Between Speech and Silence: The Problematics of Research on Language and Gender. *Gender at the Crossroads of Knowledge*, ed. M. di Leonardo, 175-203. Berkeley: University of California Press.

Gallagher, John. 1999a. Lesbian Plague? *Witness to Revolution: The Advocate Reports on Gay and Lesbian Politics, 1967 - 1999*, ed. Chris Bull, 391-5. Los Angeles: Alyson Books.

Gallagher, John. 1999b. California Explodes after Governor Kills Workplace Bias Ban. *Witness to Revolution: The Advocate Reports on Gay and Lesbian Politics, 1967 - 1999*, ed. Chris Bull, 269-74. Los Angeles: Alyson Books.

Gaudio, Rudolf P. 1996. Men Who Talk Like Women: Language, Gender and Sexuality in Hausa Muslim Society. Ph.D. Dissertation, Stanford University.

Gaudio, Rudolf P. 1997. Not Talking Straight in Hausa. *Queerly Phrased: Language, Gender and Sexuality*, ed. Anna Livia and Kira Hall, 416-29. New York: Oxford University Press.

Gluckman, Amy and Betsy Reed. 1997. The Gay Marketing Moment. *A Queer World: The Center for Lesbian and Gay Studies Reader*, ed. Martin Duberman, 519-25. New York: New York University Press.

Graf, Roman and Barbara Lippa. 1995. The Queens' English. *Beyond the Lavender Lexicon: Authenticity, Imagination, and Appropriation in Lesbian and Gay Languages*, ed. William Leap, 227-34. OPA: Gordan and Breach.

Hall, Kira. 1995. Lip Service on the Fantasy Lines. *Gender Articulated: Language and the Socially Constructed Self*, ed. Kira Hall and Mary Bucholtz, 183-216. NY: Routledge.

Hall, Kira. 1997. 'Go Suck your Husband's Sugarcane': Hijras and the Use of Sexual Insult. *Queerly Phrased: Language, Gender and Sexuality*, ed. Anna Livia and Kira Hall, 430-60. New York: Oxford University Press.

Hall, Kira, and Veronica O'Donovan. 1996. Shifting Gender Positions among Hindi-Speaking Hijras. *Rethinking Language and Gender Research: Theory and Practice*, ed. J. Bing, V. Bergvall and A. Freed, 228-66. London: Longman.

Hanks, William. 1986. Authenticity and Ambivalence in the Text: A Colonial Maya Text. *American Ethnologist* 13.4:721-44.

Hanks, William. 1987. Discourse Genres in a Theory of Practice. *American Ethnologist* 14.4:688-92.

Hurtado, A. 1989. Relating to Privilege: Seduction and Rejection in the Subordination of White Women and Women of Color. *Signs* 14.4:833-55.

Ibanez, Francisco. 1995. From Confession to Dialogue. *Beyond the Lavender Lexicon: Authenticity, Imagination, and Appropriation in Lesbian and Gay Languages*, ed. William Leap, 65-86. OPA: Gordan and Breach.

Inoue, Miyako. 2000. Gender, Language and Modernity: Toward an Effective History of 'Japanese Women's Language.' Ms.

Jaggar, A. 1983. *Feminist Politics and Human Nature*. Totowa, NJ: Rowman and Allanheld.

Joans, Barbara. 1995. Dykes on Bikes Meet Ladies of Harley. *Beyond the Lavender Lexicon: Authenticity, Imagination, and Appropriation in Lesbian and Gay Languages*, ed. William Leap, 87-106. OPA: Gordan and Breach.

Kapchan, Deborah. 1996. *Gender on the Market: Moroccan Women and the Revoicing of Tradition*. Philadelphia: University of Pennsylvania Press.

Kendall, Shari and Keller Magenau. 1998. He's Calling her Dada: Lesbian Mothers and Discursive Gender Ideologies in Child Custody Cases. *Engendering Communication: Proceedings of the Fifth Berkeley Conference on Women and Language*, ed. Suzanne Wertheim, Ashlee Bailey and Monica Corston-Oliver, 259-270. Berkeley: Berkeley Women and Language Group, University of California Berkeley.

Kuipers, Joel. 1998. *Language, Identity and Marginality in Indonesia: The Changing Nature of Ritual Speech on the Island of Sumba*. Cambridge: Cambridge University Press.

Kulick, Don. 1998. *Travesti: Sex, Gender and Culture among Brazilian Transgendered Prostitutes*. Chicago: University of Chicago Press.

Kulick, Don. 1999. Language and Gender/Sexuality. URL: www.language-culture.org/colloquia/symposia/kulick-don/.

Labov, William. 1972. *Language in the Inner City*. Philadelphia: University of Pennsylvania Press.

Leap, William. 1996. *Word's Out: Gay Men's English*. University of Minnesota Press.

Liang, A. C. 1997. The Creation of Coherence in Coming Out Stories. *Queerly Phrased: Language, Gender, and Sexuality*, ed. Anna Livia and Kira Hall, 287-309. New York: Oxford University Press.

Livia, Anna, and Kira Hall. 1997. 'It's a Girl!' Bringing Performativity Back to Linguistics. *Queerly Phrased: Language, Gender, and Sexuality*, ed. Anna Livia and Kira Hall, 3-20. New York: Oxford University Press.

McClintock, Anne. 1995. *Imperial Leather: Race, Gender and Sexuality in the Colonial Contest*. NY: Routledge.

McElhinny, Bonnie. n.d. Working away on Gender: Women and Discourse in a Blue-Collar Workplace.

McElhinny, Bonnie. In press. Armed Robbers, Assholes and Agency: Linguistic Ideologies, Gender and Police Officers. *Gendered Practices in Language*, ed. Sarah Benor, Mary Rose, Deyvani Sharma, Julie Sweetland and Qing Zhang. Stanford, CA: CSLI Press.

McElhinny, Bonnie. 1998a. Cooperative Culture: Reconciling Equality and Difference in a Multicultural Women's Co-operative. *Ethnos* 63.3:383-412.

McElhinny, Bonnie. 1998b. Genealogies of Gender Theory: Practice Theory and Feminism in Sociocultural and Linguistic Anthropology. *Social Analysis* 42.3: 164-89.

McElhinny, Bonnie. 1997. Ideologies of Public and Private Language in Sociolinguistics. *Gender and Discourse*, ed. Ruth Wodak, 106-39. London: Sage Publishers.

McElhinny, Bonnie. 1995. Challenging Hegemonic Masculinities: Female and Male Police Officers Handling Domestic Violence. *Gender Articulated*, ed. Kira Hall and Mary Bucholtz, 217-43. New York: Routledge.

McElhinny, Bonnie. 1994. An Economy of Affect: Objectivity, Masculinity and the Gendering of Police Work. *Dislocating Masculinity: Comparative Ethnographies*, ed. Andrea Cornwall and Nancy Lindisfarne, 159-71. New York: Routledge.

McElhinny, Bonnie. 1993. We All Wear the Blue: Language, Gender and Police Work. Ph.D. Dissertation, Stanford University

Mendoza-Denton, Norma. 1997. Chicana/Mexicana Identity and Linguistic Variation: An Ethnographic and Sociolinguistic Study of Gang Affiliation in an Urban High School. Ph.D. Dissertation, Stanford University.

Miller, Edward. 1995. Inside the Switchboards of Desire: Storytelling on Phone-sex Lines. *Beyond the Lavender Lexicon: Authenticity, Imagination, and Appropriation in Lesbian and Gay Languages*, ed. William Leap, 3-18. OPA: Gordan and Breach.

Moonwomon-Baird, Birch. 1996. Lesbian Conversation as a Site for Ideological Identity Construction. *Gender and Belief Systems: Proceedings of the Fourth Berkeley Conference on Women and Language*, ed. Natasha Warner, Jocelyn Ahlers, Leela Bilmes, Monica Oliver, Suzanne Wertheim and Melinda Chen, 563-74. Berkeley: Berkeley Women and Language Group, University of California Berkeley.

Moonwomon, Birch. 1995. Lesbian Discourse, Lesbian Knowledge. *Beyond the Lavender Lexicon: Authenticity, Imagination, and Appropriation in Lesbian and Gay Languages*, ed. William Leap, 45-64. OPA: Gordan and Breach.

Morris, Rosalind. 1995. All Made Up: Performance Theory and the New Anthropology of Sex and Gender. *Annual Review of Anthropology* 567-92.

Morrish, Elizabeth. 1997. 'Falling Short of God's Ideal': Public Discourse about Lesbians and Gays. *Queerly Phrased: Language, Gender, and Sexuality*, ed. Anna Livia and Kira Hall, 335-48. NY: Oxford University Press.

Morgan, Ruth and Kathleen Wood. 1995. Lesbians in the Living Room: Collusion, Co-construction and Co-narration in Conversation *Beyond the Lavender Lexicon: Authenticity, Imagination, and Appropriation in Lesbian and Gay Languages*, ed. William Leap, 235-49. OPA: Gordan and Breach.

Nicholson, Linda. 1994. Interpreting Gender. *Signs* 20.1:79-105.

Ortner, Sherry. 1991. Reading America: Preliminary Notes on Class and Culture. *Recapturing Anthropology: Working in the Present*, ed. Richard Fox, 163-90. Santa Fe: School of American Research Press.

Pateman, C. 1989. *The Disorder of Women: Democracy, Feminism and Social Theory*. Stanford: Stanford University Press.

Pharr, Suzanne. 1988. *Homophobia as a Weapon of Sexism*. Inverness: Chardon Press.

Queen, Robin. 1998. Conversational Interaction among Lesbians and Gay Men. Engendering Communication: *Proceedings of the Fifth Berkeley Conference on Women and Language*, ed. Suzanne Wertheim, Ashlee Bailey and Monica Corston-Oliver, 461-72. Berkeley: Berkeley Women and Language Group, University of California Berkeley.

Reskin, Barbara and Patricia Roos. 1990. *Job Queues, Gender Queues: Explaining Women's Inroads into Male Occupations*. Philadelphia: Temple University Press.

Rosaldo, M. 1980. The Use and Abuse of Anthropology: Reflections on Feminism and Cross-cultural Understanding. *Signs* 5.3:389-417.

Schieffelin, Bambi and Elinor Ochs. 1986. *Language Socialization across Cultures*. Cambridge, MA: Cambridge University Press.

Sedgwick, Eve Kosofsky. 1990. *Epistemology of the Closet*. Berkeley: University of California Press.

Shapiro, Judith. 1981. Anthropology and the Study of Gender. *Soundings: An Interdisciplinary Journal* 64:446-65.

Stoler, Ann Laura. 1991. Carnal Knowledge and Imperial Power: Gender, Race and Morality in Colonial Asia. *Gender at the Crossroads of Knowledge: Feminist Anthropology in the Postmodern Era*, ed. Micaela di Leonardo, 51-101. Berkeley: University of California Press.

Stoler, Ann Laura. 1995. *Race and the Education of Desire: Foucault's History of Sexuality and the Colonial Order of Things*. Durham: Duke University Press.

Strathern, M. 1988. *The Gender of the Gift*. Berkeley: University of California Press.

Strub, Sean. 1997. The Growth of the Gay and Lesbian Market. *A Queer World: The Center for Lesbian and Gay Studies Reader*, ed. Martin Duberman, 514-5. New York: New York University Press.

Weston, Kath. 1998. *Long Slow Burn: Sexuality and Social Science*. New York: Routledge.

Weston, Kath and Lisa Rofel. 1998. Sexuality, Class and Conflict in a Lesbian Workplace. *Long Slow Burn: Sexuality and Social Science*, 115-42. New York: Routledge.

Woods, James with Jay Lucas. 1993. *The Corporate Closet: The Professional Lives of Gay Men in America.* New York: The Free Press.

Woods, James. 1997. The Different Dilemmas of Lesbian and Gay Professionals. *A Queer World: The Center for Lesbian and Gay Studies Reader*, ed. Martin Duberman, 508-513. New York: New York University Press.

Yanagisako, S. and J.F. Collier. 1990. The Mode of Reproduction in Anthropology. *Theoretical Perspectives on Sexual Difference*, ed. D. Rhode, 131-144. New Haven: Yale University Press.

Yanagisako, S. and J.F. Collier. 1987. Toward a Unified Analysis of Gender and Kinship. *Gender and Kinship: Essays toward a Unified Analysis*, ed. J.F. Collier and S. Yanagisako, 14-52. Stanford: Stanford University Press.

Part Two:

Contesting Meaning in Practice

9

'Queering' Semantics: Definitional Struggles

SALLY MCCONNELL-GINET

In a famous passage from Lewis Carroll's *Through the Looking Glass*, Humpty Dumpty explains to Alice why un-birthdays should be celebrated.

'... and that shows that there are three hundred and sixty-four days when you might get un-birthday presents-'

'Certainly,' said Alice.

'And only ONE for birthday presents, you know. There's glory for you!'

'I don't know what you mean by 'glory',' Alice said.

Humpty Dumpty smiled contemptuously. 'Of course you don't – till I tell you. I meant 'there's a nice knock-down argument for you!''

'But 'glory' doesn't mean 'a nice knock-down argument',' Alice objected.

'When I use a word,' Humpty Dumpty said, in rather a scornful tone, 'it means just what I choose it to mean--neither more nor less.'

'The question is,' said Alice, 'whether you CAN make words mean so many different things.'

'The question is,' said Humpty Dumpty, 'which is to be master--that's all.'

Many students of language have drawn their own morals from this passage. In this paper, I argue that both Humpty Dumpty and Alice are partly right. Alice understands that we can't make words mean whatever we want them to: there are substantial constraints that arise from past history and from what is involved in trying to mean something. At the same time, there

Language and Sexuality: Contesting Meaning in Theory and Practice.
Kathryn Campbell-Kibler, Robert J. Podesva, Sarah J. Roberts and Andrew Wong (eds.).
Copyright © 2001, CSLI Publications.

is room for shaping and reshaping word meanings. Humpty Dumpty understands that tugs over meaning can be struggles for power. But the stakes go
far beyond who wins. Different meanings promote the pursuit of different
kinds of social action, cultural values, intellectual inquiry. Meanings, I argue,
can indeed facilitate mastery in a variety of arenas.

1 'Queer'

The word *queer* is my starting point. I highlight this particular word because it is such a powerful example of semantic indeterminacy, shift, and,
most important, contestation. The word *queer* has figured prominently in
recent years in political and theoretical discourse centered on issues of sexuality, especially sexual diversity, and its complex relation to gender. Annamarie Jagose (1996: 1) puts it quite nicely:

> Once the term *queer* was, at best, slang for homosexual, at worst, a term of
> homophobic abuse. In recent years, *queer* has come to be used differently,
> sometimes as an umbrella term for a coalition of culturally marginal sexual
> self-identifications and at other times to describe a nascent theoretical
> model which has developed out of more traditional lesbian and gay studies.
> What is clear is that queer is very much a category in the process of for-
> mation. It is not simply that queer has yet to solidify and take on a more
> consistent profile, but rather that its definitional indeterminacy, its elastic-
> ity, is one of its constituent characteristics. ... [P]art of queer's semantic
> clout, part of its political efficacy depends on its resistance to definition,
> and the way in which it refuses to stake its claim.

In a real sense, I want to argue, many words are queer; that is, they resist
definition and it is their definitional intractability that gives them much of
their real bite, their efficacy as tools for thought and action. What is the
source of such malleability? Like all words, *queer* figures in discursive
history, a history that is never fully determinate and that looks back to
sometimes conflicting assumptions and forward to a range of alternative
possibilities. Noting the importance of the history of its deployment, Judith
Butler (1993: 228, 230) claims that the semantic indeterminacy of *queer* is
essential to its political utility.

> If the term *queer* is to be a site of collective contestation, the point of de-
> parture for a set of historical reflections and futural imaginings, it will have
> to remain that which is ... never fully owned, but always and only rede-
> ployed, twisted, queered from a prior usage and in the direction of urgent
> and expanding political purposes ... [T]he term *queer* has been the discur-
> sive rallying point for younger lesbians and gay men and, in yet other
> contexts, for lesbian interventions and, in yet other contexts, for bisexuals
> and straights for whom the term expresses an affiliation with anti-
> homophobic politics.

As the passages from Jagose and Butler demonstrate, queer theorists are
unlikely to be surprised by my two main claims. (1) Particular meanings are

better or worse suited for various kinds of enterprises: to use Jagose's language, 'semantic clout' can be significant but it is variable. To put it a different way, questions of semantics are often not 'just' semantics. (2) The historically contingent character of meaning--its dependence on discursive practice in a range of contexts--is critical to its power. Many linguists and philosophers of language, however, may find these claims initially puzzling, indeed quite queer. In this paper, I sketch a skeletal framework for thinking about the interconnections of linguistic meaning and discourse. The aim is to further understanding of the role language plays in human plans and projects, especially but by no means only those of our plans and projects that connect directly to gender and sexuality.

Let us begin by examining some sample attempts to define *queer*. Table 1 has definitions from several different dictionaries or similar volumes, slightly abridged in some cases.

For many speakers of English, the word *queer* seems pejorative, and several of the entries describe its application as 'derogatory'. Random House puts no such label on any of the uses it describes, and in 1985 *A Feminist Dictionary* noted that the word was sometimes used 'appreciatively', though also noting its 'depreciative' uses. Obviously, what is derogatory depends on who is using the word of whom and from what kind of position. The citation in *A Feminist Dictionary* is from a 1975 piece by Charlotte Bunch:

> One of the ways to understand better [what heterosexism is] ... is to 'think queer,' no matter what your sexuality. By 'think queer', I mean imagine life as a lesbian for a week. Announce to everyone — family, roommate, on the job, everywhere you go — that you are a lesbian. Walk in the street and go out only with women, especially at night. Imagine your life, economically and emotionally, with women instead of men. For a whole week, experience life as if you were a lesbian, and you will learn quickly what heterosexual privileges and assumptions are, and how they function to keep male supremacy working.

There is a long tradition of disagreement over whether *queer* is a label to embrace or to shun. Historian George Chauncey (1994) reports that *queer* was the preferred term of self-reference in New York City in the early part of the twentieth city for men whose primary identification was their sexual interest in other men. And yet the *Encyclopedia of Homosexuality* (Dynes 1990) forecast the imminent death of the word *queer*. The encyclopedia did note that *queer* was still the preferred self-designator for some gays, although its entry indicates some incredulity that the term could be seen as 'value-free'.

queer adj. 1. Deviating from the expected or normal; strange. 2. Odd or unconventional in behavior; eccentric. 3. Arousing suspicion. 4. *Slang.* Homosexual. 5. *Slang.* Fake; counterfeit. -n *Slang.* 1. A homosexual. 2. Counterfeit money. -tr. v. 1. To ruin or thwart. 2. To put into a bad position. [Perhaps from German *quer*, perverse, cross. ... See *terkw-* .]

terkw-   To turn. 1. Variant form **t(w)erk-* in Germanic **thwerh* , twisted, oblique, in a. Old High German *dwerah*, *twerh*, oblique: QUEER. *American Heritage Dictionary* (1969).

queer adj. and n. A. adj. 1. Strange, odd, eccentric; of questionable character, suspicious. early 16th c. 2a. Bad; worthless. mid 16th. b. Of a coin or banknote: counterfeit, forged. *Criminals' slang.* mid 18th c. 3. Out of sorts; giddy, faint, ill. 4. Esp. of a man: homosexual. *slang, derog.*, late 19th c. B. n. 1. Counterfeit coin. Also (US), forged paper currency or bonds. *Criminals' slang.* early 19th c. 2. A (usu. male) homosexual. *slang derog.* Early 20th c. Special collocations and combinations [of particular relevance]: **queer-basher** *slang* a person who attacks homosexuals; **queer-bashing** *slang* physical or verbal attack on homosexuals; **queerdom** n. (*slang, derog.*) the state of being a homosexual mid 20th c. **queerness** n. (a) strangeness; (b) (*slang, derog.*) homosexuality: late 17th c. *The New Shorter Oxford English Dictionary* (rev. ed., 1993).

[Note: the 1971 edition of the full OED gives nothing explicitly connected to sexuality in either the main entry or the appendix. It gives essentially the etymology of the AHD, though expressing some skepticism as to the validity because of *queer*'s early 16th c. appearance in Scots]

queer adj. 1. strange or odd from a conventional viewpoint; unusually different; singular. 2. of a questionable nature or character; suspicious; shady. 3. Not feeling physically right or well; giddy, faint, or qualmish. 4. mentally unbalanced or deranged. 5. *Slang* a. homosexual. b. bad, worthless, or counterfeit. v.t 6. to spoil; ruin. 7. to put (a person) in a hopeless or disadvantageous situation as to success, favor, etc. 8. to jeopardize. n. *slang* 9. a homosexual. 10. counterfeit money. *Random House Dictionary* (1966).

queer almost archaic The word's declining popularity may ... reflect today's visibility and acceptance of gay men and lesbians and the growing knowledge that most of them are in fact quite harmless ordinary people. [Although in 20th c. America] *queer* has been the most popular vernacular term of abuse for homosexuals, even today some older English homosexuals prefer the term, even sometimes affecting to believe that it is value-free. *Encyclopedia of Homosexuality* (1990)

queer Perhaps from German *quer*, 'crosswise' in the orginal sense of 'crooked,' 'not straight,' to modern English via Scots beggars cant. Means singular, strange, odd, differing from what is 'ordinary.' Generic slang term used depreciatively and appreciatively to mean homosexual (also means 'counterfeit' as in *queer as a two-dollar bill*). *A Feminist Dictionary* (1985)

Table 1. 'Queer'

Certainly, until the late 1980s *queer* as a positive term was nearly invisible to people outside communities with a focus on same-sex desire. Before the term *gay* spread widely as a non-clinical designator of homosexuals, *queer* did have some currency among some American heterosexuals as 'politer' than words like *faggot*, *fruit*, *fairy*, *dyke*, or *butch* and, of course, less clinical than *homosexual*. This is not to say that it was positive in those uses. In the early 1970s, a former colleague of mine, a straight-identified woman, described another former colleague, a man, as 'queerer than a two-dollar bill.' In doing so, she was certainly condescending and homophobic, and I recall vividly my shock that she would say *queer* rather than *homosexual*. At the same time, however, she clearly saw herself as simply 'telling it like it is' as opposed to engaging in overtly hostile 'name-calling' as she would have been if she'd used *faggot* or *fruit* or *fairy*. Her use of *queer* probably reflected a growing discomfort with other available terms, a discomfort that was manifest both among anti-homophobic activists and among vaguely 'progressive' straight-identified people. Jagose (1996: 75) quotes James Davidson, writing in the London Review of Books in 1994: '*Queer* is in fact the most common solution to the modern crisis of utterance, a word so well-traveled it is equally at home in 19th-century drawing-rooms, accommodating itself to whispered insinuation, and on the streets of the Nineties, where it raises its profile to that of an empowering slogan.'

As the Random House entry in Table 1 indicates, the term tended to be used primarily for men. One fear many self-described lesbians and other nonstraight women have expressed is that this androcentric pattern will persist even as other features of the term's use shift. Certainly the related term *gay* has often not been construed gender inclusively, as the frequent conjunction *gays and lesbians* in all kinds of public discourses indicates. In spite of such fears, however, *queer* has become very widespread in self-reference among political activists as an umbrella term for gay men, lesbians, bisexuals, transgender and transsexual people and others who challenge heteronormative views of sexuality. A turning point was the birth of Queer Nation, with its in-your-face politics and its defiant and memorable slogan: 'We're here; we're queer; get used to it.' Interestingly, definitions of *queer* are missing from some places one might expect to find them. For example, Part IV of *Bi any other Name: Bisexual people speak out* (Hutchins and Kaahumanu 1991) is entitled 'Politics: A Queer among Queers,' and the overview to that section begins with the following quotation from Autumn Courtney, a bi-activist speaking in 1988 at the San Francisco Lesbian Gay Freedom Day Parade Celebration. 'Hey queer! Hey you are queer aren't you? What kind of queer are you? QUEER – you know what it means – odd, unusual, not straight, gay. I am queer, not straight. And ... I am odd. Odd in the fact that I have been an *active open out-of-the-closet Bisexual* in the lesbian and gay world for the last seven years.... We must unite to fight common enemies; we must not squabble among ourselves over who is more queer or more politically correct.' The editors and other contributors to this very interesting book clearly recognized *queer* as a word applicable to self-identified bisexual people. In spite of that, the short glossary at the end of the book does not include *queer*, even though it does tackle such difficult to define expressions as *bisexual, homophobia, patriarchy*, and *sexism*. Part of the problem for the editors in defining *queer* might have lain in the tension between the kind of identity politics represented by some contributors to the volume and the dis-identity politics that theorists have so often associated with *queer*. Queer theorists tend to emphasize difference and to challenge the ideological processes that help constitute identity, even 'queer' identities.

2   'Gay'

How does *gay*, now probably the most widely used 'umbrella' term, differ from *queer*? To 'outsiders', *gay* was somewhat less familiar than *queer* as a label for a sexual identity until the gay liberation movement began in the late 1960s. It became increasingly prominent in both speech and print during the 1970s and 1980s as gay liberation became a real political force. As a label of self-identification for men, Chauncey (1994) reports that *gay* entered the New York City scene in the 1920s and 1930s and became increasingly common during the wartime period. Kennedy and Davis (1993) report that it became more prevalent as a generic term for lesbians in Buffalo, NY during the 1950s than it had been earlier. Table 2 contains some dictionary entries for *gay*.

Gay a. 1. Showing or characterized by exuberance or mirthful excitement. 2. Bright or lively, especially in color. 3. Full or given to social or other pleasures. 4. Dissolute; licentious. 5. *Slang.* Homosexual. [Middle English *gay, gai,* from Old French *gai,* from Old Provençal, probably from Gothic *gaheis* (unattested), akin to OHG *gahi,* sudden, impetuous.] *American Heritage Dictionary,* 1969.

Gay a.,adv., & n. ME [(O)Fr. *gai,* of unkn. origin.] A adj. 1. Full of, disposed to, or indicating joy and mirth; light-hearted, carefree. ME. b. Airy, offhand, casual. late 18th c. 2. Given to pleasure; freq. *euphem.,* dissolute immoral. Late ME. b. Leading an immoral life; *spec.* engaging in prostitution. *slang.* Early 19th c. 3. Good, excellent, fine. Now chiefly *dial.* Late ME. b. Of a woman: beautiful, charming, debonair. Long *arch.* & poetic. Late ME. c. In good health, well. *dial.* Mid 19th c. 4. Showy, brilliant, brightly colored. Also, brightly decorated *with.* Late ME. b. Finely or showily dressed. Now *rare.* Late ME. c. Superficially attractive; (of reasoning, etc.) specious, plausible. Late ME-Late 18th c. (now obsolete) 5. Of a quantity or amount: considerable, reasonable, fair. Chiefly Sc. Late 18th c. 6. Of an animal: lively, spirited, alert. Early 19th c. b. Of a (dog's) tail: carried high or erect. Early 20th. 7. (Of a person, sometimes *spec.* a man) homosexual; of or pertaining to homosexuals; (of a place, etc.) intended for or frequented by homosexuals. Chiefly *colloq.* Mid 20th c. *Special collocations & phrases*: **gay cat** *US slang* (a) a hobo who accepts occasional work; (b) a young tramp, *esp.* one in company with an older man. **gay dog** a man given to revelling or self-indulgence. **gay deceiver** (a) a deceitful rake; (b) in *pl.* (*slang*), shaped pads for increasing the apparent size of the female breasts. **Gay Lib, Liberation** (the advocacy of) the liberation of homosexuals from social stigma and discrimination. **gay plague** *colloq.* (sometimes [!] considered *offensive*) AIDS (so called because first identified amongst homosexuals), **get gay** *US slang* act in an impertinent or overfamiliar way. C. n. 3 A homosexual; sometimes *spec.* a male homosexual. Chiefly *colloq.* Mid 20th c. *The New Shorter Oxford English Dictionary* (rev. ed., 1993).

Gay is a Middle English word derived from the Middle French term GAI (gai). It is defined in British dictionaries as 'joyful, akin to merry, frivolous, showy, given to dissipated or vicious pleasure.' GAI became popularized in the Middle French burlesque theatre's description of effeminate, pretentious male character roles. ... English theatre began to use the word GAY to describe 'saucy, prostituting, or sexually promiscuous' characters. Since women were not at that time allowed on stage in either country, these mock feminine roles were always caricatured by men. The Scottish tradition of the word GAI (guy) was more distinctly used to describe someone different ... an astrologer, forester, or recluse. (E.g., 'I say, he is a bit gai!'). This tradition originally was not negative, but merely implied 'different or queer from the norm'. ... It is interesting to note that the word GAY was not used to describe 'homosexual' women until it found its way to the Americas. Today the terms LESBIAN and SAPPHIC are still the tradition in Europe. In the 1920s and 1930s the word GAY surfaced in the underground homosexual subculture as a term of identification among homosexual men. Expressions such as 'You're looking gay tonight,' or 'That's a gay tie you have there' were used to establish mutual identity in social situations. Finally, in the late 1990s, the term GAY was taken up by the Gay Liberation Movement in its attempt to affirm 'a truly joyous alternative lifestyle' and throw off the sexually objectifying term 'homosexual'. Entry quoted from Jeanne Cordova (1974) in *A Feminist Dictionary*, 1985.

Table 2. 'Gay'

Gay as a designator for homosexuals had many fewer negative associations in the minds of those outside the homosexual community than *queer*. This is partly because it was less familiar in such uses and partly because its other uses were generally more positive than the other uses of *queer*. It is probably for such reasons that it very quickly established itself as the most general 'polite' form for outsiders to use in referring to self-identified homosexuals. By the 1990s even mainstream politicians were talking publicly about 'gays,' especially in contexts where they wanted to be seen as inclusive. Even in 2000, however, *queer*, though widely used by academic theorists and political activists, was still taboo in contexts like presidential candidates' speeches. And large numbers of people who do not identify themselves as belonging to sexual minorities still assume that *queer* is fundamentally 'derogatory', although they might use it among familiars as a 'milder' form than some others available.

3 'Lesbian'

In contrast to *queer* and *gay*, the term *lesbian* has no generally familiar uses outside the domain of sexual identity and politics. It has, however, for a very long time been used in speech and in writing as the least marked way to refer to women whose sexual desires are primarily directed towards other women. More accurately, *lesbian* has been the least marked designator outside communities of such women. Elizabeth Kennedy and Madeline Davis (1993: 6-7) comment on terms of self-reference among the women they interviewed for their groundbreaking ethnohistorical study of the working class lesbian community in Buffalo, NY from the 1930s through the 1950s.

> We use the term 'lesbian' to refer to all women in the twentieth century who pursued sexual relationships with other women. Narrators, however, rarely used the word 'lesbian,' either to refer to themselves or to women like themselves. In the 1940s the terms used in the European-American community were 'butch and fem,' a 'butch and her girlfriend,' sometimes a 'lesbian and her girlfriend.' Sometimes butches would refer to themselves as 'homos' when trying to indicate the stigmatized position they held in society. Some people ... would use ... 'gay girls' or 'gay kids' to refer to either butch or fem. In the 1950s, the European-American community still used 'butch' and 'fem' [but other] terms became more common. Sometimes butches of the rough crowd were referred to as 'diesel dykes' or 'truck drivers.' They sometimes would refer to themselves as 'queer' to indicate social stigma. In the African-American community 'stud broad' and 'stud and her lady' were common terms, although 'butch' and 'fem' were also used. . . The term 'bull dagger' was used by hostile straights as an insult, but was sometimes used by members of the African-American community to indicate toughness. . .[L]anguage usage was not consistent and a white leader in the 1950s says that she might have referred to lesbians as 'weird people.'

(This discussion makes it clear that it is within particular communities of practice that patterns of language usage develop and that it is important to consider localized as well as broader patterns; see Eckert and McConnell-Ginet 1992, 1995 for discussion of the notion 'community of practice' in application to language and gender research.)

As Kennedy and Davis point out (p. 7-8), at least four distinct kinds of erotic relationships existed between women in the 19th and 20th centuries: (1) women who passed as men, some of whom were erotically involved with other women; (2) middle-class married women with intense passionate friendships with other women, some erotic (though few genital); (3) middle-class unmarried women who 'built powerful lives around communities of women defined by work, politics, or school'; (4) 'women . . . who socialized together because of their explicit romantic and sexual interests in other women.' Does/should *lesbian* apply to all these women? For some, the word was unavailable; only those in group (4) were likely to think that the word might apply to them (although they may not actually have used it). Such questions are among those that have animated discussion of the term during the past several decades.

Standard dictionary entries don't go much beyond the Isle of Lesbos, where Sappho lived in the 6th c. BC, and the idea of same-sex desire among females. There has been, however, considerable dispute about how to construe *lesbian*. Is it a sexual or a political identity or does it point to a continuum of woman-identified practices and attitudes? Does it allow for diverse sexual practices or is it normativizing? Are fems *really* lesbians–or, conversely, are they the only *genuine* lesbians? Is there a transhistorical notion of *lesbian* or does the term presuppose consciousness of sexual preferences and practices being constitutive of personal identity, a consciousness that arguably developed as a real possibility only in the late 19th century? Table 3 includes a number of entries from *A Feminist Dictionary* which give some idea of the range of these disputes. As with *gay*, the entry leads off with a quote from Jeanne Cordova's 1974 article 'What's in a Name?'.

Although the choice between *gay* and *homosexual* certainly has political overtones, neither of those words has been the site of as much ideological struggle as *lesbian*, with its connections not only to anti-homophobic but also to anti-sexist politics. Indeed, there is a tendency, as noted in some of the citations in Table 3, to conflate feminism and lesbianism. The quotes from Mary Daly and from Marilyn Frye take being a lesbian to require not only defiance of male dominance but also a focus of attention on women in all areas of life. On this kind of view, *lesbian* certainly resists assimilation into some gender-neutral 'gay' category. Some lesbian theorists (e.g. Jeffreys 1993), have even seen gay men as more invested in patriarchy than straight men, arguing that their erotic preference for men stems from a thoroughgoing misogyny. In my view, although gay men, like some women, are not immune from misogyny, this particular charge seems profoundly misguided. Not only have many men active in gay liberation also been active in anti-sexist efforts. It is also clear that erotic preferences are far more complex than the equation of a man's male-directed desires with his disdain for women would allow.

This is not to deny that gender and sexual oppression are linked in many different ways. Heterosexual desire (or at least norms promoting such desire) can lead women to cooperate in their own subordination, especially in cultural contexts that eroticize female vulnerability and male strength. These connections are part of what has led some to see lesbianism as the only path to female emancipation. Opting out of what Barrie Thorne (1993) and Penelope Eckert (1996) call the 'heterosexual marketplace' can be a liberating move for some girls and young women. And being not dependent on men sexually can make it easier to avoid other kinds of dependence on them (and also the deference that dependence often brings). But equating lesbianism and feminism risks obscuring the specificity both of sexualities and of gender dynamics. The equation can be particularly problematic because it resonates all too well with persisting conflation in the dominant culture of heterosexual eroticism with male dominance and female subordination. Many feminists, among them many lesbians, want to open up more discursive space for sexual desire and erotic activity involving strong female agency no matter whether the sexual object might be female or male. Farwell (1988) treats definitions like Daly's and Fry's as 'simply' metaphoric since they treat genital sexual activity between women as insufficient for applying the label *lesbian* and require a certain (feminist) stance toward men and male dominance. I return below to this and other metaphoric uses of identity labels, but at this point I simply want to note that such uses, even if seen by all as special and 'non-literal', are nonetheless often implicated in attempts to promote certain kinds of social norms and values or pursue certain kinds of political strategies.

lesbian

'The word LESBIAN comes to us as a British word derived from the Greek 600 BC Isle of Lesbos and 'the reputed female homosexual band associated with Sappho of Lesbos'. (*Webster's Seventh New Collegiate Dictionary*). Etymologically speaking, the word LESBIAN, rather than the word 'gay', is the more correct term when speaking of women-identified women.' (Jeanne Cordova, 1974)

Mary Daly ... prefers 'to reserve the term LESBIAN to describe women who are woman-identified, having rejected false loyalties to men on all levels. The terms *gay* or *female homosexual* more accurately describe women who, although they relate genitally to women, give their allegiance to men and male myths, ideologies, styles, practices, institutions, and professions.' (Mary Daly, 1978)

'A lesbian is the rage of all women condensed to the point of explosion.' (Radicalesbians, 1970)

'I, for one, identify a woman as a lesbian who says she is.' (Cheryl Clarke, 1981)

'Lesbian is the only concept I know of which is beyond the categories of sex (woman and man), because the designated subject (lesbian) is *not* a woman, either economically, or politically, or ideologically.' (Monique Wittig, 1981)

Those who 'have a history of perceiving them Selves as such, and the will to assume responsibility for Lesbian acts, erotic and political.' (Janice Raymond, 1982)

One who, by virtue of her focus, her attention, her attachment is disloyal to phallocratic reality. She is not committed to its maintenance and the maintenance of those who maintain it, and worse her mode of disloyalty threatens its utter dissolution in the mere flicker of the eye. (Marilyn Frye, 1983)

Lesbian continuum includes 'a range — through each woman's life and throughout history — of woman-identified experience; not simply the fact that a woman has had or consciously desired genital sexual experience with another woman.' Adrienne Rich wants to expand the concept of lesbian to 'many more forms of primary intensity between and among women, including the sharing of a rich inner life, the bonding against male tyranny, the giving and receiving of practical and political support.' (Adrienne Rich, 1980)

Lesbianism means that 'you forget the male power system, and that you give women primacy in your life — emotionally, personally, politically.' (Rita Mae Brown, 1976).

'Feminism is the complaint, and lesbianism is the solution.' (Jill Johnston, 1975)

Joan Nestle challenges this slogan, on the grounds that it invalidates lesbian herstory. Pre-Stonewall lesbians, though not lesbian feminists as currently defined, were nevertheless feminists. 'Their feminism was not an articulated theory, it was a lived set of options based on erotic choice.' Further the playing out of butch-fem roles, now considered oppressive, was actually a mode of adventuring produced by their social and sexual autonomy from mainstream culture. (Joan Nestle, 1981).

'For most women – especially of my age – it is not a choice. Being attracted to women sexually is a unique and precious response.' (Chrystos, 1981)

lesbian politics of naming

'The attempt to criminalize lesbianism through a clause in the 1921 [UK] Criminal Law Amendment Bill (to place it on a par with the 1885 criminalisation of male homosexuality) foundered on the conviction that drawing attention to the existence of a practice unknown to most women might itself incite the practice.' (Lucy Bland, 1983)

'The denial of lesbians is literally Victorian. The Queen herself was appalled by the inclusion of a paragraph on lesbianism in the 1885 Criminal Law that sought to penalize private homosexual acts by two years' imprisonment. She expressed a complete ignorance of female inversion or perversion and refused to sign the Bill, unless all reference to such practices was omitted.' (Blanche Cook, 1977)

'It is not ethical to call yourself a feminist when you mean lesbian, or to use those words interchangeably.' (Thyme Siegel, 1983)

Table 3. 'Lesbian'

Even if we stay with sexualities, the citations make clear that there have been many disputes on just what being lesbian might amount to. Is it a matter of sexual behavior or of sexual desire or of sexual identity? Is it impossible to be lesbian if one does not embrace that identity whole-heartedly? Can someone whose sexual fantasies include both other women and men be lesbian? Can someone who engages in sexual activity with both women and men be a lesbian? Can a woman become a lesbian at the age of 50 or stop being a lesbian at the age of 30? Questions like these have been actively debated and were particularly prominent during the 1970s and 1980s. They have faded somewhat in importance as activists have tended to move away from identity politics, although they are by no means dead.

4 Comparisons of *Queer*, *Gay*, and *Lesbian*

Both *gay* and *lesbian* have tended to focus on identities, often modeled on ethnic identities. In contrast, *queer* has been mobilized in the past decade or so to cut across a range of sexual identities. One aim has been to bring together those who *dis*-identify with heteronormativity; i.e., those who challenge sexual norms that assume potentially reproductive sexual encounters as a standard, with other kinds of sexual activity at best a substitute for the 'real thing' or, more often, somehow distasteful or morally wrong. Unlike the self-affirming uses of *gay* and *lesbian*, however, the reclamation of *queer* is pretty much limited to gay-affirmative groups or to academic contexts like this book. As noted earlier, the word is not used by presidential candidates in their speeches or in New York Times reporting on gay rights issues. A number of my students have reported not knowing that *queer* could be used to speak about diverse sexualities without thereby derogating them. Thus the reclamation of *queer* is certainly still not a complete one, being limited to certain communities of practice.

In contrast to *queer*, both *gay* and *lesbian* are widely seen as nonjudgmental terms, quite useable in contexts where they might be heard by those they designate. Of course, this does not mean that there is no 'taint' of homophobic attitudes associated with these words. Those of my students who thought that *queer* was always somewhat negative and that *gay* and *lesbian* were the preferred neutral terms were nonetheless familiar with the relatively recent use of *gay* as an all-purpose derogatory descriptor, roughly glossable as 'uncool' or 'gross'. This use, very common among elementary school kids, is not reflected in the dictionary entries above. It seems quite likely, however, that the third graders' sneering 'That's so gay' ultimately has arisen from contemptuous talk about gay sexuality, even though the third graders themselves generally do not make a connection to sexual orientation (and may never even have heard the kind of homophobic talk that gave birth to their own usage).

So we have here a cluster of related words – *queer*, *gay*, and *lesbian* – each of which has a cluster of (more or less) related senses or patterns of use, and each of which has a history not just of change from earlier patterns but of ongoing tension among them. There are many more words that are related to these: e.g., *homosexual, heterosexual, monosexual, bisexual,* and *straight.* In his influential *Keywords,* social theorist Raymond Williams pointed to the sociocultural significance of distinct but connected interpretations for particular words. His entry for the word *culture* contains the following discussion (Williams 1983: 91, 92):

> Faced by this complex and still active history of the word, it is easy to react by selecting one 'true' or 'proper' or 'scientific' sense and dismissing other senses as loose or confused... It is clear that, within a discipline, conceptual usage has to be clarified. But in general it is the range and overlap of meanings that is significant. The complex of senses indicates a complex argument about the relations between general human development and a particular way of life, and between both and the works and practices of art and intelligence. . . [T]he range and complexity of sense and reference indicate both difference of intellectual position and some blurring or overlapping. These variations, of whatever kind, necessarily involve alternative views of the activities, relationships, and processes which this complex word [i.e., *culture*] indicates. The complexity, that is to say, is not finally in the word but in the problems which its variations of use significantly indicate.

Similarly, the complexity we find in *queer* and its kin points to the wide array of issues involved in thinking about sexual practices, sexual identities, sexual norms and values.

5 Word Meaning and Social Practice

What I want to do in the rest of this paper is explore some of the mechanisms through which the shaping and reshaping of word meanings emerge as part and parcel of the shaping and reshaping of social and political practices. There are four independent but related ideas about language and word meaning I want to draw on. (1) Natural languages are in important ways like formal linguistic systems or logics in which basic expressions—the word-like units—are not given fixed meanings but must be assigned interpretations when the system is used. (2) The cognitive structure underlying the concept a (content) word labels is less like a definition or a prototype than like a theory (or family of theories) in which that concept plays a key role. (3) Interpretations draw on preceding discourse understandings and on projections of future plans. (4) Linguistic communication involves bringing about some kind of change in the discourse-produced picture of how things are (or might be or should be or ...).

5.1 Words as 'empty' forms

The first idea—that a natural language is in many ways very like a formal linguistic system—is common to a number of approaches to semantics in linguistics and philosophy. Formal semantic theories offer considerable insight into combinatorial semantics—how word meanings fit together to express thoughts. There is significant work done on the semantics of function words like *and*, *not*, *if*, *every*, and *the*. From a slightly different but also relatively formal perspective, there is very illuminating investigation of such features of word meaning as the argument structure of verbs—e.g., the role of a verb's direct object or its subject. Formal semantics has also offered insight into the meaning of plurality, tense and aspect, possessives, and other grammatical morphemes and constructions. But formal semantics has rather little to say about the meanings of the basic content-ful expressions, about words like *woman* or *tree* or *water* or *laugh* or, of course, expressions like *queer*, *gay*, and *lesbian*. There may be some things to be noted about truth-conditional relations among words; e.g., perhaps *Kim is a lesbian* entails *Kim is a woman* which in turn entails *Kim is not a man*. Such connections, however, are limited and do not offer us much insight into the conceptual complexity of basic vocabulary items. (I will return to the question of why and how sometimes even such entailments seem to be missing.)

Among the more content-ful analyses of lexical items are those that identify semantic features on the basis of contrasts: e.g., *woman* contrasts with *man* in being +female, with *girl* in being +mature, and so on. The idea that what a word means is, at least in part, a matter of how it contrasts with certain other words in the same semantic field is an important one that informs many empirical explorations of word meaning. The status and utility of semantic features or components is a matter of some dispute, but there is no question that lexical contrasts have to figure in any guide to word usage and that speakers must incorporate them somehow in their understanding of linguistic practice.

There are also, of course, other ways to shed light on word meanings. So-called cognitive semantics looks less at particular words and more at metaphorical patterning, at the recurrence of certain abstract identifications. For example, Caitlin Hines (2000) explains the evolution of dessert terms to refer to women in terms of such identifications as WOMEN ARE SWEET, ACHIEVING A DESIRED OBJECT IS GETTING SOMETHING TO EAT. And George Lakoff (1987) has an interesting discussion of the complex and changing conceptual structure(s) associated with the word *mother* as reproductive technologies and women's increased participation in the waged labor force allow more varied kinds of relations between women and children. The evolving and competing meanings he identifies are, of course, embedded in evolving and contested social practices of reproduction and parenting. (Note that the recent emergence of *parent* as a verb is part of feminist-inspired moves to involve men more actively in responsibility for childcare.)

An approach in which word meaning is relatively empty and is filled in as part of ongoing discursive processes can indeed draw on insights from cognitive semantics or from componential analysis into semantic features. What is important is that the empty vessel view of words does not assume that there will be available anything like a necessary and sufficient set of conditions for applying the word. Nor does it assume that the word's meaning is somehow encapsulated in something like a prototypical exemplar. On the view I am proposing, words do not really *have* (much) meaning—word meanings are underspecified—but they are given meaning as they are deployed to do things in ongoing discourse. Humpty Dumpty was on the right track.

5.2 Words anchored by 'theory'

But now we must turn to the remaining ideas I mentioned. Of course, words are as not completely 'empty' as I may have seemed to suggest, free to be used in just any old way. People do attach some kind of concepts, some sort of cognitive structures, to the content words of their language. And, just as important, people often take their uses of those words to be 'regulated' in certain ways that may go beyond what is in individual users' heads, their individual lexical concepts. What has been called the 'theory-theory' of lexical concepts draws on recent work in psychology and also on some ideas from the philosophy of language. In his influential 'The Meaning of "Meaning",' philosopher Hilary Putnam (1975) posited a 'linguistic division of labor' for regulating our use of words. Putnam notes that many English speakers might have both the words *elm* and *beech* in their lexicons, knowing nothing about them other than the fact that they are trees. To know whether someone has spoken truly if she says 'Hildegard's yard has two elms in it,' speakers turn to those with botanical expertise. We use others to access the scientific theory that elucidates the distinction between elms and beeches. In this attenuated sense, then, tree-theory underlies these lexical concepts, but particular individuals may know only that there is a relevant tree-theory, whereas others may have some mental representation of this theory (though perhaps even then deferring to experts on fine points). At the same time, Putnam suggests, individual language users may access a 'stereotype' that guides them fairly well in regulating their own usage. For example, even people who believe that certain bodily features are 'really' criterial for applying the terms *woman* and *man* to individuals may rely on things like clothing, hairstyles, facial hair, and linguistic and behavioral style to guide their own labelling of people as women or men. Putnam's basic idea has been adopted by a number of cognitive and developmental psychologists. Keil (1989), e.g., notes that the child seems to shift from an early belief that the stereotypical features are what counts to later recognition, at least for biological kinds, that there is stuff 'below the surface' that counts more than what is readily apparent.

What neither Putnam nor the psychologists influenced by him point out is that the stereotype may be allied with a theory of social norms: this is how women 'should' dress, wear their hair, speak and act. Such norms can then be drawn on for helping to interpret expressions like *womanly*. Even generic statements about *women* are often not simple statistical generalizations but generalizations that mark those who deviate from them as somehow deficient as women, as not 'true' women, as 'queer' in some way or other. Socially normative theories may be in competition with one another, and language users may recognize a number of alternative uses of a word, each of which 'fits' better with some theories than with others. The standard 'theory-theory' does not consider the possibility of competing theories. It might be that for some lexical concepts like tree names, ceding semantic authority to scientific experts is unproblematic. Who is master matters much more, however, when we turn to words and concepts that play a more central role in our informal, everyday theories of ourselves and our social worlds, our cultural values and ideologies. What I propose is that words may be associated with a family of theories, some of which are in direct competition with one another, others of which are simply deployed for alternative purposes. 'Theory' may weight the balance too much towards notions of scientific expertise. Perhaps it might be better to say that words are associated with families of discursive practices that give them their real force.

5.3 Words shaped by history

The third idea is that interpretations draw on the past and project to the future. One might be introduced to the word *lesbian* by being told that it's a term for female homosexuals, but the concept would be enriched and complicated in many different ways. Social stereotypes of various kinds can get added. As one of my self-identified lesbian students said sarcastically, 'Of course we're all Birkenstock-wearing vegetarian dykes with extremely short hair who hate men.' And, as the citations in Table 3 show, political and moral attitudes of various sorts also get loaded in. The lexical concept in some sense organizes potentially accessible discursive history. Some parts of the history are seen as grounding 'literal' meaning (perhaps quasi-scientific theories of women's erotic attraction to other women) and others are seen as having a different kind of connection, relating to the role the word plays in various other kinds of theories and debates.

Where Humpty Dumpty went astray was in assuming that he could do anything at all with any word. When Humpty Dumpty says something to Alice, he is entitled to assume that they can both access (1) a linguistic system and certain words in it, (2) patterns of using those words to do particular things, (3) background beliefs and other attitudes, (4) assumptions about the current situation and some of its likely developments. It is through a (more or less) shared discursive history that (1)-(3) are guaranteed—it is a common past that is important. If Humpty Dumpty and Alice have not had much prior personal contact, the assumptions they can make about access to patterns of word use and to background beliefs and other attitudes will be limited to what they have reason to think is relatively conventional or at least very widespread in discursive practices in the larger society to which they belong. On the other hand, if they are long-time coparticipants in some local community of practice, they may well be able to assume access to many more distinctive word uses and particularized attitudes. What (4) involves includes not only standard assessments of current surroundings and why linguistic exchange is occurring but also appraisals of interlocutors' social relationship to one another and their relevant capacities and interests and resources. So, for example, even though *queer* might have long carried a presumption of derogation and an air of gay-bashing in the discursive history of most interlocutors, those who heard activists chanting 'We're here, we're queer, get used to it!' were not thereby misled into thinking that these folks using *queer* to refer to themselves were abjectly confessing to self-hatred. Rather it was clear that by publicly and assertively using the term in self-reference queer activists were explicitly challenging the contempt and the attempts to control them that had fueled others' use of *queer* as a term of abuse. Indeed, the challenge would not have been so insistently issued had they used a word that did not have a readily accessible history of use in gay-bashing. 'We're gay; get used to it' or 'We're homosexual; get used to it' or 'We're not straight; get used to it' would have been far less effective. And of course it was not just the history of *queer* in homophobic practices but also its suggestions of 'strange' and 'odd' and 'not ordinary' that helped give the slogan its punch, its in-your-face effectiveness. *Queer* can insist on the 'specialness' of those so labeled. (Some may have also appreciated the fact that English *queer* sounds a lot like French *cuir* 'leather', creating a bonus joke for those in the know; my colleague Nelly Furman reminded me of this crosslingual wordplay.)

Examining a very different cultural context, Andrew Wong and Qing Zhang (2000) discuss the appropriation of the word *tongzhi*, widely employed in Chinese revolutionary discourse and usually glossed as 'comrade', as a term for members of the 'imagined' queer community being constructed by a Chinese gay and lesbian magazine. The word *tongzhi* brings its Chineseness and its revolutionary associations with it; it does not have the clinical feel of the medical term *tongxinglian zhe* 'homosexual', allowing it to emphasize ties with others rather than some kind of deviance. Its use in the magazine creates a quite different sense of community than would the use of imported western terminology like *queer*, translated into Chinese as *ku-er*, literally something like a 'cool person'. The word *tongzhi* did have some negative associations from its history in Communist discourse, but the new uses managed to ameliorate the word and reclaim it as an appropriate self-designator for members of a home-grown queer community. But amelioration was by no means completely successful. As Wong (this volume) shows, the term in its recently acquired sexual identity uses is undergoing new pejoration. The word *tongzhi* is now also used in the mainstream press to apply to Chinese gays and lesbians, but a large proportion of those uses are negative. Not only is sexual orientation often highlighted inappropriately, but there is frequently a kind of 'mocking' of the *tongzhi* and their relationships to one another. These detailed case studies illustrate beautifully that what words can convey and the impact they can have is firmly rooted in their connection to past histories and to conceptions of future possiblities. It also shows how different and competing perspectives on social practices and values affect linguistic practice. The pejoration of *tongzhi* occurs in opposition to attempts to push toward a future of sexual tolerance and inclusiveness and get beyond the still predominant idea of deviance that infects talk and thinking about Chinese sexual minorities.

5.4 Words as tools for acting

This gets us to the final and central idea—namely, that linguistic communication is a kind of action. More specifically, to say something is generally to attempt to bring about a change in the mutually available picture of how things are or might be or should be. This important insight is at the heart of the picture of meaning and communication developed by the philosopher Paul Grice (Grice 1989 collects most of Grice's papers on meaning and related issues). Humpty Dumpty claims that when he said 'There's glory for you' he meant 'There's a nice knock-down argument for you'—i.e., that he intended to get Alice to recognize that the possibility of 364 gift days rather than just a single one provided an irrefutable argument in favor of celebrating unbirthdays. Unlike the Queer Nation activists, however, Humpty Dumpty was not able to draw on a rich context that would make it clear that this is what he intended to do. Just wanting *glory* to mean 'nice knock-down argument' is not enough to endow it with that meaning: the past history plus the present context must support what a language user tries to do with words. Of course, Humpty Dumpty is right that we do occasionally simply stipulate that we are using old words in new ways, but if stipulation is needed a reliable communicator will preface her comments with the stipulation. Without stipulation, which is always a rather special move and of course a part of establishing the current context, interlocutors must rely on what can be accessed from discursive history and readily accessible features of the current context. These features include assumptions about the others' knowledge, cleverness, and so on. It is clear that Humpty Dumpty did not think Alice could actually figure out what he had meant (nor could he reasonably have done so). On the Gricean account of what it is for a speaker to mean something to an addressee, Humpty Dumpty could not really have meant to Alice 'there's a nice knock-down argument for you'. Humpty Dumpty can expect Alice to ignore past discursive history only if he has explicitly asked her to do so for purposes of the current exchange. And even then, it's pretty hard to get interlocutors to stick to a stipulative definition of a familiar word. But the Queer Nation slogan shows that there are indeed questions of 'mastery' or power involved. To use *queer* both to affirm difference from heterosexual norms and to refuse efforts to eliminate or reduce such differences is to claim a kind of 'mastery', to refuse the conjunction of abuse and attribution of homosexuality so prominent in the discursive history of the word *queer*. At the same time such moves typically meet with resistance. It is hardly surprising that we do not find a general 'acceptance' of *queer* as affirmative.

Notice that we can have metaphorical interpretations that arise contextually and contribute to discursive history but do not have the same kind of effect on default interpretations as, e.g., the gay-affirming uses of *queer*. For example, when Monique Wittig says *a lesbian is not a woman* (see Table 3), she is not really challenging earlier discourses that put particular lesbians in the category *woman*. She is not, e.g., saying that a lesbian does not have two X chromosomes or does not have ovaries or a vagina. As she goes on to say, her point is that 'economically, politically, ... a lesbian is not a woman.' Similarly, Lord Baden-Powell is reputed to have said, after meeting with a group of African political leaders one of whom was female, 'the only man in the room was that woman.' His point, of course, was that she was the only one who showed the kind of courage and intelligence he took as characteristic of men and not of women. He was not commenting on her bodily configuration or that of her male companions. So we might still maintain that language users 'know' that *being a lesbian* entails *being a woman*, which entails *not being a man*, even though we can understand Wittig and Baden-Powell when they deny those entailments. We recognize their uses of *woman* and *man* as somewhat special, as non-literal and metaphorical, mainly because their utterances do have something of a shock value--and are clearly intended to seem paradoxical. Wittig is forcing us to confront various aspects of men's control over wives and female lovers and to see lesbianism as breaking such bonds. Baden-Powell is heaping contempt on the African men who did not seem to live up to his standards and doing so by comparing them invidiously with their female compatriot, whom he lauds but in a somewhat problematic way. Such metaphorical uses can, of course, become literalized , as in the words *womanly* and *manly*.

Marilyn Farwell (1988) has discussed *lesbian* as a metaphor for female creative energy. As Farwell says (p. 110), the metaphor 'remains within the tradition that highlights sexuality as the core of creativity, but because it privileges a female sexuality that does not need or want male energy, it radically revises the symbolic order.' Adrienne Rich's writings have been especially influential and also very controversial in developing this metaphor: 'It is the lesbian in us who is creative, for the dutiful daughter of the fathers in us is only a hack' (Rich 1979: 201). This use is not far from the definitions of Daly and Frye, discussed earlier, which see the lesbian as the one who has turned attention towards women and away from 'the fathers'. In her very important article introducing the notion of the 'lesbian continuum', Rich highlights 'forms of primary intensity between and among women' (see Table 3) and seems at times to erase sexuality from the picture. We take Wittig's claim that a lesbian is not a woman as metaphorical in the sense that it is supposed to have a certain shock value and to direct us to the pervasive and debilitating dependence of women upon men in all kinds of realms. Similarly, we take Rich's focus on the non-erotic to be intended to direct our attention to a positive kind of ideal of women-centered activities and concerns and, at the same time, to infuse fresh and positive meaning into the term *lesbian*. Is it also an exhortation to women whose sexual desires center on other women to pay more attention to women's needs and interests in other domains? Probably, though it is probably more widely addressed and intended to push all women towards increased concern for one another. Can we read Rich as exhorting women who care about women's welfare to direct their erotic energy only towards other women? This seems much less clear and interpreters have not agreed (nor have they always read her as 'exhorting' rather than 'describing').

Ferguson, Zita and Addelson (1981) each discuss what Farwell has called Rich's metaphoric lesbian. Ferguson seems to take Rich to be speaking literally and criticizes her use of *lesbian* as ahistoric and problematically desexualized, rendering it unable to discriminate among contemporary forms of sexual identity. Zita agrees that Rich may have strayed too far from sexuality in her conception of the lesbian continuum. At the same time, Zita thinks that Ferguson fails to appreciate the power of heterosexism as an institution and has missed the challenge that Rich's notion offers to polarized heterosexist conceptions. Like Rich, Zita takes women's bonding to be crucial to their resistance to male dominance. Addelson (p.195) finds the notion of the lesbian continuum useful for examining 'the past (and present) not in terms of hierarchical institutions but in terms of women's own understandings within the historical contexts of life patterns they were creating,' although she disagrees that effective resistance to male dominance has always involved women bonding with one another. She points out that by its nature *lesbian* will be understood from (at least) two perspectives. In the dominant culture, it (still) designates a 'deviant' identity, one that is institutionalized as 'abnormal', whereas lesbian communities themselves have a positive perspective and a critique to offer of the dominant view. But she also offers a cautionary note (p. 199): 'the terms defining willingness to [engage politically in resistance to both heterosexism and male dominance] should not be made into a procrustean bed against which to measure the resistance of women throughout history or throughout our own society.'

As Addelson makes clear, disputes over interpretations show the ways in which alternative theories and ideologies and strategies get enmeshed with how words are understood. It is because words are used to do things, to have effects, that people often endorse or promote one construction of a word over alternative ways that they also recognize of construing it. So though some people use *queer* as simply equivalent to 'gay male or lesbian,' politically there can be real utility in creating alliances with other people outside heterosexual norms: e.g., those who identify themselves as bisexual or transsexual. Queer activism promotes such alliances. What seems an obvious difference of the word *queer* from compound designators like 'lesbian and gay' or 'lesbian, gay, bisexual' or 'lesbian, gay, bisexual, transsexual' is that it does not draw definitive boundaries. It leaves room to welcome those who identify with none of the standard categories of sexual minorities but nonetheless feel excluded by dominant heterosexual norms. In some contexts it even embraces those who just want to promote sexual tolerance or non-restrictiveness though their own sexual dispositions might seem to categorize them as *straight*. Such inclusiveness is often seen as a political advantage. It can, however, also be seen as a shortcoming: namely, such a sweeping use of *queer* obscures the special burden born by those whose sexual inclinations are heavily stigmatized. A rather different political objection to *queer* as an umbrella term is that it does not fit well with an assimilationist gay politics since it seems to insist on the peculiarity, the difference, of those who do not identify as straight.

Queer theory grew out of lesbian and gay studies, and several of the papers in this volume address its relevance to linguistic inquiry. Teresa de

Lauretis is often credited with coining the term in a special 1991 issue of *differences: A Journal of Feminist Cultural Studies*, but the thinking it embodies goes back considerably further. Queer theory questions – queries? – the notion of essential or innate sexual identities. It points to the historical and cultural specificity of sexual practices and categories, criticizing the assumption that the world 'naturally' splits into homosexual and heterosexual people. It treats both gender and sexual identities as 'performative', constituted through discursive histories of repeated acts of self- and other-identification. It often emphasizes the ongoing 'polymorphous perversity' of sexual desire and practice. It examines the constraining effects of naming and the effects of identity formations. There is, of course, not a single queer theory but a family of related queer theories. And the possibility of accessing these theories is part of what underlies the lexical concept of *queer* for many of us academics who are trying to explore productive ways for feminism and queer theory to 'meet.'

I have emphasized the elusiveness and elasticity of *queer*. Do we always want such fuzziness in our concepts? For certain kinds of purposes, rigidifying interpretations can be useful. This is why we find specialized uses of everyday words so often in theoretical discourses. In linguistics, e.g., we try to impose on our students an understanding of *dialect* in which everyone speaks a dialect, even though in ordinary uses *dialect* is reserved for language varieties that are seen as either defective or at best suited only for certain kinds of informal uses. Sometimes of course new terminology is introduced for technical purposes, but even when this happens there can be an ongoing process of trying to develop definitions that will elucidate the patterns in which the investigators are interested, with one way of marking out the patterns often more useful than another. A classic article of the 1930s is called 'On Defining the Phoneme.' For both *lesbian* and *feminist*, there have been extensive arguments about what kind of 'definition' best fits both the needs of intellectual (esp. historical) inquiry and of current political strategizing. (For *lesbian*, see, e.g., Rich 1980; Ferguson, Zita, and Addelson 1981; Farwell 1988. For *feminist*, see Offen 1988.)

6 Defining

Defining is often an attempt to direct thought along certain theoretical lines, to push a particular strategy for political action. Definitions draw boundaries around a concept. When the concepts involved are ones connected to personal identities, some people are included and others excluded by defining. Defining is seldom 'just' semantics but is consequential precisely because words are key resources for thought and action, central players in theory and in politics. Kulick (2000) argues that 'queer linguistics' is too slippery a notion to be useful in sociolinguistic inquiry, that the elasticity so celebrated by queer theorists promotes confusion and equivocation when used in studies of linguistic phenomena. Certainly, any particular study that aims to enrich our understanding of how talk enters into the construction of sexual identities will need to offer some explicit discussion of the people and practices being examined. But that kind of particularized explicitness is not inconsistent with seeing the study as part of a broader (and not clearly bounded) inquiry into 'queer linguistics'.

Queer certainly does in many of its uses recognize openness and indeterminacy in interpretation. At the same time, it recognizes the need to continue questioning names and strategies as they change their directions in the course of discursive history. Humpty Dumpty's dream of being fully 'master' is illusory, but shifting alliances can indeed use words to mean and to do new things.

References

Butler, Judith. 1993. *Bodies That Matter: On the Discursive Limits of 'Sex'*. New York: Routledge.

Chauncey, George Jr. 1994. *Gay New York: Gender, Urban Culture, and the Making of the Gay Male World, 1890-1940*. New York: HarperCollins.

Dynes, Wayne R. 1990. *Encyclopedia of Homosexuality*. New York: Garland Publishing.

Eckert, Penelope. 1996. Vowels and Nail Polish: The Emergence of Linguistic Styles in the Preadolescent Heterosexual Marketplace. *Gender and Belief Systems: Proceedings of the Fourth Berkeley Women and Language Conference*, ed. Natasha Warner, Jocelyn Ahlers, Leela Bilmes, Monica Oliver, Suzanne Wertheim and Melinda Chen, 183-190. Berkeley, CA: Berkeley Women and Language Group.

Eckert, Penelope and Sally McConnell-Ginet. 1992. Think Practically and Look Locally: Language and Gender as Community-based Practice. *Annual Review of Anthropology* 21: 461-490.

Eckert, Penelope and Sally McConnell-Ginet. 1995. Constructing Meaning, Constructing Selves: Snapshots of Language, Gender, and Class from Belten High. *Gender Articulated*, ed. Kira Hall and Mary Bucholtz, 469-507. London and New York: Routledge.

Farwell, Marilyn R. 1988. Toward a Definition of the Lesbian Literary Imagination. *Signs: Journal of Women in Culture and Society* 14.1:100-118.

Ferguson, Ann, Jacquelyn N. Zita, and Kathryn Pyne Addelson. 1981. On 'Compulsory Heterosexuality and Lesbian Existence': Defining the Issues. *Signs: Journal of Women in Culture and Society* 7.1:158-199.

Grice, Paul. 1989. *The Ways of Words.* Cambridge, MA: Harvard University Press.

Hines, Caitlin. 2000. Rebaking the Pie: The 'WOMAN AS DESSERT' Metaphor. *Reinventing Identities: The Gendered Self in Discourse,* ed. Mary Bucholtz, Anita Liang, and Laurel Sutton, 145-162. New York and Oxford: Oxford University Press.

Hutchins, Loraine and Lani Kaahumanu, eds. 1991. *Bi Any Other Name: Bisexual People Speak Out.* Boston: Alyson.

Jagose, Annamarie. 1996. *Queer Theory: An Introduction.* Melbourne: Melbourne University Press and New York: New York University Press.

Jeffreys, Sheila. 1993. *The Lesbian Heresy: A Feminist Perspective on the Lesbian Sexual Revolution.* Melbourne: Spinifex Press.

Keil, Frank C. 1989. *Concepts, Kinds, and Cognitive Development.* Cambridge: MA: MIT Press.

Kennedy, Elizabeth Lapovsky and Madeline D. Davis. 1993. *Boots of Leather, Slippers of Gold: The History of a Lesbian Community.* London and New York: Routledge.

Kramarae, Cheris and Paula Treichler with assistance from Ann Russo. 1985. *A Feminist Dictionary.* London: Pandora Press.

Kulick, Don 2000. The Future of 'Queer Linguistics.' Paper presented at the International Gender and Language Association. Stanford University.

Lakoff, George. 1987. *Women, Fire and Dangerous Things.* Chicago: University of Chicago Press.

Offen, Karen. 1988. Defining Feminism: A Comparative Historical Approach. *Signs: Journal of Women in Culture and Society* 14.1, 119-157.

Putnam, Hilary. 1975. The Meaning of 'Meaning'. *Language, Mind, and Knowledge,* ed. by Keith Gunderson, 131-193. Minneapolis: University of Minnesota Press.

Rich, Adrienne. 1979. 'It is the Lesbian in Us ...' *On Lies, Secret, and Silence: Selected Prose, 1966-1978,* 199-202. New York: Norton.

Rich, Adrienne. 1980. Compulsory Heterosexuality and Lesbian Existence. *Signs: Journal of Women in Culture and Society* 5.4, 631-60.

Thorne, Barrie. 1993. *Gender Play: Girls and Boys in Schools.* New Brunswick, NJ: Rutgers University Press.

Williams, Raymond. 1983. *Keywords: A Vocabulary of Culture and Society,* rev. ed. London: Fontana Paperbacks and New York: Oxford University Press.

Wong, Andrew. This volume. The Semantic Derogation of *Tongzhi:* A Synchronic Perspective.

Wong, Andrew and Qing Zhang 2000. The Linguistic Construction of the *Tongzhi* Community. *Journal of Linguistic Anthropology* 10.2, 248-278.

10

The Semantic Derogation of *Tongzhi*: A Synchronic Perspective

ANDREW WONG

1   Introduction

In the last few decades, many studies have examined the social processes through which semantic derogation takes place. For instance, Schultz (1975) suggests that prejudice is the main reason why the female pair of many English terms (e.g., *mister* vs. *mistress*) gained negative connotations. Furthermore, McConnell-Ginet (1989) proposes a discourse-based theory to explain how the micropolitics of daily discourse between ordinary individuals can lead to the semantic derogation of women. However, since the object of study is diachronic change, it is often difficult to recapture the discourse conditions under which semantic derogation occurred. As a result, few studies have provided concrete evidence on how language use contributes to semantic derogation. To address this issue, this study examines the on-going semantic change of the Chinese term *tongzhi*. The original meaning of this term is 'comrade.' By looking at change in progress, I believe it is possible to gather enough language-use evidence to show the social mechanism underlying semantic derogation. *Tongzhi* was a general address term in Communist China, but it has become disfavored due to its original political connotations (Fang and Heng 1983). Nevertheless, since the late 80s, it has been appropriated by the gay and lesbian communities in Hong Kong and Taiwan as a reference term for 'gay and lesbian Chinese,' and it

Language and Sexuality: Contesting Meaning in Theory and Practice.
Kathryn Campbell-Kibler, Robert J. Podesva, Sarah J. Roberts and Andrew Wong (eds.).
Copyright © 2001, CSLI Publications.

has the positive connotations of respect, equality and resistance (Wong and Zhang 2000). In the last three years, *tongzhi* has also been used in mainstream newspapers to refer to 'gay and lesbian Chinese.' However, I argue that the way in which it is used in mainstream newspapers leads to the pejoration of the term.

This chapter is divided into three parts. The first part of the chapter provides a diachronic perspective on the use of the term *tongzhi*. In the second part, I give an overview of the types of articles in which the term *tongzhi* is used in *Oriental Daily News* – the most widely circulated newspaper in Hong Kong. In the third part, I present a textual analysis of a typical article in which this term is used. My goal is to show the way in which this term is currently used in *Oriental Daily News* may lead to the semantic derogation of *tongzhi*.

2   Background

The term *tongzhi* was initially used in the works of Dr. Sun Yat Sen, leader of the 1911 Chinese democratic revolution. Originally, it meant 'followers,' but it acquired political and revolutionary connotations during the Communist Revolution. It gained the new meaning 'comrade' and it was adopted as a general address term among the masses. In the last two decades, with the rapid social and economic changes in China, *tongzhi* has become disfavored due to its original political and revolutionary meanings (Fang and Heng 1983). However, this term has been re-appropriated by the Chinese gay and lesbian community since the early 90s. In particular, the most popular Chinese gay and lesbian magazine – *G&L* (published in Taiwan) – uses it as the equivalent of 'gay and lesbian Chinese.'

A comparison between the situation that communist revolutionaries faced half a century ago and what gay and lesbian Chinese face today can shed light on why this term is appropriated by gay and lesbian Chinese. Both the revolutionaries and gays and lesbians are marginalized groups living under oppression. They are united by shared beliefs and a striving for a shared cause – for communist revolutionaries, the establishment of an egalitarian socialist state and for gay and lesbian Chinese, the promotion of equal rights. Joining either the revolutionary army or the gay and lesbian community can mean, for some, rejection of their biological family, involving breaking up with family members, friends, or spouses. In addition, like the revolutionaries who worked undercover in the nationalists' occupied territories, people with same-sex desire sometimes live undercover, that is remain in the closet – both living in darkness, wondering whether there are other *tongzhis* out there.

The above comparison shows that gay and lesbian Chinese make a conscious and strategic choice to use *tongzhi* to symbolize their community. By exploiting the revolutionary connotations of intimacy, equality, respect and striving for liberty, gay and lesbian Chinese use the term to call upon each other to respect themselves and to join the common endeavor of fighting for equality in a heterosexual society. Nevertheless, they do not adopt the term *tongzhi* in its entirety: although certain positive connotations (e.g., equality and resistance) are kept, the association of *tongzhi* with the Chinese Communist Party (in particular, its attitude toward homosexuality) has been ignored. The re-appropriation of the term *tongzhi*, therefore, involves the language users' strategic adoption and rejection of different meanings associated with the term.

3   An Overview

From a synchronic perspective, the meaning of *tongzhi* is by no means fixed; rather it is widely contested. This study focuses on the use of the term in *Oriental Daily News*. Though not known for its political commentary, *Oriental Daily News* is the most widely circulated newspaper in Hong Kong. It sells more than 350,000 copies and boasts a seven-figure readership (Cohen 1997). To look for the use of *tongzhi* as a reference term for 'gay and lesbian Chinese,' I examined all the articles in two sections: (1) local news; and (2) news from China and Taiwan, and these articles were published between November 1998 and February 2000. I decided to focus on these two sections because it is in these two sections that the use of the term *tongzhi* to refer to 'gay and lesbian Chinese' is most expected. Furthermore, the putative objectivity of news reporting is often underscored in these two sections. On the other hand, it is more acceptable for journalists to express their personal opinions in other sections (e.g., entertainment section) and in other types of articles (e.g., social commentaries and editorials).

Since the use of the term *tongzhi* to refer to 'gay and lesbian Chinese' is a relatively recent phenomenon, it is understandable that there are only 28 articles in which the term is used. However, it is important to point out that this term is often used in highly sensationalized news stories. By looking at the general themes and the headlines of the articles, as well as the type of information that they provide, it is not difficult to see that gay and lesbian Chinese are usually cast in a bad light.

Table 1 summarizes the general themes of the articles in which the term tongzhi is used to refer to 'gay and lesbian Chinese'. Notice that 20 out of

	Date	Section	General Theme	Representation of *Tongzhi*
1.	11/23/98	Taiwan	Suicide	Negative
2.	11/29/98	Taiwan	Robbery	Negative
3.	12/22/98	Taiwan	Lewd Conduct	Negative
4.	1/4/99	Hong Kong	Review of a Musical Performance	Neutral
5.	1/7/99	Hong Kong	Theft	Negative
6.	1/21/99	Hong Kong	Lewd Conduct	Negative
7.	1/23/99	Hong Kong	Safe Sex Campaign	Neutral
8.	2/1/99	Taiwan	*Tongzhi* Bookstore	Positive
9.	2/10/99	Taiwan	Internet Websites	Neutral
10.	3/2/99	China	Murder	Negative
11.	3/4/99	Hong Kong	Domestic Dispute	Negative
12.	3/11/99	Hong Kong	Domestic Dispute	Negative
13.	4/16/99	Hong Kong	Fist Fight	Negative
14.	5/16/99	Hong Kong	Exposé on *tongzhi* Sex Clubs	Negative
15.	5/20/99	Hong Kong	Lewd Conduct	Negative
16.	5/23/99	Taiwan	The Sale of Used Underwear to *tongzhi*s	Negative
17.	6/3/99	Hong Kong	The Designation of the Dragon Boat Festival as *Tongzhi* Day	Neutral
18.	6/18/99	Hong Kong	The Designation of the Dragon Boat Festival as *Tongzhi* Day	Neutral
19.	6/18/99	Hong Kong	Survey (Public Attitudes Toward Homosexuality)	Neutral
20.	7/2/99	China	Murder	Negative
21.	7/5/99	Taiwan	Domestic Dispute	Negative
22.	7/5/99	China	Volunteers became *tongzhi*'s Venting Targets	Negative
23.	7/11/99	Hong Kong	Domestic Dispute	Negative
24.	9/13/99	Hong Kong	Domestic Dispute	Rather Positive
25.	9/14/99	China	The 'Marriage' of Two Female *tongzhi*s	Negative
26.	10/21/99	Hong Kong	Gay and Lesbian Organizations	Rather Negative
27.	11/12/99	Taiwan	Transvestite	Negative
28.	2/16/00	Hong Kong	Drug Sale in *tongzhi* Establishments	Negative

Table 1. Types of Articles in which the Term *tongzhi* is Used (shaded cells indicate articles with negative representations of *tongzhi*)

the 28 articles contain negative representations of *tongzhi*. Six of these articles are about domestic disputes of gay and lesbian couples, three are about lewd conduct of 'male homosexuals,' two are about murder, and one is an exposé on *tongzhi* sex clubs. Just by looking at these articles, one might get the impression that *tongzhi*s are often those who engage in sexual conduct in public bathrooms, and they often have domestic disputes which lead to attempted suicide.

With regard to headlines, Alan Bell (1991:181-191) and a host of others have pointed out that they serve two main functions (cf. Iarovici and Amel 1989). The first function is a semantic one – that is, a headline is like a summary of a news story; it informs the reader about the content or the nature of the subsequent text. The second function is a pragmatic one – that is, headlines serve the purpose of attracting the reader's attention. The pragmatic function may be intensified by the use of common rhetorical devices such as alliteration, punning, and pseudo-direct quotes. In the articles that I examined, however, most of the headlines tend to attract the reader's attention by exaggerating the negative aspect of the news stories, and this is done through the use of evaluative and value-laden lexical items. As Alan Bell (1991:156) explains, deviance is a negative characteristic with proven news interest. Table 2 shows the headlines of the articles in which the term *tongzhi* is used. Some examples of the use of value-laden lexical items are *kong4 tan1* 'swallowing madly' in the headline of Article 23 and *gwai2 wan6* 'frolicking' in the headline of Article 6.[1] One may wonder why 'frolicking' instead of a term like 'lewd conduct' needs to be used in the headline of Article 6.

Furthermore, some of the headlines single out *tongzhi*, even though the *tongzhi* aspect of the news story is only a secondary detail. Article 16 is about a new trend of selling used underwear in Taiwan. The headline is *seui3-go1 yi6-sau2 noi6-fu3 fung1-mo1 tung4-ji3* '*Tongzhi*s obsessed with used underwear of handsome men.' Although the article is mostly about this particular kind of fetish and the sale of women's used underwear to straight men, the journalist highlights the sale of men's used underwear to men. It appears that the journalist is under the assumption that the sale of used underwear to *tongzhi*s can emphasize the negativity of the news story, thereby increasing the news value of the article.

---

[1] The Chinese equivalent of 'comrade' is *tongzhi* in Mandarin and *tung4-ji3* in Cantonese. The romanization of Chinese characters in this chapter is based on the Yale system. Tones are indicated as follows: 1 – High level, 2 – High rising, 3 – Mid level, 4 – Low falling, 5 – Low rising, and 6 – Low level.

Article	Date	Headline (English Translation)
1.	11/23/98	*Tongzhi* jumps to death in fit of jealousy
2.	11/29/98	*Tongzhi* thief robbed, reveals plot within plot
3.	12/22/98	Naked visitor from Hong Kong arrested in Taiwanese *tongzhi* health club
5.	1/7/99	*Tongzhi* caught stealing cosmetics awaits judgment
6.	1/21/99	Two *tongzhi*s caught frolicking in public toilet
8.	2/1/99	*Tongzhi* bookstore in Taiwan well-integrated in neighborhood
11.	3/4/99	Female *tongzhi* attacks 'boyfriend', attempts suicide by slashing wrist
12.	3/11/99	Female *tongzhi* slashes wrists, disappears from hospital
13.	4/16/99	Six female *tongzhi*s embroiled in fierce battle with three men in bar
14.	5/16/99	Private club transformed into *tongzhi* veranda
16.	5/23/99	*Tongzhi*s obsessed with used underwear of handsome men
17.	6/3/99	Wat Yun suffers injustice? Dragon Boat Festival designated *Tongzhi* Day
19.	6/18/99	70% of youths object to *tongzhi*'s kissing
20.	7/2/99	Female *tongzhi* strangles lover to death
21.	7/5/99	*Tongzhi* identity of husband discovered only after 10 years of marriage
22.	7/5/99	Volunteers tragically become venting targets of homosexuals
23.	7/11/99	Female *tongzhi* suspects girlfriend of 'infidelity', writes 'farewell letter,' unconscious after swallowing painkillers madly
24.	9/13/99	Female *tongzhi* slashes wrist with razorblade
25.	9/14/99	Female *tongzhi* awarded marriage certificate after sex change, discovered to have use someone else's sperm to have a child 23 years later
26.	10/21/99	*Tongzhi*s at Chinese University received official permission to advocate homosexuality
28.	2/16/00	Police set trap to catch *tongzhi* for drug sale

Table 2. Headlines

In addition to the general themes and the headlines of the articles, the reason why the portrayal of *tongzhi*s in these articles is far from flattering is that many of these articles provide inaccurate or biased information about gay and lesbian Chinese. For instance, the headline of Article 22 in Table 2 is *'yi6-gung1 chaam2 bin3 tung4-sing3-lyun2 syun1-sit3 deui3-jeung6'* 'Volunteers tragically become venting targets of homosexuals.' Notice the use of the stance adverb *chaam2* 'tragically' in this headline. In this article, the journalist discusses the types of people who call a certain hotline for those who have problems dealing with their same-sex desire. In particular, the journalist describes a particular case in which a male college student became interested in wearing women's clothes after watching a concert in which the performers were cross-dressers. Using an unidentified source, the journalist tries to identify the 'cause of homosexuality' by saying that many male *tongzhi*s like the way women dress. As a result, they develop their sexual attraction to men. Not only is this claim scientifically unsound, but also the journalist does not present other competing explanations.

Moreover, in most cases, the use of the term *tongzhi* and the mention of gay and lesbian Chinese may actually be gratuitous information. In other words, the sexual orientation of those in the story is not relevant information. For instance, Article 10 in Table 1 is about a murder of a female sex-worker. She was killed by one of her clients in a hotel. Although the news story itself has nothing to do with gay and lesbian Chinese, the journalist mentions that the murder took place in a hotel frequented by both female sex-workers *and* male *tongzhi*s. Again, the assumption is that the mention of male *tongzhi*s highlights the deviant nature of the news story and increases the news value of the article.

If we look at these 28 articles, one may wonder why the sexual orientation of those in the new stories should be mentioned and why a term such as *tongzhi*, which originally has positive connotations, should be used. Article 5 is about a person who was caught stealing cosmetics. The headline is *'tung4-ji3 dou4 fa3-jong1-ban2 kau3 siu2-laam3 hau6 pun3'* 'Tongzhi caught stealing cosmetics awaits judgment'. The news story itself is trivial enough. However, the main question is why this person's sexual orientation should be highlighted in the headline of the article. It is possible that this person might not even identify himself as *tongzhi*. Why should this term be used at all? Certainly, the journalist thinks that by mentioning the person's sexual orientation, he or she can emphasize the negative aspect of the story. A headline such as 'heterosexual caught stealing cosmetics awaits judgment' might not have the same effect.

4 Textual Analysis: An Example

To further illustrate how the use of *tongzhi* in *Oriental Daily News* can lead to the pejoration of the term, the third part of the paper presents a more detailed textual analysis of one of the articles. This article, Article 11 in Table 1, was published in the March 4, 1999 issue (see Appendix). It is about the domestic dispute of a lesbian couple. In the first paragraph, the two protagonists of the news story are identified as *neui3 tung4-ji3* 'female *tongzhi,*' but the newspaper's portrayal of them and the description of the event are far from flattering. Furthermore, the positive connotations that the term *tongzhi* has gained as a result of its use in Chinese gay and lesbian community are lost.

The journalist's bias against homosexuality is conveyed through several means. First of all, quotation marks are used for words such as '*naam4-yau3*' 'boyfriend' (Paragraphs I, V, VI and VII), '*neui3-yau3*' 'girlfriend' (Paragraph I), '*sing3-gaau1*' 'sexual relation' (Paragraph VI), '*kau4-oi3*' 'pursue' (Paragraph V). This stylistic device indicates that what is within the quotation marks is falsely or improperly named (e.g., the *so-called* sexual relation, the *so-called* girlfriend). As a result, it makes a mockery out of the two protagonists in the story and trivializes their relationship.

Secondly, the journalist's voice is made explicit through the use of stance adverbs in certain sentences. For instance, in describing how Lai (one of the protagonists) 'became' homosexual, the journalist states that Lai had been involved in three heterosexual relationships, but because of unpleasant experiences, she lost confidence in men. Consequently, as the story goes, she fell for one of the female colleagues who later became her '*naam4-yau3*' 'boyfriend.' In describing the female colleague's pursuit of Lai, the journalist states:

> deui3-fong1 **ging2** chan3 gei1 kau4-oi3....
> The other party (Lai's female colleague) **surprisingly** took this opportunity to pursue (or propose to) Lai.... (Paragraph V; my translation)

Notice the use of the stance adverb *ging2* 'surprisingly' in this sentence. It suggests that Lai's female colleague was ruthless enough to take advantage of the situation (i.e., Lai's misfortunes with men). The journalist portrays Lai as a victim, who despondent about failed relationships with men, fell prey to the seduction of her homosexual colleague. The journalist perpetuates yet another stereotype of gays and lesbians — that is, homosexuals constantly look for 'new recruits,' and if one is not careful enough, one can fall into their trap.

Furthermore, the journalist's value judgments toward homosexuality are manifest through the presuppositions that are implicit in the article. For instance, when describing the relationship between the two protagonists in the news story, the journalist says:

Jong1 baan6 yin2 naam4-sing3 gok3-sik1, Lai4 jak1 wai4-chi4 neui3-sing3 **bun2**-fan6.

'Jong [one of the protagonists of the news story] plays the male role, while Lai [the other protagonist] maintains her **original** female identity...' (Paragraph II; my translation, emphasis added)

By claiming that Lai maintains her '*original* female identity,' the journalist implies that Jong, who likes playing the 'male role,' shuns her 'original' identity (i.e., female). In other words, the journalist perpetuates the stereotypes associated with lesbians (and by extension, gay men) often found in homophobic discourse – that is, effeminate men are trying not to be male, while lesbians are trying not to be female.

Finally, this article is mixed with linguistic elements of news reporting and those of dramatization (See Fairclough 1995 for a discussion on interdiscursivity). Although it is supposed to be about a domestic dispute incident in the local news section, the putative objectivity of news reporting and the neutrality of the journalist have disappeared. In fact, this article sounds more like a highly dramatized story about a dysfunctional lesbian couple. In particular, notice the journalist's strategic use of various key adverbs and adjectives in the first paragraph. According to Alan Bell (1991:176), the first paragraph of a news story, often called the 'lead', is arguably the most important part of the article. The lead concentrates the news value of the story. Like the headline, it attracts the reader's attention, so that he or she will continue reading the article. Not surprisingly, to increase the news value of the story, the journalist uses many evaluative and value-laden lexical items to dramatize the story. For example, the journalist states, 'the "girlfriend's"...unstable sexual orientation...caused the "boyfriend's" *intense* jealousy. A *fierce* quarrel started in their apartment...and then, it turned into *a full-fledged fist fight*...the "girlfriend," *in fury*, slashed her wrist with broken glass.':

... yan3-hei2 'naam4-yau3' chou3-yi3 **daai6-faat3**.
... caused the 'boyfriend's' **intense** jealousy...

... faan3-sang1 **gik1-lit6** jang1-chaau2, kei4-hau6 yin2-sing4 **chyun4-mou3-hang4**....
... a **fierce** quarrel started, and then it turned into a **full-fledged fist fight**...

... 'neui3-yau3' jak1 **fan3** yi3 yung6 seui3-pin2 got3-mak6 ji6-saat3....
... 'girlfriend', **in fury,** slashed her wrist with broken glass...

The use of evaluative expressions such as *daai6-faat3* 'intense,' *fan3* 'in fury,' *chyun4-mou3-hang4* 'full-fledged fist fight,' increases the negativity and enhances the news value of the story. However, at the same time, it makes the news story sound like a parody of the lesbian couple's relationship.

5 Conclusion

To conclude, when used in a context such as the one described above, the positive connotations of *tongzhi* – respect, equality and intimacy among gay and lesbian Chinese – are lost, while negative connotations are added to the term. Many readers who were not familiar with the use of *tongzhi* to refer to 'gay and lesbian Chinese' are only exposed to it in mainstream newspapers, such as *Oriental Daily News*. Regardless of their attitudes toward gays and lesbians, readers are not made aware of the positive connotations associated with *tongzhi* when the term is used in this context. Worse still, they may regard *tongzhi* as yet another pejorative term for 'gay and lesbian Chinese.' According to *Oriental Daily News*, *tongzhi*s are often those who refuse to acknowledge their 'original gender roles' and consistently look for easy victims to recruit into their community. As McConnell-Ginet (1989:46) points out, a word becomes an insult because of the context in which it is used. After it has been used in a negative context long enough, the addressee or the reader does not need the extralinguistic context to gain access to the derogatory connotations. As a result, despite all the positive connotations that *tongzhi* has gained because of its use in the Chinese gay and lesbian community, the meaning of the term may be determined by those who have the advantage in defining the label for the wider community – that is, those who control the channels for the implementation of the semantic change. Consequently, the adoption of *tongzhi* by *Oriental Daily News* and other mainstream newspapers may lead to the pejoration of the term.

However, this does not mean that the positive connotations of *tongzhi* will be lost for ever. As Stuart Hall (1982) points out, although dominant cultures attempt to fix meanings through power and ideology, meanings can never be fixed. The questions of how a minority group should be defined and what label should be used for a minority group can always be contested. Although the positive connotations of *tongzhi* have been diluted in mainstream newspapers, gays and lesbians in Hong Kong and Taiwan can challenge the negative connotations that the expression has gained as a result of its use in the media. This example illustrates the inner dialectic nature of a living ideological sign that Voloshinov refers to, as he says in *Marxism and the Philosophy of Language* (1986:23):

> In actual fact, each living ideological sign has two faces, like Janus. Any current curse word can become a word of praise, any current truth must inevitably sound to many other people as the greatest lie. This inner dialectic quality of the sign comes out fully in the open only in times of social crises or revolutionary change.

References

Bell, A. 1991. *The Language of News Media.* Oxford: Blackwell.

Cohen, E. 1997. Hong Kong: The Future of Press Freedom. *Columbia Journalism Review.* May/June 1997.

Fang, H. and J. Heng. 1983. Social Changes and Changing Address Norms in China. *Language in Society* 12:497-50.

Fairclough, N. 1995. *Critical Discourse Analysis: The Critical Study of Language.* London and New York: Longman.

Hall, S. 1982. The Rediscovery of 'Ideology': Return of the Repressed in Media Studies. *Culture, Society, and the Media,* ed. M. Gurevitch et al. New York: Methuen.

Iarovici, E. and R. Amel. 1989. The Strategy of the Headline. *Semiotica* 77.4:441-59.

McConnell-Ginet, S. 1989. The Sexual (Re)Production of Meaning: A Discourse-Based Theory. *Language, Gender, and Professional Writing: Theoretical Approaches and Guidelines for Nonsexist Usage,* ed. F. Wattman & P. Treichler, 35-50. New York: Commission on Status of Women in the Profession, Modern Language Association of America.

Schulz, M. 1975. The Semantic Derogation of Women. *Language and Sex: Difference and Dominance,* ed. B. Thorne and N. Henley, 64-75. Rowley, MA: Newbury House.

Voloshinov, V. 1986. *Marxism and the Philosophy of Language.* Cambridge, MA: Harvard University Press.

Wong, A. and Q. Zhang. 2000. The Linguistic Construction of the *Tongzhi* Community. *Journal of Linguistic Anthropology.*

Appendix

Article from March 4, 1999 *Oriental Daily News*

女同志扑傷「男友」圖割脈死

兩同居逾年的女同志，「女友」疑性傾向不堅定，對異性仍有渴望，引起「男友」醋意大發，雙方昨晨在跑馬地寓所發生激烈爭吵，其後演變成全武行，「男友」被玻璃樽扑穿頭，「女友」則憤而用碎片割脈圖自殺，雙雙送院治療。

兩女事主分別姓鍾（廿七歲）及姓黎（廿二歲），年多前開始在景光街租住一單位共賦同居，鍾扮演男性角色，黎則維持女性本分，互以「老婆」、「老公」相稱。

被指對男性仍有遐想

據悉，鍾、黎兩人同於跑馬地一間酒吧工作，分別擔任唱片騎師及酒保。昨晨三時，兩人收工後帶黎偷看日記，甫抵家中發現她對男性仍有遐想，因瑣事發生爭執，期間更趨激烈，繼而大打出手，雙方由廳中扭打至廚房，兩人同告受傷。

至清晨五時，鄰居發現兩人遇襲及企圖自殺，出現血案，割脈自殺，代寫致電報警，警方懷疑兩人另有隱情，將兩人送往醫院治療，暫列作意外受傷及企圖自殺案處理。

記者訪問，黎表示，自己曾與異性投緣，並拍過三次拖，三心兩意，對愛情要求高，最終分手，同性戀者性傾向沒有改變，曾對異性十分傾慕，遂欣然接受鍾，令黎女感動，經常向黎女動粗。

黎女在異性戀與同性戀間周旋，醫院治療變激，不願任職，年前請黎同居，一年後因「男友」變成分產，地呼有「男友」，黎居場。

雖有同床但無「性交」

年多前，黎轉到跑馬地酒吧擔任酒保，邂逅姓鍾「男友」，不久即共賦同居，期間雙方曾多次因瑣事爭執，一度分手，直至一個月前才復合。

黎並不諱言，她與「男友」雖然同床，但只是神交，並沒有「性交」，她又讚鍾較其前「男友」溫柔。

兩人在醫院接受治療後並無大礙，更冰釋前嫌手挽手返回跑馬地「愛巢」。

Oriental Daily News, **March 4, 1999**

Female *Tongzhi* Attacks 'Boyfriend', Attempts Suicide By Slashing Wrist

An argument broke out between two female *tongzhi*s who have been living together for more than two years. The 'girlfriend' was suspected of having an unstable sexual orientation and being attracted to the opposite sex. As a result, this caused the 'boyfriend's' intense jealousy. A fierce quarrel started in their apartment in Paau Ma Dei last night, and then, it turned into a full-fledged fist fight. The 'boyfriend' was hit on the head with a bottle, while the 'girlfriend,' in fury, slashed her wrist with broken glass. Both were sent to the hospital for treatment.

The two parties are Jong (27 years old) and Lai (22 years old). They moved into their apartment on Ying-Gong Street a few years ago. Jong likes playing the male role, while Lai maintains her original female identity. They call each other 'wife' and 'husband.'

Accused of being attracted to men

According to an unidentified source, Jong and Lai work together at a bar in Paau Ma Dei, one of them is the DJ while the other one is a barback. A little drunk, they went home around 3 o'clock this morning. When they arrived, they started arguing over some insignificant matter. At that time, Jong was suspected of having read Lai's diary, and she discovered that Lai was still attracted to men. They started arguing, and the argument became more and more intense. A fist fight ensued. It started in the living room and ended up in the kitchen. Both were reported injured.

Around 5 am this morning, neighbors discovered that a fist fight broke out and they reported to the police. Jong and Lai were sent to the hospital for treatment. Both denied that they were attacked or attempted suicide. The police suspected that the story was more complicated than it was claimed. The case is temporarily listed as accidental injury and attempted suicide.

When she was at the hospital, Lai was interviewed by the reporter. She admitted that she is homosexual. She also said that she had several hetero-sexual relationships. She stated that she dated men three times. Unfortunately, she did not have any luck: they stole her love and her money. As a result, she did not have any confidence in men. Three years ago, she became a real estate agent. She was invited to a bar for female homosexuals by one of her female colleagues whom she was friendly with. She accepted her colleague's invitation. The other party surprisingly 'pursued' her. At that time, Lai was not embarrassed. On the other hand, she was very pleased and decided to see where it might go. Since the 'boyfriend' was not attentive and often abused Lai physically, they broke up after having lived together for a year.

Sharing the same bed, but no 'sexual relationship'

A little more than a year ago, Lai started working as a barback in one of the bars in Paau Ma Dei. She met her 'boyfriend' Jong. Before long, they started living together. During that time, they separated several times because of insignificant matters. They only got back together last month.

Lai did not mince words. She states that although she and her 'boyfriend' share the same bed, it is only a platonic relationship. They do not have a 'sexual relationship.' She also said that Jong was more attentive than her previous 'boyfriend.'

After having been treated at the hospital, they made peace and went back to their 'love nest' hand in hand.

11

Sharing Resources and Indexing Meanings in the Production of Gay Styles*

ROBERT J. PODESVA, SARAH J. ROBERTS AND KATHRYN CAMPBELL-KIBLER

1 Introduction

In recent years an increasing number of linguists have criticized sociolinguistic approaches to style limited to correlations between linguistic variation and pre-defined social categories. Instead, researchers such as Ochs (1991), Irvine (2001), and the California Style Collective (1993), have sought to highlight the ways in which linguistic practice produces and reproduces social meaning.

Drawing on this work, we propose a new approach to style, which centers around two important concepts. First of all, we distinguish between linguistically conveyed meanings relating directly to the immediate context of the discourse participants, and those involving the construction of personal or stylistic identities. Further, we argue that indexical relationships (in

* Our names appear in random order. We would like to thank audiences at NWAV 28, IGALA 1, and in particular the Style, Language, and Ideology Collaborative at Stanford for discussions on this material. Special thanks to Penny Eckert for encouraging us to think about the issues we explore here. We accept full responsibility for any errors this work may contain.

Language and Sexuality: Contesting Meaning in Theory and Practice.
Kathryn Campbell-Kibler, Robert J. Podesva, Sarah J. Roberts and Andrew Wong (eds.).
Copyright © 2001, CSLI Publications.

the sense developed in Ochs 1991) relate these different types of social meaning to each other, as well as to linguistic resources. Using this approach, we examine a gay activist's use of phonetic features in a radio interview to project a style which is markedly gay and yet differs from the style usually identified as gay by researchers and the culture at large.

In section two we focus on issues peculiar to the study of gay men's speech, or the speech of men perceived to sound gay. While the topic has garnered some interest over the years, only through a closer analysis of specific gay communities and identities can one address what it means for any given individual to sound gay in a particular context. We argue that it is necessary to recognize where and how gay men differ from each other in their linguistic performances, as well as to see how variables not limited to the gay community may be used within it.

We outline in section three several existing notions of style, reviewing the approaches of Labov, Bell, Irvine, and Ochs, and also detailing our own framework of style. Specifically, we explain our understanding of style as the ongoing construction of identity, built both directly through linguistic (and other) resources, and indirectly through the performance of social acts or activities, and the projection of emotive stances.

In section four we lay out the rationale and procedures of the study. We discuss the context of the radio interview from which we gathered our data, as well as its impact on the performance of the speaker we analyze. We also introduce the variables examined in the study, and review results found elsewhere for these same variables.

The results of our study are discussed in section five. We show that the speaker under investigation does not use the same variables previously reported to trigger a gay percept. Our claim is not that he is refraining from or does not command a recognizably gay style, but that he is using a different style that is neither stereotypical nor flamboyant.[1] He uses different variables to achieve a performance of competence and non-stereotypical gay identity.

2 Gay Ways of Speaking

Sociolinguistic research on the speaking styles of gay men has centered on identifying the features that constitute a monolithic speech variety, often referred to as Gay Speech or the Gay Accent. Scholars have argued that the speech of gay men, or alternatively gay-sounding speech, differentiates itself from other speaking styles on the lexical (e.g., Rodgers 1972), phonetic

---

[1] Though not all stereotypical styles are flamboyant, flamboyance is associated with stereotypical gay style.

(e.g., Crist 1997), and discourse (e.g., Leap 1996) levels. Although we do not question that some segments of the gay male community may use the features discussed in these works, we take issue with the practice of labeling them as specifically gay male features. We argue that labeling a linguistic feature as gay is at once too general and too specific.

First, the assumption that there is a singular gay way of speaking homogenizes the diversity within the gay community, erasing or at least deeming unimportant to sociolinguistic inquiry the many subcultures comprising the community. Gay culture encompasses reified categories such as leather daddies, clones, drag queens, circuit boys, guppies (gay yuppies), gay prostitutes, and activists both mainstream and radical, as well as more local communities of practice which may not even have names. Membership in one of the subcultures often takes precedence over a more general affiliation with the gay community, and social activities—and hence opportunities for linguistic exchanges—are usually organized around membership not in the gay male community at large, but in its subcultures. The distinction between the subcultures is constructed stylistically, through dress, use and choice of drugs, music preferences, and linguistic resources. The meanings of stylistic resources, linguistic or otherwise, are negotiated in these gay subcultures. Thus treating the meaning of a linguistic feature as generally as gay ignores the community that has worked to give the feature meaning.

Second, while labeling linguistic features as gay is too general, it also runs the risk of not being general enough. By simply assigning gay meanings to linguistic features, one reifies as gay certain linguistic features that are shared throughout society. For instance, Leap (1996) identifies cooperative discourse as a marker of 'Gay Men's English,' but Cameron (1998) points out that cooperative discourse also occurs among young heterosexual men. And then there are the original cooperators: women, the subject of the first discussions of cooperative discourse in the language and gender literature (e.g., Coates 1998, Tannen 1990). By labeling cooperative discourse as a specifically gay feature, one ignores its use by women and straight men. What is missing is an analysis that allows cooperative discourse to contribute to heterosexuality in some situations and to the construction of gay identities in others.

To avoid these two problems, we propose a framework for style in which linguistic features become associated with communities by indexing the stances, acts, and activities that characterize and constitute them. Such a framework moves beyond linguistic features that directly index gross demographic characteristics (e.g., gay), allowing for linguistic features that index social meaning on a micro-level. At the same time the framework enables linguistic resources to index identities through intermediary social meanings (e.g., stance of precision), and these social meanings may be shared across communities. In the following section we explicitly lay out our framework for style.

3 Style

We view style as the situational use of linguistic resources (including phonetic variables, syntactic constructions, lexicon, discourse markers) to negotiate one's place in the local communicative context as well as in society in general. Style permeates language not as a separate component or dimension but as a building block for creating and perpetuating social meaning. However since meaning is always somewhat in flux and dependent on the ever-changing contexts in which resources are used (see McConnell-Ginet, this volume), style itself is always a work in progress.

This approach differs considerably from many contemporary approaches to style. In variationist sociolinguistics, style (intraspeaker variation) is usually treated as unidimensional and linked in some way to stable social categories. Labov (1966) and others (e.g., Wolfram 1969, Trudgill 1974) regard style as a function of attention paid to speech, ranging from casual to highly monitored speech. Their methodology reveals the stratification of social categories such as class or 'sex' by correlating linguistic variation to stylistic variation. This approach shows that categories have empirical relevance to linguistic variation, but (as with any correlational approach) it does not reveal whether categories shape linguistic practice or are themselves derivative of language use. It also assumes the stability of both style and social categories; this methodology routinely elicits pre-defined 'styles' from speakers (such as Casual Style, Reading Style, etc.) and categories serve to locate a given speaker within a fixed social structure. Finally, this approach limits style to a single dimension and does not explain how situational and interactional factors, such as social power, mode of interaction, topic, setting (as discussed by Hymes 1972 and Biber 1994), contribute to intraspeaker variation.

Bell (1984) proposed an alternative unidimensional approach that treats style as interpersonal audience accommodation. Drawing on accommodation theory (Coupland and Giles 1988), Bell proposed that style represents efforts by speakers to converge with or diverge from the speech of their addressee(s). As a result, style as intra-speaker variation is derivative of inter-speaker variation (the style axiom). In a recent revision to his model (Bell 1997), he highlights the role of identity and differentiation in the production of style. He characterizes the process along the following lines:

1. Group has its own identity, evaluated by self and others.

2. Group differentiates its language from others': 'social,' or inter-speaker variation.

3. Group's language is evaluated by self and others: linguistic evaluation.

4. Others shift relative to group's language: 'style,' or intra-speaker variation. (Bell 1997:244)

Identity therefore serves as the basis of social and linguistic differentiation, and evaluation links social attitudes towards groups to the groups' patterns of variation. These attitudes then filter down to the level of intraspeaker variation: 'Style derives its meaning from the association of linguistic features with particular social groups.' (p. 243)

Bell's model however takes as its starting point predefined 'groups' which already possess their own identities. It accepts uncritically the notion, questioned by Cameron (1998) and others, that identity is a predetermined and stable fact instead of a construct constituted through social and linguistic practice. As research in the field of language and gender has often shown, identity cannot be separated from the social performances that produce and perpetuate meaning. By making style a by-product of identity, Bell precludes the possibility of style as a means of constituting group identities.

Our approach to style, in accordance with recent research on identity and the role played by language in forming identity, assumes that identity and style are co-constructed. Instead of treating stylistic variation as merely reflective of one's social address or identity, we view style as the linguistic means through which identity is produced in discourse. A style may be viewed as a collage of co-occurring linguistic features which, while unfixed and variable, work together to constitute meaning in coherent and socially intelligible ways. Style simultaneously gives linguistic substance to a given identity and allows the identity to be socially meaningful.

Irvine (2001) mentions that distinctiveness underlies both style and identity: 'Whatever 'styles' are, in language and elsewhere, they are part of a system of distinction, in which a style contrasts with other possible styles, and the social meaning signified by the style contrasts with other social meanings' (p. 77). Along these lines, we need to examine a style not just in relation to others it may draw on, but also in relation to those other styles to which it opposes itself—particularly in the local, situational contexts in which styles are produced. In the case of gay styles one would need to consider how a given style opposes itself to other perceived gay styles (such as those associated with the various subcultures mentioned in the previous section), in addition to the obvious opposition between gay and straight. An approach to gay speech that posits a single dimension of identity or 'gayness' independent of local context misses not only much of the diversity within the gay community but also ignores Zwicky's (1997:31) observation that variables are employed by 'different speakers, in different places, on different occasions.'

Ochs (1991) proposes an explicit framework for understanding how linguistic resources are linked to abstract categories or groups. Most resources are not correlated directly to social categories. Rather they bear pragmatic information about particular situations. Certain resources may contribute to stances and acts that impact the immediate speech situation; for instance, 'tag questions may index a stance of uncertainty as well as the act of requesting confirmation/clarification/feedback' (Ochs 1991:335). At the same time, speakers derive from past experiences an understanding that these resources are differently used across society and therefore develop 'norms, preferences, and expectations regarding the distribution of this work *vis-à-vis* particular social identities of speakers, referents, and addressees' (Ibid, p. 342). As a result, resources may indirectly index abstract social categories in a constitutive sense; for instance, one may lay claim to a female identity by using tag questions to produce a stance of hesitancy, which in some communities is normatively associated with female identity.

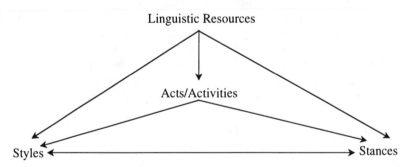

Figure 1. Indexical Relations Between Linguistic Resources and Social Meanings

So while a few variables directly index a given category (such as the indexing of male gender by the pronoun *he* or the use of *gay* to index a putative gay category), most index categories only indirectly and function primarily to express pragmatic meanings relating to local context. We have diagrammed the indexical relationship between these meanings and style in Figure 1. The meanings that contribute to style may either derive directly from the use of linguistic resources or indirectly via the speech acts, activities (socially-defined speech events such as debate or prayer), or stances that speakers perform in the course of conversation.

For instance, /in/ vs. /iŋ/ variation (as in *workin'* vs. *working*) is a classic example of a variable which expresses a stance of informality, contributes to working class styles, and is meaningful ideologically in contrasting a friendly, close-knit working class group against a more institutionally-based middle class (Eckert 2000). This approach allows us to incorporate Labov's concern for formality/informality (which he characterized as attention paid to speech) while distancing variation from simple demographic characteristics. Conversely, styles that are legibly associated with certain social groups may be used to enact certain stances. Cheshire (1997) discusses the case of a teenaged boy increasing his use of vernacular markers in a school setting relative to his out-of-school speech, in contrast to his friends, who decrease their use of the variables at school. In this case he uses his vernacular style to display a stance of resistance against the authority of the school.

Our priorities, as set forth by this approach to style, would include the identification of linguistic resources that are used to constitute different gay styles, an analysis of how these resources are used to index different meanings, and speculation on how a particular style may index more than a single category at the same time—as one's identity as gay is hardly independent from other possible identities relevant to a given context. In the data presented below, we examine what might be termed 'mainstream gay activist style,' which is here constructed in the setting of a radio discussion, primarily in opposition to a straight audience, as well as to a more flamboyant gay style. Gay identity is highly salient for representatives of gay political organizations, especially in public discussions. But at the same time, participants are frequently warned against sounding 'too gay.' We suggest that the style displayed is an attempt to portray at once strong gay identity and professional competence—as evaluated by a mainstream, mostly straight audience.

4 The Study

The radio discussion selected as a data source for this study occurred on a popular National Public Radio talk show and dealt with a politically sensitive gay issue: namely, whether private voluntary organizations reserve the right to ban gays from their membership. Our study focuses on the speech of speaker A, an openly gay attorney and reasonably famous gay rights activist. We chose to examine his speech because it evoked a strong gay percept and because his contribution was of suitable length for phonetic analysis. When he appeared on the radio program, he was representing in court an individual who had been dismissed from such an organization. Although the host introduced issues directly bearing on gay identity at the outset of the program, the debate mainly revolved around an intricate discussion of antidiscrimination laws. Speaker A's contribution foregrounded his expertise in interpreting law and repeatedly named the ousted individual as his professional 'client.' For the most part, he was speaking more as an attorney than as a gay man.

We contrast Speaker A's speech with that of Speaker B, his opponent in the debate. Speaker B was a representative of a libertarian organization, and his speech did not evoke a gay percept. Their primary point of contestation did not revolve around gay rights but rather concerned the role of government in regulating the internal affairs of private organizations. Speaker B, in fact, made it clear that he did not personally favor the discrimination. Since the issue structuring the opposition between the two speakers called on Speaker A's legal expertise instead of his experience as a gay man, Speaker A's role as attorney was emphasized.

An acoustic analysis was conducted on the speech of speakers A and B, concentrating on the following variables:

1. Durations of /æ/, /eɪ/

2. Durations of onset /s/, /l/

3. Fundamental frequency (f0) properties (max, min, range, and value at vowel midpoint) of stressed vowels

4. Voice onset time (VOT) of voiceless aspirated stops

5. Release of word-final stops

Though we have opted to call these phonetic features variables, we do not use the term in the traditional sociolinguistic sense. Rather than coding data categorically, we have quantified values acoustically. For example, the duration of a segment is coded in milliseconds rather than with a perceptual label, such as short or long. With the exception of word-final stop releases, all variables considered here are continuous.

Following Crist (1997), who reported that for five out of six male speakers the segments /s/ and /l/ were longer in gay stereotyped speech, we examined the duration of /s/ and /l/ in onset position. Rogers, Smyth, and Jacobs (2000) have since duplicated Crist's finding, showing that sibilants (both /s/ and /z/) and the lateral approximant (/l/) exhibit greater duration in gay-sounding speech.

The pitch properties of speakers A and B were also investigated, since high pitch and wide pitch ranges are often anecdotally associated with gay styles of speaking. Though Gaudio (1994) found that neither pitch range nor pitch variability provided sufficient cues to yield a gay percept, Jacobs, Rogers, and Smyth (1999) have recently found that listeners are more likely to identify speakers as gay if they have large pitch ranges, regardless of whether the speakers are gay or straight. Four measures of fundamental frequency (f0), the acoustic correlate of pitch, were taken for each stressed vowel: maximum f0, minimum f0, f0 at vowel midpoint, and f0 range.

The variables discussed thus far—the durations of onset /s/ and /l/ and the four measures of fundamental frequency—have been associated with stereotypically gay speech, but as mentioned above, speaker A does not employ a flamboyantly gay style. We have therefore identified a number of other variables that could potentially be used in an activist style based on our impressionistic judgments from radio interviews with six gay activists. These variables included the durations of the vowels /æ/ and /eɪ/, the duration of voice onset time (or aspiration) for voiceless stops, and the release of word-final stops. Unlike the continuous variables discussed above, the release of word-final stops was coded as a boolean: marked for the presence or absence of a burst. Long voice onset time (VOT) and the frequent release of word-final stops exemplify hyperarticulation, a feature identified by Walters (1981), as cited by Barrett (1997).

We now turn to a discussion of Speaker A's stylistic construction of identity using the phonetic features reviewed in this section.

5   Results

The variables we examined fall into roughly three categories. We first discuss segment duration of onset /s/, onset /l/, /æ/, /eɪ/, and aspiration of voiceless stops. These variables group together naturally as the findings for any one segment cannot be analyzed without looking at the others, given the strong influence of overall speech rate. Next, we present the findings related to f0: the high and low for each vowel (stressed vowels in multisyllabic words), the range (difference between them), and the f0 at the midpoint of the vowel. Finally, we give the results for the frequency with which each speaker released final stops.

The duration variables do not lend themselves to straightforward analysis, due to the confounding factor of overall speech rate. Table 1 summarizes the results for the duration variables. Speaker A has a higher mean for three of these five variables: /æ/, /s/, and VOT. Given this trend, it would be inadvisable to interpret these specific duration variables as individually significant in this context. Instead we suggest that speaker A merely has an overall slower rate of speaking than does speaker B, and these variables are not being used independently of rate. Thus the vowel /eɪ/, which contradicts this trend, is being used as a meaningful variable, or correlates with a meaning distinct from overall speech rate. This correlation may indicate a relationship between words in which this vowel appears and topics which inspire emphatic stress or shifts in speed. Throughout the interview both speakers vary their speech rates to color their points. In addition, they both use repetition of particular key lexical items freely as a rhetorical device, and the selection of words to repeat (and stress) may influence these duration results.

	Mean		Standard Deviation	
	A	B	A	B
/æ/	93*	76	44	39
/eɪ/	107	131*	46	53
/s/	111*	100	36	30
/l/	70	66	20	31
VOT	73*	59	25	23

* Significantly longer (alpha level = 0.05)

Table 1. Results for the Duration Variables (in ms)

Use of this strategy is evidenced in the duration of /eɪ/ in the word *gay*. Hypothesizing that this word could serve as a locus of performance or meaning, we looked at the duration values of Speaker A's tokens of /eɪ/ in *gay*, in all other words, and in other words in which it is the final segment. The results are shown in Table 2. Speaker A's tokens of /eɪ/ occurring in the word *gay* are significantly longer than those that do not, and have a higher mean than speaker B's overall mean. A similar lexical analysis could not be conducted on Speaker B's speech, as he avoided the term *gay*, using it only twice during the hour-long program.

	Mean	Standard Deviation
tokens of *gay*	162.2	68.2
other tokens of /eɪ/	102.4	39.8
other tokens of word-final /eɪ/	101.5	50.3
all tokens of /eɪ/	107.8	46.2

Table 2. Speaker A's Durations of /eɪ/ (in ms)

As mentioned previously, the durations of /l/ and of /s/ have been linked to stereotypically gay performances (Crist 1997). We found no difference in the duration or the variance of /l/ between the two speakers. Speaker A does have a significantly longer mean for duration of /s/ than does Speaker B. This may indicate some stylistic use of this variable, or it may result from an overall speech rate difference, as discussed above.

Another commonly cited factor in establishing a gay percept is f0, the results for which are summarized in Table 3. Speaker B has higher average levels for maximum f0, minimum f0, and f0 at vowel midpoint, as well as a higher variance for all of these values. This suggests both that speaker B has a generally higher voice than speaker A (whether through biology or effort), and that his f0 is more variable across tokens.[2]

	Mean		Standard Deviation	
	A	B	A	B
V midpoint	131	137*	31	39*
max	142	152*	33	41*
min	122	130*	128	36*
range	21	21	19	18

* Significantly higher (alpha level = 0.05)

Table 3. Results for Fundamental Frequency (f0) Variables (in Hz)

The two speakers exhibit no difference in the f0 range, calculated as the difference between the maximum and minimum values within each vowel. This shows that neither speaker exceeds the other in use of 'swoopy voice,' a feature commonly associated with gay men.

Overall, Speaker A uses neither a higher pitch nor a wider f0 range relative to his counterpart to perform a gay identity. These results establish that speaker A does not use pitch in ways usually attributed to gay-sounding men. Nonetheless, speaker A is self-presenting as a gay man, and is immediately perceptible to listeners as such. We conclude that the type of gay style speaker A is performing differs from the other styles that have been investigated. Further, the way that his style differs from this more recognized style is not merely idiosyncratic (or inexplicable) variation, but a deliberate and common response to the meanings associated with wide pitch variation and especially its use by gay men. In particular, we propose that higher pitch and even more, wide pitch ranges, form part of a recognizably flamboyant gay style. We use flamboyant here, not to describe the intensity of the social meaning, but as an integral part of the meaning itself. It is frequently tempting to see broad demographic categories as essential basic meanings, and variation within them as aligned along a continuum.[3] In this case, the continuum might place the stereotypical 'queen' at the far extreme

---

[2] Either Speaker B is using a variable pitch as a facet of his radio performance, or Speaker A is deliberately controlling his use of pitch as a variable, or both. With two speakers interacting, however, such a distinction is not useful, as they will respond to one another.

[3] This notion is discussed by Irvine and Gal (2000) under the name 'fractal recursivity,' wherein an opposition between two large groups is repeated within the groups, often to indicate better or worse representatives of the category. For example, if men are on average taller than women, this may be reified into the opposition 'men are tall, women are short.' In turn, this opposition may be repeated, such that height is a masculine and desirable trait in a man, and an unfeminine and undesirable trait in a woman.

of gayness. Others who deviate from that image, either in terms of body-related characteristics such as race, disability status, weight, or linguistic performance, are then cast as less gay. We question this arrangement, and suggest that the speaker under investigation, while striving not to sound too gay, is not bound to the continuum, but is rather inhabiting a different space altogether. That is, using high f0 and wide f0 ranges is not simply a flamboyant way of being gay in the world, but rather a way of being flamboyantly gay. It is precisely this performance which speaker A is avoiding, both as a result of his goals for the show (which include being non-threatening and competent) and the paths along which the discussion runs, focusing primarily on legal questions, and as a result, requiring him to speak with authority on serious topics.

In addition to duration and pitch, we investigated the release of word-final stops for both speakers. Speaker A has a significantly higher percentage of released stops than speaker B, as shown in Table 4. This result does not mean, however, that this variable directly indexes gay for this speaker, as sexual orientation is hardly the only difference between the two speakers, or even the only difference made relevant by the context and topics of discussion. To look for the meaning of this variable in one context, it is useful to see where and how it is used by other people in other contexts. Bucholtz (1996) mentions this same feature as forming a part of a geek girl style, and that it has a particular link to education and literacy for these speakers. Ashburn (2000) discusses its use by members of the science fiction convention community, as does Benor (in press) among Orthodox Jews, again with similar implications.

	A	B
	(N = 248)	(N = 202)
released	22.4%	12.9%
unreleased	77.6%	87.1%

$\chi^2 = 7.04, df = 1, p = 0.004$

Table 4. Percent of Released Word-Final Stops

We propose that this variable has a culture-wide relationship to education or precision, and that speaker A is using it for this purpose. This use accomplishes two goals. In the first place, as a lawyer he has an interest in establishing his identity as an educated and competent representative of the profession especially in a context where he is answering questions on specifically legal issues. And secondly he may be trying not to sound too gay, a goal often explicitly discussed by activists and speakers in the gay community as important when appearing before a mainstream, mostly straight audience. We posit that the phenomenon of not sounding too gay is not merely a function of dampening general features that say 'gay', but a different performance entirely. 'Too gay' here is, in fact, a code. It is code for other social meanings associated with gay men and particular gay styles such as frivolity, promiscuity, and excitability. While speaking to potentially hostile audiences, activists often construct themselves in opposition to these images, as well as the other meanings populating the social space around them. Invoking cultural ideas concerning education and authority is one way to distance oneself from these qualities.

6 Conclusion

Our findings further problematize the notion of a singular gay way of speaking, as discussed in §2. First, we have demonstrated that speaker A is not exploiting pitch or the duration of /l/ to produce a gay style, even though these phonetic features have been linked to stereotypically gay speech. We argue that speaker A is performing an entirely different kind of gay identity, one which strongly contrasts with a stereotypically gay style. Although high pitch, wide pitch ranges, and prolonged /l/s index a gay style, they index only one of many gay styles. Speaker A is performing a non-stereotypical gay identity, and his performance illustrates that linguistic styles—including gay styles—are as diverse as the individuals and communities producing them. Second, speaker A uses the release of final stops, a feature which also constitutes part of a geek girl style, in the production of his gay identity. This finding illustrates how a linguistic feature may be employed without evoking solely a gay meaning and also highlights the importance of contextualizing features that express social meaning.

We would like to emphasize that there is a need for additional studies investigating how sets of variables cluster together to form gay styles and all linguistically constructed styles. If we can demonstrate patterns similar to those observed in this study for a number of speakers, and in particular if we observe those speakers cross-situationally, we will be able to abstract over individual idiosyncrasies and arrive at a more complete understanding of how variables group together to index different kinds of identities. The overall picture would express much more complexity than an approach assuming simple oppositions, such as gay vs. straight. With a focus on style as an indexically constituted social meaning, we are better equipped to analyze how the individual negotiates identity across situations and how groups may co-vary in interesting and perhaps unexpected ways.

References

Ashburn, Karyn. 2000. Mainstream Perceptions of SF [Science Fiction]. Panel discussion at Minicon 35, Minneapolis.

Barrett, Rusty. 1997. The 'Homo-genius' Speech Community. *Queerly Phrased: Language, Gender and Sexuality*, ed. Anna Livia and Kira Hall, 181-201. Oxford: Oxford University Press.Bell, Allan. 1984. Language Style as Audience Design. *Language in Society* 13.145-204.

Bell, Allan. 1997. Language Style As Audience Design. *Sociolinguistics: A Reader and Coursebook*, ed. Nikolas Coupland and Adam Jaworski, 240-250. New York: St. Martin's Press.

Benor, Sarah Bunin. In press. Sounding Learned: The Gendered Use of /t/ in Orthodox Jewish English. *University of Pennsylvania Working Papers in Linguistics* 7.

Bucholtz, Mary. 1996. Geek the Girl: Language, Femininity, and Female Nerds. *Gender and Belief Systems*, ed. J. Ahlers, L. Bilmes, M. Chen, M. Oliver, N. Warner, and S. Wertheim, 119-132. Berkeley: Berkeley Women and Language Group.

Byber, Douglas. 1994. An Analytical Framework for Register Studies. *Sociolinguistic Perspectives on Register*, ed. Douglas Byber and Edward Finnegan, 31-56. New York: Oxford University Press.

California Style Collective. 1993. Variation and Personal/Group Style. Paper presented at New Ways of Analyzing Variation 21, Ottawa.

Cameron, Deborah. 1998. Performing Gender Identity: Young Men's Talk and the Construction of Heterosexual Masculinity. Coates 1998a, 270-284.

Coates, Jennifer. 1998a. *Language and Gender: A Reader*. Oxford: Blackwell.

Coates, Jennifer. 1998b. Gossip Revisited: Language in All-female Groups. Coates 1998a, 226-253.

Coupland, Nikolas and Howard Giles 1988. Communicative Accommodation: Recent Developments. *Language and Communication* 8.175-327.

Crist, Sean. 1997. Duration of Onset Consonants in Gay Male Stereotyped Speech. *University of Pennsylvania Working Papers in Linguistics* 4.3.53-70.

Eckert, Penelope. 2000. *Linguistic Variation as Social Practice*. Malden, MA: Blackwell.

Gaudio, Rudolf P. 1994. Sounding Gay: Pitch Properties in the Speech of Gay and Straight Men. *American Speech* 69.1.30-57.

Hymes, Dell. 1972. Models of the Interaction of Language and Social Life. *Directions in Sociolinguistics*, ed. John Gumperz and Dell Hymes, 35-71. New York: Holt, Reinhart, and Winston.

Irvine, Judith. 2001. Style as Distinctiveness: the Culture and Ideology of Linguistic Differentiation. *Stylistic Variation*, ed. John Rickford and Penelope Eckert. Cambridge: Cambridge University Press.

Irvine, Judith and Susan Gal. 2000. Language Ideology and Linguistic Differentiation. *Regimes of Language: Ideologies, Polities, and Identities*, ed. Paul Kroskrity, 35-83. Santa Fe: SAR Press.

Jacobs, Greg, Henry Rogers, and Ron Smyth. 1999. Sounding Gay, Sounding Straight: A Search for Phonetic Correlates. Paper presented at New Ways of Analyzing Variation 28, Toronto.

Labov, William. 1966. *The Social Stratification of English in New York City*. Washington: Center for Applied Linguistics.

Leap, William L. 1996. *Word's Out: Gay Men's English*. Minneapolis: University of Minnesota Press.

Ochs, Elinor. 1991. Indexing Gender. *Rethinking Context*, ed. Alessandro Duranti and Charles Goodwin, 335-358. Cambridge: Cambridge University Press.

Rodgers, Bruce. 1972. *The Queen's Vernacular: a Gay Lexicon*. San Francisco: Straight Arrow Books.

Rogers, Henry, Ron Smyth, and Greg Jacobs. 2000. Vowel and Sibilant Duration in Gay- and Straight-sounding Male Speech. Paper presented at the International Gender and Language Association Conference 1, Stanford.

Tannen, Deborah. 1990. *You Just Don't Understand: Women and Men in Conversation*. New York: Morrow.

Trudgill, Peter. 1974. *The Social Differentiation of English in Norwich*. Cambridge: Cambridge University Press.

Walters, Keith. 1981. A Proposal for Studying the Language of Homosexual Males. Austin: University of Texas, ms.

Wolfram, Walter A. 1969. *A Sociolinguistic Description of Detroit Negro Speech*. Washington: Center for Applied Linguistics.

Zwicky, Arnold. 1997. Two lavender issues for linguistics. *Queerly Phrased: Language, Gender and Sexuality*, ed. Anna Livia and Kira Hall, 21-34. Oxford: Oxford University Press.

12

Camionneuses s'abstenir: Lesbian Community Creation Through the Personals

ANNA LIVIA

1 *Lesbia Magazine* and Community Values

Launched in 1980, *Lesbia Magazine*, the French monthly, currently retails for 25FF (about $4.00) and is available throughout France at magazine kiosks, mainstream bookstores and even railway stations platforms. Because of its low price, regular appearance, longevity and widescale distribution, it is the most popular lesbian magazine in France and functions as a cultural icon for French lesbians. It not only provides readers with information about lesbian activities in the Hexagon and throughout the world, but also serves as a forum for the discussion and contestation of community values.

As a Paris-based magazine, *Lesbia* necessarily has an urban, metropolitan flavor appealing particularly to middle class white lesbians with an interest in international culture and affairs. The typical reader is in her mid-thirties, college-educated, uncloseted, and living in a large city (as evidenced by the target of the commercial ads which appear in the magazine). However, since no other national lesbian magazine exists in France, lesbians who do not fit the profile outlined above rely on *Lesbia* as a source of information about regional events such as film festivals or political demonstrations, and services such as women's bookstores and women-owned bed

Language and Sexuality: Contesting Meaning in Theory and Practice.
Kathryn Campbell-Kibler, Robert J. Podesva, Sarah J. Roberts and Andrew Wong (eds.).
Copyright © 2001, CSLI Publications.

and breakfast places. Small circulation, often regionally localized magazines serving different sections of the lesbian community have appeared and disappeared in France over the last forty years. *Têtu*, for example, a gay glossy monthly, was launched in 1995. It has more cultural and less political coverage than *Lesbia*, and is read by young urban lesbians while the very hip, intellectual set read *Zoo*, launched in 1999, which is a self-proclaimed queer theory zine. In the main, however, most lesbians who are active and visible as lesbians, read *Lesbia* at least occasionally.

2 Resisting Readers

Just before I began my field research in May 2000, the collective of *Lesbia* were under fire for racist remarks made at Cineffable, a lesbian film festival they sponsor. A group of 'lesbiennes des migrations, des colonisations et descendantes de systèmes esclavagistes' (migrant lesbians, lesbians descended from colonialism and the descendants of slaves--a group composed of women of color) protested at the presence of a white woman bar owner at this festival who is infamous for refusing entrance to black lesbians at her bar. The *Lesbia* collective refused to allow the protest, dismissing the women who mounted it as 'commandos du grand sud' (*Lesbia*, December 1999). To understand this insult, one must appreciate that although the expression means literally 'commandos from the deep south,' the south so designated is not simply the south of France (not a symbolically black area) but also the continent on the other side of the Mediterranean, i.e. Africa. The phrase was taken as meaning 'black guerillas.' This controversy provoked a series of formal protests against *Lesbia* magazine which served, paradoxically, to make visible a large community of black French lesbians who are readers of the magazine.

The question of exactly who should be included as part of the community of *Lesbia* readers remains a fraught one and certainly needs to include resisting readers, or those who do not share the values propounded by the magazine. Nevertheless, these values are propagated by the monthly appearance of the magazine as well as in the discussions it occasions. The process of community building takes place throughout the magazine in a multilayered, multi-directional way. The process can be seen at work in a top-down direction, from editors to readers, overtly by the articles the editors choose to publish and the issues they decide to cover, as well as more covertly in artwork and lay-out. It works in a bottom-up direction, from readers to editors, in the letters page for many letters comment, often critically, on the values espoused by the magazine. Letters that respond to previous letters create horizontal ties, from reader to reader.

3 Personal Ads and Notes from the Keyboarder

Further complicating the picture are the personal ads that form their own section at the back, often taking up as many as seven pages of this fifty page magazine. The ads are extremely popular, and according to Christine Lemoine, a former member of the editorial team, 'The ads are read by a large number of women. Some buy *Lesbia* just for the ads, they never read the articles' (personal communication via email, March 2000). These ads are written by readers in search of a sexual and emotional partner and are ostensibly addressed to the unique being who can fulfill the writer's desires. This, of course, is a fiction. Many of the ads are disrupted, right in the middle of the text, by *notes de la claviste* (NDCs) or notes from the keyboarder at *Lesbia* magazine. These notes are separated from the wording of the ad only by parentheses.

The NDCs comment on the wording of the ad in which they are located, or the attitude it conveys. Since the personal ads are framed as private communications between the writer and the ideal addressee, they appear to occupy a position outside of the process of evaluation, contestation and reformulation taking place in the rest of the magazine. However, the invasive presence of the NDCs and their cryptic commentary on the values conveyed in the ad, serve to politicize even this apparently sheltered and individualized haven.

The NDCs are styled to represent the voice of lesbian reason, a liberal majority who despise censorship, favor free self-expression but still patrol the boundaries between the sexes. Using Penelope Eckert and Sally McConnell-Ginet's insights into communities of practice, we will see how the language of the ads and of the NDCs serve to create a cohesive lesbian community, through the process of articulation, contestation and, to some extent, re-evaluation.

4 Wording of the Ads

Personal ad writers typically provide pithy, evocative descriptions of themselves, using multiple abbreviations and references to symbolic figures and occupations. Self-descriptions (I), descriptions of the ideal other (II), and lists of exclusions (III) are presented in a tripartite structure intended to form a contrasting pattern so that the perfect lesbian partner can emerge, as may be seen in the first example (Roman numerals and bold are my addition and an English translation follows):

(1)   E66RP (I) **30 ans, balance, andro,** cherche contrepoids féminin pour
      équilibre harmonieux et calins. Souhaite (II) **poids plume, mouche
      ou moyen.** (III) **Catcheuses, camionneuses,** passez votre chemin.

E66RP (I) **30 years old, Libra, androgynous,** looking for a feminine
counterweight for harmonious equilibrium and caresses. Want (II)
featherweight, bantam weight or medium weight. (III) **Female
wrestlers, female truck drivers** go on your way. [November
1988, #66, p. 37]

She must be different from but compatible with the writer; she must correspond to the positive qualities listed; and at the same time she must not
personify any of the outlawed qualities. The ideal mate for (1), will be feminine where the author is androgynous, a lightweight, not built like a woman
wrestler.

These descriptions frequently end with a list of undesirables. Over and
over again, alcoholics are told to refrain from responding to the ad, as are
those who use drugs, suffer from various types of mental illness or malaise,
or do not participate in high culture. This type of exclusion covers:

(2)   alcoolos, incultes, mal élevées non-équilibrées, instables, vulgaires,
      caractérielles, (femmes) mal dans sa peau, paumées, en cours
      d'analyse, perturbées, névrosées, vicieuses

alcoholics, uncultured, badly brought up, unbalanced, unstable, vulgar,
temperamental, (women) not comfortable with themselves, undergoing analysis, disturbed, neurotic, vice-ridden

The most common exclusions involve sexual orientation and gender
presentation. Masculine gender presentations are frequently the subject of
exclusions in the personal ads, but because the description of undesirable
attributes works by reference to symbols of masculinity rather than by objective criteria or self-definition, they are much harder to expose, discuss or
oppose than those concerning bisexuals, for example. Butches are widely
disliked by the French lesbian community if one takes the choices and exclusions listed by *Lesbia Magazine* personal ad writers as a guide to the
community's preferences. Terms referring to butches include:

(3)   masculines, jules, hommasses, garçonnes, camionneuses, catcheuses,
      armoires, lesbiennes du ghetto

masculine women, butches, (ugly) mannish women, boyish women,
truck drivers, women wrestlers, closets (i.e. women built like a
heavy piece of furniture), lesbians in the ghetto

While some of these terms refer explicitly to masculinity: *masculines, jules, garçonnes, hommasses,* others refer to traditionally male professions and activities in which few women are involved: *camionneuses, catcheuses.* These latter are not merely masculine pursuits, but also activities that increase muscle bulk and therefore connote working class status. It is specifically working class masculinity that is shunned, and not even working class masculinity per se, but its connotations and trappings, since the implicit assumption is that no men read or write ads in *Lesbia.*

The symbolic value of the term *camionneuses* is far greater than the actual number of women truck drivers in France. It is a social category meaning butch lesbians with connotations of heavy drinking, large biceps, frequent use of obscenities, lack of education, and ignorance of high culture. Since alcoholism, low education level and preference for popular culture are already covered by other exclusions: 'alcoolo, incultes, mal élevées' (alcoholics, uncultured and badly brought up women), their undesirability reinforced by the lists of positive qualities desired: 'bcbg, bon niveau culturel et scolaire, raffiné' (bon chic bon genre (dressy and classy), good cultural and educational level, refined), one needs to delve deeper to discover the motivation for the 'camionneuses s'abstenir' envoi which ends many ads. One particularly pointed letter to the editor implores, 'plus de tatouées, cloutées, épinglées, cammionneuses et autres' ((no) more tattooed, studded, safety-pinned woman, female truckies and others [February 1997, #157, p. 48]). 'Trolls' and 'gnomes' are also asked to keep away.

Terms which are unusual in themselves may be read in context as symbolizing femininity or masculinity. Thus the woman who is looking for a 'poids plume, mouche ou moyen' (featherweight, bantam weight or medium weight) is valuing slim feminine build over masculine strength. The *ourse mal léchée* (badly-licked she-bear) is asked not to respond to the *marmotte* 'marmot' (April 1997, #159, p. 45). The bear is considered not only uncultivated and blundering, but also aggressive and predatory, like a stereotypical man. Successful decoding of these ads depends on readers being acculturated into the dominant values of the personals where the feminine is prized and the masculine despised. (See Livia 1995 for discussion of representations of butch speech in literature; see Martine Caraglio 1997 for discussion of masculinity among French lesbians; see Judith Halberstam 1999 for discussion of female masculinity in general).

In contrast, stereotypically feminine pursuits and interests are encouraged. Adjectives like *douce* 'soft', *tendre* 'tender', *câline* 'caressing' are frequent. Ad writers often describe themselves as liking typically feminine activities: 'J'aime la nature-fleurs-animaux-l'eau-voyages-balades' ('I love nature-flowers-animals-water-traveling-strolling,' [November 2000, #198, p.

46]). The hyphenated spelling, which combines six nouns into one, demonstrates that these items are intended to be taken together to typify a life style rather than as discrete activities. The author is clearly not proposing big game hunting in Africa, followed by cyclone tracking on the Indian Ocean, with a side trip to a sub-Saharan cactus garden – pursuits which would also require a fondness for nature, animals, water and travel. Descriptions of the ideal mate are often just as impressionistic: 'cherche gazelle-tendre-douce-complice pour partager mots-saveur-rêves-épices-miel' ('seeking a tender-gentle-accommodating-gazelle to share words-tastes-dreams-spices-honey,' [November 2000, #198, p. 149]). This kind of non-classifying language permits readers to interpret the ads as referring to abstract values rather than concrete phenomenon. One could, for example, respond to the 'tender gazelle' ad even if one was allergic to honey and taking medication that eliminates dream-generating REM sleep, despite the writer's desire to share dreams and honey.

5 The Humble Keyboarder

The editors of the magazine get together every week to suggest witty, supportive, or gently critical rejoinders to the personal ads. To aid them in this task, they have created the personality of the *claviste* or keyboarder who just has to make a personal response as she types up the ads. The practice of giving the humble keyboarder, who performs the lowly grunt work of the magazine, a chance to express herself (in the form of evaluative comments in the ads she types) comes from the early days of *Libération*, the French left wing daily (interview with Catherine Gonnard, former editor of *Lesbia*, Paris, May 2000). In the late 1960s and early 1970s, when social unrest was seething in the streets of Paris, the *Libé* editors decided to give even typesetters a voice. The *Lesbia* editors have turned this technique around as the 'lowly keyboarder' most often represents the more powerful collective voice. According to Christine Lemoine,

> The NDCs are a way of taking a little distance from the seriousness of 90% of the ads both for the writers of the ads and for the readers. What most of the readers didn't know [. . .] is that 'NDC' is not one person (la claviste) but several and that over the same period, even at the same time, two or three or more could write NDCs. I remember at the proof-reading sessions, everybody would suggest NDCs and it was really funny. (Personal communication via email, March 2000).

The process of composition of NDCs is, according to this description, a lighthearted, humorous affair, a communal undertaking intended to present a divergent point of view in a non-antagonistic way. Just as the myth that the ads are created for, and read exclusively by, the writer's unique soulmate, is shattered by the presence of the intrusive NDCs, so Lemoine's account of how the NDCs are really composed exposes the fiction of the lonely claviste who relieves her own solitude by responding, cryptically, to the ads.

The NDCs themselves perform various functions. They point out good matches between the ads, indicating that a writer should check out another ad in the same edition; they offer supportive comments to writers who confess to negatively regarded qualities; they make puns and other verbal jokes; and they provide covert criticism of the lists of exclusions cited above. Each one of these activities serves as community glue. Matching lesbians up with each other helps create smaller units within the larger community. Supporting writers who describe themselves as plump, as in the following example:

(4)   Femme 36 ans, cheveux longs, <<confortable>> physiquement (dodue, quoi! Ça y est, je l'ai dit) (NDC: Mais oui, n'ayons pas peur des mots)

       Woman, 36, long hair, <<comfortable>> physically, (plump, even! There you go, I said it) (NDC: Yes indeed, let's not be afraid of words) [November 1988, #66, p. 36]

promotes an ideal of a supportive community in which each member is accepted and valued despite having a less than perfect body.

6   Articulating the Stereotype

The NDC often uses puns and other jokes to point out an incongruous use of words or an odd coincidence:

(5)   Je veux et j'exige (NDC: dites-le 10 fois de suite et vous verrez si vous zozotez)

       I want and I demand (NDC: say that ten times in succession and then see if you don't end up lisping) [December 1996, #155, p. 49]

The writer of (5) is being a little too insistent in her search for her ideal love. The NDC's comment that if she repeated the phrase 'je veux et j'exige' ten times it would make her lisp, is a veiled criticism of her language use, a particularly appropriate intervention because lispers are not considered highly effective or authoritative speakers. It works against a background belief in the French lesbian community that one should seek but not demand a sexual partner. Furthermore, it plays off a masculine stereotype against a feminine one: men demand, women lisp. By warning the ad writer of the danger of lisping, the NDC subtly reinforces an ideal of masculinity elsewhere derided.

(6)   Q68-75 et petite ceinture (NDC: jaune ou noire?)

> Q Haut-Rhin-Paris and little belt, ie surrounding area) (NDC: yellow or black?) [April 2000, #192, p. 48]

The humor of (6) comes from the pun on the word 'ceinture' which means both 'surrounding area' (the writer's meaning) and 'belt.' The NDC's question as to whether the belt is yellow or black is a shorthand reference to the fact that many lesbians have taken up karate and judo. Since judo is traditionally a masculine activity, this works as a subtle acceptance of 'masculine' lesbians.

The criticism of 's'abstenir' clauses works in a similar way. The NDCs tend to be oblique, requiring the reader to work to decode them.

(7)   M26

> Femme cérébralement masculine, cherche de 30 à 45 ans amie sérieuse, douce. 43 ans, sensible aime nature, sport, ciné, désire rencontrer sur toutes régions amie fidèle, sensible tendre masculine, bi, alcoolo, androgyne s'abstenir (NDC: Où se trouve le point entre vos désirs et vos aversions? Moi je sais pas).

> Intellectually masculine woman, seeking serious partner 30 to 45 years old, gentle. Forty-three years, sensitive, love nature, sport, movies, want to meet faithful partner, sensitive tender masculine, bisexual, alcoholic, androgynous refrain from responding (NDC: Where is the boundary between your desires and your aversions? I can't tell). [November 1992, #110, p. 47]

In (7), the writer has created a long list of desirable qualities she is looking for in her ideal match. The person who responds should be faithful, sensitive and tender (three non-classifying, entirely subjective adjectives which are so often used in *Lesbia* ads that they have become clichés). The next four adjectives pose a problem: she is not looking for someone who is androgynous, for the exclusionary imperative 's'abstenir' appears immediately after this word. But what about a masculine, bisexual alcoholic? As the NDC points out, it is unclear where she draws the line between her ideal and her worst fear. A more subtle reading of the NDC is that there is in fact no line, the idealized and the despised are not that far apart, are in fact, closely imbricated. The writer describes herself as 'cerebrally masculine' so we can assume that masculinity, however defined, is not a category she automatically excludes. If masculinity is not excluded, how can androgyny be excluded? For a woman to have qualities deemed masculine is per se to appear androgynous. As for bisexuality and alcoholism, they are sandwiched between the two mentions of gender deviation, as though they were similar qualities.

This reading is born out by intertextual reference to other ads in which the exclusion is written as one multi-hyphenated word:

(8)   Amour-Tendresse

Non fumeuses-camionneuses-alcoolo-névrosées s'abstenir.

Non smokers-truck-drivers-alcoholics-neurotics refrain from responding. [June 1999, #183, p. 49]

What exactly is the role of the negative 'non' in this (dis)qualifier? Are all the nouns ruled by it, or only smokers? Must one be a non-smoker and a non-truck driver in order to be disqualified? Is the writer desperately seeking a smoker who drives a truck? Another ad writer states who she is looking for, what she is like herself, and then gives her list of exclusions in multi-hyphenated text:

(9)   Toi mignonne- très- féminine- chaleureuse- sensuelle- coquette- douce-
équil [...] tu veux F trentaine-mignonne-fém.-sensible-non bi. Pas
stables-opportunistes-vulgaires-masc.: non!

You cute-very-feminine-warm-sensual-coquettish-gentle-balanced [...]
you want 30 yr old W-cute-fem.-sensitive-not bi. Not stable-
opportunistic-vulgar-masc.: no! [June 1999, #183, p. 46]

What is the role of the dual negative in (9), the preposed 'pas' and the postposed 'non'? Do they cancel each other out, encouraging unstable vulgar masculine lesbians to reply? Or do they work like the traditional verbal bi-partite negatives 'ne' 'pas,' enclosing the matter to be negated? The ambiguity in meaning is resolved by the context: readers of (9) have already been exposed to hundreds of other *Lesbia* personal ads and know that vulgarity and masculinity are not highly prized qualities in an ideal part-ner. However, obliging readers to rely on context rather than the text itself also serves to reinforce the message which the NDCs are striving to im-part: that each ad, each lesbian seeking her soulmate, participates in a sys-tem of value-making which has repercussions for the whole of the *Lesbia* community.

Elsewhere, the NDC warns writers against responding to ads which are incompatible with their stated desires or descriptions:

(10) T46

> Qui la trentaine serait intéressée par création en moyenne montagne d'un commerce en camionnette (NDC: pas T44, elle aime pas les camionneuses!)

> Who in her thirties would be interested in creating a minivan company in the mountains? (NDC: Not T44, she doesn't like women truck drivers!) [May 1996, #149, p. 46]

The humor of the NDC in (10), revolves around the pun on 'camionnette' and 'camionneuses.' The writer of T46 is suggesting a serious business proposition selling minivans in a mountainous region. The writer of T44 has specifically excluded 'camionneuses' from responding to her ad. By drawing a parallel between the two, the NDC forces readers to think of the useful, practical side of owning and driving trucks. This is a frequent theme in NDCs which attempt to reinvest the term 'camionneuses' with its classifying, non-evaluative meaning. Another ad writer describes her desire for a 'super copine' (super girlfriend), repeating the term 'super' four times:

(11) Besoin d'une super copine pas super star mais super gentille, super (NDC: le diesel est plus économique) complice pour dialogues.

> Need a super girlfriend, not a super star but super nice, super (NDC: diesel is more economical) complicit/understanding to talk to. [September 1999, #185, p.46]

The writer of (11) has not mentioned trucks or truck drivers, yet the NDC draws readers' attention to the second meaning of 'super,' a type of gasoline which is more expensive than the diesel used exclusively in trucks. At first reading, this remark is completely irrelevant, but on a deeper level, it provides positive value to the idea of the truck driver, suggesting that the 'super' girlfriend might turn out to be butch and therefore, perhaps, more 'economical' in emotional terms.

The editors' official stance is that they wish neither to promote nor to exclude masculine lesbians. It is in the realm of gender norms, as we have seen, that the most direct confrontations occur between the ad writers and the infamous NDCs. Usually these take the form of pointing out contradictions inherent in the ad writers' position:

(12) Valeurs morales appréciées. Pas sérieuses-bi-masculines s'abstenir. (L'exclusion, ce n'est pas trop moral. NDC.)

> Good moral values appreciated. If you're not serious, bisexual or masculine, refrain from replying. (Exclusion is not very 'moral'. NDC.) [July-August 2000, #195, p. 44]

In (12), the ad writer states a preference for women with high moral values. The NDC uses this ethical attitude to point out the moral failing of discrimination and prejudice.

(13) Masculine-bi s'abstenir mais tt le reste (NDC: oui mais de beaux restes!) apprécié.

Masculine-bi refrain from replying but all the rest (NDC: yes, but what fine (sad) leftovers) appreciated. [July-August 2000, #195, p. 48]

The NDC which interrupts the flow of this ad by its insertion between noun and adjective (reste apprécié) is particularly interesting in its use of irony. The NDC comments that those who are permitted to reply to the ad, i.e. those not specifically excluded by the provision that bisexuals and masculine lesbians keep away, may consider themselves 'de beaux restes' (fine leftovers). However, this phrase begs an ironic reading since it is part of the meaning of the term 'leftover' that the best has already been consumed. Fine leftovers are, per se, dried up and useless leavings. It would take substantial pragmatic unmarking for the phrase to have a sincere interpretation. The use of irony is always significant in any study of community building since irony assumes (and requires) a homogeneous set of members who are able to read both the sincere surface message and its ironic—usually opposite—intended meaning.

7   Communities of Practice

As Eckert and McConnell-Ginet observe, a community of practice is formed when 'an aggregate of people come together around a mutual engagement in an endeavor.' When such a community forms, 'ways of doing things, ways of talking, beliefs, values, power relations emerge' (1992:463-464). As well as being a nexus of social identity, they argue that language is also a site of struggle and a producer of social relations (ibid). According to this definition, the readers and writers of *Lesbia Magazine* ads form a community of practice. In formulating their ads, and announcing their preferences, the writers are both participating in an existing social network, and disseminating its values.

The ads create a fiction of addressing only the unique individual with whom the writer wishes to spend the rest of her days. The use of *tu* (*you* singular) is frequent, as may be seen in the following: 'Je rêve de t'aimer. Je te désire féminine belle-douce-affectueuse. Je ne peux plus vivre sans toi' (I dream of loving you. I want you feminine beautiful-soft-affectionate. I can no longer live without you. [November 2000, #198, p. 50]). Although this ad is, supposedly, written only for the eyes of the idealized 'tu', it is interpreted as representing a community which prefers its women to be 'feminine beautiful-soft-affectionate.' It is this, wider, community meaning which explains the constant interjections of the NDCs which reinforce or contest the values inherent in the ad.

8   The Personal of the Month: Covert Pedagogy

The NDCs are not the only form of comment from the *Lesbia* collective, they are merely the most explicit in their criticism. *Lesbia* has created a special box for the *P.A. du mois* (personal of the month) to highlight the values prized by the collective and espoused by the magazine. These ads are chosen because of their lack of explicit exclusions and their broadening of the community conception of the desirable to include older lesbians, lesbians from outside Europe, and lesbians without financial resources, as the following examples illustrate:

(14)   Célibataire retraitée souhaite rencontrer femme de plus de 65 ans.

> Single retired woman wants to meet woman over 65. [October 2000, #197, p. 44]

The 'Célibataire retraitée' ad has been picked out purely because of its validation of women over sixty-five as sexual and romantic objects. The language is simple and straight forward, using no metaphors or non-classifying terms. It serves as a model in this covert heuristic operation which seeks to teach, by example, what type of ads are acceptable.

(15)   Recherche vieille fille apathique, de préférence vulgaire égocentrique et fauchée.

> Looking for an apathetic old maid, preferably vulgar, egocentric and broke. [January 1997, #156, p. 44].

The 'vieille fille apathique' ad has been chosen for its humor and its ironic criticism of ad writers who privilege rich, highly educated and culturally elitist women as in the following: 'Couple 40ans BCBG-bon niveau sociocult. Lance un appel aux femmes de qualité' (40 year old couple, well dressed, well-bred, good sociocultural level, launches an appeal to women of quality. [November 2000, #198, p. 46]). Since adjectives like *vulgaire, égocentrique* and *fauchée* (broke) depend almost entirely on one personal tastes and preferences, it is just as hard to find someone one can classify as vulgar as to decide definitively that a person is not vulgar.

(16) Métisee noire à main verte, commence à voir tout rouge dans un monde un peu trop gris. Parlez-moi tout bleu, je cesserai de rire jaune et verrai la vie en rose.

Black woman of mixed race with green thumb, is beginning to see red in a world that is a bit too grey. Tell me fairy tales (blue stories) and I'll stop laughing sardonically and see the world through rose-colored glasses. [March 1999, #180, p. 45]

The 'Métisee noire à main verte' ad has been selected for its humor, its punning use of color adjectives and its validation of the Black woman of mixed race as an appropriate judge of lesbian values. Women who place ads in *Lesbia Magazine* are both vulnerable, in that they present themselves as in need of companionship, and also powerful, since they decide which qualities are preferred and which denigrated, at least in the highly visible realm of the ad. This writer has followed the lead set by the wording of the NDCs and makes readers stop and consider both the denotative and the connotative meanings of highly charged terms. By lining up the descriptor 'noire' with other metaphorical color expressions like seeing red, looking out on a grey world, and wearing rose-colored glasses, she makes the reader aware of its literal and figurative meanings.

(17) Amoureuse de l'Orient, sa lumière-ses-splendeurs-ses poètes, débutante en arabe.

Woman in love with the East, its light-its-splendor-its poets, learning Arabic. [November 2000, #198, p. 46]

The 'Amoureuse de l'Orient' ad has been picked because it places high value on a region often despised by racist sections of the French lesbian community: the East. This East is not merely a geographical location, however, but a mythology in the Barthesian sense (1957). This is the east of light, splendor and poets. To appreciate this east more fully, the ad writer is learning Arabic. However, most Arabic speakers in France come not from the east, but from the south, that is to say the African Maghreb: Morocco, Tunisia and Algeria, a region often considered poor and uncivilized, without intellectual lights or great poets, as may be seen from *Lesbia Magazine's* own dismissive phrase 'commandos du grand sud.' Thus we can say that the personal ads are not only a site of struggle between writers and the collective, but also a locus in which inherent and unacknowledged contradictions are laid bare.[1]

---

[1] Although racism in personal ads has not been the main focus of this chapter, it is clear that here too there exists an unwritten policy of so far and no further. Many lesbians of color do

9 Boundary Policing

It is noticeable that the personal ad of the month never showcases ads which are positively seeking masculine lesbians (although these do occasionally appear in the main body of the ad section). Indeed, if the *Lesbia* collective feels an ad writer has erred too far along the gender continuum toward masculine identification, the NDC may intervene to question the writer's intentions as may be seen in the following:

(18) Je cherche la femme de ma vie: vraie lesbienne libre, tendre, virile. (NDC: c'est une femme ou un homme que vous cherchez?)

I am looking for the woman of my life: a truly free lesbian, tender, virile. (NDC: are you looking for a man or a woman?) [April 1997, #159, p. 44]

Since the ad writer has already stated that she is looking for a woman, from a purely informational standpoint it is unnecessary to ask which sex she seeks. But, as we have seen, little in these ads, apart from department code and box number, is intended to provide information of a factual sort. The *Lesbia* collective, acting as arbiters for the French lesbian community—in all its fractious unity—and using the NDC as its voice, is questioning the ad writer's definition of a 'truly free lesbian' as virile, and objecting by its explicit question about gender, that virility is a quality only men possess. In this way, the NDC functions to police the boundary line and ensure that Lesbia readers stay on the feminine side of it.

10 Overt Censorship

Recently, the editorial team of *Lesbia* decided to refuse ads they considered too exclusionary [January 2000, #189, p.46]. There have been many protests against this policy by readers, asking the editors not to censure the content of the ads [March 2000, #191, p. 42]. This move on the part of the editors represents a big change in direction from the witty, oblique comments of the NDC or the positive reinforcement at work in the choice of the personal of

---

advertise in *Lesbia*, typically portraying themselves with short, factual descriptors: *lesbienne martiniquaise cherche idem* (Martiniquan lesbian seek similar) or by reference to colors, smells or foods from their (ancestral) homelands such as *canelle* (cinnamon), or *couleur-thé-au-jasmin* (color of Jasmine tea). However, as we saw from the *Lesbia* editors' response to the protest by the *lesbiennes des migrations* (migrant lesbians) against the presence of a racist bar owner at a film festival, the anti-racist work of the magazine does not include support for direct political action against its own activities.

the month. It also suggests a lack of understanding of the role these exclusions play. Despite years of covert criticism from the untiring NDC, writers of personal ads have continued to end their descriptions with a coda of 's'abstenir.' In the fantasy created by the ad, only one person is a true match for the writer. The positive description of desired qualities should be enough for this 'match' to recognize herself, thus exclusions are unnecessary. One needs to ask what role these exclusions play at both the microlevel of the ad, and at the macrolevel of the *Lesbia* community.

The *Lesbia* editors find the exclusions 'discriminatory,' but searching for one's life partner necessarily involves discrimination. Although serial monogamy is the most common lesbian pattern, the fantasy remains of a single life partner. Few writers advertise for what Carol Queen, the San Francisco Bay 'sexpert' calls 'Miss Right Now,' they are looking for Miss Right. Indeed, 'baiseuses à tout vent' (women who fuck around) is also a common exclusion. It is only when one sees the ads as building blocks for the community as a whole that either the list of exclusions or the refusal to publish them make sense. The romantic vision of the 'longue balade sentimentale dans totale complicité' (long sentimental stroll perfectly in synch [November 1992, #100, p. 47]) is a metaphor not only of a relationship but also of the lesbian community. The ad writers are rejecting butches not just from their bed but from their community—this at least is the logic behind the recent decision to exclude the exclusions. But, at the same time as the ad writers attempt again and again to banish butches, the spectral butch keeps returning to the intimate realm of the ad. This is an internalisation of the non-lesbian world and its hatred of lesbians; those who are most virulent in their anti-butch stance also declare themselves to be 'hors ghetto' (outside the lesbian ghetto) 'ne fréquentant pas le milieu' (not frequenting the lesbian milieu), but they remain fascinated by what they see in this milieu, and what shocks, revolts and attracts them most is masculinity in women. This complex, homophobic reaction is unlikely to be susceptible to overt censorship; the banning of the ads is not simply heavy-handed, it doesn't tackle the real problem. The NDCs, in contrast, keep the dialogue going so that values can be contested, clarified and created by all participants.

11 Conclusion

As Judith Halberstam (1998) has pointed out, masculinity is not the exclusive property of men, nor have men been the only sex to refine and define its meaning. It is evident from the way gender markers are used, contested and refined in personal ads in *Lesbia Magazine* that the community created by these readers, writers and editors is involved in a heated debate about the value of lesbian masculinity. Although classism, ageism, cultural bias and other prejudices appear in the ads—reflecting the intimate desires of their writers—they are often countered by the NDCs. The status of 'personal ad of the month' is awarded to the ad which best reflects the values of the magazine and the community it sees itself as serving. This provides another space in which to criticise ageist or racist attitudes, by displaying an oppositional value system, often humorously phrased.

The case of anti-masculine ads is more attenuated. Some types of lesbian masculinity is prized (Livia 2001, forthcoming) especially those representing high class status such as the *garçonne*, the *dandy* or the Romaine Brooks lookalike [September 1998, #174, p. 49]). Working class masculinity is widely despised, as may be seen in responses to the diesel dyke, the woman wrestler (catcheuse) or the kitchen dresser (armoire). Although the NDCs comment negatively on the exclusion of masculine lesbians, the editors evidently feel there is a limit on how masculine a lesbian can be and still be welcome in the French lesbian community.

References

Barthes, Roland. 1957. *Mythologies*. Paris: Seuil.

Caraglio, Martine. 1997. Les lesbiennes dites 'masculines', ou quand la masculinité n'est qu'un paysage. *Nouvelles Questions Féministes* 18:57-74.

Eckert, Penelope and Sally McConnell-Ginet. 1992. Think Practically, Look Locally: Language and Gender as a Community-Based Practice. *Annual Review of Anthropology*, 21: 461-490.

Halberstam, Judith. 1999. *Female Masculinity*. Raleigh, NC.: Duke University Press.

Livia, Anna. 1995. I Ought to Throw a Buick at You: Fictional Representations of Butch/Femme Speech. *Gender Articulated: Language and the Socially Constructed Self*, ed. Kira Hall and Mary Bucholtz, 245-278. New York: Routledge.

Livia, Anna. 2001. Forthcoming. Les camionneuses et les dandies: Sexualité, genre et classe. *Attirances: Lesbiennes fems, Lesbiennes butchs*, ed. Christine Lemoine and Ingrid Renard, 122-137. Paris: Editions gaies et lesbiennes.

13

Identity and Script Variation: Japanese Lesbian and Housewife Letters to the Editor

HEIDI FRANK

2 Introduction

In 1992, 1,200 lesbian, gay and bisexual Japanese marched in the First Lesbian and Gay Parade in Tokyo. Attendees watched as women kissed each other in the streets as a demonstration of their pride in being queer (Summerhawk et al. 1998). While events such as this demonstrate the possible beginnings of the acceptance of sexual diversity in Japan, it does not mean that being openly lesbian is without its serious social repercussions.

Many lesbians, gays and bisexuals in Japan live their lives in the closet. For lesbians, however, the possibility of coming out is even less an option not only because of social isolation but because of low economic status. Even in Ni-Chome, the gay district of Tokyo, there are only 10 lesbian bars as compared to the 200 - 300 gay bars, shops and businesses. This disparity reflects the fact that women in Japan make significantly less money than men and so have less disposable income. In addition, a single woman usually lives with her parents, who often limit their daughters' movement. If a

Language and Sexuality: Contesting Meaning in Theory and Practice.
Kathryn Campbell-Kibler, Robert J. Podesva, Sarah J. Roberts and Andrew Wong (eds.).
Copyright © 2001, CSLI Publications.

lesbian does marry a man,[1] she does not usually have the freedom to frequent bars as her husband does, a restriction that increases with children.

Events such as the First Lesbian and Gay Parade and weekend retreats, organized for and by lesbians, provide women with a chance to meet other lesbians, get emotional support, and plan future activities. However, these weekends are attended by only about 30-80 women per weekend. Contrariwise, one lesbian periodical, *Labrys* (the predecessor to *Labrys Dash* discussed here) has a readership of about 1,600 (Summerhawk et al. 1998). Lesbian periodicals, like those in this paper, that circulate in Japan function to provide women, especially those in rural areas, with lesbian contact and a means for establishing a lesbian identity apart from the negative stereotypes of the larger society. Lesbian periodicals print articles on topics like monogamy vs. polygamy, give advice and print letters and life stories by readers.

Housewives in Japan follow a seemingly more traditional path than lesbians. As in many cultures, most adult women in Japan are married. Although 'love marriage' is becoming more popular, some women (or their families) still choose a marriage partner based on factors such as his family background or career prospects. Many women marry due to social pressures and economic problems single women face, especially in rural areas (Ishino and Wakabayashi 1996).

Once a woman has chosen to become a housewife, she may have a period of time (most likely before having children or taking care of aging parents) with relatively more free time. Many women take classes and through these form social networks.[2] In addition, many women take on part-time work outside the home. However, Japanese housewives with children or aging parents to care for often become isolated from their social networks. In much the same way as the lesbian periodicals discussed above, housewife periodicals like *Suteki na Okusan* and *Fujin no Tomo*, provide housewives with contact with other housewives. In these periodicals, women tell their life story, write a letter, or provide insights into organizing the domestic space. While these periodicals reinforce stereotypes of the Japanese housewife as domestically concerned or as balancing career and family, they also provide a space to express their views and negotiate identity.

---

[1] A 1989 survey of lesbians in Japan found that 25% of the women surveyed were in a heterosexual marriage. (This does not present a problem for my analysis, as I suggest individuals present themselves differently as they occupy different roles.)

[2] The school where I worked in Japan had 'housewife' classes that met during the afternoons. Some of the women in these classes also socialized outside of school. One woman, who cared for her aging in-law, often did not socialize outside of class and often complained about her isolation.

Given the important role of periodicals to lesbians and housewives in Japan, this paper will explore how these groups use this space as a means of negotiating their identity and sexuality. In particular, how do these women utilize the Japanese writing system to this end? The Japanese writing system consists of three main scripts (see Table 1). The meanings associated with each are available to both groups: Kanji is associated with erudition, the hiragana syllabary with traditional Japanese and female, and the katakana syllabary with modernity and, I argue, lesbian identity. I argue in this paper that the historical situating of the two syllabaries can be tied to the ideologies they index.

2 Script Isomorphism and Indexicality

2.1 Double meaning: extension and intension

Emile Benveniste (1985) posits that language is the only sign system that exhibits two discrete 'modes of meaning' or 'double meaning'. The first of these is *semiotic* meaning referring to the inter-connection of signs or 'the intrasystematic domain'. For example, *table* is recognized as different from *fable* by virtue of each word's semiotic meaning. By contrast, Benveniste calls *semantic* meaning that which serves to link the sign with the world outside. The link exists between an agreed upon referent of a sign (e.g., an actual tree) and the sign itself (e.g., *tree*). Semantic meaning allows for the indexing of socially created meaning through the understanding of the sign.

Similarly, scripts also possess double meaning: *extensional* and *intensional*. The extension of a grapheme is the language the script represents. Two scripts can be said to be co-extensional if and only if they share the same object language. By contrast, the intension of a grapheme or script is those features or segments of the object language that it represents. These features may be tonal, intonational, lexical, morphemic, etc. Scripts, such as cursive and print in American English, have a reciprocal relationship that can be termed *isomorphic*. That is, they are both co-extensional and co-intensional. Why would a language support two or more isomorphic scripts? One reason is that isomorphic scripts can index different contexts of usage.

In written Japanese, it is necessary to utilize up to four scripts in a text. These four scripts are exemplified in Table 1 below.

Katakana	キ セツ	Kanji	季 節
Hiragana	き せつ	Romaji	ki setsu

Table 1. Japanese Scripts for 'season'

In the Japanese mixed system of writing, all four scripts are co-extensional. However, since hiragana and katakana are also syllabic, they are also co-intensional and, thus, isomorphic. From this point, the discussion will center on these two isomorphic Japanese syllabaries.

Given that hiragana and katakana are isomorphic and following the above theory of script isomorphism, a differential relationship from these scripts to societal ideas they index should also exist. However, before discussing the indexicality of the Japanese syllabaries, I will briefly summarize the present state of scripts and script usage in Japanese.

2.2 The Japanese writing system: an overview

The Japanese writing system, as stated above, comprises four scripts: kanji, romaji, hiragana, and katakana. Because these scripts are co-extensional, they can be used to represent the same word. At the sentential level, all scripts may appear in a single sentence, but each plays a somewhat different role. Due to script co-occurrence at this level the Japanese writing system is referred to as a mixed system.

(1)　Hiroko の　　友 達　は　うどん と　ピザ が　　好き です。
　　　Hiroko no　　tomodachi wa　udon　to　piza ga　　suki desu.
　　　Hiroko GEN[3] friend　　TOP　udon　and pizza NOM like　COP
　　　'Hiroko's friend likes pizza and udon.'

In example (1), 友達 'friend' is written in kanji, うどん 'udon' and function words are in hiragana. ピザ 'Pizza' is represented in katakana and 'Hiroko' in romaji. 好き 'like' employs a mixture of kanji and hiragana.

Each of the Japanese scripts occupies a general domain of use. The following is the canonical usage of each category. Kanji is used to represent Japanese and Sino-Japanese lexical items. Katakana is employed predominantly for loanwords, but also for onomatopoeia and emphasis. Hiragana is used in the representation of Japanese vocabulary, function words, and inflectional endings. Romaji is used for emphasis, acronyms and for decorative purposes. However, some variation does occur as is evident in the analysis section of this paper.

2.3 Japanese syllabaries and indexicality

In the contemporary Japanese writing system, there is evidence that hiragana and katakana may work to index identity. More specifically, an historical analysis of hiragana and katakana suggests that the former script indexes

---

[3] Abbreviations used throughout this paper: GEN - genitive, TOP - topic, NOM - nominative, COP - copula, CONN - connective form, LOC - dative/locative.

notions of 'traditional' Japanese identity and the female, while the latter indexes modernity and lesbian identity. These proposed associations are products of modern Japanese culture and constitute only some contexts that may participate in an indexical relationship with these two scripts. The bases for these indexical relationships begin in the Meiji era (1868-1912), a time when much of the world was confronting issues of national identity. As a symbol of national identity, a language more often than a writing system fills this role. However, in nineteenth century Japan, orthographic, linguistic, and national communities were the same entity.

In 1854, just after the emergence of the modern nation-state in Europe, Westerners again came to Japan, bringing with them their form of national consciousness (Anderson 1991).[4] By 1868, just fourteen years after the arrival of Commodore Perry to Japan, the Tokugawa Shogunate had been overthrown by opposing interests within it. The new government embarked upon a campaign of cultural borrowing with a push to Westernize politically, economically, and socially. However, some Japanese felt as if their newly acquired modern identity was not their own. This discontent was exacerbated by the parallel devaluation of things Japanese (e.g. aesthetics, literature) by the government, the West, and sectors of Japanese society (Pyle 1969).

At the turn of the century, bolstered by wars in China (1894-1895) and with Russia (1904-1905), nationalism based in pre-Meiji Japanese culture was on the rise. The new centralized government, mass media, universal education, and military conquest served to consolidate Japan into a nation-state (Inoue 1994). Some influential journalistic elites, seeking to define Japan and Japanese identity, formed a group known as *Seikyohsha* 'society for political education'. Miyake Setsurei and Shiga Shigetaka of the *Seikyohsha* movement pointed to Heian era literature written by women as a component of Japanese identity. Shiga stated, '[Japan's] foundation is in harmony, which is the source of art.... We have the writing of Murasaki Shikibu....' (Pyle 1969:68-69).

Japanese women's writing became a popular literary genre around 1895 with the publication of a special issue of *Bungei Kurabu* 'Literary Club' entitled 'Women's Fiction'. The category was further fixed with the 1901 publication of *A History of Women's Literature,* which tied together literature written by women of the Heian era through the Edo era, placing the literature from these disparate periods in the same genre (Ericson 1996).

During this period, the indexical relationship of Japanese traditional identity with Heian era women and their literature was established. The women's literature of the Heian era was written predominantly in hiragana

---

[4] Portuguese Jesuit missionaries were the first to come, between 1542 and 1637.

and was known as *onnade* 'woman's hand'. Therefore, I suggest that hiragana participates in this indexical relationship not only with Japanese traditional identity but also with the female[5]. Although the literature of the later periods in *A History of Women's Literature* utilized kanji and katakana, this new historic literary genre reinforced the hiragana's indexical ties with Japanese identity and the female by the important inclusion of Heian era literature and by the continued view of this literature as Japanese classics. The definition of Japanese identity through its classical women writers and Japanese women also gained support from the state's efforts to create a unique and unified Japan.

Almost concurrent with historicization of Japanese women's writing and hiragana, the government further solidified the indexical relationship between hiragana and Japanese identity. Japanese leaders 'came to recognize that what was needed in the wake of the tremendous social upheavals following the Meiji Restoration was the fashioning and refining of that language into an instrument which would serve the nation ... as a focus of national pride, an element in a sense of nationalism' (Twine 1991:9). These reforms were partly brought about by the Gembun'itchi movement of the Meiji era. This movement sought to reduce the number of Chinese characters in use and unify Japanese speech and writing through development and standardization of colloquial style (*kohgotai*). This style consisted of a kanji/hiragana orthography based on the Tokyo dialect.

By the early 1900s Gembun'itchi was able to achieve its major goal: 'From this time on, with Ministry blessing, classical styles [in kanji-katakana mixed script] began to disappear from textbooks...and colloquial style gradually became the normal mode of expression' (Twine 1991:171). It should also be noted that in April 1946, the era of kanji-katakana mixed script in official documents also began to decline. In the MacArthur Japanese Constitution, the kanji-hiragana mixed orthography system was employed because it was considered to be the language of the Japanese people, so more appropriate for the new Japanese democratic system (Inoue 1991).

Through this brief history of hiragana, I suggest the indexical relationship between Heian women writers and national identity was created and expanded to a relationship in which hiragana indexes national identity and the female.

Katakana, as the isomorphic pair of hiragana, should also have an indexical relationship within Japanese society. This indexical relationship stems from the use of katakana for the representation of foreign words. To-

---

[5] It was pointed out that this indexical relationship between hiragana and the female can be seen in women's names, which may be assigned Chinese characters or hiragana, while men's names appear in Chinese characters.

day, Japanese contains thousands of loanwords. They have come not only from English but also languages such as French, German, and Portuguese. However, given the strong English language influences in Japan and the rise of English usage in international contexts, more loanwords are English in origin than any other single language.

Japanese	Transliteration	Translation	
		Lending Language	English
ズボン	zubon	jupon (French)	trousers, pants
パン	pan	pao (Portuguese)	bread
コレポン	korepon	correspondence (English)	correspondence
レスビアン	lesubian	lesbian (English)	lesbian

Table 2. Loanword Examples

Traditionally, katakana had been used to represent words more or less phonetically. Katakana was used to annotate Chinese texts with pronunciation guides. It was intended to reflect actual speech, moderately similar to the phonetic alphabet. Today, the main usage for katakana is in representing the many loanwords. Through this usage in representing loanwords, most of which are English in origin, katakana has come to index notions of modernity. I further argue, in section 3, for the role of the Japanese women's liberation movement in the 1970s in connecting modernity and lesbian identity, which created an extended indexicality between katakana and lesbian identity.

These indexical relationships associated with hiragana and katakana, then, should find some realization in writings of native speakers. In order to demonstrate the proposed indexicality, a study, similar to one conducted by Smith and Schmidt (1996), was carried out.

3   Script Indexicality in Practice: Subject Groups and Texts

In this study, texts from two lesbian periodicals (*Labrys Dash* and *TypeMx*) and two popular women's periodicals (*Suteki na Okusan* 'The Ideal Housewife' and *Fujin no Tomo* 'The Women's Friendship Society') were examined. The lesbian and what I term *housewife* groups were chosen because they seem to represent two ideologically divergent groups of women in Japanese society and so appear likely to exhibit differing script proportions.

Housewives and lesbians in Japan, I argue, represent divergent groups of women due to their historical positioning within Japanese culture. The notion of the 'Good Wife and Wise Mother' (GWWM), which has long been linked with the housewife, has its beginnings in the Edo era. During this period, this ideology supported women's education and increased their power in the household. In the Meiji era, however, this ideology was re-molded by the Ministry of Education, incorporating Neo-Confucianist ideas popular at the time, it became a tool for socializing women to 'mothering as the principal gendered role' (Ramusack and Sievers 1999:200). This role of child raiser and educator was situated as not only important to the family, but necessary to the development of a modern society (Koyama 1994). In post-World War I Japan, good wives and wise mothers were masters of the household responsible for the domestic sphere. In addition, under pressure from the new women's movement, the government encouraged women to work outside the home to the extent that it did not interfere with their duties as housewife. Women welcomed this change in their role as it elevated their position in the family to arguably equal with their husbands'.

While these reformulations of the GWWM ideology created a more or less favorable situation for Japanese women, today it is the Meiji reformulation that affects many women in Japan adversely. From a social perspective, there remains significant pressure to marry and have children. As stated in Koyama (1994:31), 'Today we cannot say that the image of the 'good wife and wise mother' is a thing of the past. Although the number of employed women is increasing, women are still primarily called upon to fulfill the roles of housekeeper, wife and mother.' In at least one rural area, women who are single after the age of 30 are called *katawa* 'deformed' (Ishino and Wakabayashi, 1996). From an economic view, women in Japan make on average 60% of what men do (Summerhawk et al. 1998). Because financial independence is not available, they are left with few choices for their future. By leaving women with few options but to conform to the tra-ditional role of women in Japan, the historically based GWWM ideology remains a strong influence on present day Japanese women.

The historical positioning of the modern lesbian movement in Japan finds its roots in the Women's Liberation movement of the 1970s (Ishino and Wakabayashi 1996). However, the Women's Liberation movement was not new to Japan in the 1970s. First Wave Feminism, engendered by the women's suffrage movement in the West, reached the shores of Japan in the years surrounding 1920. During this time, there was a significant influx of women's liberation theories from the West, such as Ellen Key, Charlotte Perkins Gilman. In addition, Japanese women had proved useful as workers outside the domestic sphere during the recently ended World War I. 'In 1918-19, four women, Yosan Akiko, Hiratsuka Raicho, Yamakawa Kikue, and Yamada Waka ... [set] forth the basic argument for female liberation.' (Koyama 1994:35). The concurrent process of modernization, which had begun during the Meiji era, brought together the process of modernization with what it meant to be a modern Japanese woman (i.e., child educator, wife, worker). At this time, female liberation and the GWWM ideology did not have the conflictory nature it can have today. However, as discussed above, reformulations of this ideology were not able to adapt to the new ideas infused by the feminism of the 1970s such as equal employment and birth control. I argue that, with Second Wave Feminism in the 1970s, the links between modernity, the West and feminism persisted and were reinforced due to the origination of this Second Wave, like the First Wave at the time of modernization in Japan, in the West. In addition, because the lesbian movement came out of this Second Wave Feminism, lesbian identity also became tied up with notions of modernity and, by extension, can be indexed by katakana.

Lesbians today predominately occupy a different place in society than housewives. Because the nature of the lesbian couple does not conform to traditional views of the family and most likely excludes children as a necessary component, it threatens the notion of the traditional family in a culture where 'the 'family' plays a central role in everyone's life' (Summerhawk et al. 1998:5). In addition, the media has painted a picture of lesbians as very different from the stereotypical housewife. They are described as 'women who want to be men' and portrayed on TV as foiled seducers of pretty women. The influence of lesbian pornography for and by heterosexual men has also increased the perception of lesbians as non-traditional (Ishino and Wakabayashi 1996).

As stated in the introduction, periodicals serve an important function in both of these social groups. Most relevant here is their role of providing a space for lesbians and housewives to participate in their communities despite relative isolation. Therefore, the writing samples chosen for this study were letters to the editor, editorials, and life stories.[6] These particular texts were chosen from the lesbian and housewife periodicals because they formed the largest groups of texts of roughly the same type (according to native speaker intuitions). While it was not always possible to control for the age of the authors, some of the letters provided the author's age. Writings from an author over 40 were excluded.

Lastly, I will give some information about each of the periodicals in this study. Both of the housewife periodicals enjoy wide circulation in Japan. They can be easily found at train kiosks and bookstores. *Suteki na Okusan* targets young mothers who are not employed outside the home. The content focuses on recipes, child rearing, and tips for household organization. *Fujin no Tomo*'s target audience is still mothers. However, it aims at mothers who

---

[6] I did not control for topic of the articles utilized as I did not feel I would be able to find a sufficient number of articles that had the same topic.

also work and who may be slightly older (30 and up) than the average reader of *Suteki na Okusan*. Articles in *Fujin no Tomo* focus on the difficulties of balancing family and career and tend to be more intellectual in nature. Less information is available on the lesbian periodicals due to their restricted circulation as they are obtainable only through specific channels. In general, *TypeMx* contains fashion tips and surveys, letters from readers, movie reviews and advertisements. *Labrys Dash* seems to have an older audience with more intellectual articles, lesbian news from Japan and the world, letters from readers and book and movie reviews.

3.1 Methodology

Methodology is based upon that of Smith and Schmidt (1996). Smith and Schmidt formulated a method they termed script proportion analysis (SPA). SPA is the calculation of script totals for each text where script totals are the number of characters of each script type present. Each literature set contained 8,400 characters (roughly 8-9 pages of text) excluding titles, captions, and any characters not part of the text's main body. These groups of characters were chosen randomly. However, an attempt was made to find the largest continuous groupings of characters possible in order to limit the possibility of intertextual variation. Each of the 8,400 character sets in the lesbian and housewife periodicals came from five separate texts. From the lesbian literature, two articles were from *TypeMx* and three from *Labrys Dash*. In the housewife data set, two articles came from *Suteki na Okusan* and three from *Fujin no Tomo*.

All texts were divided into groups of 200 characters. Within each group of 200 characters, individual character type sums were totaled. Following Smith and Schmidt (1996), kanji/hiragana mixed words were counted as independent tokens of each script and kanji with furigana[7] were counted as appearing in the script chosen for the furigana. As Smith and Schmidt point out, this is not an ideal solution to the problem but, because there is variation in furigana script choice, this method will suffice for now. Geminates were counted as two characters.

While it is not clear whether the script choice demonstrated in these periodicals is the result of the author's choice or if there exists a level of mediation, such as an editor, prescribing choice of script, this ambiguity is not problematic. Whether these texts show how these two groups write or how it is viewed they should write, either is an important object of study. Both direct and reported script choice are phenomena linked with the social world (Hanks 1988).

---

[7]*Furigana* is script placed above or beside kanji to indicate how the kanji is to be read and can be in hiragana or katakana.

3.2 Results and discussion

To begin, I will present some initial observations on the periodicals themselves. First, while Western books and journals open from the right and have their text printed horizontally, Japanese books traditionally open from the left with the text running vertically beginning on the right side of the page. *Suteki na Okusan* and *Fujin no Tomo* open from the left and roughly 80% of the text runs vertically beginning on the right side of the page. On the other hand, *TypeMx* and *Labrys Dash* open from the right with approximately 95% of the text running horizontally left to right. Secondly, the periodical names give an indication of the position taken in relation to Western or non-Japanese influence. The housewife periodicals' titles employ Japanese or Sino-Japanese vocabulary. However, the lesbian periodical titles utilize English. These initial observations, summarized in Table 3, provide preliminary support for the notion that housewives and lesbians occupy different spheres in Japanese society.

	Opening	Direction of Text	Titles
Housewife Literature	Left	~80% vertical	Kanji or Hiragana/Kanji
Lesbian Literature	Right	~95% horizontal	Romaji

Table 3. General Characteristics of the Periodicals

To determine statistical significance of overall script choice, independent samples t-tests and chi-square tests were run. For each set of 200, the number of katakana, hiragana, and kanji were counted, and a t-test was used to compare the numbers within each character type across the two types of literature. The lesbian literature utilized significantly more katakana than the housewife literature (t = 6.21, p < .0001). This trend is also revealed by collapsing the sets of 200, and looking at the total distrubution of katakana versus non-katakana across the whole data set. This distribution is significant (χ^2 = 305.58, df = 1, p < .0001). In relation to the kanji data, it was demonstrated that the housewife literature employed significantly more kanji than the lesbian literature (t = 8.78, p < .0001). This significance was further born out by the total distribution of kanji versus non-kanji across the entire 8,400 characters counted for each type of literature (χ^2 = 296.33, df = 1, p < .0001). The hiragana data was surprising as, while significant, it showed that the lesbian literature utilized *more* hiragana than the housewife literature (t = 2.16, p < .05). This difference is also significant when the sets of 200 were collapsed and hiragana was compared with non-hiragana (χ^2 = 24.78, df = 1, p < .001). These results are reviewed in Table 4.

	Katakana	Hiragana	Kanji
Housewife Literature	332	4951	2982
Lesbian Literature	928	5258	1964
χ^2 Test (df = 1)	$\chi^2 = 305.58$	$\chi^2 = 24.78$	$\chi^2 = 296.33$
	$p < .0001$	$p < .001$	$p < .0001$
Independent	$t = 6.21$	$t = 2.16$	$t = 8.78$
Samples T-Test	$p < .0001$	$p < .05$	$p < .001$

Table 4. Distribution of Katakana, Hiragana and Kanji

Based on the above overall numbers, literature for and by lesbians and housewives does exhibit script choice patterns that distinguish one type of literature from another. Although the hiragana data did not configure as hypothesized, the katakana data does support the theory of an indexical relationship between katakana and modern identity.

At this juncture, I would like to look at some variation that occurred within each literature type. Across the two lesbian periodicals, *Labrys Dash* and *TypeMx*, there was significant variation in the katakana ($t = 2.23$, $p < .05$). However, in an independent samples t-test conducted using the katakana data from each lesbian periodical against the katakana from each housewife periodical, the variation in katakana use remained significant with significantly more katakana appearing in the lesbian data set. The least variation was demonstrated between *TypeMx* and *Fujin no Tomo* ($t = 2.49$, $p < .01$), yet the variation remained significant. In the other three t-tests, variation was more significant.

Across the two housewife periodicals, *Suteki na Okusan* and *Fujin no Tomo*, there was significant variation in hiragana ($t = 4.65$, $p < .001$) and kanji ($t = 3.50$, $p < .001$). This variation may relate to differences in target audience. *Suteki na Okusan* utilizes a significantly higher percentage of hiragana than *Fujin no Tomo*, while the opposite is true for kanji. Given the connotations of *fujin* 'wife/housewife' as having a larger role in the nondomestic sphere than entailed by *okusan* 'housewife/wife', this might explain the differential script use.

I would like to briefly return to the surprising results attained in the hiragana analysis across the two types of literature. In an earlier pilot, I conducted a brief analysis of some literature for women's household education published in 1948. I extracted 875 successive characters and found that 73% were hiragana, 25% katakana, and 2% romaji. A change in housewife ideology could have begun in the 1970s with the United Nations' Decade for Women and the start of the Women's Liberation Movement in Japan. Housewives were encouraged to become active in the community and take part in self-improvement (e.g. study, sports). The television 'home dramas' of the 1980s reflected this change in role, portraying women as independent and as single mothers. Therefore, based in this apparent change in the attitudes of and toward women during the seventies and eighties in Japan, further study of differences between housewife literature on both sides of the 1970s divide might prove useful. In addition, it has been suggested that lesbians use more hiragana than housewives due to its relation to Heian era women writers and the female, in general. It is, in fact, possible that hiragana indexes a female ideological space and that lesbians are calling upon this notion in their writing. While I have no evidence to support this idea, it seems a plausible explanation for my findings. Because my data support only the katakana portion of my hypothesis, from this point, my analysis will focus on this data.

4 Uses of Katakana in the Lexicon

Differences in katakana usage across the two groups are so disparate that it was necessary to explore in more detail the two groups' use of this script. To this end, repetition effects and non-loanwords in katakana were analyzed.

4.1 Repetition effects [8]

If repetition had occurred often enough it could have undermined the statistical effects observed in the previous section. Therefore, a list of each lexical item in katakana from each literature type was created. Each word was listed only once. In order to statistically compare the two bodies of data, character totals were calculated for the unrepeated 106 lesbian and 51 housewife lexical items. A ChiSquare comparing the lesbian and housewife data was then run using the katakana character totals from the non-repetitive list and non-katakana characters from each entire data set (see Table 5). This difference is significant ($\chi^2 = 69.490$, df = 1, p < .001). Thus, the statistical significance in the previous section is not solely due to repetition.

	Katakana Characters in Unrepeated Items	Non-Katakana Characters
Housewife Literature	281	8068
Lesbian Literature	<u>538</u>	7472

$$\chi^2 = 69.490,\ df = 1,\ p < 001$$

Table 5. Katakana in Unrepeated Lexical Items

---

[8] There are problems here with changing analysis level from characters to words. However, given the high statistical significance and large sample size, I do not think this issue is problematic.

4.2 Non-loanwords in katakana

Because it is obligatory for loanwords appear in katakana and some contexts call for more loanwords than others, it is possible that topic is affecting the use of katakana seen in the lesbian texts. Therefore, each of the lists of katakana lexical items from both data sets was divided into loanwords and non-loanwords. These character totals were tabulated and a ChiSquare test demonstrated significance (χ^2 = 15.506, df = 1, p < .001).

	Katakana in Non-Loanwords	Non-Katakana Characters
Housewife Literature	24	8068
Lesbian Literature	60	7472

$$\chi^2 = 15.506, df = 1, p < .001$$

Table 6. Katakana in Non-Loanwords

Based on the results in Table 6, I suggest that, while this may be influenced by the intimacy of the lesbian community, it also demonstrates that katakana utilization is seeping into areas of usage which are not conventional for written Japanese. I further suggest that this may be due to the desire of some members of the lesbian community to ally with modernity and lesbian identity associated with this script.

It has been pointed out that within the set of lexical items appearing in katakana that the housewife literature uses a greater percentage of loanwords (~87%) than the lesbian literature (~80%). This difference, however, is not statistically significant (χ^2 = 1.36, df = 1, p < 1.0).

4.3 Potentially free morphemes

The last section of the analysis pertains to the mixed use of scripts within a lexical item. More innovative uses of katakana may be an indicator of non-standard uses of this syllabary and so may index modernity and lesbian identity. I would like to emphasize that script mixture occurs only at morpheme boundaries. Thus, the mixing of scripts is not random. However, shifts in script choice tend to occur only when both morphemes are potentially free. These shifts were not common, though, with less than a dozen appearing across both data sets. (In the following examples, katakana script is underlined.)

A predominant number of loanwords in Japanese are nouns; this was borne out by my data. However, this does not mean that loanwords must be used as nouns in every context. One common way of making loanwords or non-loanwords into verbs in Japanese is by adding the verb *shimasu* or 'to do'/'to make' after a lexical item. An example of this construction is provided in (2). This *shimasu* mix was the only script mixture type found in the housewife data set.

(2)　ペス　ダウン　し　て
　　　pesu　da u n　shi　te
　　　pace　down　to do/make-CONN
　　　'to slow down' (one's lifestyle) (Fujin no Tomo, 1999:35)

This construction was used in both types of literature. In example (2), *shite* is a form of *shimasu* which acted here as a connective form in a compound sentence.

Compound words are another type of lexical item that employs script mixing. Kanji and katakana mixing was quite common in both literature types, but hiragana/katakana compound words were found only in the lesbian literature. In these mixed script lexical items, the loanword appears in katakana and the Japanese word in either hiragana or kanji (3a-b).

(3)　a.　**イベント　情報**
　　　　i　be n　to　jo ho
　　　　'event information' (TypeMx, 1999:36)
　　b.　レズ　も　の
　　　　re zu　mo　no
　　　　'lesbian things' (Labrys Dash, 1997:33)

The last class of katakana use between potentially free morphemes involves the rendering in katakana of a compound word of which one component is a loanword and one is a Japanese word, as in (4). This type of construction was found only in the lesbian literature.

(4)　**ギョーカイ**　　　　　**ライフ**
　　　gyo　ka i　　　　　**ra i fu**
　　　professional sphere/society　life
　　　'professional life' (Labrys Dash, 1997:35)

4.4 Obligatorily bound morphemes

It was remarkable to find changes in script choice at boundaries with obligatorily bound morphemes. Due to these morphemes' status as dependent upon a potentially free morpheme, a change in script choice seemed much less likely between multiple bound morphemes. There were only three examples of script change at a bound morpheme boundary. In example (5), the first morpheme is from English and the second from Japanese.

(5)　ノン　ケ
　　　no n　ke
　　　non　tendency (shortened colloquial version)
　　　'a non-tendency' (TypeMx, 1999:34)

The next two examples do not involve loanwords as any component of the lexical item. They do, though, demonstrate innovative uses of katakana.

(6)　a.とくに　住んで ても　OK なら 写真送 ります　ケ ド。
　　　Toku ni　sunde　temo　OK nara shashin okurimasu **ke do**
　　　Far-LOC live　even if OK if　photo　send　　　though
　　　'Even if (s/he, you) live far away, if it is OK, I will send the photo though.'
　　　(TypeMx, 1999:36)

　　　b. とにかく　　　眠い　ッス。
　　　to ni kaku　　　nemui　**ss**
　　　in any case/anyhow sleepy
　　　'In any case, (I'm) sleepy.' (TypeMx, 1999:34)

Examples (6a-b) use katakana to represent a Japanese bound morpheme.

Lastly, I found an instance of compound script mixing which was particularly innovative because, while tokens, like those in (4), can be separated and retain basically the same meaning, this is not so with (7).

(7)　本 ト
　　　hon **to**
　　　'true, actual' (TypeMx, 1999:34)

When used in other contexts *hon* can mean 'real' while *toh* whose kanji is 当 means 'justice, fairness.' It should also be noted that the *to* of *hontoh* is usually written using a geminate (i.e. *hontoh* not *honto*). These examples involving script change at a boundary with an obligatorily bound morpheme demonstrate further innovative script choice involving katakana.

In this section, evidence has been provided for the theory that lesbian literature employs more katakana and does so more innovatively and deviates significantly from the canonical usage of katakana in written Japanese.

5   Conclusion

The data in this paper have provided support for the proposed indexical relationship the katakana syllabary with modernity and lesbian identity. This support was found in the overall high occurrence of katakana in Japanese lesbian literature at the level of characters. Furthermore, at the level of the lexicon, the aforementioned indexical relationship was further bolstered by the lack of repetition effects, the significantly differential use of Japanese words appearing in katakana in the lesbian as opposed to the housewife literature, and the innovative uses of katakana in the lesbian literature.

As stated earlier, these periodicals assist in linking lesbians across Japan into a community, much like Anderson's imagined community (1991). They function as a social space for lesbians to interact with other lesbians and, in general, participate in the community from which they may be isolated. In this space, writing takes the place of spoken language as an identity marker and to be lesbian in this space is to write on topics relevant to the lesbian community and, more significantly for this discussion, with a certain mixture of Japanese scripts. It is also clear that housewives utilize their respective written social space in a manner that is not so different from lesbian writers. Although this paper does not provide an analysis of this data, it does indicate that to be a housewife participating in this space is, like for lesbians, to write in a certain manner.

On a broader level, this analysis carries important implications for the study of written language as distinct from that of spoken. In spoken language, when a given lexical item is uttered, its dependency upon its written instantiation for any extralinguistic information is greatly diminished, if not erased. This is due, at least in this case, to a lack of effect of script type upon the pronunciation of a lexical item. However, by examination of written language, these indexical relationships can be accessed. Thus, this project emphasizes the important contribution the study of written language, as a social space for accessing linguistic ideologies, can make to the field of sociolinguistics.

References

Anderson, Benedict. 1991. *Imagined Communities: Reflections on the Origin and Spread of Nationalism.* London: Verso Publishing.

Benveniste, Emile. 1985. The Semiology of Language. *Semiotics: An Introductory Anthology*, ed. R. Innis, 226-46. Bloomington: Indiana University Press.

Ericson, Joan E. 1996. The Origins of the Concept of 'Women's Literature'. *The Women's Hand: Gender and Theory in Japanese Women's Writing*, ed. P.G. Schalow and J.A. Walker, 74-115. Stanford: Stanford University Press.

Fujin no tomo (The Women's Friendship Society). 1995. Yoko Utsunomiya, ed. Tokyo: Fujin no Tomo-sha. v. 5.

Hanks, W.F. 1988. Text and Textuality. *Annual Review of Anthropology* 18:95-127.

Inoue, Kyoko. 1991. *MacArthur's Japanese Constitution: A Linguistic and Cultural Study of its Making.* Chicago: University of Chicago Press.

Inoue, Miyako. 1994. Gender and Linguistic Modernization: Historicizing Japanese Women's Language. *Cultural Performances: Proceedings of the Third Berkeley Women and Language Conference,* ed. Mary Bucholtz, A.C. Liang, Laurel Sutton, and Caitlin Hines, 322-33. Berkeley: Berkeley Women and Language Group, University of California Berkeley.

Ishino, S. and N. Wakabayashi. 1996. *Unspoken Rules: Sexual Orientation and Women's Human Rights.* London: International Gay and Lesbian Human Rights Commission.

Koyama, Shizuko. 1994. The 'Good Wife and Wise Mother' Ideology in Post-World War I Japan. *U.S.-Japan Women's Journal, English Supplement.* 7:31-52.

Labrys dash. 1997. Tsu-chi, China, Chu, and Iri, eds. Tokyo: Labrys Dash. v. 4.

Pyle, Kenneth B. 1969. *The New Generation in Meiji Japan.* Stanford: Stanford University Press.

Ramusack, B. and S. Sievers. 1999. *Women in Asia: Restoring Women to History.* Bloomington: Indiana University Press.

Smith, Janet S. and David Schmidt. 1996. Variability in Written Japanese: Towards a Sociolinguistics of Script Choice. *Visible Language* 30.1:46-71.

Summerhawk, Barbara, Cheiron McMahill, and Darren McDonald. 1998. *Queer Japan.* Norwich: New Victoria Publishers.

Suteki na okusan (The Ideal Housewife). 1999. Kiyoshi Kurosaka, ed.. Tokyo: Shufu to Seikatsu-sha. v. 6.

Twine, Nanette. 1991. Language and the Modern State: The Reform of Written Japanese. London; New York: Routledge.

TypeMx. 1999. Mika Ma-san, ed. Tokyo: TypeMx. v. 4.

14

Skirting Around: Towards an Understanding of HIV/AIDS Educational Materials in Modern Israeli Hebrew[*]

HARRIS SOLOMON

' . . . public health educators have to understand the principles which govern AIDS-related discourse in American English contexts and in other language domains. Linguists can help in this regard, first by identifying these principles as they occur in different discourse settings, then by describing how their presence affects the form and content of discourse within those domains.'

-William Leap (1991:286)

'I've slept with a lot of men – a lot. Figure it out – over two months, an average of three a day. I know that what I do is very, very dangerous, with AIDS . . . But, look, I try to use as many preventatives as possible, and to pay attention to the guidelines of the AIDS Task Force, and all that bullshit – how to be careful, what not to do, what to do, all sorts of things like that.'

-'Amit', a male sex worker interviewed Fink and Press (1999:118)

[*] I am indebted to Rae Moses, Judith Levi, Gregory Ward, Lane Fenrich, Bill Leap, and Benjamin Junge for their guidance and insight that helped coax this project along from its inception to its realization. Thanks also to the participants at the First International Conference on Gender and Language, held at Stanford University in May 2000, whose comments were especially helpful.

Language and Sexuality: Contesting Meaning in Theory and Practice.
Kathryn Campbell-Kibler, Robert J. Podesva, Sarah J. Roberts and Andrew Wong (eds.).
Copyright © 2001, CSLI Publications.

1 Introduction

Although Israel continues to expand its medical resources for treating those citizens affected by HIV/AIDS, only modest efforts have been realized in comprehensive AIDS education. Existing socio-religious taboos and a lack of public health educational funding have hindered individuals in their choice of informative materials. The Israel AIDS Task Force (IATF) estimates that as many as 10,000 men, women, and children are living with HIV in Israel (IATF 2001). Of these, approximately 2,200 are registered with the Ministry of Health as living with HIV; the remainder of the estimated 10,000 people includes those who are believed to be carrying the virus but are unaware of their HIV-positive status. The IATF estimates that every day three Israelis become infected with HIV (IATF 2001).[1]

Despite numerous obstacles exacted upon widespread educational efforts by religio-political forces in the Israeli government, state-sanctioned educational programs do exist in many public schools, and AIDS education curricula are planned for a number of other state institutions. However a lack of funding, staff, and any official state-approved educational model has effectively demonstrated a large unmet need for AIDS education for the population at large. With little monetary support, several grassroots organizations have enacted AIDS education programs using informative pamphlets as a key strategy to disseminate a health education message. What this paper addresses in detail is the grammatical dimension of written discourse in selected Hebrew AIDS educational pamphlets, and how grammatical particulars and wider-level discursive trends in the texts reflect the temperament of AIDS education in Israel. Attending to the roles of the texts in consolidating images of AIDS and reproducing incomplete or incorrect knowledge about AIDS, the analyses reveal a disparity in the amount of information 'entrusted' to the reader based upon gender. Further, the language of the texts depicts AIDS (aside from other embodiments) as a beast of a corporeal nature for gay men and as an assault on the psyche for women.

After briefly discussing recent studies in AIDS discourse events and the evolving story of AIDS in Israel, I explore the diacritic-less Hebrew format used in selected AIDS educational pamphlets through morphological analysis and a consideration of style. I address ways in which the obscuring ef-

---

[1] Walzer (2000: 37-38) keenly describes the highly contested issue of actual AIDS cases in Israel. Anonymous testing, a recent phenomenon in Israel, only adds to the confusion in producing an agreed-upon prevalence figure. The Israel AIDS Task Force claims the highest number of actual cases (upwards of 10,000). Others, including Dr. Tzvi Ben-Yishai, head of the government's National Steering Committee on AIDS, believe that the actual number of cases is between four and five thousand. A detailed discussion of AIDS policy issues in Israel appears in Ben-Yishai, 1996.

fects of nonvocalic written Hebrew are exploited to reach an audience of both men and women, as well as ways in which the written language differs in style and tone between audiences based upon gender. Utilizing the complementarity of diacritical analysis and discourse analysis, I discuss the semantically complex AIDS-related educational messages found in the pamphlets. Finally, I propose possible contributing factors that affect the choice of language recruited by the authors of these pamphlets. My aim is to present a country-specific context of AIDS education through the analysis of materials from an international health education program, thereby enriching the already burgeoning field of study of medical discourse.

2   Discourse as Intervention

A discursive study of written materials about HIV/AIDS may inspire a variety of conclusions about how the disease is understood by existing as an intermediary between author and audience. Written discourse about AIDS provides a means for the reader to negotiate a sense of identification with the illness (Clark 1996). This identification may intersect the reader's dynamic construction of his or her sexuality as a result of exposure to certain medical terminology, or may aid the reader's perception of HIV through various discrete metaphorical concepts.

Negotiating an identity connected to AIDS is inextricably linked with an understanding of the construction of the disease on a societal level. According to Adam (1989), AIDS is a 'pure case' in the social construction of disease, for AIDS was very much unanticipated by epidemiologists and the general public – neither predicted the arrival of an epidemic disease whose mode of transmission is largely sexual. Understanding AIDS as a disease of pandemic proportions greatly interests scholars, for existing taboos about sex, drug use, and homosexuality all have been attached to AIDS. According to Gusfield (1981: 53), the study of AIDS is the study of how 'uncertain, inconsistent, and inaccurate' knowledge is 'fashioned into a public system of certain and consistent knowledge in ways which heighten its believability and its dramatic impact.' Critical discourse analysis is a useful tool in examining the discourse events that emerge from such systems of knowledge and beliefs. Van Dijk (1993: 252) asserts that critical discourse analysis 'is primarily interested and motivated by pressing social issues.' Fairclough (1995) explains that discourse is constitutive of ideology, but its operations are constrained by complex political, economic, and social regimes that are evident in the real world.

The situation of language in a dynamic relation to reality is articulated in its reflexivity, where language concurrently constructs and reflects particular situations in which it is used (Gee 1999). Gee describes a number of connected components of such situations, which include material aspects (the bodies and physical locality of an interaction), political aspects (the distribution of power and status), and sociocultural aspects (the various levels and types of knowledge and identities involved in an interaction). These aspects together constitute a system, or a 'situation network', where each component or aspect gives meaning to the other components and also receives meaning from them (Gee 1999: 83).

This theoretical framework is particularly helpful in considering AIDS discourse, in English and in other languages, in which multiple and interconnected social, political, and cultural meanings of the body, illness, gender, and sexuality may exist. These meanings are further negotiated on both personal and societal levels, thus constituting a complex system that necessarily requires a method of analysis rooted in intertextuality. Since analysis of AIDS-related discourse also aims to reveal much about sexuality, it is critical to note that communication about sexuality and AIDS is only partially expressed in overt language. What is concealed or suppressed is often more relevant than what has been expressed in words (Leap 1991). It should also be noted that this analysis is concerned with written language, and not spoken discourse. Numerous differences exist between spoken and written discourse (see Georgakopoulou and Goutsos 1997), and among those differences is the element of planning and consideration that goes into written discourse events. Accordingly, the pragmatic suppression of overt meaning may not be expressed in written text as it is in spoken discourse.[2]

What was not concealed in the emergent written and spoken discourse of AIDS (at the time it first filtered into the public arena in the United States) was its focus on sexuality. This discourse addressed risk groups based on specific behaviors, and subsequently the locus of the disease was attached to homosexuals early on; as a result, this group (among other similarly labeled 'risk groups') has yet to escape such stigmatized labeling. AIDS has been predominantly categorized as a sexually transmitted disease much like syphilis or gonorrhea, as opposed to solely a viral disease such as hepatitis B (which is transmitted through vectors similar to HIV's modes of

---

[2] Also see Brundson 1990 and Morley 1980. I recognize that this analysis is carried out in isolation from audience reception; however, as Fairclough asserts:

'there is a danger ... of throwing out the baby with the bathwater, by abandoning textual analysis in favour of analysis of audience reception. The interpretation of texts is a dialectical process resulting from the interface of the variable interpretative resources people bring to bear on the text, *and* properties of the text itself. Textual analysis is therefore an important part, if only a part, of the picture, and must be defended against its critics' (1995: 9).

transmission).[3] Donovan (1997: 119) concludes that 'the medical definition of AIDS as an STD practically insured that issues such as prevention and treatment would involve a policy debate centering on moral as well as medical judgments.' Allan Brandt supports the significance of this categorization in his social history of venereal disease in America by noting that 'Medical and social values continue to define venereal disease as a uniquely sinful disease, indeed, to transform the disease into an indication of moral decay' (1985: 186).

These medical definitions in question have often taken the rhetorical form of metaphor, and have filtered into popular linguistic constructions of AIDS in English and often in other languages as well.[4] Treichler (1999) premises that AIDS is a point of intersection for multiple meanings, stories, and discourses to overlap, reinforce, and subvert one another. Highly charged language and imagery surrounding the organization of our understanding and experience with AIDS contribute to such intersecting discourse. Treichler, reacting to Sontag (1988), effectively calls for an AIDS intervention on the linguistic level:

> No matter how much we may desire, with Susan Sontag, to resist treating illness as metaphor, illness is metaphor, and this semantic work – this effort to 'make sense of' AIDS – has to be done. Further, this work is as necessary and often as difficult and imperfect for physicians and scientists as it is for 'the rest of us'. (1999: 359)

This sort of 'linguistic intervention' will directly implicate the promulgation of (and the identification with) specific messages designed to educate communities about AIDS.

3   From Modesty to Action

Jewish law and tradition play a crucial role in many aspects of Israeli society, and are key players in the arena of AIDS education. Condoms are not condoned as a proper method of birth control by Orthodox Jewish law; using a condom constitutes a 'spilling of the seed' which is outlawed in the Old Testament. Recently, however, many rabbis have ruled that if a married man is found to have AIDS or to be an HIV carrier, he should use condoms with his wife during intercourse with her if he does not agree to divorce his wife to save her from infection (Siegel-Itzkovich 1999).

---

[3] Cindy Patton also notes that 'the diseases which served as analogues for AIDS – hepatitis B and syphilis – suggested that there would be much less time from infection to symptoms' (1999: 401). Conceptualizations of the progress of HIV infection in the body, namely how much 'healthy time' remains, directly pertain to the analysis presented here.

[4] For discussion on qualitative research issues including collection of linguistic data about AIDS, see, for example, Bolton 1992; Parker 1992; and Parker and Carballo, 1990.

Israel's Minister of Health, Rabbi Shlomo Benizri, decided in 1999 that the streets of Jerusalem 'would be desecrated' by the sight of rolled-up condoms on publicity posters for World AIDS Day (Siegel-Itzkovich 1999: 1455). Benizri ordered health officials to destroy posters and pamphlets with the 'embarrassing' objects and to replace them with others that do not show condoms. Health Ministry official Yair Amikam said that Benizri was responding to 'public demand for modesty while educating in detail' about sexually transmitted diseases (Fishman 1999: 1887). Another Health Ministry spokesman declared that 'Israeli citizens – Jewish, Arab, religious, secular – have indicated that pictures of condoms are offensive and embarrassing' (Fishman 1999: 1887). Fishman describes how this spokesman told *The Lancet* 'many booklets, films, demonstrations, and advertisements throughout the media, sponsored or produced by the Ministry, contain explicit detail about the value and use of condoms without having to show pictures of someone holding a rolled-up condom in his hand' (1999: 1887). In summing up his view of the climate of AIDS education in Israel, the head of the Israel AIDS Task Force stated that:

> If you are talking about health and medical care, Israel is similar to Europe, but if you are talking about prevention and education, Israel is more similar to Africa. In the States, Europe, and Australia they spend US$1.69 per capita per annum. In Africa it's seven cents and in Israel it's about 13 cents. (Fishman 1999: 1887)

In the face of such hindrances to sound and effective educational efforts, several successes are worthy of mention. In 1998, the Israeli government approved plans to begin funding the multi-drug combination antiviral treatment commonly known as 'the cocktail' for people infected with HIV (Henderson 1998). The Minister of Health at the time, Yehoshua Matza, enhanced the announcement by classifying AIDS as a 'serious disease'. Under the plan, Israelis covered by the national medical insurance (a privilege extended to all citizens) would have access to a therapy that costs an estimated 48,000 shekels (US$13, 150) per year. The ministry also noted that the 'significance of the decision is that people infected with HIV or AIDS carriers needing treatment by "cocktail" medications will receive full funding from health funds' (Henderson 1998). The privately-run funds are to be reimbursed by the state.

The Israel AIDS Task Force, perhaps the most successful of all programmatic-focused AIDS action groups, has secured a niche for education, counseling, and international cooperation. The Task Force is a voluntary organization, founded in 1985, whose purpose is to provide support and assistance for people living with HIV and AIDS and to provide information on the virus and how to prevent its transmission. IATF draws from a pool of over 200 volunteers, including doctors, nurses, researchers, social workers, alternative therapists and people living with HIV. The Israel AIDS Task Force is recognized today as the largest organization in Israel dedicated to the fight against AIDS. The Task Force maintains close contact and cooperation with all the AIDS centers and hospitals in Israel, the Health Ministry, the Education Ministry, local government bodies and other relevant organizations through the Israeli AIDS Coalition of Human Right Organizations, which was initiated by IATF. On an international level, IATF works with the International Committee of AIDS Organizations, the Global Network of People Living with HIV and with European and American AIDS organizations (IATF 2001).

As a core element of its educational program initiatives, the IATF makes use of informative pamphlets to purvey a health education message. The advantage to using pamphlets is that they can be distributed in large numbers to an array of people, thus reaching diverse communities in Israel. It is the language of these pamphlets that is the primary element of this study.

4 Finding Gender

Before examples of Hebrew-language AIDS discourse are examined here, I present a brief explanation of the relevant Hebrew grammatical categories – particularly gender – that form the basis of this analysis. As is typical of Semitic languages, Hebrew employs diacritical markings to represent most of its vowel sounds and to distinguish between certain consonantal alternations. Such markings are orthographically placed around consonantal letters to delineate the sounds of the word itself, which can signal a variety of grammatical morphemes, including gender morphemes.[5] For reasons of clarity, I have chosen to represent Hebrew words in this analysis without diacritical markings by including a nonvocalic transliteration into English. These transliterations appear in capital letters, and serve to convey the notion of a somewhat semantically ambiguous nonvocalic Hebrew consonantal skeleton (thus *K T V T* for /katavt/, 'she wrote').[6]

---

[5] I represent Hebrew consonants by their closest English-letter approximation. The exceptions are the Hebrew letters 'chaf' and 'chet', which delineate a gutteral 'h' (similar to the *ch* in German *Loch*). I assign the English letter *x* to this sound, to avoid confusion with other pronunciations of *ch*.

[6] Note that the consonantal skeleton is not necessarily equivalent to the morphological stem of the word. The skeleton *K T V T* represents /katavt/, 'she wrote'. The skeleton *K T V* can represent the masculine form of the same verb in the past tense, /katav/, 'he wrote'. However, *K T V* also could be interpreted as the morphological stem in Hebrew, or *shoresh* ('root'). Thus, the three-letter root *K-T-V* is the base of words such as /kitovet/, 'address', /ketubah/, 'marriage contract', /katvanit/, 'typist', etc. Glinert (1994: 29) explains that the *shoresh* may have from two to five consonants and implies a 'distinct, but not necessarily a very precise meaning'. The

Every noun in Hebrew is assigned a single grammatical gender, either masculine or feminine (Glinert 1994). Gender assignment is generally arbitrary although the morphophonological shape has some predictive value. Feminine words are marked by a suffixal *–a* and *–t* (as in /talmida/, 'pupil' [f.sg.], or /soferet/, 'writer' [f.sg.]), while masculine words carry either a zero or *–e* suffix (as in /talmid/, 'pupil' [m.sg.], /sofer/, 'writer' [m.sg.], or /ole/, 'immigrant' [m.sg.]). As noted by Ravid (1995), number and gender are inherent in the nouns, from which agreement spreads out to other categories; in Hebrew, these include both verbs and adjectives. Nevertheless, a basic distinction exists between the expression of number and expression of gender in nouns.

Syntactically, gender is a feature that is attached to the noun stem in the lexicon and thus appears on the noun at all levels of syntactic representation (Ritter 1993). A diagram of a Hebrew determiner phrase (DP), from Ritter (1993), follows:

(1) $[_{DP}$ Det $[_{NumP}$ Num $[_{NP}$ N$]]]$

                                    |

                ... X-[gender] ...

Ritter's claim that gender is a feature on the lexical stem in Hebrew – more specifically, on N (as opposed to Num) – is largely rooted in the fact that switching from masculine to feminine in Hebrew is a common productive method for deriving new nouns from existing nouns. Bat-El (1986) shows the regularity of this method with the following examples of derivation of new words from masculine nouns via addition of the feminine suffixes *–et*, *-it,* and *a(t)*:

	Masculine Nouns	Feminine Nouns
a.	*magav*, 'wiper'	*magev-et*, 'towel'
	magav-im, 'wipers'	*magav-ot*, 'towels'
b.	*maxsan*, 'warehouse'	*maxsan-it*, 'magazine'
	maxsan-im, 'warehouses'	*maxsani-ot*, 'magazines'
c.	*amud*, 'page'	*amuda*, 'column'
	amud-im, 'pages'	*amud-ot*, 'columns'

Table 1. Word Formation Via Feminine Suffixation.

---

shoresh in this example, *K-T-V*, implies a sense of writing. Other *shorashim* are not always so precise in their field of meaning. Glinert provides *K-B-L* as an example: it yields /kibel/, 'he received' but also /kaval/, 'he complained'.

According to the paradigm as illustrated by Bat-El, these examples demonstrate not only the derivational nature of these nouns, but also the fact that the feminine markers shown have no inherent semantic content, so the meaning of the derived forms is not compositional.

The following examples introduce the nature and value of vowel diacritics in Hebrew, using words which have identical consonantal skeletons, but different vowel markings:

(2a) /xaval/
     'pity'

(2b) /xevel/
     'rope'

In everyday written Hebrew, the diacritics are generally left out; native speakers are capable of recognizing – and disambiguating – words without the markings. However, there exist instances where the absence of the vowel markings generates ambiguity in discerning the word:

(3)   X V L
      ? /xaval/

      ? /xevel/

In (3), the absence of the diacritics makes identifying the word difficult; as written, it appears only as /xvl/, which could be read as either /xaval/ or /xevel/. Normally, contextual clues are the most useful resource for resolving such ambiguity. For example, in the Hebrew sentence /xaval she lo bata/ (which transliterated from a nonvocalic form into English might appear as 'XVL SH L BT'), '(it's a) pity that you didn't come', the rest of the sentence makes it clear that this cannot be read as 'rope that you didn't come'.

This kind of ambiguity frequently arises in forms that express gender agreement – which includes all tensed verbs and all adjectives, and thus the vast majority of Hebrew sentences. Some examples follow:

(4a) /l'xa/
     'to you$_m$'

     /lax/
     'to you$_f$'

(4b) /katavta/
     'you wrote$_m$'

     /katavt/
     'you wrote$_f$'

(5a) LX
    ? /l'xa/
    ? /lax/
    'to you$_{unspec}$'

(5b) KTVT
    ? /katavta/
    ? /katavt/
    'you wrote$_{unspec}$'

Thus in (5a) and (5b), which show the nonvocalic forms as they would be transliterated into English, the lack of the diacritics that normally would signify masculine or feminine gender marking makes the intended gender of the word unclear. Even when these words appear in written text, there often are not enough clues to disambiguate these very common forms. Therefore, the reader must guess at which gender(s) the writer intended.

It is important to note that in Hebrew, as in many other gender-specific languages, the masculine gender is considered the default. gender. Consequently, in vocalizing written Hebrew without diacritics, a speaker would normally utter the masculine form of the word in question. However, in some public health educational brochures (including literature on AIDS and breast cancer), it has become increasingly more common to adapt a system of explicitly demarcating gender either by including the vowel diacritics or by writing both masculine and feminine forms. The ambiguity that results from a lack of gender transparency can prevent a reader from identifying with the intended message. As medical discourse, AIDS educational materials contain a message written by authors who ideally share the salient goal of fostering reader identification with the message. This identification and subsequent understanding of a safer-sex message could lead a reader to change his or her risky practices that perhaps could lead to HIV infection. It is for this reason that the gender marking options chosen by health educators are so critical for AIDS education and prevention.

5 AIDS: 'Just Like You'

The pamphlets used in this study were taken from the resource library of the Israel AIDS Task Force. The years of publication for the pamphlets in this study vary, but all were published in the mid- to late- 1990s (no exact dates of publication appear on the pamphlets).[7] However, many pamphlets first

---

[7] I thank Ravit Tolidano for aiding me in the difficult task of performing 'background checks' on the pamphlets.

published in the early 1990s continue to be distributed, unchanged, to the public. Until the IATF began to publish its own materials (which often target a general audience regardless of gender or sexual orientation), the majority of AIDS educational pamphlets were produced by a group called *Bela Doeget*. *Bela Doeget* (a Hebrew acronym for 'Bisexual, Lesbians, and Gays for Change in AIDS Education') is a branch of the Association of Gay Men, Lesbians, Bisexuals, and Transgendered People in Israel (known in Hebrew as 'the *Agudah*', or 'The Association') devoted to HIV/AIDS outreach efforts, which was founded when HIV began its spread in Israel.

The most common mode of information presentation in these educational pamphlets is the question-and-answer format. Often the first paragraph of the pamphlet explains that individuals 'just like you' (the gender of 'you' varies with the intended audience) will provide answers to the questions posed therein. These individuals are presented as either HIV-positive or who are in advanced stages of AIDS. The questions are nearly always asked from the first-person point of view, e.g. 'Why should *I* get tested? How will *I* deal with this?'. As will be discussed, this format places a strong emphasis on how AIDS affects the individual, as opposed to the community.

Other pamphlets employ a narrative form, attempting to tell a complete story on the nature of the disease, how it is transmitted, what effects it has on the body, and why the reader should consider being tested. The pamphlets frequently end with a listing of Israeli HIV/AIDS resources such as telephone hotlines, support groups, and a list of HIV-testing centers (both governmental and private) throughout the country.

6 Audience (Un)Accommodation

Selected excerpts from the pamphlets demonstrating gender ambiguity via the absence of diacritics are presented and annotated below. The first pamphlet under consideration was authored by the Israel AIDS Task Force. The remaining three pamphlets were authored by *Bela Doeget*. The subscripts in the given texts delineate marked (or unmarked) Hebrew gender on the singular pronouns and verbs in question: *m* for masculine, *f* for feminine, and *unspec* for unspecified gender.

One should bear in mind that the syntactic structures and lexicalization of the Hebrew original text may not match those of the English translations. For example, the pronoun in the English 'you engaged' is absent in the Hebrew form */kayamt(a)/* (as it is in many other verbs in the past and future tense). This is because the 'you' is recoverable from verbal morphology.

Pamphlet 1: 'An Anonymous AIDS Test: The Result is in Your$_{unspec}$ Hands'

'If you engaged$_{unspec}$ in full sexual relations and not protected (sex), that is to say, penetration without a condom, it is possible that you have been infected$_{unspec}$ with the HIV-virus (the virus that causes AIDS).'

Here gender ambiguity is present in the various forms of the singular verbs appearing in the text:

(6a) KYMT
/kayamt(a)/
'you engaged$_{unspec\ sg}$'

(6b) NDBKT
/nidbakt(a)/
'you have been infected$_{unspec\ sg}$'

The text, opting for verbs that could be realized in either masculine or feminine forms, targets an audience of both genders. This general-audience targeting is more specifically demonstrated in Pamphlet 2:

Pamphlet 2: 'You$_f$ are not alone // You$_m$ are not alone'

'Perhaps you received$_{unspec}$ a positive answer to your $_{unspec}$ HIV-test recently and perhaps this was known to you$_{unspec}$ for a long time already but this is the first time that you are searching$_{m/f\ sg}$ for information or help. You$_{unspec}$ should know; you$_{m/f\ sg}$ are not alone.'

This text leaves out the diacritics for most of the opening paragraph that is translated above, but at the end of the opening statement the texts begins to employ **both** the masculine and feminine forms of the 2nd person singular pronoun as well as of the verbs.

It should be noted that the full forms of both the masculine and the feminine are not necessary to indicate that both genders are included. Rather than presenting both forms in full, the full masculine form is given; then, because the feminine form has the same stem as the masculine but a different suffix, only the suffix is given after the slash:

(7) MXPS/T
/mixapes/et/
'searching$_{m/f\ sg}$'

This contracted combined-gender form of expression can also be accomplished with the singular forms of the pronoun 'you' (which in Hebrew is marked for both gender and number), as shown here, although in this case the suffix turns out to indicate the masculine form /ata/ (the feminine form is simply /at/).

This pamphlet is clearly directed towards a mixed gender audience, as the missing diacritics are accounted for by the inclusion of separate masculine/feminine forms.

Pamphlet 3: 'An AIDS Test. To know in order to live.'

'If you discover$_m$ tomorrow that you $_m$ are a carrier (i.e., HIV positive), this does not mean that you$_m$ need$_m$ to run and to tell it to your friends (lit., 'the gang'). Think$_m$ about it a little, take$_m$ your$_{unspec}$ time – and you$_{unspec}$ have time.'

This pamphlet makes almost exclusive use of explicitly masculine forms for pronouns and verbs, indicating a male target audience. It does not include diacritics at all, which accounts for the unspecified form of 'your'. This pronoun is orthographically identical for masculine and feminine forms (SHLX could either be /shelxa/, 'you$_{m\ sg}$' or /shelax/, 'you$_{f\ sg}$'). As far as verbs are concerned, the text employs only the masculine form:

(8a) /tigale/
'you will discover$_{m\ sg}$'
(as opposed to /tigali/, 'you will discover$_{f\ sg}$')

(8b) /tzarix/
'need$_{m\ sg}$'
(as opposed to /tzrixa/, 'need$_{f\ sg}$')

(8c) /taxshov/
'think$_{m\ sg}$ (imp)'
(as opposed to /taxshevi/, 'think$_{f\ sg}$ [imp])

This pamphlet, published by *Bela Doeget*, targets a gay male audience. Although this intent is not wholly unambiguous from the text itself since the masculine forms could be read as 'generic' gender, an examination of the graphic art in the text provides support for this claim. Arguably, pictures of half-clothed young men dancing together in nightclub settings suggest that this pamphlet is intended for those who self-identify as men who have sex with men.[8]

Pamphlet 4: 'HIV+ . This is not the end of you$_f$'

'Perhaps you received$_{unspec}$ a positive answer to your $_{unspec}$ HIV-test recently and perhaps this was known to you$_{unspec}$ for a long time already but this is the first time that you are searching$_{f\ sg}$ for information or help. This pamphlet is intended to clarify for you$_{unspec}$ basic ideas about the virus and to help you$_{f\ sg}$ to find ways to cope with it.'

---

[8] See Nelson (1994) for further analyses of graphic presentations in AIDS educational materials.

This text, similar to Pamphlet 2, begins with unspecified address, but continues to employ the feminine form of *searching* and then uses the feminine form of *you*:

(9) */mixapeset/*
    'searching$_{f sg}$'

(10) */la'azor lax/*
    'to help you$_{f sg}$

This example is in contrast to Pamphlet 2, which includes 'searching' in both masculine and feminine forms. This pamphlet is specifically geared to women, as indicated by its title which explicitly uses feminine-inflected *you*.

7 Body or Soul?

Just as the analysis of missing vowel diacritics helps to establish exactly *who* is (or, perhaps, is not) being addressed by the authors of the pamphlets, a discursive analysis of the message itself reveals *how* the authors introduce AIDS to the reader of a pamphlet. Different texts discursively present the HIV/AIDS education message in distinctly different ways, depending upon the intended audience. For the pamphlets targeted towards gay men, the literature is mainly geared towards encouraging the reader to consider an HIV-antibody test (incorrectly referred to in the literature as an 'AIDS test'). These pamphlets include little or no mention of the emotional factors that enter into the process of acknowledging one's HIV-positive status. The general tone of the texts is very much focused on the physical nature of the virus; that is, the texts address AIDS in terms of the virus and the body (and thus not on the mind or spirit).

Indeed, the questions themselves (posed by the authors, a group of self-identified HIV-positive gay men) are themselves focused on the body; most are focused on physical treatment and how it works:

'Who has the strength to deal with the medications?'

'Why should I be tested now? When I feel bad, I'll go to the doctor and he'll give me the cocktail.'

'For how long do these medications help?'

'Will they discover a cure in the end?'

'If the future is so bright, why should I use a condom?'

'Do you (the authors of the texts) have a sex life?'

Questions such as these are answered by assuring the reader that the medications are effective and comprehensive, that safer sex is enjoyable, and that being HIV-positive does not preclude a healthy sex life.

In the pamphlets geared towards women, the texts employ a considerably different tone. The following passages are taken from a pamphlet entitled 'You are not alone. This is not the end of you':

> If you are angry, this is fine. You have reasons to be angry and you are permitted to express it, for this small virus is attacking your very existence. If you are full of fears – ask yourself what they are. There's no point in running from them. Don't aggravate yourself too much; don't think that you have to be strong. Nothing is required of you.

Another passage directly addresses loss:

> Perhaps you feel that you lost something, that many of the supports in your life are now in the hands of the doctors, clinics, or 'experts of that type' that think that they know what you need to do and how you need to do it. This is likely to cause you to feel that you have lost control of your life and to incite great anxiety within you.

Pamphlets that address *both* a male and female audience similarly sustain the emotional burden that accompanies HIV-infection, and offer advice about changing one's life after being informed of one's HIV-positive status:

> It's possible that your list of priorities may change in a meaningful way. If this happens to you, be certain that you are doing this only with consideration and understanding. Many HIV-positive [people] changed their lives. Many weaned themselves from habits such as smoking or excessive drinking. Some of them ended unhealthy relationships or left work that they hated. Coming to terms with the possibility of disease changed the lives of many of us for the good and even made [our lives] more healthy.

What educational messages may be extrapolated from these texts? I argue that the texts geared solely toward gay males focus primarily on the sexual nature of AIDS, using discourse to place a distinct emphasis on sexual activity. With discourse that only obliquely attends to the emotional aspects of AIDS, it is unproblematic for a reader to dismiss the fact that emotional duress is a likely occurrence as part of coming to terms with being HIV-positive. Utilizing purely pathological discourse offers a blurred portrayal of treatment options as well. It is far easier for a reader to think that if he or she is going to be affected only physically, then the only course of treatment must be a physically therapeutic approach. The psychological effects of disease are arguably as dangerous as the physical effects, and by simply dismissing these wholly inevitable outcomes, the texts of the pamphlets proffer an incomplete educational message.

In contrast, the pamphlets that address a female audience place emphasis on the emotional aspects of AIDS. Taking the approach of 'counseling' the reader, these texts are far more affect-focused than the ones intended for a gay male audience. Issues emphasized include fear, loss of control, and the worries of everyday life for an HIV-positive woman. The educational message is quite complete; aside from all concerns physical, the discourse in these texts does not fail to address the formidable emotional burden of being HIV-positive. This presents AIDS as a disease that is extremely onerous, for it is conveyed as having far-reaching physical as well as psychological effects. From the perspective of those who advocate prevention as an effective means of retarding the number of people infected with HIV, this educational method is considered superior to methods that address AIDS only in the somatic domain.

8 White Lies

In regard to written discourse, Herbert Clark asserts 'it is the institution – the ad agency, drug company, or legislature – that is ultimately responsible, approved the wording as faithful to the institution's collective intentions' (1996: 7). For those seeking informative materials pertaining to HIV and AIDS, it is the hope of each reader that the information he or she encounters will be accurate and affirming – two goals that an institution with sound educational ideals would be assumed to endorse. However, in the case of the materials examined for this study, it was evident that the architects of discourse for many of the educational texts failed to present a well-formed educational message. Instead, these authors proffered a message that either fell short of mentioning vital information, or contained information that was demonstrably incorrect.

One factor observed in the materials geared towards a gay male audience was the casual approach used in presenting the 'cocktail', a combination antiviral therapy against HIV-infection, to men questioning possible medical treatment for HIV. These pamphlets quickly introduce text about the cocktail in discussing how one can treat HIV; this is not surprising, as the cocktail has prolonged the lives of numerous HIV-positive people. However, in the Hebrew materials, the cocktail is discursively underscored as a therapy much akin to a cure. There is no mention of side effects, the fact that many patients cannot tolerate the medication, or the fact that the therapeutic effects of the cocktail may be short-lived.

In one of the pamphlets that targets a gay male audience, a question arises as to why one should pursue an HIV-antibody test if there is no cure. The answer provided follows:

> It was a little hard for doctors to answer this [question] for someone who asked it five years ago. There exists an effective therapy known as 'the cocktail' for AIDS treatment. The cocktail, composed of three or four different medications, succeeds in dramatically lowering the concentration of the virus in the blood. In most of those treated with the cocktail, the immune system recovers satisfactorily. If you are [HIV] positive, this therapy

can remove you from all danger, to delay and perhaps to prevent the progression of the disease.

The message that this discourse conveys is, at once, both false and dangerous to those seeking information about the disease. The passage above purports a release of anxiety as the primary function of the cocktail. Additionally, worry and fear are addressed at the purely corporeal level; a medicine that acts upon the body and not the mind is used to assuage any fear the reader may harbor. By consigning psychic predicaments to the physical body, this description recapitulates the discourse trend set in the U.S. in the 1980s of defining the gay male body through AIDS. Treichler notes that

> Whatever else it may be, AIDS is a story, or multiple stories, read to a surprising extent from a text that does not exist: the body of the male homosexual. It is a text people so want – need – to read that they have gone so far as to write it themselves. (1999: 361)

In valorizing the cocktail as a 'miracle drug', the pamphlet's text does not abandon its laissez-faire tone in regards to testing. To the question: 'Who has the strength to deal with medications?', the authors of the text (self-identified HIV-positive gay men) respond:

> If you discover that you are negative (that you have not been infected with AIDS), you can forget about [taking a number of pills every day for the rest of your life]. If you discover that you are positive, it is possible that you don't need to begin treatment immediately. It is plausible to assume that you will have enough time to prepare for a change that will necessitate [this] medical treatment.

To add to the misleading nature of the educational message, the text now assures the reader of a number of implausible outcomes. First, a negative result to an HIV-antibody test does not at all guarantee that the person tested is HIV-negative. Unlike virtually all of the materials sampled in this study, most AIDS-related pamphlets printed in the U.S. at the same time as these Israeli materials include the fact that one must be tested three to six months after the first test (and not engage in risky behaviors) to be sure that one is HIV-negative. A reader of the Hebrew pamphlet may incorrectly assume that he is negative when in fact he may be positive but has not yet developed serum antibodies to HIV – antibodies that are key in determining a person's HIV-positive status. Furthermore, for all of the advice offered in the text of this pamphlet, not once is a doctor's visit encouraged. Timing of first antiviral treatment remains a highly contested issue in the medical community. To date there still exists no consensus on protocols for primary treatment for HIV infection, and thus as in any medical situation each case should be dealt with on an individual basis by consulting with a knowledgeable doctor.

The text concerning the cocktail in the pamphlet targeting a female audience is accurate and informative compared to the pamphlet aimed towards a gay male readership. In the section entitled 'What does the cocktail do to you?', the authors of the woman-targeted text state the following:

> The therapy includes a number of pills per day and is capable of causing side effects that many women experience and some women do not. Most of the most severe side effects occur in the first months of treatment and if they do not pass and the woman treated feels that it's difficult for her [to cope] with them, it is recommended to consult with a physician about the ending of the treatment.
>
> If you decide to trust your doctor's recommendation to begin with the treatment, it behooves you to organize yourself for the beginning of a strict medical regimen. It is important that you understand: Ending the therapy or carelessness in taking the pills will cause the virus in your body to develop resistance to the medications.

This text is thorough in describing the cocktail; it makes the concrete point that it is imperative to seek a physician's advice in thinking about beginning such a treatment. Further, the text supportively advises a woman who has decided to undergo treatment that she must adhere meticulously to the treatment, and also clarifies that fact that failure to adhere to the regimen of medications may result in developing a resistance to the drugs.

9 Conclusion

There is a clear difference in the presentation of a cogent Israeli Hebrew AIDS educational message based upon the gender of the intended audience. This linguistic engineering creates discourse geared towards an audience of readers based upon gender and/or sexual orientation. Use of marked personal pronouns and verb forms provides a means for conveying the gender-specific message. Missing information adds to the nebulousness of the message conveyed, and this trend is most readily apparent in pamphlets targeting a gay male audience. Comparable pamphlets targeted towards a female audience, on the other hand, do not employ such techniques of obscuring information, and are the most successful in presenting a cogent educational message. These pamphlets geared towards women address both the psychological as well as the physical aspects of testing for HIV, consulting a physician, and embarking upon a course of therapy. Conversely, the pamphlets that target a gay male audience or an audience of mixed genders fail to accomplish the task of fully describing the many facets (emotional as well as somatic) of HIV infection.

It is unclear whether the authors of the pamphlets consciously decided to include or exclude diacritic markings in the text. Certainly, the diacritics were used to create emphasis and to remind the reader that he or she is being specifically addressed. However, within these pamphlets there does not seem to be a unifying reason that accounts for the instance of marked language in one instance and ambiguous nonvocalic language in another. Predominant Israeli concepts of masculinity, femininity, and homosexuality may have been influential in the accentuation of the various messages. Though beyond the scope of this analysis, a vigorous examination of notions of gender and sexuality in Israel that are situated in broader political economic trends could evidence forces that have shaped the discourse of these and other AIDS educational materials. Furthermore, a historical focus on the course of AIDS in Israel could contextualize the results of this analysis by elucidating putative changes in the perceptions of HIV. The pamphlets examined here were published in the mid-1990s, when the discovery of combinatory anti-retroviral therapies could have altered the perception of AIDS from a death sentence to a disease that can be managed over the course of one's lifetime. An examination of AIDS in Israel along so many disciplinary lines would, at its very minimum, require extensive personal interviews with key players in AIDS education on both private and governmental levels. In addition, though the language in the pamphlets provides a glimpse at gender-specific discourse, larger corpora of data (including spoken language data) would be required to establish more grounded connections between language and gender constructions.

On a macro-level, the navigation of the political scene by Israeli gay groups in the mid-1980s can perhaps serve as a starting point to explain why AIDS was relegated to the domain of the individual body in the texts aimed at gay male populations. Walzer (2000) proposes that the gay community in Israel chose to disconnect AIDS from discussions of homosexuality because Israeli society in the 1980s was not receptive to the gay community. He asserts that this disjuncture developed into an educational tactic of bypassing any links between 'AIDS' and 'gay' which continued until the late 1990s, when many in the gay community believed that the separative discourse of this tactic was having an adverse impact on gay men's safer-sex practices.[9] An analysis of this discourse of exclusion could begin to explain the emphasis on the individual body in AIDS educational pamphlets for gay men and preclusion of any mention of community (be it the gay community or the general community).

As educational efforts changed, and pamphlets began to be published for lesbian and heterosexual audiences, the discourse changed. Perhaps the authors of these newer pamphlets harbored less fear of the social stigma connected to gay men than did previous pamphlet authors. This could ac-

---

[9] *HaZman HaVarod*, a monthly gay newspaper, adorned its March 1997 issue with the headline '2,800 Gays in Israel Don't Know They're Infected' (Kaner 1997). Walzer (2000) contends that though the country's sodomy law had been repealed in 1998 and gays were increasingly seen as part of the Israeli population at large, many gays did not seem to think that they could develop HIV infection 'just like everyone else'.

count for the fact that the discourse of these newer pamphlets invoked the psychological and social facets of AIDS in addition to its somatic aspects. Further analysis of AIDS-related discourse in written Hebrew, especially of discourse targeted at groups with much less visibility than gay men (such as Israeli lesbians and gay and lesbian Arabs), may lead to a clearer understanding of these texts. Delving more deeply into the domain of gender and sexuality identity politics in Israel would provide a rich contextual background and a source of reference for current and future engineers of written AIDS educational discourse.

Another useful and insightful direction for future study is a comparative analysis of HIV/AIDS educational materials in languages other than Israeli Hebrew. More specifically, an exploration of semantic targeting and hiding techniques in a language such as English (which does not morphologically mark gender as Hebrew does and instead must rely upon lexical techniques of obscuring or specifying gender) may prove a useful addition to nascent linguistic examinations of this domain of public health education. As medical therapies for HIV and AIDS progress in their efficacy, it is also imperative to realize successful and comprehensive AIDS educational campaigns that honestly and thoroughly inform the public about a disease which affects the world in increasingly epidemic proportions.

References

Adam, Barry. 1989. The State, Public Policy, and AIDS Discourse. *Contemporary Crises* 13(1): 1-14.

Azaiza, Faisal and Adital Tirosh Ben-Ari. 1997. Knowledge of and Attitudes to AIDS Among Arab Professionals in Israel. *International Social Work* 40(3): 327-341.

Bartholet, Jeffrey. 1996. A New Kind of Blood Libel. *Newsweek*, 12 February 1996, 127(7): 40.

Bat-El, Outi. 1986. Extraction in Modern Hebrew Morphology. Master's thesis, UCLA, Los Angeles, California.

Ben-Yishai, Tzvi. 1996. National AIDS Policy of Israel. *AIDS Education*, ed. Schenker, I., Sabar-Friedman, G., and Sy, F. New York: Plenum Press.

Bolton, Ralph. 1992. Mapping Terra Incognita: Sex Research for AIDS Prevention – An Urgent Agenda For the Nineties. *In the Time of AIDS: Social Analysis, Theory and Method*, ed. Herdt, G. and Lindenbaum, S. Newbury Park, CA: Sage.

Brandt, A.M. 1991. AIDS and Metaphor: Toward the Social Meaning of Epidemic Disease. *In Time of Plague: The History and Social Consequences of Lethal Epidemic Disease*, ed. Mack, A. New York: New York University Press.

Brundson, C. 1990. Television: Aesthetics and Audiences. *Logics of Television*, ed. Melancamp, P. Bloomington: Indiana University Press.

Clark, Hebert H. 1996. *Using Language*. Cambridge: Cambridge University Press.

van Dijk, Teun A. 1993. Principles of Critical Discourse Analysis. *Discourse and Society* 4(2): 249-285.

Davidson, Alan G. 1991. Looking for Love in the Age of AIDS: The Language of Gay Personals, 1978-1988. *The Journal of Sex Research* 28(1): 125-137.

Davidson, Brad. 1998. Interpreting Medical Discourse: A Study of Cross-linguistic Communication in the Hospital Clinic. Ph.D. Dissertation. Department of Linguistics, Stanford University.

Donovan, Mark C. 1997. The Problem with Making AIDS Comfortable: Federal Policy Making and the Rhetoric of Innocence. *Journal of Homosexuality* 32(3/4): 115-144.

Fairclough, Norman. 1995. *Critical Discourse Analysis: The Critical Study of Language*. London and New York: Longman.

Fink, Amir Sumaka'i and Jacob Press. 1999. *Independence Park: The Lives of Gay Men in Israel*. Stanford: Stanford University Press.

Fishman, Rachelle. 1999. Condoms Banned From Israel's Anti-AIDS Campaign. *The Lancet*, 27 November 1999, 354(9193): 1887.

Gantz, Walter and Bradley S. Greenberg. 1990. The Role of Informative Television Programs in the Battle against AIDS. *Health-Communication* 2(4): 199-215.

Gee, James Paul. 1999. An Introduction to Discourse Analysis: Theory and Method. London and New York: Routledge.

van Gelder, Paul. 1996. Talkability, Sexual Behavior, and AIDS: Interviewing Male Moroccan Immigrants. *Human Organization* 55(2): 133-140.

Georgakopoulou, Alexandra, and D. Goutsos. 1997. *Discourse Analysis: An Introduction*. Cornwall: Edinburgh University Press.

Glinert, Lewis. 1994. *Modern Hebrew: An Essential Grammar*. London and New York: Routledge.

Goldin, Carol S. 1994. Stigmatization and AIDS: Critical Issues in Public Health. *Social Science and Medicine* 39(9): 1359-1366.

Gusfield, J. 1981. *The Culture of Public Problems*. University of Chicago Press: 53.

Henderson, Charles W. 1999. AIDS Knowledge and Attitudes of Pupils Attending Urban High Schools in Israel. *AIDS Weekly Plus*, 10 May 1999.

Henderson, Charles W. 1998. Israel to Fund 'Cocktail' Drugs for AIDS Patients. *AIDS Weekly Plus*, 1 June 1998.

Hymes, Dell. 1987. Communicative Competence. *Sociolinguistics: An International Handbook of the Science of Language and Society*, ed. Ammon, U. Berlin: de Gruyter.

Israel AIDS Task Force.. Accessed on 17 February 2001.

Jones, Rodney H. 1998. Two Faces of AIDS in Hong Kong: Culture and Construction of the 'AIDS Celebrity'. *Discourse and Society* 9(3): 309-338.

Kaner, Oren. 1997. AIDS in Israel: A Gay Disease. *HaZman HaVarod*, March 1997: 3- (in Hebrew).

Leap, William L. 1991. AIDS, Linguistics, and the Study of Non-Neutral Discourse. *Journal of Sex Research* 28(2): 275-287.

Leap, William L. 1996. *Word's Out: Gay Men's English*. Minneapolis: University of Minnesota Press.

Lupton, Deborah. 1994. *Medicine as Culture: Illness, Disease and the Body in Western Societies*. London: SAGE Publications.

Lupton, Deborah, Sophie McCarthy and Simon Chapman. 1995. 'Doing the Right Thing': The Symbolic Meanings and Experiences of Having an HIV Antibody Test. *Social Science and Medicine* 41(2): 173-180.

Lyttleton, Chris. 1994. Knowledge and Meaning: The AIDS Education Campaign in Rural Northeast Thailand. *Social Science and Medicine* 38(1): 135-146.

Morley, David. 1980. *The 'Nationwide' Audience*. Television Monograph, No. 11. London: British Film Institute,

Myrick, Roger. 1998. AIDS Discourse: A Critical Reading of Mainstream Press and Surveillance of Marginal Identity. *Journal of Homosexuality* 35(1): 75-93.

Nelson, Steven D. 1994. Wear Your Hat: Representational Resistance in Safer Sex Discourse. *Journal of Homosexuality* 27(1/2): 285-304.

Oklahoman Staff. 1985. State Blood Group Testing For AIDS. *The Daily Oklahoman*, 15 March: 22.

Parker, Richard. 1992. Sexual Diversity, Cultural Analysis, and AIDS Education in Brazil. *In the Time of AIDS: Social Analysis, Theory, and Method,* ed. Herdt, G. and Lindenbaum, S. Newbury Park, CA: Sage.

Parker, Richard, and M. Carballo. 1990. Qualitative Research on Gay and Bisexual Behaviour Relevant to HIV/AIDS. *The Journal of Sex Research* 27: 497-525.

Patton, Cindy. 1999. Inventing 'African AIDS'. *Culture, Society, and Sexuality*, ed. Parker, R. and Aggelton, P. London: UCL Press.

Ravid, Dorit. 1995. Neutralization of Gender Distinctions in Modern Hebrew Numerals. *Language Variation and Change* 7(1): 79-100.

Ritter, Elizabeth. 1993. Where's Gender? *Linguistic Inquiry* 24(4): 795-803.

Saville-Troike, Muriel. 1989. *The Ethnography of Communication*. Oxford: Blackwell.

Siegel-Itzkovich, Judy. 1999. Israel Health Minister Bans AIDS Campaign Promoting Condoms. *British Medical Journal*, 4 December 1999, 319(7223): 1445.

Sontag, Deborah. 2000. A Pop Diva, A Case of AIDS and an Israeli Storm. *The New York Times*, 29 February 2000. Section A, p. 16, Column 1.

Sontag, Susan. 1989. *Illness as Metaphor and AIDS and Its Metaphors*. New York: Doubleday.

Taylor, Christopher C. 1990. The Pathogenesis of Metaphor. In Feldman, D. (Ed.) *Culture and AIDS*. New York: Prager.

Toufexis, Anastasia. 1987. Ads That Shatter an Old Taboo; Fear Over AIDS Puts Condom Commercials on TV. *Time*, 2 February 1987, 129: 63.

Treichler, Paula. 1999. AIDS, Homophobia, and Biomedical Discourse: an Epic of Signification. *Culture, Society, and Sexuality*, ed. Parker, R. and Aggelton, P. London: UCL Press.

Walzer, Lee. 2000. *Between Sodom and Eden: A Gay Journey Through Today's Changing Israel*. New York: Columbia University Press.

15

Playing the Straight Man: Displaying and Maintaining Male Heterosexuality in Discourse

SCOTT F. KIESLING

1   Language, Gender, Sex and Desire

In this chapter I explore the connections between language use on the one hand, and that part of a person's identity that has to do with sex and desire. I define identity as the relationship an individual creates, through his or her everyday practices, with other people in society, whether those people are directly in front of them, or some imagined stereotypical other. Identities in this view are quite complex and entail an interaction among all of the relationships a person has. One aspect of such relationships is gender. This kind of relationship is based on the sexual dimorphism of the human species, but transcends, emphasizes, and negates the 'original biology to create a system of social practices defined and recreated by those practices' (see Connell 1987: 78-82). Moreover, the practices of gender can have consequences for the body: 'We may say, then, that the practical transformation of the body in the social structure of gender is not only accomplished at the level of symbolism. It has physical effects on the body; the incorporation is a material one' (Connell 1987:87).

One of the practices that is regulated by gender relations is desire, especially sexual desire, desire being a relationship that can obtain between two

Language and Sexuality: Contesting Meaning in Theory and Practice.
Kathryn Campbell-Kibler, Robert J. Podesva, Sarah J. Roberts and Andrew Wong (eds.).
Copyright © 2001, CSLI Publications.

people or groups of people. In this case sexual desire usually organizes relations between genders. In recent western history, sexuality has become an identity category as well. An (academic) dichotomy between 'queer' and 'straight' identities has developed, where straight indicates traditional (generally heterosexual) gender practices, and queer denotes non-straight. One could argue that this is simply a separate identity category of sexuality, not necessarily part of gender. However, it is impossible to define queer without reference to the normative gender practices to serve as the 'unmarked' straight category; in a structuralist sense, without straight, there is no queer. In any view, these are all aspects of a person's identity, and the separation of taxonomies of gender, sexuality, class, race, ethnicity, etc. could be argued to be simply an academic exercise that rarely enters the everyday practice of speakers going about the business of creating identities. So connections among different aspects of identity will always exist; I argue that gender and sexuality are particularly intertwined.

In this chapter I explore the discourse of heterosexuality: how a group of men define, police, and display heterosexual relationships within their same-sex group, and how these practices also help to create and display relationships among the men – relationships of homosocial desire and dominance.

The heterosexual identities I explore are not just displays of difference from women and gay men. They are also, more centrally, displays of power and dominance over women, gay men, and other straight men. A discourse of heterosexuality involves not only difference from women and gay men, but also the dominance of these groups. In fact, we will see that, through the use of address terms, men display *same-sex* dominance by metaphorically referring to other men as 'feminine', thus drawing on the cultural model of the heterosexual couple to index a homosocial inequality.

2 'Greek' Society and Compulsory Heterosexuality

The men's discursive indexing of their heterosexuality is embedded in a community of practice that is organized around heterosexuality and sexual difference. Thus, not only the practices within speech activities, but also the organization, purposes, and rituals of speech events and activities in this community help to create a heterosexual and homosocial community.[1] This heterosexual organization begins with a separation of genders: The 'greek' letter society system is arranged through an ideology of sexual difference, such that fraternities are all-male, sororities all-female.

---

[1] I am using speech activities to denote actions smaller than a speech event but larger than a speech act. Speech activities can be made up of several speech acts; speech events are longer in duration and are made up of speech activities.

The system also polices heterosexuality through its organization and naming of social speech events and activities. The most obvious example of this is a 'mixer' speech event, at which one fraternity and one sorority hold a joint party, and 'mix' with one another. This terminology also reinforces an ideology of difference: Men and women are metaphorically different ingredients that must be mixed.

'Open' parties, while not being so overtly focused on heterosexual desire, nevertheless are similar in their focus on sex and alcohol. This focus is seen most in how the men evaluate parties, as Flyer does in the following excerpt. He is speaking during a meeting held to discuss fraternity problems. In this context, he compares his fraternity's parties to another's:

01 Flyer: I- I- I went-
02　　　I even went to a party the other night to investigate
03　　　just to see who was gone
04　　　not that I really wanted to go there
05　　　I didn't have a great time
06　　　I tried to get the fuck outta there but my ride dumped me.
07　　　I went to- what the fuck-
08　　　I went to see what happened.
09　　　it was fuckin packed.
10　　　it was wall to wall chicks.
11　　　chicks hookin' up with guys everywhere
12　　　they're havin such a great time
13　　　they decided to fuck on the floor or whatever (??)
14 ??:　(who?)
15 Flyer: this was Sig Ep OK.
16　　　and this- what this-
17　　　I- I thought *Jesus Christ.*
18　　　this was our parties.
19　　　good music,
20　　　they had a couple of trash cans of beer
21　　　and a couple bottles of liquor.
Excerpt 1. Flyer.[2]

---

[2] Transcription conventions are as follows:

I I	Bounds simultaneous speech.
=	Connects two utterances produced with noticeably less transition time between them than usual.
(number)	Silences timed in tenths of seconds.
#	Bounds passage said very quickly.
^	Falsetto.
TEXT	Upper case letters indicate noticeably loud volume.

In this excerpt, Flyer is in fact implying that Gamma Chi Phi's parties have become too focused on drinking and homosocial activity, by suggesting another fraternity's party was better primarily because *it was wall to wall chicks* (*chicks* is the term the men most often use for women, especially young women to whom they are sexually attracted). Moreover, these women are *hookin' up* with the men, and are having such a great time, claims Flyer, that they *decided to fuck on the floor.* Thus it is because of this heterosexual activity that the party is rated highly - notice that Flyer goes out of his way to suggest that the drinks were not special (line 20: *they had a couple trash cans of beer*). This high evaluation of heterosexual activity creates a social context in which heterosexual sex is glorified as an end in itself, thus creating an ideology of heterosexual desire as an important social goal.

Some heterosexually organized speech activities constitute these larger speech events, and have been named by the men and women. Flyer's phrase *hook up* is an example. These named sexual speech activities were explained to me by Saul in an interview:

```
01 SK:    there's hookin' up, there's scamming,
02        what other words are there like that?
03 Saul:  throwin' raps hhhhhhh
04 SK:    I never heard that one, what's that?
05 Saul:  throwin' a rap is just basically
06        you go up to a girl you think is attractive and uh
07        y'kno:w you try to be as outgoing as you can. normally-
08        the best way
09        that I've found
10        to get a girl
11        to hold a conversation
12        #is to entertain em.#
13        an' basically throwing a rap is entertaining a girl
14        *with* the intent to try to bring her back that night he he he he
```

°	Indicates noticeably low volume, placed around the soft words.
Text	Italics indicates emphatic delivery (volume and/or pitch).
-	Indicates that the sound that precedes it is stopped suddenly.
:	Indicates the sound that precedes it is prolonged.
,	Indicates a slight intonational rise.
?	Indicates a sharp intonational rise.
he, ha	Laughter.
(text)	Transcript enclosed in single parenthesis indicates uncertain hearing.
((comment))	Double parenthesis enclose transcriber's comments.

15 SK:　　yeah

16 Saul:　*or* with the intent of eventually setting something up.=

17 SK:　　=is there any difference,

18　　　　like if you just go an t- an an an

19　　　　and talk to her

20　　　　like is there is there any way that *she* knows that?

21　　　　lin that throwing rapsl

22 Saul:　lthe smart　　　　　l the smart girls do he he he he he he

23　　　　they they they know that um::

24　　　　but...we do our best to say, y'know

25　　　　like, we'll throw in all kinds of disclaimers when we're talkin y'know

26　　　　'y'know hey::'

27　　　　'y'know but we you know what I mean'

28　　　　'y'know what I'm sayin?'

29　　　　that kind of things

30　　　　and you'd even say that to a girl.

31　　　　You'll be talkin'

32　　　　and you'll say somethin' a little promiscuous maybe like

33　　　　'aw you know know what I mean' type of deal so-

34　　　　so yeah

35 SK:　　OK, so, and hookin' up is- is that different?

36　　　　that's more of a ... after the fact kind of thing

37 Saul:　tha- tha- that's the action. he he he he he

38　　　　that's the action and that's uh...uh

39　　　　ah:I mean y'know you find a gir:l,

40　　　　you throw your rap,

41　　　　you hook up,

42　　　　and uh, usually no strings attached.

43　　　　but a lot of times- not a lot of times-

44　　　　depending on who the girl is

45　　　　if it happens to be a drunk thing

46　　　　and it's late night

47　　　　and you hook up

48　　　　it's usually something you try to keep as a drunk story.

49　　　　but um, but, I mean, sometimes hookin' up leads to y'know

50　　　　y'know you li- you end up likin' the girl y'know

51　　　　and then you go into your commitment thing.

52 SK:　　yeah all right now then there's some other ones like scamming.

53　　　　do you guys use that at all?

54 Saul:　yeah:: well

55　　　　scamming is interchangeable with throwing a rap.

```
56 SK:     is that uh-...
57         in my experience that's more of a female term.
58 Saul:   yeah gir- girls- yeah that's the way to look at it
59         if I go to a girl, I'm throwin a rap.
60         but if I'm a girl, getting the rap thrown to me,
61         and I'm catching on to this,
62         this guy's scamming on me.
63 SK:     OK
64 Saul:   so...that's- I guess that's the bound
65         that's the fine line between the two.
66 SK:     do people do that a lot?
67 Saul:   oh yeah. oh:: yeah.
68         e- even- even w-
69         I remember when I had a girlfriend and,
70         y'know we were committed,
71         and I liked her a lot but we had our problems and
72         y'know I'd see a girl I though was atttractive
73         and if I could talk to her,
74         I'd throw her a rap.
75         not knowing- not thinking I was gonna hook up with her that night
76         but to let her know that I'm around and
77         eventually I- y'know I knew I'd be free and I could come  back then
78         'hey you remember me?'
79         'let's go do something sometime,' y'know
80         (0.5)
81         try to leave an impression.
82         that's what throwin a rap does is tryin to leave an- an impression.
```
Excerpt 2. Saul.

In this excerpt, Saul explains a constellation of terms describing heterosexual speech activities: *throwin' raps*, *scamming*, *hookin' up*. He also names some different kinds of heterosexual relations without describing them in detail: *a drunk thing* and *do your commitment thing*. The latter two illustrate the distinction the men make between short- and long-term relationships respectively, and their importance as immediate goals of the fraternity men. Saul comments that a *drunk thing* is an experience *you might want to keep as a drunk story* (for 'Gavel', as described below). This way of viewing 'one-night stands' suggests that they are as much for the homosocial enjoyment of the fraternity, and a display of sexual prowess, as they are actual sexual attraction (although sexual attraction should be understood socially as well). The *commitment thing*, on the other hand, implies that the man actually likes the woman and enjoys her companionship whether or not sex is involved. In fact, men were often ridiculed by other members for spending too much time with their girlfriends at the expense of the fraternity.

The men thus have a range of named heterosexual speech events, activities, and sexual relationships. Other social displays, such as the display of posters of nude or nearly-nude women in their apartments and dorm rooms, are similarly heterosexually-focused. In sum, the institutions of greek society, the speech events that make up this society, and the speech activities within those events are constructed principally around the display of sexual difference and heterosexual desire. They reflect the cultural models for men and women as different and unequal: men as dominant and hunting for sex, women as submissive and existing as sexual prey for the men.

3 The Heterosexuality of Homosociability in the Fraternity

Now let us turn to how the men talk in these interactions, and how this talk serves to create and reinforce the heterosexual model. The men use several different strategies to police and construct sexuality. However, most involve the taking or assigning of specific stances either to themselves or to others, including women and subordinated men. specifically, one revolves around the telling of stories, both performed in meetings and told in more private conversations. Another type is speech in which men take on roles of women and homosexual men - or have these roles forced upon them. A man is 'assigned' the role of a woman or gay man when he is in a subordinate position.

3.1 Cultural models of sex in interaction: Public valorization of 'man as hunter for sex'

Many of the stories the men tell present women and men in sexual relationships. These stories comprise a recognized, ratified genre in which men display sexual relationships. This 'genrification' of such narratives is an important component for policing/reinforcing hegemonic heterosexuality, because it means that one kind of sexual relationship is valorized in narrative performances.

This genre is a linguistic object, and its importance in the verbal repertoires of the men is a way of valorizing this kind of heterosexuality. There is status (and solidarity) to be gained from telling a story of this sort, or in being a character of one of these stories. In investigating how identities are created and how social values are transmitted, we need to look at the deployment of genres in the community, which includes the content of these genres. For example, in the academic community such story-telling as is found in the fraternity Gavel round is not valued. Horvath (1987) has compared the kinds of texts (genres) told at a working-class women's party and a middle-class women's lunch, and found that there is a significant difference in the kinds of texts told by these different people, and that they reflect cultural differences. In addition, certain *forms* of speaking are likely to co-occur with these genres, so they thus become an explanatory concept as well.

3.2 'Fuck stories' in gavel

Gavel is a story round at the end of Sunday meetings in which men often tell of their sexual exploits over the weekend. These are explicitly named by the men as 'fuck stories.' They can be particularly graphic, and portray women as sexual objects for the men, including for men who are voyeurs. The gavel stories were one of the highlights of the week for the men; they were performances for the entertainment of the members, usually told at the expense of the performer or one of the other members. (Fuck stories are not the only kind of narrative; another common type is the 'drunk story,' in which one member tells about the usually embarrassing actions of another member while very intoxicated; drunk stories and gavel stories are often the same.)

During most of my research I was not permitted to tape-record gavel. This fact shows how important this story round is for the social cohesion of the group – it is a form of ritual gossip which may never leave the group. They are a powerful way of creating a cultural model and placing value on it.

3.3 Conversational narrative and alternate sexual identities

While fuck stories are perhaps the most overt and obvious genre in which a certain heterosexual norm is reproduced, the men do not see this as the only kind of relationship with women, although it is the most 'public' representation their relationships with women. Let's have a look at one of the members who displays this public/private dichotomy. First, consider a portion of Hotdog's report to Mack of his trip to Atlanta, in which he creates a stance with respect to women similar to that in gavel stories. This excerpt is from the beginning of the narrative, on the day Hotdog arrived in Atlanta.

```
01 Hotdog: Then we went to a Ma:ll
02         and just like sat in the food court
03         and just looked at all the beautiful fuckin' hot ass chicks
04 Mack:   (are they) really dude.
05 Hotdog: Oh my go:d
06 Mack:   Where was it?
07 Hotdog: In Atlanta
08 Mack:   I know but what school?
```

09 Hotdog: Ahh Georgia Tech.
10 Mack:　I'm movin' to Atlanta dude
11 Andy:　We're movin' there
12 Hotdog: We weren't like at the school
13　　　　we were like
14　　　　we were like in like the business district
15 Mack:　Oh
16 Hotdog: So it was just like all business ladies dressed up
17　　　　and they're like (.) *in*credible.
18　　　　then that night we registered
19　　　　that's that *first* night is when we went to Lulu's,
20 Mack:　Let's move to Atlanta when we graduate　|dude.
21 Hotdog:　　　　　　　　　　　　　　　　　　|I want to. I *de*finitely
　　　　want to. Definitely.
22 Andy:　I told you I wanna move down there.
23　　　　I'm movin down there as soon as I graduate.
Excerpt 3. Hotdog, Mack and Andy.

In this excerpt, Hotdog evaluates a shopping mall in Atlanta by describing the physical appearance of the women he sees there. We can see the impact of this evaluation and the importance of the appearance of women through the reaction of the men: Just this description of the women prompts them to talk about moving there when they graduate. This response constructs Hotdog's evaluation, then, as the highest compliment for the city.

Contrast this positioning with the one Hotdog presents in the interview situation, and with only myself present. The following excerpt begins after I have asked Hotdog about his plans for the future, specifically marriage.

01 Hotdog: I don't ever intend to be close to getting married any time soon.
02 SK:　　You think you'll get married eventually?
03 Hotdog: Yeah.(0.8)Probably (1.0)*let's see today's ninety three*
04　　　　I probably could see myself getting married by like
05　　　　nineteen ninety seven nineteen ninety eight.(1.4)
06　　　　So about (.) four years.
07 SK:　　Wow. Do you- I mean- do want to or is that just a matter of-
08 Hotdog: No I-
09　　　　it's not that I want to I have I have had a girlfriend sinc:e
10　　　　*I guess we were*
11　　　　I was in high school we've been datin' on and off.
12　　　　Kinda got a little more serious *once* we went away believe it or not.
13　　　　and uh (.) yknow if things stay the same way with her,

14   I could see us getting married like: ninety seven ninety eight
15   but if: we-
16   if things don't stay the same
17   I can't see u- me gettin' married
18   until after the year two thousand (laughing).
19   ISo. I
20 SK: ILaughI (1.7) So you guys are pretty close then.
21 Hotdog: Yeah. We're very close.

Excerpt 4. Hotdog.

Because Hotdog evaluates all the women he sees in the Atlanta mall as sexual objects, we would get an impression that his status on the heterosexual marketplace is unattached: For most of the men, the definition of having a 'girlfriend' is monogamy with that person. Thus, if Hotdog publicly shows a face of sexual voracity, it would be logical to think that he does not have a girlfriend. However, he *does* have a girlfriend, one with whom he is 'very close,' and one whom he is considering marrying in the near future. So Hotdog represents himself with respect to women and that he represents his sexuality quite differently in two different situations with different audiences and purposes: he performs two different kinds of identity in each of these situations.

In fact, it seems that he is a little unsure of exactly how to perform his identity with me in the interview. My status is not one he is familiar with: I am similar to a member, but not quite a member. At the beginning of this excerpt, Hotdog seems to want to present the same kind of identity as he did in the Atlanta recount. He denies quite strongly an interest in getting married: *I don't ever intend to be close to getting married any time soon.* But after I rephrase the question, he reveals that marriage may only be four years off. It takes several moves on my part before Hotdog tells me about his girlfriend, even though he later says 'we're very close' (line 19).

Hotdog's relationship with me has shifted over these turns, so has his identity. He begins with a stance similar to the one he takes publicly in the fraternity, and eventually admits to having a close, loving relationship with a woman. We thus see how the linguistic construction of sexuality for these men is based not just on the actual relationships they have with women but also on the relationships they are creating with other men. This allows the men to `have' in fact more than one (hetero)sexual identity.

3.4 Metaphorical representations of other members as women

Morford (1987) and Hall and O'Donovan (1996) show that an address term indexes not simply such things as power and solidarity, but specific cultural models which are part of speakers' knowledge, and which interact with context to create local relationships between speakers. To the extent that speakers share these cultural models and scripts, the address terms are interactionally successful. Address terms in the fraternity work in this way as well, on several levels of linguistic and cultural awareness. All of the address terms I consider position a man as subordinate through the use of a female address term.

In the first case, the address term occurs within a culturally recognized phrase, thus indexing a certain heterosexual cultural model. It occurs while the men are playing monopoly, in which players pass through other players' property and pay rent. I will particularly focus on line 26, but I reproduce here some relevant context as well.

```
09 ((Pete rolls, moves))
10 Dave:       Nice. pay me. (2.3)
11 Pete:   I can't. Aren't you in jail or something?
12         Don't I not have to pay you this time?
13             IFree pass.I
14 Boss: You  Igot a    I free pass.
15         He's got one more.
16 Dave: No that's your last one.
17 Pete:   I have one more.
           I've got one left.
18 Dave: No that's it
19 Pete:   I have one left. I've only used two.
20 Dave: That's right. And these over here. OK.
21 Pete:   The deal was for fi:ve.
22 Dave: God damn I needed that money too you son of a *bitch*.
23 ((Dave rolls))
24         The deal was for TWO.
25 (4.3)
26 Pete:   HI: HI: hi: honey I'm home.
27 Boss: I'm gonna blow by Dave right here.
28 ((Boss rolls))
```
Excerpt 5. Dave, Pete and Boss.

The phrase 'Hi Hi honey I'm home' in line 26 does a large amount of contextually-dependent identity work for Pete. First, we need to understand the game situation: Pete has landed on a property owned by Dave, which would usually mean that Pete has to pay rent to Dave. However, because of an earlier deal in which Dave gave Pete a number of 'free passes,' Pete is allowed to 'stay' at Dave's property without paying rent. Pete draws on this metaphor and extends it. The metaphor taunts Dave and puts him down, in part by metaphorically vandalizing Dave's property, but also through the phrase 'Hi Hi honey I'm home.'

Without the correct background knowledge and cultural ideologies, the remark makes no sense, especially as a taunt. The phrase brings to mind the stereotype of a husband returning from work to a 'housewife' in a stereo-typical American nuclear family, in which the woman is an unpaid house-worker. So it metaphorically positions Pete not only as one of the family staying for the night, but as 'the man of the house,' in a dominant position over his wife. This interpretation was confirmed through an informal poll of the members. Dave is then put in a metaphorically subordinate position as a housewife in a particular stereotype of a family. It thus makes sense as a taunt because Pete is not only staying for free but claiming that Dave is in a servant position to him. Without this background knowledge, the phrase makes little sense. Thus it reinforces an ideology as a woman/wife in that subordinate servant role for the man/husband, even as it is constructing a local dominance relationship between Pete and Dave.

This kind of dominance relationship was even clearer in the naming of one of the pledges. During the pledge period, the members gave all the pledges nicknames which were often insulting or highlighted the subordi-nate position of the pledge. One pledge was given the name 'Hazel,' and was made to perform household cleaning duties for several of the members for a few weeks. Here again, the name of the subordinate male is female. But it also refers to a 1950s television show of the same name, about a character of the same name who is a domestic worker for a nuclear-family household. The men draw on the show and the larger cultural metaphor of women as domestic workers, to name a structurally subordinate position for 'Hazel.'

One of the most common examples of this kind of positioning is the use of *bitch* to insult another man. I collected several examples of this, and heard many more which I did not record or note down. In the next excerpt, Pete uses bitch in the prototypical way. It takes place during the chapter correspondent election. Like several other members (including Mack), Pete suggests three offices and the proper candidate for each. Mick reminds him not to argue for other offices and Pete then argues he can say whatever he wants when he has the floor.

```
01 Mick:    Pete
02 Pencil:  You're a moron ((to Mitty, who just spoke))
03 Pete:    Kurt for chapter correspondent,
04          IRitchie for sch-olarship,
05 ?:       Ino                              no:::::
```

06 Pete: and Ernie for hilstorian.
07 ?:   IRitchie for chaplain.
08 Pete: allright well Ritchie for historian,
09   and Ernie for scholarship.
10 Mick: We're on one vote right now.
11 Pete: Hey I get to say my piece I got the floor bitch.
12 Mick: Darter.

Excerpt 6. Mick, Pencil and Pete.

Here we see Pete clearly in opposition to his addressee, here Mick. He finishes his statement by calling Mick 'bitch,' normally a term used to refer derogatorily to a woman (or a female dog, from where the insult derives). This insults Mick both through the 'conventional' manner of calling him a dog, and by drawing on a social ideology of female as subordinate.

We have evidence that 'bitch' is associated with this subordinate role through another derogatory term used by the men: 'bitch boy.' This term is loaded with dominant-subordinate meaning: first through 'bitch,' and second through the term 'boy', also used to refer to a servant. First let's look at how it is used in a meeting by Speed:

01 Speed: All right look.
02   first of all, you guys need to realize
03   we do *not ha:ve* to ne- necessarily make a:ll the new brothers,
04   put them in positions right away.
05   a *lot*_of the new brothers already have positions.
06   they can get elected next year *or* next semester.
07   there *are* some positions that are semesterly.
08   we don't have to make sure that every one of them has a position.
09   they need time to *learn* and grow-
10   it's better that Ithey're-   Ithat they're=
11 ?:   I(I need an assistant,) I
12 Speed: =SHUT THE F:UCK UP.
13   it's better that they're-
14   that they're almost like I was with Tex.
15   I was Tex's like little bitch boy, graduate affairs,
16   and I learned a lot more there,
17   than I would if I got stuck in some leadership role,
18   so *fuck`em,

Excerpt 7. Speed.

Here Speed refers to the fact that he was Rex's assistant in the graduate affairs position, doing any tedious work Rex gave him. It is clearly a subordinate role, and therefore 'bitch' in its subordinate, servant meaning fits in. In addition, we have the story of the origin of the term from Mack:

01 Mack:	So bitch boy um
02	Chicken hawk and I don't know if you've ever met him KW um
03	one time was tellin a story
04	and I don't know if there were other people around
05	or if he's just told this story so many times
06	but um he apparently was at another school I think
07	maybe with his brother,
08	he was in a bar with his brother,
09	the details of it I'm not- I don't remember very well.
10	Anyway he was at this bar
11	and I think maybe he was talking to this- he was talking to a girl.
12	another guy some strange guy bigger than K though
13	um came over and started hassling him
14	either about the girl or he was standing in his place
15	you know the normal bar nonsense. and um
16	so K kinda left it be for a while and uh
17	he he I think he mentioned it to his brother
18	now they were there with a friend of his brother's
19	and apparently this friend of his brother's
20	they were at the bar
21	this friend of his brother's was quite a big man
22	very large you know
23	like six four you know like two hundred and fifty pounds or something
24	strong
25	big guy
26	and um so K went back over I think to talk to this girl
27	and uh apparently this same guy started giving him problems again
28	eh and this guy this big friend of Ks brother
29	comes up behind- behind this guy this guy that's bothering K,
30	and just puts his arm around him very gently
31	and kind of pulls him in close
32	and starts talking to him r:::really kind of
33	y- you know I don't even wanna I don't even wanna try and do the voice
34	that K does you're gonna have to ask K for it.

35   but t- he starts really talkin to him
36   like he's pimpin this guy or somethin' you know
37   and he goes you know what we gon do?
38   You gon be my bitch boy fa the rest of the night
39   and then he just went down the list of things that he's gonna make=
40   this guy do for him an
41   it wasn't- it was demeaning things like
42   you know you gonna get me drinks
43   your gonna come in and wipe my ass and
44   you know nothing nothing like
45   I'm gonna kick your ass or anything like that.
46   he spoke real calmly and real coolly and
47   you know You gon be my bitch boy tonight. you know
48   and so that's where it came from and
49   bitch boy you know it's pretty self explanatory
50   you know it's just a little boy
51   who's gonna do all the bitch work for me I dunno
Excerpt 8. Mack.

The bitch boy relationship is clearly one of dominance. Not a dominance of actual physical violence, but one of potential violence symbolized
by the things the dominant male makes the subordinate do. But it also has an
essential sexual component as well, one that on the surface looks to be homosexual. Under the surface, though, the relationship is a metaphorical male
dominant - female subordinate metaphor. Notice in line 31 that Mack says
'he starts talking to him like he's pimpin' this guy,' indicating he's treating
him like a prostitute under his care. Here we see clearly Mack equate *bitch*
with *woman*, stating that the relationship is metaphorically a heterosexual
one, not homosexual. So in using one of the most overt named dominance
relationships in the fraternity group, the men use a term that not only has a
lexical association with women (*bitch*), but also draws on the metaphor of a
woman as a (sexual) servant to a (physically) powerful, dominant man.
Thus, the meaning of bitch boy, which Mack claims is 'pretty self explanatory' in line 44, is only self explanatory if you have access to this cultural
script of heterosexual relationships of this type. Moreover, the use of the
term presupposes an understanding of this relationship and through its repetition reifies the existence of the dominance heterosexual model. The 'male'
half of the term (*boy*) also helps to create the subordinate position of the
addressee through age and race hierarchies. *Boy* is clearly an address term
used with a younger and less powerful person; a male who has not yet made
it to his full dominant position. It also indexes a racial cultural model in

which powerful White men address Black men with the term, such as in Ervin-Tripp's (1969) example of an exchange between a Black physician and a White police officer. The fraternity men, then, when they use *bitch boy*, are creating a number of different identities and relationships. Most immediately for the discourse, they are creating a relationship between who is the bitch boy and who is his dominator. However, they are also crucially drawing on a shared an ideology of gender relationships in which a woman is dominated by a man.

What about other address terms, especially those which are more clearly (heterosexual) male? Consider again the address terms in the monopoly game, where we saw Pete use 'Hi honey I'm home' to taunt Dave. Notice that Pete also uses the address term *dude*, particularly in line 5: `Dave, dude, dude Dave,' in which he is clearly playing with language by using alliteration and chiasmus. Pete is here having fun with language given the resources of the game. But the relationship he has - and wants to construct - with Dave is quite different. In the *dude* situation, Pete is not clearly dominating Dave, but rather Dave has something Pete wants (the red property). So Pete is constructing a solidary and perhaps even a subordinate relationship with Dave. This is the way the two clear 'masculine' address terms are used in the fraternity (*dude* and *man*): as solidarity indexes to focus on cooperative actions, and even to diffuse tensions during confrontations. So the generic masculine address terms focus on equality and solidarity, whereas the female terms are terms of dominance and insult. Thus, not only are male and female separated, they are treated unequally. Moreover, through the term *bitch boy* (and similar creative terms such as 'Hazel') male and female are related metaphorically through an assumed heterosexual ideology.

The address terms I have considered thus do more than just position a man as a woman. They position a man as a woman *in a narrative* - a cultural script. This woman, moreover, is clearly in a subordinate position in the narrative: as a housewife, as a prostitute, as a domestic servant. Each use of the address term makes sense only if the interlocutors share access to the cultural script.

This has implications for the way we understand language to index social identity. The standard assumption is that a certain variant of a variable becomes associated with a recognized cultural group, and people who identify with that cultural group are statistically more likely to use the variant. This is the 'acts of identity' model of language and identity (LePage and Tabouret-Keller 1985). It requires a knowledge of groups and the way they act, and a direct, one-to-one indexing of linguistic form to group identity. What we see here is that heterosexual identities and ideologies are being created in a much more complex way: there is really no separated group of heterosexuals in the dominant culture. This group, like men a few decades ago, is considered the norm, and is indeed hardly a coherent group. But as we have seen here that we can identify heterosexuality as part of these men's socially constructed identity. We must therefore have a model of language and identity that is itself much more complex than the acts of identity model, one that can take account of mocking and metaphorical positionings within a group that perpetuate its ideologies.

Such a model would recognize a multilayered social indexing of language, similar to Silverstein's (1996) orders of indexicality. The model would index at least four levels of social relationship: a local stance within an ongoing speech event, a position within an institution, a status in wider society, and, potentially at least, a place within a cultural model or script. And we have seen that there could be indexing within these levels as well, as local dominance relationships are indexed by a primary indexing of the cultural model.

4 Summary

We have seen how language is used by the men to reproduce a hegemonic heterosexuality which is embedded in the larger context of hegemonic masculinity. We saw that their society (Greek-letter society) is organized around an ideology of difference and how the speech activities which make up this society – both mixed and single sex – are based on the notion of sexual difference and heterosexuality. There is an elaborate cultural script around different kinds of heterosexuality, and these have led to the naming of these scripts and speech activities: throwing raps, scamming, a drunk story, the commitment thing. One of the most secret and sacred genres of the fraternity is centered around narratives of heterosexuality: fuck stories. In interaction, men metaphorically represent other men as women in order to claim dominance over that man (even in play), as we saw for the 'Hi honey I'm home' line, as well as 'bitch.' The metaphorical assignment of homosexuality worked in a similar way. These two metaphors find a complex but telling synthesis in the term 'bitch boy'. Importantly, in all of these examples the men were performing relationships for the men. We thus see that heterosexuality is embedded in the more important relationships of male dominance hierarchies and homosociability.

Similar practices of cathexis have been discussed by ethnographers of other European cultures. For example, Almeida (1996) describes a variant of the 'fuck story' genre told by the men he studied in a Portuguese village. He also describes a similar dichotomy of heterosexuality focusing on women as sexual partners and women as marriage partners. The fraternity men and the

Portuguese men show how much time and effort go into displaying these kinds of heterosexuality: For both groups of men, these stories are central to their socializing, and are something exalted and enjoyed, not merely expected.

Most importantly, these speech strategies of heterosexuality are how men in both cultures create status among their peers. Heterosexuality is thus not just about sexual object choice, but it also has a social construction that is primarily used by social actors to compete within same sex groups. This pattern suggests that patterns of male domination are not simply about men dominating women. Rather, in both cultures, male domination in heterosexual displays is about men displaying power *over* other men (and women) *to* other men. The stories and other forms of heterosexual display therefore represent same-sex status competition in which heterosexual gender differentiation and dominance is not the goal, but one strategy with which to construct a hegemonic masculinity. This finding suggests that in order to understand language and gender patterns, we need to understand how language is used to create difference and status within gender groups.

References

Almeida, Miguel Vale de. 1996. *The Hegemonic Male: Masculinity in a Portuguese Town*. Providence, RI: Berghahn Books.

Connell, Robert. 1987. *Gender and Power*. Stanford, CA: Stanford University Press.

Ervin-Tripp, Susan. 1969. Sociolinguistics. *Advances in Experimental Social Psychology*, ed. Leonard Berkowitz, Vol. 4, 93-107. Academic Press.

Hall, Kira and Veronica O'Donovan. 1996. Shifting Gender Positions among Hindi-speaking Hijras. *Rethinking language and Gender Research: Theory and Practice*, ed. Victoria Bergvall, Janet Bing, and Alice Freed, 228-66. London: Longman.

Horvath, Barbara. 1987. Text in Conversation: Variability in Story-Telling Texts. *Variation in Language: NWAV-XV at Stanford. Proceedings of the Fifteenth Annual Conference on New Ways of Analyzing Variation.* ed. Keith Denning, Sharon Inkelas, Faye McNair-Knox, and John Rickford. 212-223. Stanford, CA: Stanford University Linguistics Department.

LePage, R. B. and Andree Tabouret-Keller. 1985. *Acts of Identity: Creole-based Approaches to Language and Ethnicity.* Cambridge, New York: Cambridge University Press.

Morford, Janet. 1987. Social Indexicality in French Pronomial Address. *Journal of Linguistic Anthropology* 7:3-37.

Silverstein, Michael. 1996. Indexical Order and the Dialectics of Sociolinguistic Life. *SALSA III: Proceedings of the Third Annual Symposium About Language and Society -- Austin*, ed. Risako Ide, Rebecca Parker, and Yukako Sunaoshi, 266-95. Austin, Texas: University of Texas Department of Linguistics.

16

'Open Desire, Close the Body': Magic Spells, Desire and the Body Among the Petalangan Women in Indonesia

YOONHEE KANG

1   Introduction

How do people perceive their bodies and talk about them? How do people experience and make sense of their desires? How are their bodies and desires represented and projected in language practices? This study aims to discuss the interplay among language practices, desire,[1] and the body through an analysis of magic spells that are used among the Petalangan people of Indonesia.

As one of several indigenous ethnic groups living in the remote Kampar river hinterlands on the eastern part of Sumatra, Petalangans are well known for their practices of magic spells. They use magic spells in nearly every activity and for almost every pursuit. There are magic spells for farming, hunting, healing, promoting beauty, courtship, child-birth, and even for sexual intercourse.

---

[1] According to a dictionary (Merriam Webster's Collegiate Dictionary, 10th edition), desire is defined as 1) conscious impulse toward something that promises enjoyment or satisfaction in its attainment, 2) longing, craving, 3) sexual urge or appetite. Although the definition of desire in the sense of 'sexual urge or appetite' is a modality of desires, I use 'desire' mostly in the sense of sexual appetite or lust throughout this paper.

Language and Sexuality: Contesting Meaning in Theory and Practice.
Kathryn Campbell-Kibler, Robert J. Podesva, Sarah J. Roberts and Andrew Wong (eds.).
Copyright © 2001, CSLI Publications.

This paper will focus on a Petalangan women's genre of 'obscene magic spells' called *Monto Cabul* to discuss the discursive construction of the body and desire. Many married women in Petalangan society told me that they perform this genre of love charms in order to enhance their sexual capacity for their husbands' sexual satisfaction.[2] Based on Judith Butler's notions of discursive construction of gender and the body (Butler 1990, 1993), I will analyze the texts and social uses of women's love charms to examine how cultural notions of the body and desire are linguistically constituted through performances of magic spells.

Inspired by Butler's notions of gender as performance (Butler 1990), recent language and gender studies have paid increasing attention to the performative power of language[3] in relation to gender and sexuality (Hall and Bucholtz 1995, Livia and Hall 1997). According to Butler, gender is not a pre-given or fixed attribute of a subject, but rather an identity category created and constituted through the subject's 'repetition of acts' where the subject repeatedly 'cites' and 'performs' conventional traits and features of a specific gender so as to be culturally recognized as having specific attributes of men or women (Butler 1990: 140). Gender conventions, thus, are enabling as well as constraining factors for gender performativity.

By the same token, Butler argues that the materiality of the (sexed) body is also discursively constructed (Butler 1993). Focusing on the intelligibility and accessibility of sex and the body, she argues that sex (that is, biological attributes of men and women) always presupposes its social significance (that is, gender). People recognize a person's body either as male or female based on the presupposition of conventional or stereotyped features of the male and female bodies. According to Butler, even the materiality of the body, that is, the 'fixity of the body; its contours; its movements' (p. 2), corporeal elements that are assumed to exist prior to cultural construction of gender, are also bound up with signification. She argues that the issue of the body is neither presuming nor negating materiality (p. 30). Instead, she calls attention to the fact that the process of delimiting and contouring the body as prior to any signification itself constitutes materiality (ibid). The (sexed) body, or its materiality then is not a biologically pre-given basis of gender, but emerges as a product or effect of gender (p. 3).[4]

---

[2] Men are also reported to use magic for sexual intercourse. Unlike women's *Monto Cabul*, however, men's magic is said to enhance their sexual stamina. Men's magic is more likely to use medicine or exercise, while women's magic uses spells.

[3] Originating from Austin's speech act theory (Austin 1962), the term 'performative' refers to a constitutive or creative function of an utterance. The words are not just descriptive; they also act upon the world (cf. Searle 1969). For a discussion of 'performativity,' see Hall (2000).

[4] Butler's discussion does not imply that materialization is caused or originated by language, but rather implies that language mediates materialization, which is itself constitutive of materiality.

Criticizing Butler's universalized notion of a discursive construction of gender and the body (cf. Hall and Bucholtz 1995, Livia and Hall 1997), this study analyzes ethnographic accounts of specific language practices and their social contexts to demonstrate more localized and culturally specific ways that the body and desires are discursively constructed. I begin by examining Petalangan notions of language as action (Austin 1962) and associated cultural notions that mediate the transformations of 'words to the world' (Searle 1979). In doing so, I discuss three main questions.

First, how are the Petalangan magic spells internally organized? An a-lyzing linguistic features and patterns of these spells will reveal how a speaker's utterances are embedded in an unchanging formula of 'ancestors' words.' The highly formalized and poetic structure of magic spells renders a situated performance that transcends immediate authority by invoking ancestral authority.

Second, how do Petalangan women both recognize and represent their bodies and desires in magic spells? By applying Butler's emphasis of 'citation' or 'reiteration' of social conventions in materialization of the body (Butler 1993: 20), I will examine how women's magic spells project the female body by appropriating Petalangan conventional notions of female body, which are mostly based on male perspectives.

Third, how do women contest the dominant Petalangan gender ideology through the performances of magic spells (cf. Abu-Lughod 1986, Raheja and Gold 1994)? In contrast to the dominant Petalangan gender ideology that describes the relation of men and women as the dichotomy between 'reason' (*akal*) and 'desire' (*nafsu*) (Tsing 1993, Peletz 1996), women's uses of magic spells reveal the women to be 'rationally' in control of their desires. I will discuss how women perceive and represent their desires and the female sexuality[5] not as biologically ascribed but as a social requisite in achieving idealized wifely qualities. Differing with the conventional Western notion that desires and the body emanate from the individual, Petalangan women view desires and bodies as fully realized in their social relations.

This analysis suggests a critique of the idea that a biologically distinct individual 'self' or 'subject' is the presumed locus of agency[6] (cf. Ortner 1984), and similarly calls into question the idea that the subject's individual intention is a condition of agency (cf. Hall and Bucholtz 1995, Livia and Hall 1997). The subjective 'I' appears as a subject of sex and desire in spells, but only if it claims its agency in 'the ancestors' voices' that are em-

---

[5] By *sexuality* in this paper, I refer to the quality or state of being sexual (Merriam Webster's Collegiate Dictionary, 10th edition). In Petalangan society, however, there is no equivalent term for sexuality; they only have terms for men (*jantan*) and women (*betino*) respectively.

[6] By *agency*, I refer to the capacity of acting (cf. Ahearn 2000).

bedded in a specific type of magic formula while denying individual intentions. Petalangan women's agency is not located in their claiming of control over action. Rather, it is found in the very act of ascribing their agency to higher sources of power.

The data presented in this paper is based on a collection of magic spells that I gathered during twelve months of ethnographic and linguistic field research among the Petalangan people from 1998 to 1999. The majority of the spells were collected at Desa Betung, a Petalangan village in Kampar district. Through consultation and interviews with people from other villages, I found that practices of magic spells are common throughout the Petalangan society, and that the textual structures of the magic spells are similar in spite of some lexical variations from spell to spell.

2 Ethnographic Background: Men and Women of Petalangan Society

The Petalangan people in Sumatra (see Figure 1) constitute one of the indigenous ethnic groups that are categorized as *pedalaman* by neighboring ethnic groups. The term *pedalaman,* which literally means 'people of the interior,' implies a geographically remote and socially isolated people.[7] Because of their lack of transportation and communication with outsiders, Petalangan society has been deemed relatively 'backward' or 'primitive' compared to other communities in Riau (Tenas Effendy 1997, Turner 1997).

Historically linked to both the Minangkabau of West Sumatra and to the Malay of East Sumatra, on the other hand, Petalangan society has been influenced by the Minangkabau matrilineal system as well as by a patriarchal Malay Islamic culture (Andaya 1993). Petalangan society is thus an interesting example of male dominance within a matrilineal system. As a matrilineal society, each clan (*suku*) of Petalangans claims same ancestry through a female line, and these matrilineal descent groups consist of practical units in people's everyday lives. As a patriarchal Islamic society, only male members of the clan are allowed to control and enact customary law (*adat*), rules, and regulations of everyday life.[8]

Historically linked to both the Minangkabau of West Sumatra and to the Malay of East Sumatra, on the other hand, Petalangan society has been in-

---

[7] Since the previous Malay kingdoms of Riau used to have their main cities and towns along the rivers, the term *Pedalaman* (inland people) has been used to refer to the people who lived far from riversides and far from the centers of the kingdoms.

[8] From the Riau Malays' points of view, Petalangans' mixed culture demonstrates that they are not 'truly Malays' (Tenas Effendy 1997). See Peletz 1996 for another case study of the matrilineal Malay Muslim society.

Figure 1. Map of the Petalangan Region

fluenced by the Minangkabau matrilineal system as well as by a patriarchal Malay Islamic culture (cf. Andaya 1993). Petalangan society is thus an interesting example of male dominance within a matrilineal system. As a matrilineal society, each clan (*suku*) of Petalangans claims same ancestry through a female line, and these matrilineal descent groups consist of practical units in people's everyday lives. As a patriarchal Islamic society, only male members of the clan are allowed to control and enact customary law (*adat*), rules, and regulations of everyday life.[9]

For most Petalangans, rice cultivation, fishing and collecting rubber are the main sources of livelihood. Men undertake occasional but highly intensive and visible works, such as fishing and cutting trees in the forest,[10]

---

[9] From the Riau Malays' points of view, Petalangans' mixed culture demonstrates that they are not 'truly Malays' (Tenas Effendy 1997). See Peletz 1996 for another case study of the matrilineal Malay Muslim society.

[10] Men usually build their own houses on the river or in the forest and live there while doing work such as fishing and cutting trees for timber companies. Once a week, they will return home to the village where their wives and children live.

while women engage in less intensive but ongoing and unremarked upon tasks, such as farming, rubber-collecting, child-rearing, and other domestic works. With recent economic development, many young people have started to work at neighboring palm oil plantations. Some people, especially young adult males, leave their villages for the city to find better jobs. The most distinctive feature of men's work is mobility; it is one source of men's power.

Ideologically, people describe the relationship between men and women as that of *akal* (reason) and *nafsu* (desire) (cf. Siegel 1969).[11] These notions originate from Islamic gender ideology. *Akal* means reason, rationality, and intelligence, while *nafsu* refers to passions, desires, and bodily instincts. While animals only have *nafsu*, humans have both of these two components and *akal* controls *nafsu*. *Akal* thus distinguishes humans from the rest of the animal world. These components are associated with men and women respectively; men have more reason and women have more desire.[12] In the dominant gender discourse, therefore, women should be under the control of men, as desires are controlled by reason (cf. Tsing 1993, Peletz1996).

3 Overview of Petalangan Magic Spells

In Petalangan society, practices of magic spells accompany most activities in daily life.[13] Having a knowledge of magic spells is especially important in dealing with others and managing social relationships. People believe that magic spells have the power to control other people's wills or feelings by penetrating into their inner selves.

From the Petalangan point of view, the boundary of the person is not fixed but flexible and even exposed to outside influence. The *mayo* (life force) of a person is considered so weak and volatile that it can easily be shifted by the person or by others; it can even cross the boundary of the self. While closely related to the body and emotion, *mayo* is a spiritual concept located between the body and the mind. If someone's *mayo* is interrupted by the outside, he/she experiences changes in his/her bodily conditions or emotional states.

---

[11] Originating from Arabic, *akal* and *nafsu* refer to 'reason' and 'desire' in Indonesian as well as in Malay.

[12] See Schimmel (1997) for the detailed gender representations and images reflected in the Koran.

[13] Petalangan magic or magic spells are largely classified into two categories: *ilmu masyarakat* (magic for society), and *ilmu privadi* (magic for individuals). Magic for society includes magic for communal activities, such as farming, hunting and collecting honey, healing and child birth, and so on. Magic for individuals is used to improve personal well-being; for example, it is used to promote health, beauty, and self-protection. This category includes *ilmu pemanih* (beauty magic), *ilmu kebal* ('thick magic' to strengthen a person's body for self-protection), *ilmu pengashi* (love magic), *ilmu pembenci* (hate magic), *ilmu penunduk* (defeating magic), and so on.

The notion of *mayo* that loosens the personal boundary or even renders it boundless helps to explain people's belief in the power of magic spells to control others' feelings. Fear that others will use malicious magic to control an individual is one of the most prevalent anxieties found among Petalangan people. Accordingly, Petalangans interact with one another under constant suspicion of what others may do to them through the use of spells. A person's allusion to the knowledge of magic displays him/her as having the potential to influence others to his/her advantage, which triggers fear in other people. This, in turn, motivates people to learn spells in order to protect themselves from the willfulness of others. Most Petalangan adults, therefore, claim some knowledge of spells. Typically, men learn magic spells from male elders and women from female elders.[14]

Magic lessons take place under very private, secret circumstances, and between only two people, a student and a teacher. Custom requires the student to provide the teacher with material goods such as gold, clothes, chickens, and the like. The spells traditionally have been handed down through oral tradition, and have no written texts. It is believed that the spells must be absorbed into the performer's body, and so the spells are thought to work only if they are memorized. If a student learns the magic spells by taking notes, the notes should be burned and the ashes should be eaten so that the words become part of the body.

As indicated by the emphasis on 'words become flesh and bones (*kato jadi daging tulang*),' the idea of oneness between words and the body is prevalent and serves as a basis for the efficacy of magic spells. Reciting magic spells, for instance, gives magical power to the performer, as words and the performer become 'one breath (*satu nyawa*)'[15] when the words are uttered through the performer's voice.

Petalangans say that their spells come from their deceased ancestors, and that their ancestors' words come from God (*Allah*). In Petalangan belief, all animals were able to speak human languages when the world was created. Animals, especially birds, used to be messengers who brought God's messages to the ancestors. God's messages contained esoteric knowledge of this world and ancestors articulated God's messages into verbal formulas that living people could use. In Goffman's terms (Goffman 1981), God thus

---

[14] Most Petalangan informants report that they start to learn magic spells around the age of fifteen to seventeen. Since the Petalangans consider magic spells an important resource by which they can deal with the opposite sex in relationships, they prefer not to reveal their magic spells to the opposite sex. People say that they don't want to give *senjata* ('arms,' which means magic spells) to *musuh* ('enemy,' which means the opposite sex). Therefore, it is easier to learn such magic spells from elders of the same sex, rather than from those of the opposite sex.

[15] *Satu* means 'one' *and Nyawa* refers to 'soul' or 'spirit' that is realized and embodied by 'breath.'

becomes a principal speaker and ancestors become authors. The current speakers thus become animators who repeat the words (Figure 2).

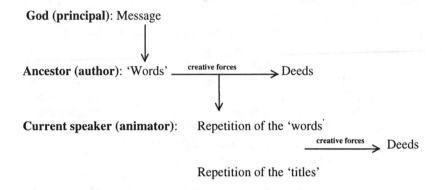

Figure 2. Petalangan Magic Spells: Creative Forces of Words

As it is believed that God creates the world through speech, ancestors' words that originated from God are thought to entail deeds within the utterance itself. Repeating the words thus carries the same creative force as the words did when uttered by the ancestors. Each Petalangan magic spell has a specific title that refers to the first owner of the spell, and it is believed that the mere utterance of the title has a magical effect (Figure 2). The practice of magic spells, therefore, is a very sacred ritual through which the performer invokes the divine power embedded in the spell.

In the following, I will focus on two types of Petalangan love charms. Many Petalangan women told me that they recite specific love charms before and after having sexual intercourse in order to increase sexual satisfaction for their spouses. Before sex, a woman recites the spell 'Opening (bodily) desires' (*buka hawa nafsu*) to herself in order to invoke her desire. Afterwards, she recites the spell called 'Locking Fatima's door' in order to 'lock the body' (*kunci badan*) for self-protection from any danger caused by the sexual intercourse.

The magic spells are recited when they take baths. Because people take a bath twice a day, in the morning and in the afternoon, they recite the 'Opening desires' during the afternoon bath prior to the night's potential sexual encounters, while 'Locking Fatima's door' is recited in the following morning bath after they have had sex. Sometimes the magic spells are recited to the water with which they take a bath. Magic spells should be recited privately and quietly so that others cannot hear the spells. Although various versions of spells may exist under the same titles, the spells show similar internal structure despite their minor variations of lexical changes; thus I have selected the most typical examples to illustrate Petalangan women's spell practices.

4 Internal Organization of Magic Spells

4.1 Parallelism

An analysis of 'The Prayer of the Seven Tastes' (Example 1) reveals special linguistic devices through which a particular speaker's utterance follows the standard structure of ancestral authority. A highly formulaic structure displays the immediate ever-changing performances as self-evident, and as having transcendental authority separate from the intentions of particular speakers.

1.	*Bismillahirahmanirrahim*	1.	In the name of God
2.	*Kunyit ku, kunyit abu*	2.	My *kunyit* (turmeric), *abu kunyit*
3.	*Di tanam di janke kayu awo*	3.	Planted at the roots of *awo* trees
4.	*Kuat sombu daging basombu*	4.	Strongly cured, flesh cured
5.	*Aku mamakai 'Tujuh Aso'*	5.	I use 'Seven Tastes'
6.	*untuk membuka hawa nafsu badan ku iko*	6.	to open desire in this my body
7.	*Kok duduk taaso-aso*	7.	If [he] stands, let [my vagina] be felt and felt [by him]
8.	*Kok togak taaso-aso*	8.	If [he] sits, let [my vagina] be felt and felt [by him]
9.	*Lubang puki aku iko*	9.	This hole of my vagina
10.	*Sataun jalan da'at*	10.	[If he goes] One year trip on land
11.	*Tigo bulan palayi'an*	11.	[If he goes] Three months fishing on the ocean
12.	*Lubang puki aku iko taaso-aso jo*	12.	Let my vagina be felt and felt [by him], too.
13.	*Sapuluh cai bini,*	13.	[Even if he] Ten times looks for wives,
14.	*Satui cai kondak*	14.	[Even if he] one hundred times finds girlfriends
15.	*Tak ado sasodap lubang puki aku iko*	15.	There is nothing as tasty as this hole of my vagina
16.	*Dik < nama>*	16.	[His] sister, <name >

17. *Barkat aku mamamkai tuju aso*	17. Bless me who uses 'Seven Tastes.'
18. *Kabul Allah, Kabul Muhammad*	18. Please bless [me], Allah, the Prophet Muhammad
19. *Kabul Bagindo Rasullullah*	19. His Majesty, the Messenger of God

Example 1. 'The Prayer of the Seven Tastes' *(Doa Tujuh Aso)*

The most commonly-found linguistic devices are framing devices (cf. Goffman 1974) through which the current speaker's speech is displayed as detached from the immediate pragmatic context of the 'here and now.' In 'The Prayer of the Seven Tastes,' the text is marked by a pair of Islamic opening and closing remarks, as shown in the following excerpt (Example 2).

1. *Bismillahirahmanirrahim*	1. In the name of God	**Opening**
18. *Kabul Allah, Kabul Muhammad*	18. Please bless [me], Allah, the Prophet Muhammad	
19. *Kabul Bagindo Rasullullah*	19. His Majesty, the Messenger of God	**Closing**

Example 2. Framing Devices: Islamic Opening and Closing Remarks

The Islamic opening and closing phrases *Bismillahirahmanirrahim* in the first line, and *Kabul Allah Kabul Muhammad, Kabul Bagindo Rasullullah* in the last line compose one of the most commonly found framing devices. Despite its minor lexical variations, most magic spells are internally framed by these Islamic phrases. These remarks frame the speaker's utterance 'in the name of God,' and locate the present speaker as an 'animator' of God (Goffman 1974).

1. *Bismillahirahmanirrahim*	1. In the name of God	**Opening**
5. *Aku mamakai 'Tujuh Aso'*	5. I use "Seven Tastes"	
17. *Barkat aku mamamkai tuju aso*	17. Bless me who uses "Seven Tastes"	**Title**
18. *Kabul Allah, Kabul Muhammad*	18. Please bless [me], Allah, the Prophet Muhammad	
19. *Kabul Bagindo Rasullullah*	19. His Majesty, the Messenger of God	**Closing**

Example 3. Repetition of the Spell's Title

The second framing device is employed through the repetition of the spell's title, found in the above Example 3 in lines 5 and 17 as shown above; *Aku memakai doa 'Tujuh Aso',* ('I use the prayer of the Seven Tastes'). These sentences define the very action in which the speaker is engaged. Framing the speech as 'Seven Tastes' allows the utterance to appear as a repeating phrase of the ancestors' words, detached from the speaker's immediate pragmatic context.

We also find the use of paired couplet from lines 2 through 5 of 'the Prayer of Seven Tastes' as shown below (Example 4). This shows a Pantun, a traditional couplet style of Malay poetry which displays an alternate rhyme pattern coupling in lines 2 and 4 and lines 3 and 5.

2.	*Kunyit ku, kunyit abu*	2.	My *kunyit* (turmeric), *abu kunyit*
3.	*Di tanam di janke kayu awo*	3.	Planted at the roots of *awo* trees
4.	*Kuat sombu daging basombu*	4.	Strongly cured, flesh cured
5.	*Aku mamakai 'Tujuh Aso'*	5.	I use 'Seven Tastes'

Example 4. Pantun (Couplets) of 'The Prayer of the Seven Tastes'

By layering the words with immediate repetitions, as in line 2, *'Kunyit ku, kunyit abu'* and line 4 *'Kuat sombu daging basombu,'* this Pantun style emphasizes the spell's poetic structure (Example 5).

2.	*Kunyit ku, kunyit abu*	2.	My *kunyit* (turmeric), *abu kunyit*
3.	*Di tanam di janke kayu awo*	3.	Planted at the roots of *awo* trees
4.	*Kuat sombu daging basombu*	4.	Strongly cured, flesh cured
5.	*Aku mamakai 'Tujuh Aso'*	5.	I use 'Seven Tastes'

Example 5. Immediate Repetition of the Words

In the following Example 6 taken from 'the Prayer of the Seven Tastes', lines 7 through 14 demonstrate the structure of canonical couplets.[16] Semantically, this spell repeats the imagined activities of the male counterpart,[17] the speaker's husband (A), expanded by diverse descriptions of the activities that he undertakes, such as 'standing,' 'sitting,' and 'going on a trip.' (In Example 6, these activities are schematically represented using A1 through A6.)

---

[16] Parallelism is one of the most prevalent forms of ritual speech found across societies. See Fox 1971.

[17] Despite the fact that indexical pronouns for the counterpart do not appear within the text, I translate the omitted subject as 'he,' based on the self-referential term, *'Dik'* in line 16. *Dik* ('younger sibling') is an everyday address term or a self-referential term for a girlfriend or a wife.

A(n): Husband's activity: (He) does (something)
A': Duration of the activity
X: Husband's sensations: (He) cannot help feeling (the speaker's body)
Y: The speaker's body

7.	*Kok duduk taaso-aso*	7. If [he] stands, let [my vagina] be felt and felt [by him]	**A1+X**
8.	*Kok togak taaso-aso*	8. If [he] sits, let [my vagina] be felt and felt [by him]	**A2+X**
9.	*Lubang puki aku iko*	9. This hole of my vagina	**Y**
10.	*Sataun jalan da'at*	10. [If he goes] One year trip on land	**A'+A3**
11.	*Tigo bulan palayi'an*	11. [If he goes] Three months fishing on the ocean	**A'+A4**
12.	*Lubang puki aku iko taaso-aso jo*	12. Let my vagina be felt and felt [by him], too.	**Y+X**
13.	*Sapuluh cai bini,*	13. [Even if he] Ten times looks for wives,	**A'+A5**
14.	*Satui cai kondak*	14. [Even if he] one hundred times finds girlfriends	**A'+A6**
15.	*Tak ado sasodap lubang puki aku iko*	15. There is nothing as tasty as this hole of my vagina	**Y**

Example 6. Canonical Organization of 'The Prayer of the Seven Tastes'

As shown in the example above, the husband's activities of the text are organized as A1 through A6. This organization is also modified by stative verbs; *teaso-aso* (be felt and felt) which is marked by X and produces the structure of [(A1+X) (A2+X)] // [(A'+A3) (A'+A4)] // [(A'+A5) (A'+ A6)]. The husband's activities are thus expanded and paired by adding the semantically equivalent description of activities, which enhances poetic structure of the magic spell.[18]

Furthermore, each pair is followed by the phrase indicating the present performer's body (Y), with the indexical words of the first person form *aku* ('my') and deictic pronoun *iko* ('this'), as shown in Example 7.

---

[18] See Keane (1997) for the importance of parallelism in ritual speech. See Fox (1988) for a review of general anthropological perspectives on parallelism.

7.	*Kok duduk taaso-aso*	7.	If [he] stands, let [my vagina] be felt and felt [by him]	
8.	*Kok togak taaso-aso*	8.	If [he] sits, let [my vagina] be felt and felt [by him]	
9.	*Lubang puki <u>aku iko</u>*	9.	<u>This</u> hole of <u>my</u> vagina	**Y**
10.	*Sataun jalan da'at*	10.	[If he goes] One year trip on land	
11.	*Tigo bulan palayi'an*	11.	[If he goes] Three months fishing on the ocean	
12.	*Lubang puki <u>aku iko</u> taaso-aso jo*	12.	let <u>this</u> hole <u>my</u> vagina be felt and felt [by him], too.	**Y**
13.	*Sapuluh cai bini,*	13.	[Even if he] Ten times looks for wives,	
14.	*Satui cai kondak*	14.	[Even if he] one hundred times finds girlfriends	
15.	*Tak ado sasodap lubang puki aku iko*	15.	There is nothing as tasty as <u>this</u> hole of <u>my</u> vagina	**Y**
16.	*<u>Dik < nama></u>*	16.	<u>Sister <name ></u>	

Example 7. Indexical Elements Embedded in Couplets (Y: Speaker's Body)

Line 16 of the above excerpt (Example 7) names and locates the speaker as '*Dik* (sister).' Given that '*Dik*' is a common Petalangan address term for a wife (cf. n.16), by naming the speaker herself as '*Dik*,' the present performer of 'I' is finally objectified and positioned as the target man's wife in a specific 'here and now.' As organized in the formulaic structure, however, the speaker 'I' remains actively embedded in the unchanging 'ancestors' words.' Figure 3 schematizes the internal organization of 'The Prayer of Seven Tastes.'

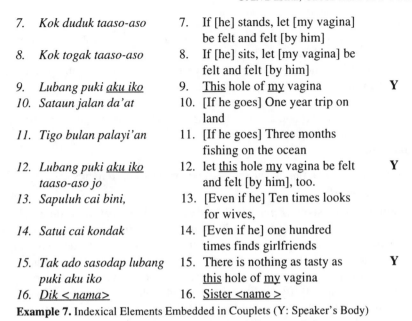

Opening: In the name of God
Title: Defining the performer's speech act

Ancestor's words — Transcendence	The target man's activities (A)	The target man's bodily experience (X)	The speaker's body (Y)	The current speaker's body: Immediate context, Situatedness
	A1+A2	X	Y	
	A3+A4	X	Y	
	A5+A6	X	Y	

Title: Defining the performer's speech act
Closing: In the name of God

Figure 3. Internal Organization of 'The Prayer of the Seven Tastes'

The internal structure of the text reveals the present speaker as an animator of ancestors and god. The highly formal and poetic internal structure of the spell provides a set of interpretive frameworks by which the present performance is understood as a recitation of the ancestors' unchanging words, and as detached from the immediate ever-changing context. Use of indexical pronouns embedded in the whole structure of framing, however, retains the link between the current speaker and the original speakers.

4.2 Social construction of the female body in relation to men's sexual experience

Another magic spell, *Kunci kati Fatima* ('locking Fatima's door') is recited to protect the female body from any possible danger of men's sexuality.[19] Given that *Fatima* is one of the most common female names in Petalangan society, this name has become a generic term for woman.[20] Fatima's door, furthermore, is metaphorically used to refer to the female genitalia (Example 8). By analyzing the second spell, I argue that the female body is socially constituted and constructed, and that its representation is mediated by conventional Petalangan notions of the female body and sexuality.

1.	*Bismillahirahmanirrahim*	1.	In the name of God
2.	*Cup takacup-kacup*	2.	*chup takacup* (sounds of jingling scissors),
3.	*Tumbuh di padang sibui-bui*	3.	Grows in the foaming field.
4.	*Takacup kacup-ku*	4.	*Takachup*, my *kacup*,
5.	*Sotollah Allah tatogak dii*	5.	In the name of Allah who stands by himself
6.	*Aku mamakai 'Kunci kati Fatima'*	6.	I use 'Locking Fatima's Door'

---

[19] In Petalangan women's view, having sex could harm the women's bodies. This perspective is frequently expressed in their anxiety that they would have a 'watery (*beaye*)' and 'not-dried (*tidak koing*)' vagina because of excessive sex, which is usually caused by the husbands' strong appetite for sexual relations.

[20] Not only in Petalangan society, but also in other Muslim societies, Fatima is a common female name. Since the biblical Fatima is the fourth daughter of Muhammad and the one most beloved by her father (cf. Schimmel 1997), many Muslims name their daughters after her.

7. *Sompit belubang ja'um*	7. <u>Tight</u> like the eye of a needle
8. *Koing abu dapur*	8. <u>Dry</u> like ashes in the kitchen
9. *Kosang sabut sekoping*	9. <u>Fresh (crisp)</u> like a chip of coconut husk
10. *Hangat sepoti tempuyung*	10. <u>Hot</u> like charcoals of palm trunk
11. *Podeh sepoti lado bepatah*	11. <u>Spicy</u> like a piece of chili
12. *Asin sepoti ga'am seisak*	12. <u>Salty</u> like a pinch of salt
13. *Lomak sepoti nio nan gulo*	13. <u>Greasy and sweet</u> like coconut milk and sugar
14. *Pintu sogo si patima*	14. *Fatima*'s heaven's door
15. *Apo nan pulang ke o'ang*	15. What returns to others are,
16. *Ambe sepoti ketopang nio*	16. Tastelessness like a coconut's hull
17. *Sojuk sepoti ayi di dapur*	17. Coldness like water in the kitchen
18. *Itulah nan pulang ke o'ang*	18. Those are what return to others
19. *Aku makai 'Kunci kati Fatima'*	19. I use 'Locking Fatima's Door.'
20. *Sotollah*	20. In the name of Allah

Use of similes (seven tastes) — bracketed beside lines 7–13.

Example 8. 'Locking Fatima's Door' (*Kunci kati Fatima*)

In 'Locking Fatima's Door'(Example 8), lines 7 through 13 show how the female body is constructed in relation to the men's sexual experience. In this spell, diverse similes describe female genital organs as having 'seven tastes[21]' or palpable characteristics, such as tight, dry, fresh (crisp), hot, spicy, salty, as well as greasy and sweet. This spell recites the names of objects that possess appropriate qualities of the seven tastes. These similes, however, describe neither the physical figures of female genitalia, nor the women's experience or feelings. Rather, the similes serve to constitute a partner's sexual experience, following conventional notions of the seven tastes of a generic woman's vagina.

6. *untuk membuka hawa nafsu badan ku iko*	6. to open desire in this my body
7. *Kok duduk <u>taaso-aso</u>*	7. If [he] stands, let [my vagina] be <u>felt and felt</u> [by him]
8. *Kok togak <u>taaso-aso</u>*	8. If [he] sits, let [my vagina] be <u>felt and felt</u> [by him]
9. *Lubang puki aku iko*	9. This hole of my vagina

---

[21] In Petalangan conventions, the female genitals have been described as having 'seven tastes (*tuju aso*).'

10. *Sataun jalan da'at*	10. [If he goes] One year trip on land
11. *Tigo bulan palayi'an*	11. [If he goes] Three months fishing on the ocean
12. *Lubang puki aku iko <u>taaso-aso</u> jo*	12. Let my vagina be <u>felt and felt</u> [by him], too.
13. *Sapuluh cai bini,*	13. [Even if he] Ten times looks for wives,
14. *Satui cai kondak*	14. [Even if he] one hundred times finds girlfriends
15. *Tak ado sasodap lubang puki aku iko*	15. There is nothing as tasty as this hole of my vagina
16. *Dik < nama>*	16. [His] sister, <name >

Example 9. Men's Bodily Sensations in 'The Prayer of the Seven Tastes'

The above Example 9 also shows how the female body is constructed through the men's sensations in 'The Prayer of the Seven Tastes.' As examined in the above section, this spell is recited in order to 'open desire' in her body (line 6). Throughout the text, however, we cannot find any description of female desire. Instead, we find the male counterpart's sexual experience as shown in lines 7 through 14. The use of stative affix of 'te(r)-' in 'teaso-aso,' which implies the passive state of feeling, such as 'cannot help feeling' in lines 7 and 8, makes the hidden subject of the sentence emerge not as an agent but as an experiencer-subject. Thus, the locus of women's desire is found not in their internal bodies or selves, but rather in men's sexual experiences.

4.3 Social construction of the female body in contrast to other women's bodies

The speaker's female body also appears in contrast to those of other women. In Example 10, lines 13 and 15 claim that the performer's sexual capacity is qualitatively superior to any other women.

13. *Sapuluh cai <u>bini,</u>*	13. [Even if he] Ten times looks for <u>wives,</u>
14. *Satui cai <u>kondak</u>*	14. [Even if he] one hundred times finds <u>girlfriends</u>
15. *<u>Tak ado sasodap</u> lubang puki aku iko*	15. <u>There is nothing as tasty</u> as this hole of my vagina
16. *Dik < nama>*	16. [His] sister, <name >

Example 10. 'The Prayer of the Seven Tastes'

15. Apo nan pulang ke o'ang	15. What returns to <u>others</u> are,
16. Ambe sepoti ketopang nio	16. <u>Tastelessness</u> like a coconut's hull
17. Sojuk sepoti ayi di dapur	17. <u>Coldness</u> like water in the kitchen
18. Itulah nan pulang ke o'ang	18. Those are what return to <u>others</u>

Example 11. 'Locking Fatima's Door'

In the above Example 11 drawing on the spell 'Locking Fatima's Door,' the performer's body is emphasized in contrast to other women's bodies, which are tasteless in line 16 and cold in line 17. The female body and desires are thus represented as constructed through men's erotic sensations as well as through a comparison with other women's bodies, drawing on conventional Petalangan representations of the 'seven tastes' of the female body.

5 Reciting Magic Spells and Shifting Values of the Female Body and Desire

What then do women do with these words? Petalangan women say that they use 'love charms' to deal with their fear of being abandoned by their husbands. Men's mobility—their freedom to go anywhere—is a threatening factor for Petalangan women. Men have more chances to meet other women outside the village, while women cannot circulate and socialize freely because of their restricted mobility. People also account for gender differences in courtship in that 'men are brave (*bo'ani*) enough to achieve desired partners, while women are ashamed (*malu*) to express their own feelings to their lovers.'

From this point of view, Petalangan women think that the use of magic spells is more 'suitable'(*cocok*) for women, because they can be performed in private and personal circumstances but are still powerful enough to activate the spiritual agents beyond women's limited social boundaries. Through the authoritative 'ancestors' words', women are said to acquire 'spiritual vision' (*pandangan batin*) that can freely move around despite women's physically restricted mobility. 'While we do not see our husbands with the eyes, we could see them in mind. Once we seize them in our "spiritual vision," then they would never leave us.'

Based on analogical thoughts, practices of magic spells are believed to have the power to absorb and to transfer specific attributes and qualities of uttered objects in the spells into the designated bodies. In the spell of 'Locking Fatima's door,' for example, 'chips of coconut husk,' 'ashes in the kitchen,' and 'a pinch of salt' are verbalized in the hope of transferring the desirable attributes of each item, such as 'crispness,' 'dryness,' and 'saltiness' to the women's bodies.

Why then do women fear being abandoned by their husbands? More strictly, women fear the shame that they would face from other family members and neighbors, who would slander and despise them if their husbands were to leave. In fact, many women in the village have been divorced or left by their husbands. They have informed me that because they have been abandoned, these women have become 'ashamed' in their social interactions with other villagers. Fear of humility and deprivation leads them to recite magic spells. Petalangan women say, 'City women put on make-up, while we wear magic spells.'

Petalangan women, therefore, believe that they must satisfy the husbands' sexual desires in order to keep their families as well as their marriages intact. They say that although they may feel a lack of sexual appetite, they make an effort to 'open desire.' They do so by appropriating the conventional notions of the female body as determined by the men's sexual experience, not as internally owned by women. By reciting magic spells, therefore, women can achieve or control their own sexual desires, allowing women to appear 'rational,' in contrast to the Islamic gender dichotomy where men represent reason, and women represent desire.

6 Conclusion – Petalangan Women's Agency: Magic Spells Revisited

The Petalangan women's genre of magic spells, therefore, reveals the women's subjective views in negotiating the dominant gender paradigm. How, then, do the women acquire agency in their language practice? To answer that question, I would like to go back to the analysis of magic spells.

1. *Bismillahirahmanirrahim* — 1. In the name of God
2. *Kunyit ku, kunyit abu* — 2. My *kunyit* (turmeric), *abu kunyit*
3. *Di tanam di janke kayu awo* — 3. Planted at the roots of *awo* trees
4. *Kuat sombu daging basombu* — 4. Strongly cured, flesh cured
5. *Aku mamakai 'Tujuh Aso'* — 5. I use 'Seven Tastes'
6. *untuk membuka hawa nafsu badan ku iko* — 6. to open desire in this my body
7. *Kok duduk taaso-aso* — 7. If [he] stands, let [my vagina] be felt and felt [by him]
8. *Kok togak taaso-aso* — 8. If [he] sits, let [my vagina] be felt and felt [by him]
9. *Lubang puki aku iko* — 9. This hole of my vagina
10. *Sataun jalan da'at* — 10. [If he goes] One year trip on land

11. Tigo bulan palayi'an		11. [If he goes] Three months fishing on the ocean
12. Lubang puki aku iko taaso-aso jo		12. Let my vagina be felt and felt [by him], too.
13. Sapuluh cai bini,		13. [Even if he] Ten times looks for wives,
14. Satui cai kondak		14. [Even if he] one hundred times finds girlfriends
15. Tak ado sasodap lubang puki aku iko		15. There is nothing as tasty as this hole of my vagina
16. Dik < nama>		16. [His] sister, <name >
17. <u>Barkat aku mamamkai tuju aso</u>		17. <u>Bless me who uses 'Seven Tastes.'</u>
18. Kabul Allah, Kabul Muhammad		18. Please bless [me], Allah, the Prophet Muhammad
19. Kabul Bagindo Rasullullah		19. His Majesty, the Messenger of God

Example 12. 'I' as an Agent, Analyzed in 'The Prayer of the Seven Tastes'

Throughout the texts, the agency of speaking subject 'I' is not apparent. 'I' as an agent only appears in lines 5 and 17 of 'the Seven Tastes' (Example 12), and line 6 and 19 in 'Locking Fatima's Door' (Example 13).

1. Bismillahiramanirahi		1. In the name of God
2. Cup takacup-kacup		2. *chup takacup* (sounds of jingling scissors),
3. Tumbuh di padang sibui-bui		3. Grows in the foaming field.
4. Takacup kacup-ku		4. *Takachup*, my *kacup*,
5. Sotollah Allah tatogak dii		5. In the name of Allah who stands by himself
6. <u>Aku mamakai 'Kunci kati Fatima'</u>		6. <u>I use 'Locking Fatima's Door'</u>
7. Sompit belubang ja'um		7. Tight like the eye of a needle
8. Koing abu dapur		8. Dry like ashes in the kitchen
9. Kosang sabut sekoping		9. Fresh (crisp) like a chip of coconut husk
10. Hangat sepoti tempuyung		10. Hot like charcoals of palm trunk
11. Podeh sepoti lado bepatah		11. Spicy like a piece of chili
12. Asin sepoti ga'am seisak		12. Salty like a pinch of salt

13. Lomak sepoti nio nan gulo	13. Greasy and sweet like coconut milk and sugar
14. Pintu sogo si patima	14. *Fatima*'s heaven's door
15. Apo nan pulang ke o'ang	15. What returns to others are,
16. Ambe sepoti ketopang nio	16. Tastelessness like a coconut's hull
17. Sojuk sepoti ayi di dapur	17. Coldness like water in the kitchen
18. Itulah nan pulang ke o'ang	18. Those are what return to others
19. <u>Aku makai 'Kunci kati Fatima'</u>	19. <u>I use 'Locking Fatima's Door.'</u>
20. Sotollah	20. In the name of Allah

Example 13. 'I' as an Agent, Analyzed in 'Locking Fatima's Door'

Given that all of these lines describe the subject's speech activity itself– as with 'I use the prayer of the seven tastes,' or 'I use locking Fatima's door'–the speaker's agency is restricted to the activity of repeating ancestors' words. Moreover, the high formality of the magic spell infuses textual authority into the spells so that it appears unchanged from generation to generation.[22] The present speaker is an animator of the original speakers. In using the name of Fatima, a collective term for women, or by framing the present utterance in the name of God, the individual speaker's agency disappears only to reappear as collective feminine subjectivity, or as coming from higher sources of authority.

In conclusion, the female body and desires in women's magic spells are constituted and constructed in relation to men's sexual sensations and in comparison to other women's bodies and desires, which are mediated by Petalangan conventional notions of the female body. As Butler argues the discursive construction of the gendered body with the concepts of 'reiteration' and 'performativity' (Butler 1993), the Petalangan case also demonstrates how the female body is construed and represented based on their discursive conventions of the female body.

By reciting the magic spells, however, Petalangan women claim their 'rational' control of their desires and sexuality, which contrasts to the dominant Islamic gender ideology of 'irrational' women. Petalangan women re-

---

[22] This process is explained by the term of *entextualization* (cf. Bauman and Briggs 1990, Kuipers 1990). According to Kuipers (ibid: 4), *entextualization* is a process 'in which a speech event is marked by increasing thoroughness of poetic and rhetorical patterning and growing levels of detachment from the immediate pragmatic context.' The authority of performance is explained as being constituted through this entextualization process.

define and represent their desires and sexuality as being socially embedded and culturally performed, which renders the Petalangan women's desires and sexuality as a social requisite in fulfilling their wifely role. Unlike Butler's universalized notions of performativity focus primarily on the 'reiteration' of discourse, paying less attention to its contextually contingent meanings, the ethnographic accounts of Petalangan women's magic spells draw attention to the multiple functions and meanings of the language practice as emergent in specific social contexts. In this respect, the analysis of Petalangan women's spell practices brings the issues of agency back to discussion, whereas Butler's emphasis on the discursive construction of gender and the (sexed) body has largely discounted the agency of the subject (Butler 1990, 1993; cf. Hall 2000:186). Petalangan women's agency operates in producing new meanings of female bodies and sexuality in specific social contexts, while embedded in the discursive limit at the same time.

Petalangan women's language practice, furthermore, demonstrates the multiplicity in forms and degrees of agency. Unlike the conventional Western notions of agency that emphasizes individual will and intentions (cf. Ortner 1984, 1996), Petalangan women acquire agency by denying their individual intentions as well as by invoking the authority of 'the ancestors' voices' embedded in a specific type of magic formula. Petalangan women's agency, therefore, is not an attribute or 'power' through which they assert control or 'authorship' over action. Rather it is found in the very act by which they ascribe their agency to the higher sources of power such as ancestors' words and God, as shown in their magic spells.

References

Abu-Lughod, Lila. 1986. *Veiled Sentiments: Honor and Poetry in a Bedouin Society*. Berkeley, CA: University of California Press.

Ahearn, Laura. 2000. Agency. *Journal of Linguistic Anthropology* 9:12-15.

Andaya, Barbara. 1993. *To Live as Brothers: Southeast Sumatra in the Seventeenth and Eighteenth Centuries*. Honolulu: University of Hawaii Press.

Austin, John. 1962. *How to Do Things with Words*. Cambridge: Harvard University Press.

Bauman, Richard, and Charles Briggs. 1990. Poetics and Performances as Critical Perspectives on Language and Social Life. *Annual Review of Anthropology* 19:59-88.

Butler, Judith. 1990. *Gender Trouble: Feminism and the Subversion of Identity*. New York: Routledge.

Butler, Judith. 1993. *Bodies that Matter*. New York: Routledge.

Fox, James. 1971. Semantic Parallelism in Rotinese Ritual Language. *Bidjra-gen Tot de Taal-, Land-. en Volkenkunde* 127: 215-255.

Fox, James, ed. 1988. *To Speak in Pairs: Essays on the Ritual Languages of Eastern Indonesia.* Cambridge: Cambridge University Press.

Goffman, Erving. 1974. *Framing Analysis.* New York: Harper and Row.

Goffman, Erving. 1981. *Forms of Talk.* Philadelphia: University of Pennsylvania.

Hall, Kira .2000. Performativity. *Journal of Linguistic Anthropology* 9:184-187.

Hall, Kira and Mary Bucholtz, eds. 1995. *Gender Articulated: Language and the Socially Constructed Self.* New York: Routledge.

Keane, Webb. 1997. *Signs of Recognition: Powers and Hazards of Representation in an Indonesian Society.* Berkeley, CA: University of California Press.

Kuipers, Joel. 1990. *Power in Performance: The Creation of Textual Authority in Weyewa Ritual Speech.* Philadelphia: University of Pennsylvania Press.

Livia, Anna and Kira Hall, eds. 1997. *Queerly Phrased: Language, Gender and Sexuality.* New York: Oxford University Press.

Ortner, Sherry. 1984. Theory in Anthropology Since the Sixties. *Comparative Studies in Society and History.* 26:126-166.

Ortner, Sherry. 1996. *Making Gender: The Politics and Erotics of Culture.* Boston: Beacon Press.

Peletz, Michael. 1996. *Reason and Passion: Representations of Gender in a Malay Society.* Berkeley, CA: University of California Press.

Raheja, G. and Ann Gold, eds. 1994. *Listen to the Heron's Words: Reimagining Gender and Kinship in North India.* Berkeley, CA: University of California Press.

Schimmel, A.1997. *My Soul is a Woman: The Feminine in Islam.* New York: The Continum Publishing Company.

Searle, John. 1979. *Expression and Meaning: Studies in the Theory of Speech Acts.* Cambridge: Cambridge university press.

Siegel, James T. 1969. *The Rope of God.* Berkeley, CA and Los Angeles: University of California Press.

Tenas Effendy. 1997. Petalangan Society and Changes in Riau. Bijdragen: Tot de Taal-, Land-, en Volkenkunde. *Deel* 153.4:630-647.

Tsing, Anna L. *1993 In the Realm of the Diamond Queen: Marginality in an Out-of-the-way Place.* Princeton: Princeton University Press.

Turner, Ashely. 1997. Cultural Survival: Identity and the Performing Arts of Kampar's Suku Petalangan. Bijdragen: Tot de Taal-, Land-, en Volkenkunde. *Deel* 153.4:648-67

Index